M. E Dunlap

Abridgment of Elementary Law

Embodying the general principles, rules and definitions of law, together with the common maxims and rules of equity jurisprudence

M. E Dunlap

Abridgment of Elementary Law
Embodying the general principles, rules and definitions of law, together with the common maxims and rules of equity jurisprudence

ISBN/EAN: 9783337315047

Printed in Europe, USA, Canada, Australia, Japan

Cover: Foto ©Suzi / pixelio.de

More available books at **www.hansebooks.com**

ABRIDGMENT

OF

ELEMENTARY LAW:

EMBODYING THE

GENERAL PRINCIPLES, RULES AND DEFINITIONS OF LAW,
TOGETHER WITH THE COMMON MAXIMS AND RULES
OF EQUITY JURISPRUDENCE,

AS STATED IN THE

STANDARD COMMENTARIES OF THE LEADING
ENGLISH AND AMERICAN AUTHORS;

EMBRACING

THE SUBJECTS CONTAINED IN

A REGULAR LAW COURSE.

COLLECTED AND ARRANGED SO AS TO BE

MORE EASILY ACQUIRED BY STUDENTS, COMPREHENDED
BY JUSTICES, AND READILY REVIEWED BY
YOUNG PRACTITIONERS.

BY M. E. DUNLAP,
COUNSELLOR AT LAW.

ST. LOUIS:
SOULE, THOMAS & WENTWORTH,
1876.

Entered according to Act of Congress, in the year 1876, by
M. E. DUNLAP,
in the office of the Librarian of Congress, at Washington.

Electrotyped by STRASSBURGER & DRACH,
St. Louis, Mo.

PREFACE.

When Mr. Wilberforce asked the advice of Lord Eldon as to the course to be pursued by the young Grants in their legal studies, the advice was, "to live the life of a hermit, and work like a horse." That has been, and no doubt still is, sound advice in England, to make a great lawyer; and in some measure it is, and perhaps will be more so, in the United States. But we are a different race of people, or rather a like race under different circumstances. The labor of the profession is not divided here as it is in England, and probably never will be; the consequence is, that to make a great lawyer one may have much less learned lore, and must have much more knowledge of men and things in general.

There is no spot on the earth where the legal profession calls for such varied and extensive acquirements, as it does in this country. A lawyer here, to be eminent, ought to know everything which can be known, for there is no kind of knowledge that he may not be required to bring into use. With these facts in view, this volume has been prepared to aid the student in the thorough mastery of his course of *legal studies,* and to some extent obviate the loss of time during his final preparation for admission to the bar; also to give him some practical hints touching the best methods of acquiring a knowledge of the law and its practice. Many of the Suggestions to Students, herein presented, are taken, like the Abridgment itself, from some of the leading English and American writers in the arena of legal science; they were found to be so elegantly and learnedly written, that the author felt there was no room left for even slight improvement; besides this, age has given to them, as to precedents in the law, a veneration and potency unattending later efforts in the same direction. The chief design of this work is to give in the fewest pages, the principles and definitions of law and equity, to furnish a review or note book and *vade mecum* for LAW STUDENTS and young practitioners. It is said that "the substance of any science consists of certain elementary rules or first principles, which, as they are generally the pure dictates of reason, and short and simple in their phraseology, find an easy access to the mind. These rules are necessarily numerous, and, with their exceptions, constitute the entire learning of any science." Principles, owing to the universality of their expression, their reason and application, glide almost imperceptibly into the mind, and, once seated in the memory, seldom or never abandon it. That which is forcibly impressed on the understanding, because fully comprehended, is not liable to forsake us; hence those rules which have been repeatedly tested by reason, and successfully applied to an infinite variety of cases, and finally adopted as principles, have a particular congeniality with the mind, and are welcomed to the memory as the offspring of philosophy. This compendium, presenting in a condensed form, pruned of all redundancies, the leading and important principles, rules, and definitions of law and equity, as laid down in the standard elementary works, will be found far more accurate and systematic than notes hastily taken by the student while reading the course, to say nothing of the immense saving of time, and the advantage of print over writing. It contains the pith of all the important branches of the law student's course, accurately collected from Blackstone's Commentaries and leading authors on Evidence, Contracts, Pleadings, and Equity. No index is furnished, because the work is, to some extent, an index itself; besides, it is the desire of the author that the student shall not consider it as a book to be "tasted," merely, but to be thoroughly "chewed and digested;" he can scarcely skim it over if he would, for it is the cream of the law, gathered from the purest and highest sources known to legal science, and the diligent student will find it richer to his professional taste as he partakes of it from day to day. The author wishes here to repeat his closing remarks in the preface to the first edition, that this work is not intended as a substitute for text-books, but simply to lighten the labors and shorten the work of the student when he shall have carefully read the WHOLE COURSE, and commenced his *review*, preparatory to final examination for the bar.

M. E. D.

FEBRUARY, 1876.

"The LORD is our *judge*, the LORD is our *law-giver*, the LORD is our King." *Isaiah xxxiii.*

LAW. "Her seat is the bosom of God; her voice is the harmony of the world; all things in heaven and earth do her homage, the very least as feeling her care, and the greatest as not exempt from her power." *Hooker.*

THE SEVERAL DEPARTMENTS OR BRANCHES OF LAW

MAY BE THUS SHOWN:

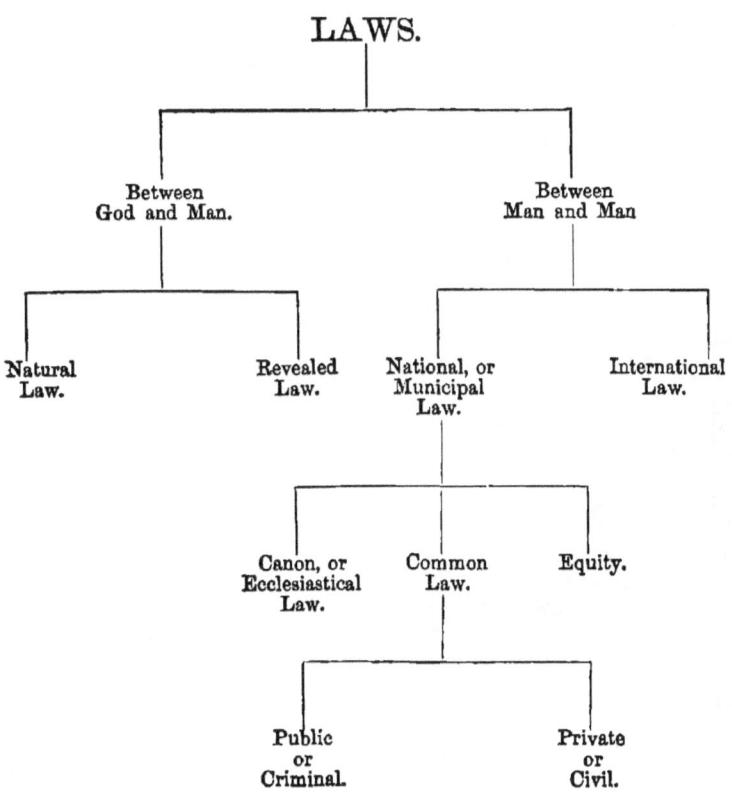

SIR WILLIAM BLACKSTONE was born in Cheapside, London, July 10th, 1723,—the third son of a silkman and bowyer.

Being in early life deprived of both parents, proved, in its consequences, the reverse of misfortune; as to that circumstance probably he was indebted for his future opportunities for advancement.

He was educated at Oxford, under the care and assistance of his uncle. Entered the Bar in 1746; and was chosen Vinerian Professor at Oxford in 1758. Was a member of Parliament; and in 1770 a judge of the Common Pleas.

He died February 14th, 1780, in the fifty-seventh year of his age,—a member of the Established Church.

BLACKSTONE began to execute his lectures on the Laws of England in 1753.

The first volume under the title of *Commentaries on the Laws of England* appeared in 1765.

COMMENTARIES

ON THE

LAWS OF ENGLAND,

BY

BLACKSTONE.

ABRIDGED.

BLACKSTONE'S

ARRANGEMENT OF THE COMMENTARIES

IS AS FOLLOWS:

INTRODUCTION.
Of the *study* of the law.
The *nature* of laws in general.
The *grounds* and foundations of the laws of England.
The *countries* subject to those laws.
The *objects* of the laws of England; which are

RIGHTS AND WRONGS.

VIZ:

THE RIGHTS OF PERSONS,	*Book I.*
THE RIGHTS OF THINGS,	*Book II.*
PRIVATE WRONGS,	*Book III.*
PUBLIC WRONGS,	*Book IV.*

THE NATURE OF LAWS IN GENERAL.

LAW is a rule of action prescribed by superior power.
In its most general and comprehensive sense, it signifies a rule of action dictated by some superior, and which the inferior is bound to obey. It is applied indiscriminately to all kinds of action, whether animate or inanimate, rational or irrational; as for example, we speak of the laws of motion, of gravitation, of optics, or mechanics, as well as the laws of nature, and of nations.

In its more confined sense, it denotes the rules, not of action in general, but of human action or conduct; that is, the precepts by which man, a creature endowed with both reason and a free will, is commanded to make use of those faculties in the general regulation of his behavior.

Law is " the perfection of reason : it always intends to conform thereto, and that which is not reason is not law."

Justinian reduces the whole doctrine of law to these three general principles: "Live honestly; hurt nobody; and render to everyone his just due."

Natural law is the Will of our Maker; and regarded as a rule of human action or conduct, as prescribed by Him in Nature, it is the eternal and immutable law of good and evil,— *discoverable* by the light of reason, and founded in those relations of justice that existed in the nature of things antecedent to any positive precept.

Divine or revealed law, considered as a rule of action, is also the law of nature, imparted by God himself.

The law of nations is a system of rules deducible from reason and natural justice, and established by universal consent, to regulate the conduct and mutual intercourse between independent states.

It is also called " that code of public instruction, which defines the rights, and prescribes the duties of nations in their intercourse with each other."

MUNICIPAL OR CIVIL LAW is "a rule of civil conduct prescribed by the supreme power in a state, commanding what is right and prohibiting what is wrong."

It is called a rule, *first*, because it is not a transient or sudden order from a superior to, or concerning, a particular person; but something permanent, uniform, and universal; *second*, to distinguish it from advice or counsel; *third*, to distinguish it from a compact or agreement, for a compact is a promise proceeding from us; law is a command directed to us.

It is called a rule of civil conduct, to distinguish it from the natural and revealed law; the former being the rule of *moral* conduct, and the latter the rule of moral conduct and of *faith*.

It is a rule prescribed, because a bare resolution confined in the breast of the legislator, without manifesting itself by some external sign, can never be properly a law.

It is prescribed by the supreme power in a state because legislation is the greatest act of superiority that can be exercised by one being over another.

Society is formed for the protection of individuals; and is founded in their *wants* and *fears*.

Governments and states are formed for the preservation of society. They are all reducible to three regular forms of government, viz:

A Democracy,—which generally has more public virtue, or goodness of intent than other forms, but may be deficient in wisdom to contrive, and strength to execute.

A Monarchy,—which is the most powerful, and dangerous of all governments.

An Aristocracy,—which is supposed to have more wisdom than the other forms of government, but less honesty than a republic, and less strength than a monarchy.

The British form of government partakes of the advantages of these *three*: the King, or Queen, representing the monarchical form; the House of Lords, the aristocratic form; and the House of Commons, the democratic form, of government; these three elements *united* constituting the English *Parliament*, or supreme power, of that state.

A law consists of four parts; viz: the *declaratory*,— which defines what is right and wrong; the *directory*,—which consists in commanding the observation of right, or prohibiting the commission of wrong; the *remedial*,—whereby a method is pointed out to recover private rights, or redress private wrongs; and the *vindicatory* part—which signifies what punishment shall be incurred by wrong-doers; and *in this* consists the main strength and force of a law.

To interpret a law, we must enquire after the will or intention of the maker; which is collected from the words, the context, the subject-matter, the effects and consequences, or the spirit and reason of the law.

Words are generally to be understood in their most known and usual signification; their general and popular sense. Terms of art, or technical terms, must be taken according to the acceptation of the learned in art, trade, and science.

The context may aid in establishing the meaning of words, still dubious.

The subject-matter; words are always to be understood as having a regard thereto;—for it is always supposed to be in the eye of the legislator, and all his expressions directed to that end.

Of the effects and consequences, the rule is, that when words bear either none or a very absurd signification, if literally understood, we must a little deviate from the received sense of them.

The reason and spirit of a law, considered, is the most universal and effectual way of discovering its true meaning; or the causes which moved its enactment,—for *when the reason ceases, the law itself ought to cease.*

EQUITY arises from this method of interpreting laws, by *the reason and spirit of them.* Grotius defines equity to be, "the correction of that wherein the law (by reason of its universality) is deficient."

The object of Equity is, to give a more specific relief than can sometimes be had, through the generality of both the unwritten and written law, in matters of private right.

Equity *depends,* essentially, upon the particular circumstances of each case; hence there can be no established rules and fixed precepts of equity laid down, without destroying its very essence, and reducing it to *positive* law.

Courts of Equity are necessary, because when the general decrees of the law come to be applied to particular cases, there should be vested somewhere the power of defining those circumstances which, had they been foreseen, the legislator himself would have expressed; but, the liberty of considering all cases in an equitable light must not be indulged in too far, lest thereby we destroy all law, and leave the decision of every question entirely in the breast of the judge.

The purposes for which our courts of equity are established, and the matters with which they only are conversant, are: to *detect* latent frauds and concealments, which the process of the courts of law is not adapted to reach; to *enforce* the execution of such matters of trust and confidence as are binding in conscience, though not cognizable in a court of law; to *deliver* from such dangers as are owing to misfortune or oversight; and to give a *relief*, more specific and better adapted to the circumstances of the case, than can always be obtained by the generality of rules of the *positive* or *common law*.

They are only conversant in matters of property, or private right.

OF THE LAWS OF ENGLAND; the municipal law of England is divided into two kinds: the *lex non scripta*, the unwritten or common law, and the *lex scripta*, the written or statute law.

The unwritten or common law includes: *general customs*, or the common law properly so called; *particular customs* of certain parts of the kingdom; and those *particular laws* that are, by custom, observed only in certain courts and jurisdictions.

General customs, or the common law, properly so called, are founded upon immemorial universal usage, whereof judicial decisions are the evidence; which decisions are preserved in the public records, explained in the year-books and reports, and digested by writers of approved authority.

The unwritten or common law, then, derives its *binding power* and the *force of law*, from long and immemorial *usage*, and universal *reception* throughout the kingdom.

The degree of antiquity necessary in a custom to entitle it to weight and authority is, that it must have been used time out of mind, or in the solemnity of our legal phrase,—time whereof the memory of man runneth not to the contrary.

The maxims and customs of the common law are to be *known* and their *validity determined* by the *judges*, in the courts of justice. They are the depositaries of the laws, the living oracles, who must decide in all cases of doubt, and who are bound by oath to decide according to the law of the land.

Of precedents; the doctrine of the law is, that they *must be followed*, unless flatly absurd, unjust, unreasonable, or clearly contrary to the *divine* law;—for, though the reason be not obvious at first view, yet we owe such a deference to former times as not to suppose they acted wholly without due consideration.

PARTICULAR CUSTOMS are those which are only in use within some particular districts; as gavel-kind, the customs of London, etc.

The rules relating to particular customs are: *first*, they must be proved to exist; *secondly*, they must appear to be legal;—that is, immemorial, continued, peaceable, reasonable, certain, compulsory, and consistent; and *thirdly*, they must, when allowed, receive a strict construction.

The seven necessary requisites to make a particular custom good or legal are: *first*, that it hath been used so long that the memory of man runneth not to the contrary; *secondly*, it must have been continued; for any interruption would cause a temporary ceasing, and the revival would give it a new beginning, which will be within time of memory, and thereupon the custom will be void; *thirdly*, it must have been peaceable, and acquiesced in, not subject to contention and dispute; *fourthly*, customs must be reasonable, or rather, taken negatively, they must not be unreasonable; *fifthly*, customs ought to be certain; *sixthly*, customs, though established by consent, must be (when so established) compulsory, and not left to the option of every man, whether he will use them or not; and *seventhly*, customs must be consistent with each other; one custom cannot be set up in opposition to another.

The decisions of the courts of justice are the *evidence* of what is common law.

The *law*, and the *opinion of the judge*, are not always convertible terms, or one and the same thing; since it sometimes may happen that the judge may mistake the law.

The reports containing the decisions of the courts of England are extant in a regular series from the reign of Edward II (1307) inclusive; and from his time to that of Henry VIII (1509), they were taken at the expense of the crown, and published *annually*, whence they are known as *The Year-Books*.

Particular laws are such as by special custom, are adopted and used only in certain peculiar courts, under the superintendence and control of the common and statute law : viz, the Roman *civil*, and *canon* law.

By the civil law is generally understood the civil or municipal law of the Roman empire, as comprised in the Institutes, the Code, and the Digest of the Emperor Justinian, and the novel constitutions of himself and some of his successors. The former were compiled by Tribonian and other lawyers, by direction of Justinian, about A. D. 533. It took them three years, and consists of: *first*, the *Institutes*, which contain the elements or first principles of the Roman law, in four books; *secondly*, the *Digests or Pandects*, in fifty books, containing the opinions and writings of eminent lawyers; *thirdly*, a new *Code*, or collection of imperial constitutions, in twelve books; and *fourthly*, the *Novels*, or new constitutions posterior in time to the other books, and amounting to a supplement to the code, containing new decrees of successive emperors:—the whole, forming the body of the *Roman Civil Law*.

The canon law is a body of Roman ecclesiastical law, relating to such matters as that Church either has or claims to have the proper jurisdiction over. It consists of the compiled opinions of the ancient Latin Fathers, the decrees of general councils, and the decretal epistles and bulls or edicts of the Holy See.

The written or statute law—the *lex scripta*,—is made by the supreme power in the state, to supply the defects, or amend what is amiss, of the unwritten law.

The courts in which the civil and canon laws are permitted to be used, are : the courts of the Arch Bishops and Bishops, and their derivitive officers; the Military Courts; the Admiralty Courts; and the Courts of the Two Universities; but they are all under the superintendency of the *Courts of Common Law*.

Statutes, are either general or special, public or private; and are declaratory of the common law, or remedial of small defects therein

The rules to be observed in the construction of statutes, are :

1st. There are three points to be considered in the construction of all remedial statutes : viz, the *old law*, the *mischief*, and the *remedy*.

2d. A statute which treats of things or persons of an *inferior* rank, cannot, by any general words, be extended to those of a *superior*.

3d. *Penal* statutes must be construed strictly.

4th. Statutes against *frauds*, are to be *liberally* and *beneficially* expounded.

5th. One part of a statute must be so construed by another, that the *whole* may stand,—if possible.

6th. A *saving*, totally repugnant to the body of the act, is void.

7th. Where the common law and a statute differ, the common law gives place to the statute; and an old statute gives place to a new one.

8th. If a statute that repeals another, is itself repealed afterwards, the first statute is thereby revived, without any formal words for that purpose.

9th. Acts of parliament derogatory from the power of subsequent parliaments, bind not.

10th. Acts of parliament that are impossible to be performed, are of no validity.

THE TERRITORY OF ENGLAND, is divided into *Ecclesiastical*, and *Civil* or Lay.

The ecclesiastical part is divided into provinces, dioceses, arch-deaconries, rural deaneries and parishes.

The civil divisions are, into counties or shires, of which some are *palatine ;* then into rapes, lathes, or tithings; next, into hundreds or wapentakes; and lastly, into towns, vills, or tithings. Ten families of freeholders made a *town* or *tithing ;* ten tithings composed a *hundred ;* and an indefinite number of these hundreds, formed a *county* or *shire*.

Counties palatine were so called, because the owners thereof had in those counties royal powers as fully as the King in his palace.

THE OBJECTS OF THE LAWS of England, are *Rights* and *Wrongs*.

Rights are privileges; they are *commanded* to be observed by law; and are subdivided into the *rights of persons*,—being those which concern and are annexed to the persons of men; *and* the *rights of things*,—which are such rights as a man may acquire over external objects or things unconnected with his person.

Wrongs are the privation of right; they are *prohibited* by law; and are divided into, *private wrongs*,—which, being infringements of particular rights merely, concern individuals only, and are called *civil injuries;* and *public wrongs,* which being breaches of general and public rights, affect the whole community, and are called *crimes,* and *misdemeanors.*

ANALYSIS OF BOOK I.

The Rights of Persons; which are
1. Natural persons, whose rights are
    1. Absolute, viz: the enjoyment of
        1. Personal security,
        2. Personal liberty,
        3. Private property.
    2. Relative; as they stand in relations
        1. Public; as
            1. Magistrates; who are
                1. Supreme,
                    1. Legislative, viz: the Parliament,
                    2. Executive, viz: the King wherein of his
                        1. Title,
                        2. Royal family,
                        3. Councils,
                        4. Duties,
                        5. Prerogative,
                        6. Revenue.
                            1. Ordinary, viz:
                                1. Ecclesiastical,
                                2. Temporal.
                            2. Extraordinary.
                2. Subordinate.
            2. People; who are
                1. Aliens, or
                2. Natives; who are
                    1. Clergy, and
                    2. Laity; who are in a state
                        1. Civil,
                        2. Military,
                        3. Maritime.
        2. Private; as
            1. Master and servant,
            2. Husband and wife,
            3. Parent and child,
            4. Guardian and ward.
2. Artificial persons, viz: bodies politic, or corporations;
    1. Ecclesiastical, or
    2. Lay; either of which may be
        1. Aggregate, or
        2. Sole.

BOOK I.

THE RIGHTS OF PERSONS, being such as concern and are annexed to the persons of men, when the person *to whom* they belong or are due is regarded, are called (simply) *rights*, in the popular acceptation; but when we consider such as are due *from* every citizen, they are denominated (civil) *duties*.

Persons are divided by law, into *natural* persons, or such as the God of nature formed us; and *artificial*, or such as are created by human laws for the purpose of society and government, which are called *corporations*, or bodies politic.

The rights of natural persons, are; *absolute*, or such as belong to individuals; and *relative*, or such as are incident to them as members of society.

The absolute rights of individuals are those rights which are so in their primary and strictest sense; such as would belong to their persons merely in a state of nature, and which every man is entitled to enjoy, whether out of society or in it.

To protect individuals in the enjoyment of these absolute rights which were vested in them by the immutable laws of nature, is the principal aim of society.

To maintain and regulate these absolute rights of individuals is the first and primary end of human laws.

Liberty is the general appellation for the natural rights of man; and every man gives up a part of his *natural liberty*, when he enters into society, as the price of so valuable a purchase.

Political or civil liberty is natural liberty so far restrained by human laws, as is necessary for the good of society.

The absolute rights of Englishmen have been declared and established, *first*, by the Charter of Liberties, obtained from King John, called *Magna Charta*; *afterwards*, by the statute *confirmatio chartarium*, directing the great charter to be allowed as the common law; *next*, by a multitude of corroborating statutes;

then, by the Petition of Right, the *habeas corpus* act, and other salutary laws passed under Charles II; *again*, by the Bill of Rights of 1688; and *lastly*, by the Act of Settlement.

The absolute rights or civil liberties of men are principally three: viz, the right of personal security; the right of personal liberty; and the right of private property.

The right of personal security consists of a person's legal and uninterrupted enjoyment of his life, his limbs, his body, his health, and his reputation.

By limbs are meant, only those members which may be useful to him in fight, and the loss of which alone amounts to mayhem by the common law.

Duress per minas is where a man, through fear of death or mayhem, is prevailed upon to execute a deed, or to do any other legal act: these may be afterwards avoided, if forced upon him by a well grounded fear of losing his life, or even limbs, in case of his non-compliance.

Civil death occurs when any man is banished by the process of common law, or abjures the realm, or enters into religion, i. e. into a monastery and becomes a professed monk; in which cases he is absolutely *dead in law*, and his next heir shall have his estate.

The right of personal liberty consists in the free power of locomotion, without illegal restraint or banishment.

Lawful imprisonment is effected by process from the courts of judicature, or by warrant from some legal officer having authority to commit to prison;—which warrant must be in writing, under the hand and seal of the magistrate, and express the cause of commitment, in order to be examined into by a *habeas corpus* if necessary. Coke says, "the *law* judges, like Festus, the Roman governor, that it is unreasonable to send a prisoner, and not to signify withal the crimes alleged against him."

Habeas corpus is a writ requiring the body of a person imprisoned to be brought before the Court of King's Bench or Common Pleas, who shall determine whether the cause of commitment be just.

The right of private property consists in the free use, enjoyment and disposal of one's acquisitions, without any control or diminution, save only by law.

The relative rights, or relations of persons, as members of society, are either *public* or *private*.

THE PUBLIC RELATIONS are those of *magistrates* and *people*, the most universal relation by which men are connected together being *government*.

Prerogative is that special pre-eminence which the King hath over and above all persons, and *out* of the ordinary course of the common law, in right of his regal dignity.

The people are divided into natives, or natural-born subjects, aliens, and denizens.

Aliens are such as are born out of the realm, or allegiance of the King.

Denizens are such born as aliens, but who have obtained letters patent (naturalization) to make them subjects.

Natives, or natural-born subjects, are such as are born within the dominions of the crown of England; that is, within the ligeance, or, as it is generally called, the *allegiance* of the King.

The rights of natives are natural and perpetual; those of aliens local and temporary only, unless made denizens.

The natives, or people proper, are divided into the *clerical* or *ecclesiastical*, which includes all persons in holy orders or offices; and the *laity*, which comprehends all the rest of the nation.

The laity are divided into the civil, the military, and the maritime.

The civil state is divided into the *nobility* and *commonalty*, and includes all the nation except the clergy, the army, and the navy.

The degrees of the nobility are: dukes, marquises, earls, viscounts, and barons.

The degrees of the commonalty are: vidames (now quite out of use), knights, colonels, sergeants-at-law, doctors, esquires, gentlemen, yeomen, tradesmen, artificers and laborers.

Allegiance is the duty of all subjects, being the reciprocal tie or *ligamen* which binds the subject to the King, in return for that protection which he affords them.

The oath of allegiance was the oath taken to a superior lord, or lord paramount, only, *without* any saving or exception whatever, to bear faith to one's sovereign lord, in opposition to all men, &c.

Fealty was the obligation on the part of the vassal to *his immediate* and superior lord.

The oath of fealty, or the feudal oath of fidelity, was the parent of our oath of allegiance, and was couched in almost the same terms as the oath of allegiance, but contained a *saving* or exception, of the faith or allegiance due to the superior lord, or King; hence it was the oath taken to the *inferior* lord.

Homage was the *submission* of the tenant or vassal to his lord, coupled with the oath and promise; and was performed by openly and humbly kneeling, ungirt, uncovered, and holding up his hands between those of the lord, and swearing that he "became his man from this day forward, for life, for limb, and worldly honor, and unto you shall be true and faithful and bear you faith for the land I hold of you," &c., and then received a kiss from his lord.

THE PRIVATE RELATIONS of persons in society are: those of master and servant, husband and wife, parent and child, and guardian and ward.

Servants are menial or domestic; *apprentices*, are usually bound for years; *laborers*, are hired by the day or week, and are not part of the family; and *stewards, factors,* or *bailiffs*, the law considers as servants *pro tempore*.

The master has a property in the service of his servant, and must be answerable for such acts as the servant does by his express or implied command or assent.

Marriage the law regards in no other light than as a civil contract, and holds it good, where the parties were able, willing, and did actually contract in the proper forms and solemnities required by law.

Disabilities to marriage, are canonical, or civil.

Canonical disabilities are: pre-contract; consanguinity, or blood relationship; affinity, or relationship by marriage; and some corporeal infirmities. They are sufficient, by the ecclesiastical law, to avoid the marriage in a spiritual court; but in our law, they only make it voidable, and not *ipso facto* void until sentence of nullity be obtained.

The civil disabilities are: a prior marriage; want of age; non-consent of parents or guardians, where requisite; and want of reason. They render the marriage void *ab initio*, and not merely voidable.

Marriage is dissolved by death or divorce. Divorce is of two kinds, *a vinculo matrimonii*, or from the bond of matrimony, which is total; and *a mensa et thoro* or from bed or board, which is partial only.

Children are of two sorts, *legitimate*, and *spurious* or *bastards*.

The duties of parents to their children are: maintenance, protection, and education.

Legitimate children are those born in lawful wedlock, or within a competent time thereafter.

Bastards are those born out of lawful matrimony.

The main end and design of marriage, is to ascertain and fix upon some certain person to whom the care, protection, maintenance, and education of children should belong.

Guardian and ward, a temporary relation between persons which the law hath provided, is a kind of artificial parentage, to supply the deficiency when it happens of the natural.

We have guardians *by nature*, or the parents; guardians *for nurture*; guardians *in socage, or by the common law*,—which last two are only until the infant attains the age of fourteen,—and guardians *by statute*, assigned by the father's will.

Full age in an infant, male or female, is twenty-one; which age is completed on the day preceding the anniversary of a person's birth.

An infant may be sued only under the protection and joining the name of his guardian; and an infant may sue either by his guardian, or *prochein amy* or next friend, who is not his guardian, but any person who will undertake the infant's case.

An infant in respect to his tender years, has various *privileges*, and various *disabilities* in law; chiefly with regard to suits, crimes, estates, and contracts.

An infant in ventre sa mere is considered in law, for many purposes, as born. It is capable of having a legacy, or a surrender of a copyhold estate, made to it; it may have a guardian assigned to it; and it is enabled to have an estate limited to its use, and to take afterward, by such limitation, as if it were then actually born.

CORPORATIONS, bodies politic or corporate, are *artificial* persons established for preserving in perpetual succession certain rights, which, being conferred on natural persons only, would fail in process of time.

Their primary division is into *aggregate*,—consisting of many members; and *sole*,—consisting of but one; as a king, bishop, or parson.

Corporations sole or aggregate are either *ecclesiastical* or *spiritual,*—erected to perpetuate the rights of the church; or *lay,* as a college, &c.

LAY CORPORATIONS are *civil,*—erected for many temporal purposes; or *eleemosynary,*—erected to perpetuate the charities of the founder.

Corporations are created generally by act of parliament, by royal charter, and by prescription,—of which the city of London is an instance; it has existed so long.

The powers incident to corporations are: to maintain perpetual succession; to act in their corporate capacity like an individual; to purchase and hold lands; to have a common seal, by which the corporation acts and speaks only; and to make by-laws or private statutes for its own government and regulation.

A corporation's privileges and disabilities are: it must always appear by attorney, being, as Coke says, "invisible;" it cannot maintain or be made defendant in a battery or like personal actions; nor commit crime in its corporate capacity, for it is not liable to corporeal penalties; it cannot be an executor, or perform any personal duties, for it cannot take the oath of due performance; it cannot be seized of lands to the use of another, for such kind of confidence is foreign to the end of its institution; it cannot be committed to prison, outlawed, or excommunicated.

Corporations, as they cannot be arrested, are made to appear by distress on their lands and goods.

The duty of corporations, is to answer the ends of their institution, which may be enforced by visitations.

A corporation may be dissolved by act of parliament; by natural death of all its members; by surrender of its franchises; and by forfeiture of its charter, through negligence or abuse of its franchises.

ANALYSIS OF BOOK II.

The Rights of Things; which consist in dominion over
1. THINGS REAL; in which are considered
    1. Their several kinds, viz:
        1. Corporeal, or
        2. Incorporeal.
    2. The tenures by which they may be holden, viz:
        1. Ancient, and
        2. Modern.
    3. The estates therein; with respect to
        1. The quantity of interest; viz:
            1. Freehold,
                1. Of inheritance, or
                2. Not of inheritance,
            2. Less than Freehold, and
            3. On condition.
        2. The time of enjoyment; viz: in
            1. Possession,
            2. Remainder, or
            3. Reversion.
        3. The number and connection of the tenants; who may hold in
            1. Severalty,
            2. Joint tenancy,
            3. Coparcenary, or, in
            4. Common.
    4. The title to them; which may be gained or lost, by
        1. Descent, or by
        2. Purchase, which includes
            1. Escheat,
            2. Occupancy,
            3. Prescription,
            4. Forfeiture, and
            5. Alienation, by common assurances; which are by
                1. Deed, or matter IN PAIS; wherein of its
                    1. General nature, and
                    2. Several species.
                2. Matter of record,
                3. Special custom, and by
                4. Devise.
2. THINGS PERSONAL, or chattels; in which are considered
    1. Their distribution,
    2. Property therein,
    3. Title to them; which may be gained or lost, by
        1. Occupancy,
        2. Prerogative,
        3. Forfeiture,
        4. Custom,
        5. Succession,
        6. Marriage,
        7. Judgment,
        8. Gift or Grant,
        9. Contract,
        10. Bankruptcy,
        11. Testament,
        12. Administration.

BOOK II.

THE RIGHTS OF THINGS, are those rights which a man may acquire in and to such external things as are unconnected with his person.

Property, or the dominion of man over external objects, has its *origin* from the *Creator*, as his gift to mankind.

The *substance* of things was, at first, common to all; yet a *temporary* property in the *use* of them might even then be acquired and continued *by occupancy*. In process of time a *permanent* property was established in the *substance*, as well as the *use*, of things; which was also originally acquired by occupancy only.

Lest this property should determine by the owner's dereliction, or death, whereby the thing would again become common, societies have established conveyances, wills, and heirships, in order to continue the property of the first occupant: and where by accident such property becomes discontinued or unknown, the thing usually results to the sovereign of the state, by virtue of the municipal law.

Things are divided into *things real*, and *things personal*.

THINGS REAL are such as are of a permanent, fixed, and immovable nature, and cannot be carried out of their place, as lands and tenements.

Things personal, are such as goods, money, and other movables, which may attend the owner's person wherever he may choose to go.

Things real, are *usually* said to consist in lands, tenements, and *hereditaments*.

Land is a term comprehending all things of a permanent, substantial nature, being a word of very extensive signification.

Land has in its legal signification an indefinite extent upwards as well as downwards, *cujus est solum ejus est usque ad cœlum* ; so that the word *land* includes not only the face of the earth, but everything under it, or over it; and by the name of *land*, everything terrestrial will pass.

Tenement is a word of still greater extent than land, and in its original proper and legal sense, it signifies *anything that may be holden,* provided it be of a permanent nature, whether it be of a substantial and sensible, or of an unsubstantial, ideal kind.

Hereditament is by much the largest and most comprehensive expression; for it includes not only lands and tenements, but *whatsoever may be inherited,* be it corporeal or incorporeal, real, personal or mixed.

All the several kinds of things real are reducible to one of these three, viz: lands, tenements or hereditaments; whereof the second includes the first, and the third the first and second.

Things real may be considered with reference to their several *kinds;* the *tenures* by which they may be holden; the *estates* therein, and their *title,* or the means of acquiring and losing them.

THE KINDS OF THINGS REAL are *corporeal* or *incorporeal;* which is also the division of *hereditaments*—the most comprehensive denomination of things real.

Corporeal Hereditaments are such as affect the senses, may be seen and handled by the body; they consist wholly of *permanent* and *substantial objects,* all of which may be comprehended under the general denomination of *land* only.

Incorporeal hereditaments are not the objects of sensation; can neither be seen nor handled; are creatures of the mind, and exist only in contemplation. *They are rights,* issuing out of things corporate, whether real or personal; or concerning, or annexed to, or exercisable within the same.

They are principally of ten sorts, viz: advowsons, tithes, commons, ways, offices, dignities, franchises, corodies or pensions, annuities and rents.

An advowson is the right of presentation to a church or ecclesiastical benefice: either *appendant, i. e.,* annexed to the possession of the manor (lords of manor being originally the only founders and patrons of churches); or *in gross,* as where separated from the *property* of the manor and annexed to the *person* of the owner, and not to his manor or lands.

Advowsons are also either *presentative,* where the patron has a right of presentation, and to demand of the bishop to institute his clerk if qualified; *collative,* where the bishop and patron are one and the same, in which case the bishop cannot present to himself, but does by the act of collation; all that is done by institution and induction, or *donative*, as where the king, or any subject by his license, doth found a church, and ordains that it shall be merely in the gift or disposal of the patron, subject to his visitations only, and not that of the ordinary, and vested absolutely in the clerk by the patron's deed of donation, without presentation, institution, or induction.

Tithes are the tenth part of the yearly increase arising and renewing from the profits of lands, the stock upon lands, and the personal industry of the inhabitants.

"Time of memory" has long ago been ascertained, by law, to commence from the beginning of the reign of Richard II.

Tithes are either *predial*, as corn, grass, hops and wood; *mixed*, as wool, milk, pigs, &c.; or *personal*, as of manual occupations, trades, fisheries, and the like.

Common is a right or profit which a man has in the lands of another; as to feed his beasts, catch fish, dig turf, and the like. It is chiefly of four kinds, viz:

Common of pasture is a right of feeding one's beasts on another's land; and is either *appendant*, as when inseparably incident to the grant of the lands; *appurtenant*, where it arises from no connection of tenure or absolute necessity, but *may* be annexed to lands, or extended to other beasts besides such as are generally commonable, as hogs, goats, &c., which neither plow nor manure the ground; *of vicinage*, where the inhabitants of two contiguous townships have intercommoned to prevent suits; or *in gross*, where it is annexed to a man's person, instead of to land.

Common of piscary is a right of fishing in another man's water.

Common of turbary is a right of digging turf on another's ground.

Common of estovers, or botes, is a right of taking necessary wood from off another's estate.

Ways are a right of passing over another's ground, and has reference only to private ways. They may be founded on permission, grant and prescription; or may arise from act and operation of law.

Offices are the right to exercise a public or private employment, and to take the fees and emoluments pertaining thereto.

Dignities are titles to honor, and bear a near relation to offices.

Franchises are a royal privilege, or branch of the king's prerogative, subsisting in the hands of the subject.

Franchise and *liberty* are used as synonymous terms.

Corodies are allotments of provisions for one's sustenance, which may be converted into *pensions*.

Annuity is a yearly sum of money charged upon the *person*, and not upon the lands, of the grantor.

Rents are certain profits issuing yearly out of lands and tenements corporeal. The rents at common law were rent-service, rent-charge, and rent-seck.

Rent-service is so called because it has some corporeal service incident to it; as, at least, fealty or the feudal oath of fidelity.

Rent-charge is where the owner of the rent has no future interest or reversion expectant in the land: and it is called a rent-charge, because the land was charged with a distress for the payment of the rent.

Rent-seck, or barren rent, is a rent reserved by deed, but without any clause of distress.

Rents of assise are the certain established rents of the freeholders and ancient copy-holders of a manor, which cannot be departed from or varied. Those of the freeholders were frequently called *chief-rents*, and those of both indifferently denominated *quit-rents*, because thereby the tenant goes quit and free of all services. When the quit-rents were reserved in silver, they were called *white-rents*, in contradistinction to rents reserved in work, grain or baser money, which were called *black-mail.*

Rack-rent is a rent of the full value of the tenement, or near it.

A fee-farm rent is a rent-charge issuing out of an estate in fee, of at least one-fourth of the value of the lands at the time of its reservation.

TENURES BY WHICH THINGS REAL MAY BE HOLDEN.

The English doctrine of tenures is derived from the *feudal law* or *system:* which had its origin from the military policy of the Northern or Celtic nations,—the Goths, Huns, Franks, Vandals, Lombards, &c.; who, all migrating from the same *officina gentium,* poured themselves in vast quantities into all the regions of Europe, at the declension of the Roman Empire. Bringing this policy from their own countries, they continued it in their new acquisitions, as the most likely means of securing them.

Feuds, *fiefs,* or *fees,*—in their original synonymous,—were allotments of large districts or parcels of land made by the conquering chief or general, to the superior officers of their armies, and by *them* dealt out again, in smaller parcels, to the inferior officers and most deserving soldiers, under them.

The appellation, *feud, fief,* or *fee,* signified in the Northern language, a conditional *stipend* or *reward,* and the condition annexed to them being, that the possessor should do service faithfully for them, to him who gave them, both at home and in wars; for which purpose he took the feudal oath of fealty; and in case of breach of this oath or condition the lands reverted to him who granted them.

The universality and early use of this feudal plan among all those nations, which in complaisance to the Romans we still call barbarous, may appear from what is recorded of the Cimbri and Teutons, nations of the same Northern origin as those we have been describing, at their first irruption into Italy, about a century before the Christian era. They demanded of the Romans stipendiary lands or feuds, to be allotted to them, to be held by military and other personal services, whenever their lord should call upon them. *This* was evidently the same constitution that displayed itself more fully about seven hundred years afterwards, when the Salii, Burgundians, and Franks, broke in upon Gaul; the Visigoths on Spain, and the Lombards upon Italy, and introduced with themselves this Northern plan of polity, as best serving to distribute and protect the territories they had newly gained. Hence the Emperor Alexander Severus took the hint of dividing lands conquered from the enemy among his generals and victorious soldiery, on condition of receiving military service from them and their heirs forever.

The wisdom and efficiency of this policy of the victorious Northerners, alarmed all the princes of Europe, and made them think it necessary to enter into the same plan, with *their* subjects, whose possession before was perfectly *allodial,* that is independent, and held of no superior; and thus **in a few years the feudal constitution or doctrine of tenures extended itself over all the western world**, which alteration of landed property in so material a point, drew after it an alteration of laws and customs; so that the feudal laws soon drove out the Roman, which had hitherto so universally obtained, but now became for many centuries lost and forgotten.

But this feudal polity thus by degrees established over all

Europe was not received universally into that part of the island called *England*, until the reign of William the Norman; for the Saxons were firmly settled in the island as early as the year 600, and it was not till two centuries after that feuds arrived at full vigor in Europe.

This introduction of the feudal tenures into England by King William, does not appear to have been effected immediately after his conquest, nor by the mere arbitrary will and power of the conqueror, but to have been gradually established by the Roman barons, and others, and afterwards universally consented to by the great council of the nation, long after his title was established,—upon the principle of self-security.

In consequence of this change, it became a fundamental *maxim* and *necessary principle*,—though in reality a mere *fiction*,—of our English tenures, "that *the King* is the universal lord and original proprietor of all the lands in his kingdom, and that no man doth or can possess any part of it, but what has mediately or immediately been derived as a *gift from him*, to be held upon feudal services."

In this system of tenure, in general, *the grantor* was called the proprietor, or *lord*, and retained the dominion or ultimate property of the feud or fee; and the grantee who had only the use or possession, was styled the feudatory or *vassal*; which was only another name for the tenant or holder of the lands.

The King,—the *original* grantor,—was styled the *lord paramount* or over all; those who held immediately under him being styled his tenants in *capite*, or in chief; and they who held under these *mesne* or middle lords, were styled tenants *parvail*, or the lowest tenants who made the *avail* or profit from the land.

The feudatories were styled *pares curtis*, or *pares curiæ* because the lord was the legislator and judge over his feudatories.

The manner of granting a feud, was by words of gratuitous and pure donation; being perfected by the ceremony of corporeal investiture, or open and notorious delivery of possession in the presence of the other vassals; called *livery of seizin*.

Feuds were not at first hereditary, though frequently granted by favor of the lord, to the children of the former possessor, till, in process of time it became unusual, and was, therefore, thought hard, to reject the heir, if he were capable to perform the service; and therefore infants, women, and monks, who were incapable of bearing arms, were also incapable of succeeding to a genuine feud, and it was for *this* reason that women did not receive the attention, consideration, or privileges pertaining to property, that men did, and many of their disabilities in law to this day, may be traced back to this origin; for previous to the introduction of this system, the privileges of women in England, were generally about the same as those of the men. This succession of the children to their father's feud, or *descent* of the feud, originally extended to *all* the males alike; but being found inconvenient, and also tending to weaken the strength of the feudal union, by multiplicity of these divisions among so many heirs, *honorary feuds*, or *titles of nobility*, were introduced, which were not divisible, and could only be inherited by the eldest son, *in imitation of military feuds*.

Neither lord nor vassal could alien his estate without the consent of the other, because the feudal obligation was looked upon as reciprocal.

The feudatories often found it necessary to commit part of *their* lands to inferior tenants, and obliged such to make *returns* in service, corn, cattle, or money; which returns were the origin of *rents*, which were called improper feuds.

THE ANCIENT ENGLISH TENURES;—or the manner in which lands, tenements, and hereditaments were held until the middle of the last century.

Tenure denotes the manner of *holding* or possessing property.

Tenement is the thing holden.

Tenant, the *person* holding lands or tenements by any title.

The *distinction* of tenures, consisted in the *nature* of the services or renders, that were due to the lords from their tenants.

The services, in respect of their quality, were either *free* or *base*; and in respect of their quantity and time of exacting them were either *certain* or *uncertain*.

Free services were such as were not unbecoming the character of a soldier or a freeman to perform; as to serve under his lord in the wars, to pay a sum of money, and the like.

Base services were such as were only fit for peasants or persons of a servile rank; as to plow the lord's land, make his hedges, &c.

Certain services, whether free or base, were such as were stinted in quantity, and could not be exceeded on any pretense; as to pay a stated annual rent, or to plow such a field for three days.

Uncertain services depended upon unknown contingencies; as to do military service in person, pay an assessment in lieu of it, or wind a horn whenever the Scots invaded the realm, which were free services: or to do whatever the lord should command, which was a base or villein service.

From the various combinations of these services have arisen the four principal species of ancient lay tenures which subsisted in England till the middle of the last century; and three of which subsist to this day. Hence *the feudal clogs, though greatly lessened, still cling to English property.*

Bracton, who wrote under Henry III, gives the clearest account of these ancient tenures, of which the following is an outline or abstract, viz:

"**Tenements** are of two kinds, *frank-tenements* and *villenage*.

"**Of frank tenements**, some are held freely in consideration of homage and *knight-service*; others, in *free-socage*, with the service of fealty only.

"**Of villenages**, some are *pure*, and others *privileged*; he holding in *pure villenage* doing whatever is commanded of him, and always bound to an *uncertain* service; and in *privileged villenage*, or *villein-socage*, the villein-socmen do villein services, but such as are *certain* and determined."

From the sense of which, the four principal kinds of *ancient* English tenures appear to have been, viz:

Tenure in chivalry, or by knight-service, where the service was *free* but *uncertain;* as military service, with homage.

Tenure in free-socage, where the service was not only *free* but *certain;* as, fealty only, or by rent and fealty.

Tenure in pure villenage, where the service was *base* and *uncertain.*

Tenure in privileged villenage, *or villein-socage,* where the service was *base,* but reduced to a *certainty.*

The most universal ancient tenure, was that in chivalry, or by *knight-service;* to make which a determinate quantity of land was necessary, called a knight's *fee—feodum militare—*and differed in but very few points from a pure or proper feud; being entirely military, the tenant or knight being bound to attend his lord, forty days in every year, if called upon, as his *reditus* or return, or his rent, or service, for the lands he held. It was granted by livery and perfected by homage and fealty.

The seven fruits and consequences of knight-service,

or tenure in chivalry, inseparably incident to it, were: aids, reliefs, primer-seizen, wardship, marriage, fines for alienation, and escheat.

Aids were principally *three*;—to ransom the lord's person if taken prisoner; to make the lord's eldest son a knight; and to marry the lord's eldest daughter, by giving her a suitable portion. Aids were originally mere *benevolences* granted by the tenant to the lord in times of difficulty and distress; but in process of time they grew to be considered as a matter of right and not of discretion.

Reliefs were a fine, or composition with the *lord* for taking up the estate which by the feudal law was lapsed or fallen in, by the death of the tenant.

Primer-seizin was a right which the *King* had whenever any of his tenants *in capite* died seized of a knight's fee, to receive of the heir, if he were of age, a whole year's profits of the lands, if they were in possession; and half a year's profits, if in reversion expectant on an estate for life.

Wardship: when the heir was under age, the lord was entitled to wardship, and was called guardian in chivalry. It consisted in having the custody of the body and lands of such heir, without any account of the profits, till the age of twenty-one in males, and sixteen in females, for the feudal law considered him incapable of knight service, till of age, or twenty-one.

Marriage, or the tendering of a suitable match to their infant wards, was another right the lord had, which if they refused, they forfeited the value of the marriage to their guardian. This custom grew from a fear of their marrying the lord's enemy.

Fines were due the lord for every alienation of the tenant, whenever he had occasion to make over his land to another,— which he could not do, however, without the consent of the lord. The lord, also, could not alien his seigniory without the consent of his tenant, which consent was called his *attornment;* for the feudal obligation was looked upon as reciprocal.

Escheat is the determination of the tenure, or dissolution of the mutual bond between the lord and tenant, from the extinction of the blood of the latter, by either natural or civil causes; in which case the land *escheated* or fell back to the lord of the fee.

Tenure by grand-serjeanty, was where the tenant was bound to do some special *honorary* service to the King in *person*, as to carry his banner, his sword, or the like; or be his butler, champion, or other officer, at his coronation.

Tenure by cornage was a species of grand-serjeanty, and consisted of winding a horn when the Scots and other enemies entered the land, in order to warn the king's subjects.

Escuage, or scutage, was a *pecuniary* satisfaction instead of military service which tenants found means of *substituting* in lieu of the more troublesome *personal attendance* of knight-service; this pecuniary substitute came at last to be levied by assessments, at so much for every knight's fee; but by the laws of Edward I, and Magna Charta, no *scutage* could be levied without the consent of parliament; these *scutages* being the groundwork of all succeeding subsidies, and the *land tax* of later times. By this degeneration of *personal* military duty into *pecuniary* assessments, the advantages of the feudal constitution were destroyed.

THE MODERN ENGLISH TENURES are those of the ancient or original English tenures which remained after the destruction of the military or most oppressive of the feudal tenures, which was accomplished at a single blow by the statute 12, Charles II, whereby all tenures except frankalmoigne, grand-serjeanty, and copyholds, were reduced to one general species of tenure, called *free and common* socage.

This statute of Charles II was even a greater acquisition to the civil property of the kingdom than Magna Charta itself; since that only pruned the luxuriances that had grown out of the military tenures, and thereby preserved the vigor of them; but the statute of Charles II extirpated the whole, and demolished both root and branch.

The word *socage*, is derived from the Saxon appellation *soc*, which signifies liberty or privilage, and being joined to a usual termination, is called *socage;* in Latin *socagium,* signifying a *free* and *privileged tenure.*

Socage, in its most general and extensive signification, seems to denote a tenure by any certain and determinate service.

This tenure includes petit serjeanty, tenure in burgage, and gavel-kind.

Free socage tenures partook strongly of the feudal nature, as well as those in chivalry; the lands being holden subject to some *service,* at least to fealty, and suit of court; and subject to reliefs, wardships, and escheat, but not to marriage. They were also formerly subject to aids, primer-seizin, fines for alienation, and escheat,—except in gavel-kind.

Socage tenures were plainly the relics of Saxon liberty, retained by such persons as had neither forfeited them to the King, nor been obliged to exchange them for, as it was called, the more honorable, but more troublesome, tenure of knight-service. This is peculiarly remarkable in the tenure prevailing in Kent, called *gavel-kind,* which is generally acknowledged to be a species of socage tenure; the preservation whereof from the innovations of the Normans is a fact universally known.

The service must be *certain,* to denominate it *socage,* and the important distinction between tenure by knight-service and tenure in socage is, that where the services were *free* and *honorable,* but *uncertain* as to the *time of their performance,* as military service, cornage, and the like, it was called *tenure in knight-service,* or *chivalry;* but where the service was not only *free,* but also *certain,* as by fealty only, or by rent and fealty; this was *tenure by free-socage,* or *liberum socagium.*

Petit-serjeanty consisted of holding lands of the King, by the rendering to him annually some small implement of war; as a bow, sword, lance, arrow, and the like. It differs from grand-serjeanty in that the latter was a *personal service,* instead of a *tribute service* or *render.* Their resemblance is, that both tend to some purpose relative to the King's person.

Tenure in burgage, is where the King or other person is lord of an ancient borough in which the tenements are held by a rent certain. It is a kind of *town* socage; as common socage, by which other lands are holden, is usually of a *rural* nature.

Borough English is an incident of Burgage tenure, and provides that the *youngest,* instead of the eldest son, shall succeed to the burgage tenement on the death of his father; by reason of the custom of *marcheta.*

Gavel-kind is also a species of socage tenure, modified by the customs of the country; the lands being holden by *suit of court* and *fealty,* a service in its nature *certain.*

The distinguishing *properties* of *gavel-kind,* (which before the Norman conquest was the general custom of the realm) are various, the principal of which are; that the tenant is of age sufficient to alien his estate by feoffment, at the age of *fifteen.* The estate *does not escheat* in case of an attainder and execution for felony. In most places the tenant could *devise his lands* by will,

TABLE OF TENURES.

I. Frank-tenement, or freehold.

LAY TENURES.

1. Military tenures (abolished, *except* grand-serjeanty, and reduced to free-socage tenures).
   1. Knight-service proper, or tenure in chivalry.
   2. Grand-serjeanty, one species of which is Cornage.

2. Free-socage, or plough service.
   1. Petit-serjeanty.
   2. Tenure in burgage.
   3. Gavel-kind.

II. Villenage.

1. Pure villenage (whence copyholds at the lord's [nominal] will, which is regulated according to custom).
   1. Tenure in ancient.
   2. Privileged copyholds, customary freeholds, or free copyholds.
   3. Copyholds of base tenure.

2. Privileged villenage, sometimes called villein-socage (whence tenure in ancient demesne, which is an exalted species of copyhold, held according to the lord's will), and is of three kinds.

SPIRITUAL TENURES.

I. Frankalmoigne, or free alms. | II. Tenure by divine service.

before the statute for that purpose was made. The lands *descended to all the sons together;* which indeed was anciently the course of descent over all England, though in some particular places, particular customs prevailed.

That *socage tenures* partake of *feudal nature* or origin, as apparent from a comparison of their incidents and consequences with those of tenure in *chivalry,* probably arises from its more ancient Saxon original; since, as before observed, feuds were not unknown among the Saxons, though they did not form a part of their military policy; nor were they drawn out into such arbitrary consequences, as among the Normans.

Villeins were a sort of people in downright servitude, under the Saxon government, who were not only used and employed in the most servile works, but *belonged,* both they and their children and effects, to the lord of the soil, like the cattle or stock upon it. They were either *regardant,* that is, annexed to the manor or *land;* or else *in gross,* or *at large,* that is, annexed to the *person* of the lord. They were transferable by deed from one person to another, but could acquire no property in land or goods. The law however protected the *persons* of villeins as the King's subjects, against atrocious injuries of the lord.

Pure villenage, then, was a precarious and *slavish* tenure, at the absolute will of the lord, upon *uncertain* services of the *basest* nature.

Copyhold tenures were the tenures of those descended from, or who were originally villeins, but who by a long series of immemorial encroachments on the lord, have at last established a customary right to those estates, which before were held absolutely at the will of the lord: which customs were evidenced by the rolls of the courts baron, in which they were entered and kept on foot by the constant immemorial usage of the manors in which the lands lay; so they began to be called *tenants by copy of court-roll,* and the tenure, a *copy-hold.* These tenures were subject like *socage* tenures, to service, relief, and escheat; also to *heriots,* wardship, and fines upon descent and alienation.

Privileged villenage, or villein-socage, is an exalted species of copyhold tenures upon *base,* but *certain,* services. The tenants could not alien or transfer their tenements by grant or feoffment, any more than pure villeins could. It was a tenure subsisting only in the ancient demesne of the crown; whence it is also denominated the *tenure of ancient demesne*. These exalted species of *copyhold tenures of ancient demesne* have divers immunities annexed to them, but are still held by copy of court-roll; but according to the custom of the manor, and not the will of the lord.

Ancient demesne consists of those lands or manors, which, though now perhaps granted out to private subjects, were actually in the hands of the crown in the time of Edward the Confessor, or William the Conqueror; and so appear to have been, by the great survey called Doomsday-book, compiled about the nineteenth year of William I.

Tenure in Frankalmoigne, or *free-alms*, is that whereby a religious corporation, aggregate or sole, holdeth lands or the donor to them and their successors forever.

ESTATES IN THINGS REAL.—An estate in lands, tenements, or hereditaments, signifies such *interest* as the tenant has therein; to ascertain which we consider the *quantity of interest*, the *time of enjoyment*, and the *number and connection of the tenants*.

The quantity of interest is measured by its *duration* and *extent*: thus, either the tenant's right of possession, is to subsist for an uncertain period of his own life, or the life of another: to determine at his own decease, or to remain to his descendants after him: or it is circumscribed within a certain number of years, months, or days: or lastly, it is infinite and unlimited, being vested in him and his representatives forever. This occasions the primary division of estates into *freehold*, and *less than freehold*. There is also *another* species, called estates *upon condition* (whether freehold or otherwise), whose existence depends upon the happening or not happening of some uncertain event.

An estate of freehold, *liberum tenementum,* or *frank-tenement*, is such as is created by *livery of seizin* at common law; or in tenements of an incorporeal nature, by what is equivalent thereto.

Estates of freehold are divided into estates *of inheritance*, and *not of inheritance*.

Estates of inheritance are divided into **inheritances absolute**, or *fee-simple;* and **inheritances limited**, or *limited fees*.

Of inheritances absolute or fees-simple; in freehold estates of inheritance,

A tenant in fee-simple, or *tenant in fee*, is he that hath lands, tenements, or hereditaments, to hold to him and his heirs forever; generally, absolutely, and simply: without mentioning what heirs, but referring that to his own pleasure, or the disposition of the law.

Fee, (*feodum*), in its **true and original meaning,** is the same as *feud,* or *fief,* and in its primary sense, was taken in contradistinction to *allodium,*—as now used. *Fee,* then meant that which was held of some superior, on condition of rendering him service, and in which superior the ultimate, property, or real ownership of the land resided. A subject therefore had only the usufruct, and not the absolute property of the soil. We express the strongest and highest estate that *any* subject can have, by the words; "he is seized thereof, *in his demesne, as of fee.*" It is a man's *demesne,* or property, since it belongs to him and his heirs forever; yet it is his demesne *as of fee,* because it is not purely and simply his own, since it is held of a superior lord in whom the ultimate property resides.

A *fee* therefore, in general, signifies an estate of inheritance; being the highest and most extensive interest that a man can have in lands.

A tenant in fee-simple is he that hath lands and tenements to hold to him and his heirs forever.

Fee-simple *now* signifies a lawful or pure inheritance. *Fee,* signifying inheritance; and *simple* is added for that it is descendible to his heirs *generally,* that is *simply,* without restraint. The word *simple* is also annexed *to distinguish it from other fees,*—as fee-tail, fee-conditional, and the like.

A fee, then, is an estate of inheritance in law, belonging to the owner, and transmissible to his heirs, and is an estate that may continue forever.

In order to make a *fee* or *inheritance,* the word "*heirs*" is necessary in the grant, for if lands be given to a man forever, or to him and his assigns forever, this vests in him but an estate for life only. The *exceptions* to this rule are: devises by will; fines and recoveries, considered as a species of conveyance; in creations of nobility by writ, though when by patent the word must be inserted; in grants to sole corporations; and in case of the King.

Inheritances limited or limited fees, are divided into *qualified* or *base* fees; and fees-*conditional,*—so called at common law;—and afterwards, in consequence of the statute *de donis,* fees-*tail.*

Limited fees are such estates of inheritance as are clogged and confined with conditions or qualifications of any sort.

A base or qualified fee is one having a qualification subjoined thereto, and which must be determined whenever the qualification annexed to it is at an end: as, if a grant be made to A and his heirs, *tenants of the Manor of Dale*, whenever the heirs of A cease to be tenants of that manor, the grant is entirely defeated.

A conditional fee, at the common law, was a fee *restrained to some particular heirs*, exclusive of others; as to the *heirs of a man's body*, by which only his *lineal* descendants were admitted, in exclusion of collateral heirs; or to the *heirs male of his body*, in exclusion of both collaterals, and lineal females also.

It was called a conditional fee, by reason of the condition expressed or implied in the donation of it, that if the donee died without such particular heirs, the land should *revert* to the donor.

Now the *condition* annexed to these fees, by the common law, when performed, is entirely gone, and the fee to which it was before annexed and *qualifying*, became *absolute*; e. g. a gift to a man and the heirs of his body was a gift upon condition that it should revert to the donor if the donee had not the heirs prescribed; but to remain to him, if he had such heirs. Hence as soon as the donee had the required heirs born to him, his estate was no longer conditional, but became absolute by the performance of the condition.

It was therefore construed at common law to be, and called, a fee-simple, on condition that the donee had the heirs prescribed.

The donee of a conditional fee had the power to *convey*, or *alien in fee*, as soon as the condition was *performed*, and *thereby debar his own issue*, and also the possibility of a *reversion* to the donor. Now this right of alienation by the donee was repugnant to the nobility, who were anxious to perpetuate their possessions, and they alleged that it was a breach of the condition of the grant or gift. They therefore procured the passage of the Statute of Westminster the Second (1272), commonly called the statute *de donis conditionalibus*, for the express purpose of preventing the donee of a *conditional fee* from aliening the land as soon as issue was born; and for the further purpose of securing the *reversion* to the grantor. This statute therefore provided that the lands or tenements given to the donee, and the heirs,—or certain heirs,—of his body, should, in every event, go to such *issue*, if there were any; or if none, should *revert* to the donor.

The origin of fee-tail and reversion is from the construction given by the judges to this statute *de donis*, they determining that the donee had no longer a *conditional fee-simple*, which became absolute, and at his own disposal the instant any issue was born; but **they divided the estate into two parts, leaving in the donee a new kind of particular estate, which they denominated a fee-tail**; and vested in the donor the *ultimate* fee-simple of the land, *expectant* on the failure of issue; which expectant estate we now call a *reversion*.

A fee-tail, then, in its original, **was a conditional fee shorn of the right of alienation after condition performed, and vesting in the donor an indefeasible reversion.**

Donor is, properly, one who gives lands to another in *tail*.

A *fee-tail* is so called because it is *entailed;* that is, *limited* as to how long it shall continue.

The word "*body*," or some other words of procreation, are necessary to make a *fee-tail*, in order to ascertain to *what* particular heirs the fee is limited, or restrained.

So if a grant be made to a man and his *issue of his body*, to a man and his *seed*, to a man and his *children* or *offspring*, all these are only estates for life, there wanting the words of inheritance, "his heirs."

Estates-tail are either *general* or *special*, *male* or *female*, or given in *frank-marriage*.

Tail-general is where lands and tenements are given to one and *the heirs of his body begotten*,—because how often-soever such donee may be married, his issue in general by all and every such marriage is in successive order capable of inheriting the estate-tail, *per formam doni*.

Tail-special is where the gift is restrained to *certain* heirs of the donee's body, and does not go to all of them in general; as if lands be given to a man and the heirs of his body, *on Mary his now wife to be begotten.*

Tail-male general is where lands are given to a man and his *heirs male of his body begotten.*

Tail-female special is where lands are given to a man and the *heirs female, of his body, on his present wife begotten.*

In case of an entail *male,* the heirs female shall never inherit; nor any derived from them; nor *e converso,* the heirs male in case of a gift in tail-female.

Frank-marriage is where tenements are given by one to another, together with a wife, who is the daughter or cousin of the donor, to hold in *frank-marriage.* By such gift, though nothing but the word *frank-marriage* is expressed, the donees shall have the tenements to them and *the heirs of their two bodies begotten,*— that is, they are tenants in *special tail.*

The inconveniences resulting from this tying up of the landed property by *estates tail* were avoided about two hundred years after the enactment of the statute *de donis,* by the invention of *fines* and *common recoveries,* which removed the limitations upon them, and passed an absolute and pure fee-simple.

Freehold estates not of inheritance are *for life* only. They are either *convention al,* expressly created by the act of the parties; or *legal,* created by construction and operation of law.

Conventional estates for life are created by an express deed or grant, whereby a lease of lands or tenements is made to a man to hold for the term of his own life, or for that of any other person; or for more lives than one; in any of which cases he is called *tenant for life:* when he holds the estate by the life of another, he is usually called tenant *pur auter vie.*

It is a rule of law that all grants are to be taken most strongly against the grantor; unless in the case of the King.

An estate is granted to one for the term of his "natural life" generally, because it may be determined by his *civil* death, if granted for "his life" only; but one's natural life can only be determined by his *natural* death.

Incident to *all* estates for life, are *estovers* and *emblements.*

If a tenant for life sows the land and dies before harvest, this is a determination of the term by the act of God, and he, or rather his personal representatives, are entitled to the *emblements,* or growing crops.

The legal estates for life are *tenancy in tail, after possibility of issue extinct; tenancy by the curtesy of England;* and *tenancy in dower.*

Tenancy in tail after possibility of issue extinct occurs where one is a tenant in special tail, and a person from whose body the issue was to spring dies without issue; or having left issue, that issue becomes extinct.

Tenancy by the curtesy *of England* is where a man marries a woman seized of an estate of inheritance, that is, of lands and tenements in fee-simple or fee-tail, and has by her issue born alive, which was capable of inheriting her estate; in this case he shall, on the death of his wife, hold the lands for his natural life, as *tenant by the curtesy.*

The four *requisites* necessary to make a tenancy by the curtesy of England are: *marriage, seizin of the wife, issue, and death of the wife.*

Tenancy in dower in where a woman's husband is seized of an estate of inheritance, of which her issue might by any possibility have been heir, and the husband dies; in this case the wife shall have the third part of all the lands and tenements whereof he was seized at any time during coverture, to hold for her natural life.

Dower was either *by common law,* or that just described; *by particular custom,* as, that the wife should have half the husband's lands, or in some places, the whole, and in some only a quarter; *dower ad ostium ecclesiæ,* which is where the person openly at the church door endowed the wife with such quantity as he pleased of his lands, to be enjoyed after his death; or *dower ex assensu patris,* which is only a species of the kind last mentioned, and is made when the husband's father is alive, and the son by his consent endows his wife with parcel of his father's lands.

The most usual species of dower was that by common law.

Dower may be barred or prevented in various ways; the most usual method being by jointure.

Jointure, which was in lieu or satisfaction of dower, is a competent livelihood of freehold for the wife of lands and tenements, to take effect, in profit or possession, presently after the death of the husband, for the life of the wife at least.

If the jointure was made *after* marriage, she had her election after her husband's death to accept or reject it, and betake herself to her dower at common law; for she was not capable of consenting to it during coverture.

ESTATES LESS THAN FREEHOLD are: estates for years; estates at will; and estates by sufferance.

An estate for years is a contract for the possession of lands or tenements for some *determinate* period. Every estate which must expire at a *period certain* is an estate for years.

Where a man seized of lands and tenements letteth them to

another for a certain period of time, which gives the tenant or lessee a right of entry on the lands only, which right is called his *interest in the term,* and he is possessed not properly of the land, but of the *term of years,*—the possession or seizin of the land remaining in him who hath the freehold,

It is called a term, because its duration is bounded, limited, and determined.

The legal difference betwen *the term,* and *the time,* of a lease, for years, is that the word *term* does not merely signify the *time* specified in the lease, but the *estate* also, and *interest* that passes by that lease; therefore the *term* may expire during the continuance of the time, as by surrender, forfeiture, and the like.

Where an estate for years is determined by any uncertain or unforseen contingency, as by an act of God, the tenant or his executors shall have the *emblements,* as in case of tenant for life; but not, if determined by his own act.

An estate at will is where lands and tenements are let by one man to another to hold at the will of both parties; and the lessee enters thereon.

Under this estate the tenant shall have the *emblements,* unless the estate be determined by his own act.

An estate at sufferance is where one comes into possession of land by lawful title, but keeps it afterwards without any title at all.

ESTATES UPON CONDITION, whether freehold or otherwise, are such whose existence depends upon the happening, or not happening, of some uncertain event, whereby the estate may be either originally created, or enlarged, or finally defeated.

Estates upon condition are divided into those upon condition *implied,* and those upon condition *expressed,*—the latter including estates held in *vadio,* gage, or pledge; estates by statute staple, or statute merchant; and estates held by *elegit.*

Estates upon condition implied *in law,* are where the grant of an estate has a condition annexed to it inseparably from its essence and constitution, although no condition be expressed in words; as if a grant of an office be made to a man, generally, without adding other words, the law tacitly annexes thereto a secret *condition* that the grantee shall duly execute his office.

Estates upon condition expressed in the grant itself

are estates granted in fee-simple or otherwise, with an express qualification or provision annexed, whereby the estate shall either commence, be enlarged, or defeated, upon the performance or breach of such qualification or condition.

Conditions expressed are either *precedent*,—such as must happen or be performed *before* the estate can vest, or *subsequent*, —such as by the failure or non-performance of which an estate, *already* vested, may be defeated.

A condition in law is one *impliedly* annexed by law to the grant.

A condition in deed is one *expressly* mentioned in the deed or contract between the parties; and the *object* of them is either to avoid or defeat an estate.

A condition in deed is either *general* or *special*. The former puts an *end* altogether to the tenancy *on entry*, for the breach of the condition; the latter only authorizes the reversioner to enter on the land and take the profits, and *hold the land by way of pledge*, until the condition be performed.

Persons who have an estate of freehold subject to a *condition* are *seized*, and may *convey or devise the same*, though the estate will continue defeasible or subject to the condition till the condition be performed, destroyed, or released.

A limitation in law is where an estate is so expressly confined and limited by the words of its creation that it cannot endure for any longer time than till the contingency happens upon which the estate is to fail.

The material distinction between a condition in a deed and a limitation in law consists in this: that a *condition* (in deed) does not defeat the estate although it be broken, the law permitting it to endure, unless the grantor or his heirs or assigns *enter* and take advantage of the breach of the condition; but it is the nature of a *limitation* (in law) to determine the estate when the period of limitation *arrives, without entry*, or claim, no act being requisite to vest the right in him who has the next expectant estate.

It is a rule of law that he who enters for a condition broken becomes seized of his first estate, and he avoids all intermediate charges and incumbrances.

An estate *for years* ceases as soon as the condition is broken, but an estate *of freehold* does not cease after condition broken *until entry*, or claim.

Words of limitation mark the *period* which is to determine the estate; **words of condition** render the estate *liable* to be defeated.

The one specifies the *utmost* time of continuance; and the other marks some event, which, *if* it takes place in the course of that time, will defeat the estate.

A conditional limitation, is where *a condition subsequent* is followed by a limitation over to a third person, in case the condition be not fulfilled, or there be a breach of it.

A collateral limitation gives an interest for a specified period, but makes the right of enjoyment to depend on some collateral event; as where an estate is limited to a man and his heirs, tenants of the manor of Dale.

Estates in gage, vadio, or pledge are estates granted as a security for money lent, and are of two kinds; *vivum vadium*, or living pledge; and *mortuum vadium,* or dead pledge, or *mortgage*.

Vivum vadium, or living pledge, is where a man borrows money of another, and grants him an estate at so much per annum to hold till the rents and profits shall repay the sum borrowed. This is upon condition, to be void on repayment of the loan, and the land or pledge is said to be *living*, as it subsists and survives the debt, and on discharge of the same the land results back to the borrower.

Mortuum vadium, dead pledge, or mortgage, is where a man borrows money of another and grants him an estate in fee, on condition that if he, the mortgagor, shall repay the mortgagee the sum borrowed, on a certain day mentioned in the deed, that then the mortgagor may re-enter on the estate so granted in pledge; but in case of non-payment at the time limited, the land put in pledge is, by law, forever dead and gone from the mortgagor, and the mortgagee's title is absolute.

Equity of redemption was a reasonable time or advantage allowed to mortgagors by courts of equity to redeem their lands.

Foreclosure was where the mortgagee either compelled the sale of the estate, in order to get the whole of his money immediately; or called upon the mortgagor to redeem his estate presently, or in default thereof, to be forever *foreclosed* from redeeming the same; that is, lose his equity of redemption.

Estates by statute merchant and statute staple are very nearly related to *vivum vadium*, being also estates conveyed to creditors, in pursuance of certain statutes, till their profits shall discharge the debt.

Both are securities for money; the one entered into before the chief magistrate of some trading town, pursuant to the statute 13, Edward I, *de mercatoribus*, and thence called *statute merchant;* the other pursuant to statute 27, Edward III, before the mayor of the staple; whence called *statute staple*.

Estates by elegit are another kind of conditional estates, created by operation *of law*, for the security and satisfaction of debts.

Elegit, (he has chosen), is the name of a writ founded on the statute Westminster Second, by which, after a plaintiff has recovered judgment for his *debt*, at law, the sheriff gives him possession of one-half of the defendant's lands and tenements, to be occupied and enjoyed until his debt and damages are fully paid; and during the time he so holds them, he is called *tenant by elegit*.

TIME OF THEIR ENJOYMENT.—Estates are either in *possession* or *expectancy;* the *latter* being created at the same time, and are parcel of the same estates as those upon which they are expectant.

Estates in possession, *or executed,* are those whereby a *present* interest passes; and not being dependent on any subsequent circumstances, there is but little to be said of them, all hitherto considered being estates of this kind.

Estates in expectancy, *or executory,* are such as are to be enjoyed in the *future,* and depend on some subsequent circumstance or contingency.

They are of two kinds: *Remainder,*—created by *act of the parties;* and *Reversion,*—created by act or *operation of law*.

An estate in remainder is an estate limited to take effect and be enjoyed *after* another estate is determined: as where lands are granted to A for twenty years, *remainder* to B in fee.

Both these *interests* are but different *parts of one whole* estate, or inheritance: they are both created, and may subsist *together;* the one in possession, the other in expectancy; hence no remainder can be limited after the grant of an estate in fee-simple; because the tenant in *fee* hath in him the *whole* of the estate.

The three rules of law to be observed in the creation of Remainders are; *first,* there must necessarily be some particular estate *precedent* to the estate in remainder; *secondly,* the remainder must commence or pass out of the grantor, at the time of the creation of the particular estate; *thirdly*, the remainder must vest in the grantee during the continuance of the particular estate, or *eo instanti* that it determines.

The precedent estate spoken of in the first rule, is called the *particular* estate, being only a small *part*, or *particula*, of the inheritance, or fee.

The use or necessity of the precedent particular estate was to prevent an abeyance of the freehold,—as at common law an estate of freehold could not be created to commence *in futuro;* and for that the *remainder,* as its name implies, was but a *part* only of the thing disposed of.

It was a rule of the common law that an estate of freehold could not be created to commence *in futuro,* but that it ought to take effect *presently* (immediately), either in *possession* or *remainder;* because **at common law no freehold in lands could pass without livery of seizin;** which must operate *immediately,* or not at all.

In granting, then, an estate of freehold to be enjoyed *in futuro,* it is necessary to create a previous, or precedent particular estate, to subsist *till that period;* and for the grantor to deliver *immediate* possession of the land to the tenant of this particular estate, which is *construed* to be giving possession *to him in remainder,* since his estate and that of the particular tenant are *one* and the same estate *in law.*

The whole estate passes at once from the grantor to the grantees; the remainder man being seized of his remainder at the same time that the termor is seized of his term.

While the enjoyment of the remainder is deferred, it is to all intents and purposes an estate commencing *in præsenti,*—though occupied and enjoyed *in futuro.*

The particular estate is said to *support* the remainder; hence it is generally true that if the particular estate is void in its creation, or by any means defeated afterwards, the remainder supported by it is defeated also.

Remainders are of two kinds; *vested* or *contingent.*

Vested remainders are where the estate is fixed to remain to a *determinate person,* after the particular estate is spent.

An estate is vested when there is an immediate right of present enjoyment, or a present fixed right of future enjoyment. It gives a legal or equitable seizin.

It is the present *capacity* of taking effect in possession, if the possession were to become vacant, that distinguishes a vested from a contingent remainder.

Contingent remainders are such where the estate in remainder is limited to take effect, either to a *dubious or uncertain person*, or upon a dubious or *uncertain* event.

Contingent remainders, if they amount to a freehold, cannot be limited on an estate for *years*, or on any particular estate *less* than a freehold.

It is not the uncertainty of enjoyment in the future, but the uncertainty of the *right* to that enjoyment, which marks the difference between a vested and contingent interest.

There must be a particular estate to precede a remainder, for it necessarily implies that a part of the estate has been already carved out of it, and vested in immediate possession in some other person.

The reason of the rule requiring a contingent remainder to be supported by a freehold, was that the freehold should not be in abeyance, and that there should be always a visible tenant of the freehold, who might be made tenant to the *præcipe*, and answer for the services required.

If the particular estate terminates before the remainder can vest, the remainder is gone forever; for a freehold cannot, according to the common law, commence *in futuro*.

If the particular estate determines, or be destroyed, before the contingency happens upon which the expectant estate depended, and leaves no right of entry, the remainder is annihilated.

The rule in Shelley's case declares, that when the ancestor, by any gift or conveyance, taketh an estate of freehold, and in the same gift or conveyance an estate is limited, either mediately, or immediately, to his heirs, in fee or in tail, "*his heirs*" are words of *limitation* of the estate, and not words of purchase.

The rule is of positive institution, and in direct variance with rules of construction; for, while the latter seek to promote the *intention* of the parties, the former subverts it.

The origin of the rule in Shelley's case is attributed to the aversion the common law had to the inheritance being in *abeyance*, and the desire to facilitate the alienation of land, and to throw it into the track of commerce one generation sooner, by vesting the inheritance in the ancestor, thereby giving him the power of disposition over it.

The policy of the rule was that no person should be permitted to raise in another an estate which was essentially an estate *of inheritance*, and at the same time made the heirs of that person *purchasers*.

In order that the *heirs* of the ancestor might, in time, enjoy the estate, as well as the ancestor himself while living, it was necessary and usual, in order to prevent him from encumbering or alienating the estate, to grant him a particular estate *for life*, and the remainder to his *heirs*. By the *fixed rule* of construction or legal interpretation, which always sought for the *intention* of the parties to written instruments, the ancestor would have only the *use* and enjoyment of the estate *for life*, and *then* it would go to his heirs, who would take it, not from the ancestor by inheritance, but as an original and independent estate from the grantor, *by purchase;* for *any* estate not acquired by inheritance is said to be acquired by purchase.

But, by a *fiction* in law,—making the word *heirs*, or *heirs of his body*, in the transfer of estates, create a fee-simple or a fee-tail,—the rule in Shelley's case declares, in substance, that the words *" his heirs,"* in the grant *merge* the life estate and the remainder, and cast the fee-simple, or whatever the estate may be, upon the ancestor, thus making him the absolute owner of the whole estate. He could then partially or totally defeat the expectations of his relatives, and the will of the grantor.

Hence we see, that when a freehold is granted to a man, and remainder to *his heirs*, it is equivalent to giving him a fee-simple, or the entire estate.

Coke says, that **"where the ancestors a freehold take, the words 'his heirs' a limitation make."**

An executory devise is such a disposition of lands, by will, that thereby no estate vests at the death of the devisor, but only on some future contingency.

An *executory devise* differs from a *remainder* in three very material points, viz : *first*, it needs not any particular estate to support it; *secondly*, by it, a fee-simple or other less estate, may be limited, after a fee-simple; and, *thirdly*, by this means a remainder may be limited of a chattel interest after a particular estate for life created in the same.

An executory devise is, in effect, a contingent remainder, without any precedent particular estate to support it;—a *freehold*, commencing *in futuro;* and such a grant or limitation would be void in a *deed*, but is good in a will, by way of *executory devise*.

An executory devise is a limitation by will of a future contingent interest in lands, *contrary* to the rules of limitations of contingent estates in conveyance.

The reason of the institution of executory devises was to support the *will* of the testator; for when the testator intended to create a contingent remainder, and it could not operate as such by the rules of law, the limitation was then, out of indulgence to wills, held to be good as an executory devise.

As by executory devise a freehold interest could pass without livery or seizin,—that is, commence *in futuro*,—it needed no particular estate to support it, the only use of which is to make **the remainder, by its unity with the particular estate, a present interest.**

As stated, by executory devise a fee, or other less estate, may be limited after a fee, as, if a man devise lands to A and his heirs, but if he dies before the age of twenty-one, then to B and his heirs, this remainder, though void in a deed, is good by way of executory devise.

There are two kinds of executory devises relating to real estate: *first*, where the devisor parts with his whole estate, but upon some contingency qualifies the disposition of it, and limits an estate upon that contingency; *secondly*, where the testator gives a future interest to arise upon a contingency, but does not part with the fee in the meantime.

Until the contingency happens, the fee passes, in the usual course of descent, to the heirs at law.

The utmost length of **time allowed for the contingency of an executory devise to happen in** is that of a life or lives in being, and twenty-one years thereafter; for the law so abhors perpetuities that it will not allow even wills to create them.

A valid executory devise cannot exist under an absolute power of disposition in the first taker.

Executory devises *differ* from contingent remainders, in that the latter relate only to lands; executory devises relate to *personal*, as well as real, estate. Contingent remainders require a freehold to precede and support them; an executory devise does not. Contingent remainders must vest, at farthest, at the instant the preceding estate determines; but an executory devise may vest after the determination of a precedent estate. A contingent remainder may be barred and destroyed by different means; but an executory devise cannot be so prevented or destroyed by any alteration whatsoever in the estate out of which, or after which, it is limited.

A reversion is the residue of an estate left in the grantor, to commence in possession, *after* the determination of some particular estate granted out by him.

Coke says, that **it is the returning of the land to the grantor or his heirs after the grant is over.**

The fee-simple of the land must abide somewhere; and if he who has before possessed of the whole, carves out of it any less estate, and grants it away, whatsoever is not granted remains in him.

Hence a reversion is never created by deed or writing, but always arises from *construction of law*.

The doctrine of merger is that whenever a greater estate and a less coincide and meet in one and the same person, in one and the same right, without any intermediate estate, the less estate is immediately annihilated, or, is said, in law phrase, to be *merged*, or drowned, in the greater.

An estate-tail is an exception to this rule; for a man may have in his own right an estate-tail, and a reversion in fee, and they will not merge, being preserved from merger by operation of the statute *de donis*.

NUMBER AND CONNECTIONS OF THE TENANTS.
—Estates may be held in *severalty* in *joint-tenancy*, in *coparcenary*, and in *common*.

An estate in severalty is where one holds lands in his own right only, without any other person being joined or connected with him in point of interest during his estate therein.

An estate in joint-tenancy is where lands or tenements are granted to *two or more persons*, to hold in any manner; in which case the law construes them to be joint-tenants, unless the words of the grant expressly exclude such construction.

The creation of an estate in joint-tenancy depends on the wording of the deed or devise by which the tenants claim title; for this estate can only arise by purchase or grant, that is, *by act of the parties*, and never by the mere act of law.

Joint-tenants, therefore, are persons who own lands by a joint title, created expressly by one and the same deed or will. They hold uniformly by purchase.

The properties of an estate in joint-tenancy are derived from its *unity*, which is fourfold, viz: unity of interest, unity of title, unity of time, and unity of possession. In other words, joint-tenants have one and the same interest, accruing by one and the same conveyance, commencing at one and the same time, and held by one and the same undivided possession. They are said to be seized *per my et per tout,*—by the half or moiety, and of all; that is, they each of them have the entire possession, as well of every parcel as of the whole; therefore, **upon the decease of one joint-tenant, the entire tenancy remains to the survivors**, and, eventually, to the last survivor. This is the nature and consequence of the *unity* and *entirety* of their interest, and is called the doctrine of survivor-ship, or *jus accrescendi.*

This estate may be dissolved by destroying any one of its constituent unities.

An estate in coparcenary is where an estate of inheritance descends from the ancestor to two or more persons.

They are called parceners, for brevity and because they may be constrained to make partition.

It arose at *common law,* where a person died and his next heirs were two or more females, as daughters, sisters, aunts, cousins, or their representatives; and by *particular custom,* as where lands descend, as in gavel-kind, to *all* the males in equal degree, as sons, brothers and uncles. In either case these *co-heirs* were called *parceners;* they *all* inherit, and together make but *one* heir, and have but one estate among them.

Estates in coparcenary are in some respects like those in joint-tenancy, having the same *unities* of *interest, title,* and *possession;* but *differ* in that they always claim *by descent,* whereas joint-tenants always claim *by purchase.* Though having a *unity,* they have not an *entirety,* of interest; they are seized *per my,* and not *per tout,* hence there is no survivor-ship among them.

The law of Hotch-pot,—"the word *seemeth* in English to mean a *pudding,* in which are put not one thing alone, but one thing with other things together,"—was a metaphor used by our ancestors, denoting that the lands given in frank-marriage and those descending in fee-simple should be mixed and blended together, and then divided equally among the daughters, *if* the donee in frank-marriage so wished.

An estate in coparcenary may be dissolved by destroying any of its three constituent unities: as by partition, which disunites the possession; by alienation of one parcener, which disunites the title, and may disunite, the interest; or by the whole at last descending and vesting in one person, which brings it to an estate in severalty.

An estate in common is where two or more persons hold lands, possibly by distinct titles, and for distinct interests; but by unity of possession, because none knoweth his own severalty.

Tenants in common hold, therefore, by *unity of possession,* (without survivor-ship, being seized *per my,* and not *per tout,*) but have no unity of title, time, or interest.

Tenancy in common may be created by the destruction of the constituent unities of the two former estates, or by special limitation in a deed.

They may take by purchase or descent, and are deemed to have several and *distinct freeholds.*

They are also compellable to make partition of their lands and to account for profits arising from the same.

Tenancies in common differ in nothing from sole estates but merely the blending and unity of possession.

TITLE TO THINGS REAL, IN GENERAL.—A title is the means whereby a man has the just possession of his property.

The stages or degrees requisite to form *a complete title* are: naked *possession, right of possession,* and *right of property,* which, when united, form a complete or *legal* title.

Title to things real, or estates in lands and tenements, are acquired or lost *by descent,* where the title is vested in a man by the single operation of the law; or *by purchase,* where the title is vested in him *by his own act* or agreement.

Title by descent, or *hereditary succession,* is where a man, on the death of his ancestor, acquires his estate by right of representation, as his heir at law.

An ancestor is one that an inheritance of lands or tenements can be derived from, only by his having had *actual seizin* of such lands, either by his own entry, or by the possession of his own or the ancestor's lessee for years; or by receiving rent from a lessee of the freehold; and in incorporeal hereditaments, by his having what is equivalent to corporeal seizin.

An heir is he upon whom the law casts the estate immediately on the death of the ancestor.

Right heirs mean **direct or lineal heirs.**

Heir apparent is one whose right of inheritance is indefeasible if he outlive the ancestor.

Heir presumptive is one who, if the ancestor should die immediately, would, in the present circumstances of things, be the heir; but whose right of inheritance may be defeated by the contingency of some nearer heir being born.

An inheritance is the estate descending from the ancestor to the heir.

Affinity is relationship by marriage.

Consanguinity, or *kindred,* is the connection or relation of persons descended from the same stock or common ancestor. It is either *lineal* or *collateral.*

Lineal consanguinity is where one kinsman is descended, in a *direct* line, from the other.

Collateral consanguinity is where the kinsmen descend from the same stock or ancestor, but *not* in direct line, one from the other.

Degrees of relationship are computed by beginning at the common ancestor and reckoning *downwards,* and in whatever degree the two persons, or the most remote of them, is distant from the common ancestor, *that is the degree* in which they are related to each other.

The rules of descent by the laws of England are as follows:

Inheritances shall lineally *descend* to the issue of the person last actually seized, *in infinitum,* but shall never lineally ascend.

The male issue shall be admitted before the female.

Where two or more males are in equal degree, the eldest only shall inherit; but the females all together.

The lineal descendants, *in infinitum,* shall represent their deceased ancestor, that is, shall stand in the same place as he himself would had he lived.

On failure of lineal descendants, the inheritance shall descend to the collateral relations of the blood of the first purchaser, subject to the three preceding rules:—to evidence which blood there are two rules, viz:

The collateral heir of the person last seized must be his next collateral kinsman of the whole blood.

THE RECKONING

OF DEGREES OF

KINDRED OR RELATIONSHIP

IS AS FOLLOWS:

I.—LINEAL.

CONSANGUINITY.
- *Ascending.*
  1. Father, mother.
  2. Grandfather, grandmother.
  3. Great grandfather, great grandmother, and so on *ad infinitum.*
- *Descending.*
  1. Father, mother.
  2. Son, daughter.
  3. Grandson, granddaughter, and so on *ad infinitum.*

AFFINITY.
- *Ascending.*
  1. Father-in-law, mother-in-law.
  2. Step-father, step-mother.
- *Descending.*
  1. Father-in-law, mother-in-law.
  2. Son-in-law, daughter-in-law.

II.—COLLATERAL.

CONSANGUINITY.
1. Brother, sister.
2. Brother's children, sister's children.
3. Uncle, aunt.

AFFINITY.
1. Brother's wife, sister's husband.
2. Uncle's wife, aunt's husband.

In collateral inheritances, the male ancestral stock shall be preferred to the female, unless the lands have descended from a female.

TITLE BY PURCHASE, or *perquisition*, **is the possession of lands which a man hath by his own act or agreement**, and not by the mere act of law, or by descent. It includes every other method of coming to an estate but that by inheritance. This embraces title by Escheat, by Occupancy, Prescription, Forfeiture, and Alienation.

Title by escheat (signifying *chance* or *accident*) denotes an obstruction of the course of descent, and a consequent determination of the tenure by some unforeseen contingency, in which case the land naturally resulted back by a kind of reversion to the original grantor, or lord of the fee.

Escheat resulted from either natural or civil causes, as by the death of the tenant without heirs, or by his blood becoming attainted, etc.

The law of escheat is founded upon the principle that the blood of the person last seized in fee-simple is by some means utterly extinct or gone.

Title by occupancy is the taking possession of those things which before belonged to nobody.

This title was founded upon the rule of the ancient common law, that what belonged to nobody is given to the occupant by natural right.

The law of alluvion and dereliction, that is, where land was *made* by the *washing up* of earth and sand by the sea, rivers, etc., and by the sea *shrinking back* below the usual water-mark, was, that if an island arose in the middle of a river, it belonged in common to the owners of the lands on each side of it; but if nearer to one bank than the other, it belonged to the proprietor of the nearest shore.

It was probably taken from the *civil law*.

But if the *alluvion* or *dereliction* was sudden and considerable, it belonged to the King, at common law; and by the civil law, to the first occupant.

Jetsam is where goods are cast into the sea, and there sink and remain under water.

Ligan is where they are sunk in the sea, but tied to a cork or buoy, in order to be found again.

Flotsam is where they continue swimming on the surface of the water.

Title by prescription is where a man can show no other title to what he claims than that he and those under whom he claims have *immemorially* used to enjoy it.

All prescription must be in a man and his ancestors, or in a man and those whose estate he hath, which last is called prescribing in a *que estate*.

Usage is *long* and *uniform practice*.

Custom is *local* usage that has acquired the *force* of law.

Prescription is immemorial *personal* usage, that is, usage beyond the "time of memory."

The principal distinction between custom and prescription is, that one is a *local*, and the other a *personal* usage.

Estates gained by prescription are not, of course, descendible to the heirs general, like other purchased estates, but are an exception to the rule. For, properly speaking, the prescription is rather to be considered as an evidence of a former acquisition, than as an acquisition *de novo*.

Nothing but incorporeal hereditaments can be claimed by prescription, as a right of way, a common, etc.

No prescription can give a title to lands and other corporeal substances, of which more certain evidence may be had.

A prescription must always be laid in him that is tenant of the fee.

A tenant for life, for years, at will, or a copyholder, cannot prescribe, by reason of the imbecility of their estates.

A prescription cannot be for a thing which cannot be raised by grant; for the law allows prescription only in support of the loss of a grant, which it presupposes to have existed.

If a man prescribes in a *que estate*, nothing is claimable but such things as are *incident appendant*, or *appurtenant*, to lands.

Incident means depending upon, appertaining, or naturally relating or belonging to.

Appendant is where a right, or thing, is inseparably,—from the very nature of it,—*incident* to a grant.

Appurtenant rights or things arise from no such absolute or necessary connexion; but only *may* be annexed or attached.

Title by forfeiture arises where a punishment is annexed by law to some illegal act, or negligence, in the owner of things *real*, as lands and tenements, whereby he loses all his interest therein, his estate being transferred to another, generally the injured party, who thus acquires the *title* to the same.

Forfeitures were occasioned by crimes, by alienation contrary to law, as in *mortmain;* by lapse, by simony, by non-performance of conditions annexed to estates, by waste, by breach of copyhold customs, and by bankruptcy.

Alienation in mortmain, or in *mortua manu,* was an alienation of lands or tenements to any corporation, sole or aggregate, ecclesiastical or temporal. This, the statute *De Religiosis,* 7 Edward I prohibited, and to avoid the statute the religious houses invented common recoveries.

Disclaimer is where a tenant disclaims to hold of his lord. This was a *civil crime,* and one of the crimes which occasioned forfeitures of lands upon reasons most apparently feudal.

Lapse is a forfeiture of the right of presentation to a vacant church, by neglect of the patron to present within the time prescribed.

Simony is the corrupt presentation of any one to an ecclesiastical benefice, as for money, gift, or reward,—whereby that turn becomes forfeited.

Waste is a spoil, or destruction, in any corporeal hereditaments, to the prejudice of him that hath the inheritance. Whatever does *lasting* damage to the freehold is *waste.*

It is either *voluntary,* which is a crime of *commission,*—as pulling down a house; or it is *permissive,* which is a matter of *omission* only,—as by suffering it to fall, from want of repairs.

A bankrupt is a trader who secretes himself, or does certain other acts, tending to defraud his creditors.

By *bankruptcy,* or the act of becoming a bankrupt, the *title* of all the estates of the bankrupt is transferred to the assignees of his commissioners, to be sold for the benefit of his creditors.

Title by alienation, *conveyance* or *purchase,* comprises in its more limited sense any method whereby estates are transferred, or voluntarily resigned, by one man and accepted by another, whether by sale, gift, marriage-settlement, devise, or other transmission of property, by the mutual consent of the parties.

Originally this could not be done without the mutual consent of both lord and vassal.

All persons are *prima facie* capable of conveying and purchasing, unless the law has laid them under particular disabilities.

Conveyances and purchases by idiots, persons of non-sane memory, infants, and persons under duress, are *voidable,* but not actually void.

Common assurances of the kingdom, as they were called, are the legal evidences of alienation, or transfer, of property, whereby every man's estate is *assured* to him, and all controversies, doubts, and difficulties are either prevented or removed.

Alienation by common assurances are of four kinds, viz.:

By deed, or matter *in pais,* which is an assurance transacted between two or more private persons *in pais* (in the country); that is, according to the old common law, upon the *very spot.*

By matter of record, which is an assurance transacted only in public courts of record.

By special custom, obtaining in some particular places relating to some particular species of property only.

By devise, as contained in the last will and testament of a decedent.

Alienation by deed, or *assurances by deed,* may be considered with reference to their general nature, and their several species.

As to their general nature: they are regarded as the *solemn act* of the parties.

A deed is a writing, sealed and delivered by the parties. It may be a deed indented, or *indenture;* or a deed-*poll.*

An indenture is now only *a name* given to a species of deeds, though formerly, when deeds were more concise than at present, it was usual to write both parts of the deed (as they originally consisted of two parts, or instruments) on the same piece of parchment, with some words or letters of the alphabet written between them, through which the parchment was cut, either in a straight or indented line, in such a manner as to leave half the words on one part, and half on the other; but at length indenting only came into use.

A deed-poll is a plain deed, made by one party only, not indented, but polled or shaved quite even, and therefore called a deed-poll, or single deed.

The requisites of a deed are as follows:

Sufficient parties: that is, parties competent to contract; and proper subject-matter.

A good and sufficient consideration.

Must be written or printed, on parchment or paper.

Legal and orderly parts, properly set forth.

Reading it, if desired.

Sealing and signing it.

Delivery, by the party himself or his attorney; and Attestation, or execution in the presence of witnesses.

The legal, or formal and orderly parts of a deed, that is, the words sufficient to specify the agreement and bind the parties, are: the premises, the *habendum*, the *tenendum*, the *reddendum*, the conditions, the warranty, the covenants, and the conclusion.

The premises in a deed are used to set forth the number and names of the parties, with their additions or titles.

The habendum expresses what estate or interest is granted by the deed.

The tenendum, "and to hold," is now of but little use, and only kept in by custom.

The reddendum is a reservation, whereby the grantor doth create or reserve some new thing to himself out of what he had before granted; as rent, or the like.

The conditions are clauses of contingency, on the happening of which the estate granted may be defeated.

The warranty is that clause or part whereby the grantor doth, for himself and his heirs, warrant and secure to the grantee the estate so granted.

Warranties are *implied* or *expressed*, and *lineal* or *collateral*.

An implied warranty is such as the law presumes or concludes every grantor or vendor to make in disposing of property; as, for instance, that he has the *right* to make such disposition.

An express warranty in the transfer of lands and tenements is an *express clause* binding the grantor and his heirs; it is a kind of covenant real. These express warranties were introduced to evade the strictness of the feudal doctrine of non-alienation without the consent of the heir.

Lineal warranty was where the heir derived, or might by possibility have derived, his title to the land warranted, either from or through the ancestor who made the warranty.

Collateral warranty was where the heir's title to the land neither was, nor could have been, derived from the warranting ancestor.

The covenants are clauses of agreement contained in the deed, whereby either party may stipulate for the truth of certain facts, or may bind himself to perform or give something to the other.

A covenant real is where the covenanter covenants for himself and his *heirs,* upon whom it descends, and who are bound to perform it, provided they have assets by descent.

The conclusion of a deed mentions the execution and date of it.

Considerations are divided into *good* and *valuable.*

A good consideration is such as that of blood, or natural love and affection; as where a man grants an estate to a near relative.

A valuable consideration is such as money, marriage, or the like.

A deed takes effect only from its delivery. A deed without date is good, if the date when it was executed or delivered can be proved.

Attestation is necessary rather for preserving the evidence than for constituting the essence of the deed.

If a man covenants, not only for himself and his heirs, but also for his executors, and administrators, his personal assets, as well as his real, are likewise pledged for the performance of the covenant, which makes *such* a covenant better than any warranty.

A deed may be avoided by the want of any of the above mentioned requisites, or by subsequent matter; as erasure or alteration, defacing its seal, cancelling it, disagreement of those whose consent is necessary, or by judgment of a court of justice.

An escrow is a deed delivered to a third party, to hold as a *scrowl,* or writing that is not to take effect as a deed until some conditions be performed by the grantee.

As to the different species of deeds: some serve to *convey* real property, and others only to *charge or discharge* it.

Deeds serving to alien or convey real estate are called *conveyances,* which conveyances are either by common law, or by statute.

Of conveyances by common law: some are *original* or *primary,* and others are *derivative* or *secondary;*—the former are those by means whereof the benefit or estate is created, or first arises; and the latter, those by which the benefit or estate, already created, is *enlarged,* restrained, transferred, or extinguished.

The original, or primary conveyances are: Feoffment, Gift, Grant, Lease, Exchange, and Partition.

The **derivative, or secondary conveyances** are: Release, Confirmation, Surrender, Assignment, and Defeasance.

A **feoffment** is the transfer or gift of any corporeal hereditament to another, perfected by *livery of seizin*, or delivery of bodily possession, to the feoffee, without which no freehold estate therein could be created at common law. Strictly speaking, it refers to the conveyance of an estate *in fee*. He that so gives, or enfeoffs, is called the *feoffor*, and the person enfeoffed is denominated the *feoffee*.

Livery of seizin is the *feudal investiture*, or delivery of corporeal possession, of the land or tenement. It was either *in deed* or *in law*.

Livery in deed was performed by the feoffor delivering to the feoffee (all other persons being out of the ground), a clod, twig, or some part of it,—as a ring, or latch, if a house,—with the words, "I deliver these to you in the name of seizin of all the lands and tenements contained in this deed."

Livery in law is where the same is not made *on* the land, but in *sight* of it only, the feoffor saying to the feoffee, "I give you yonder land; enter and take possession."

A **gift**,—*donatio*,—differs in nothing from a feoffment, but in the nature of the estate passing by it, being properly applied to the creation or conveyance of an estate tail, as feoffment is to that of an estate in fee.

A **grant**,—*concessiones*,—is the regular method, by the common law, of conveying incorporeal hereditaments, or such things whereof no livery can be had. It is now used also in the transfer of real estate, the words "grant, bargain, and sell," being express covenants for title.

A **lease** is properly a conveyance in consideration of *rent*, or other recompense, of lands and tenements, for life, for years, or at will, but always for a less time than the lessor hath in the premises; for, if it be for the whole interest, it is more properly an *assignment* than a lease.

An **exchange** is the mutual conveyance of equal interests, the one in consideration of the other.

A **partition** is the division of an estate held in joint-tenancy, in coparcenary, or in common, between the respective tenants, each taking his distinct part to hold in severalty.

A **release** is the discharge or conveyance of a man's right in lands or tenements to another that hath some former estate in possession therein. It is the descending of a *greater* estate upon a *less*.

A confirmation is the conveyance of an estate or right *in esse*, whereby a voidable estate is made sure, or a particular estate is increased and the words of it are "have given, granted, ratified, approved, and confirmed." It is of a nature nearly allied to a release.

A surrender is the yielding up of an estate for life, or years, to him that hath the immediate remainder or reversion, wherein the particular estate *surrendered* may merge.

It is of a nature directly opposite to a *Release;* for as that operates by the greater estate descending upon the less, a Surrender is the falling of a less estate into a greater. The words used are, "have surrendered, granted, and yielded up."

An assignment is the transfer, or making over to another, of the whole right one has in any estate; but usually in a lease, for life or years.

A defeasance is a collateral deed, made at the same time with the original conveyance, containing certain conditions upon the performance of which *the estate created* may be defeated or undone.

Conveyances by statute depend much on the doctrine of *uses* and *trusts*, which, in their nature and origin, are the same,—the old doctrine of *uses* being revived under the denomination of *trusts*.

A use or trust was a confidence reposed in another, who was *terre-tenant*, or tenant of the land, that he would dispose of the land according to the wishes of the *cestuy que use,* or *cestuy que trust*, to whose *use* it was granted, and suffer him to take the profits.

Uses and trusts originated in ecclesiastical ingenuity, the notion being transplanted from the civil law into England by the ecclesiastics, near the close of the reign of Edward III (about 1370), to evade the statutes *of mortmain*, by obtaining grants of lands, not to religious houses *directly*, but to their *use;* thus distinguishing between the *possession* and the *use*.

Uses are not always to be executed at the time the conveyance is made; hence we have what are called *future* uses, which are as follows:

Shifting, or secondary uses, take effect in derogation of some other estate, and are either limited by the deed creating them, or authorized to be created by some person named in it.

Thus: If an estate be limited to A and his heirs, with a proviso that if B pay to A one hundred dollars, by a given time, the use of A shall cease and the estate go to B in fee, the estate is vested in A, subject to a shifting or secondary use in fee in B.

Springing uses are limited to arise on a future event, where no preceding estate is limited, and they do not take effect in derogation of any preceding interest, as if a grant be to A in fee, to the use of B in fee after the first day of January next.

Future, or contingent uses, are limited to take effect as remainders. As, if lands be granted to A in fee, to the use of B, on his return from Rome. This is a future contingent use, because it is uncertain whether B will ever return.

Resulting uses are where the use limited by deed expires, or cannot vest, or was not to vest but upon a contingency, which has not happened, the use *results* back to the grantor.

There are also resulting trusts *implied* by law, from the manifest intention of the parties and the nature and justice of the case; as where an estate is purchased in the name of A and the price is actually paid at the time by B; here is a resulting trust implied by law in favor of B.

Contingent uses are subject to the same rules as contingent remainders.

Springing or contingent uses *differ* from an *executory devise*, in that there must be a person seized to such uses at the time when the contingency happens, else they can never be executed by the statutes; and, therefore, if the estate of the feoffee to such use be destroyed, by alienation or otherwise, before the contingency arises, the use is destroyed forever; whereas, by an executory devise, the freehold itself is transferred to the future devisee.

The statute of uses having transferred all uses into actual possession, or rather, having drawn the possession to the use, gave birth to other species of conveyances, viz: a covenant to stand seized to uses, a bargain and sale of lands enrolled; a conveyance by lease and release; deeds to lead or declare uses, that is, the use of other more direct conveyances; deeds of revocation of uses.

A covenant to stand seized to uses is that by which a man covenants that, in consideration of blood or marriage, he will stand seized of lands to the use of another,—as to the use of his child, wife, or kinsman.

On executing the covenant, the other party becomes seized of the use of the land, and the statute of uses immediately operated by annexing the possession to the use, or as it is called, "executes" at once the use or estate.

Deeds of revocation of uses were the execution of a *power reserved* at the creation of the use of recalling at a future time the use or estate so created.

These last species of conveyances owe their operation principally to the statute of uses.

In time *trusts* superseded or were made to answer in general all the beneficial ends or purposes of *uses*, without their inconveniences or frauds.

A trust, in the general and enlarged sense, is a *right* on the part of the *cestuy que trust* to receive the profits and dispose of the lands in equity.

They are of two kinds: *executed*, when either the legal or equitable title passes; or *executory*, when it is to be perfected at some future time, by conveyance or settlement.

No particular *form* is requisite to create a trust; it is sufficient if the terms of the trust can be duly ascertained by the writing.

The courts now consider a trust estate as equivalent to the legal ownership, governed by the same rules of property and liable to every charge in equity which the other is subject to in law.

Deeds which do not convey, but serve only to *charge* or *discharge* real property, are: Obligations or bonds, Recognizances, and Defeasances.

A bond or obligation is a deed whereby a person, the obligor, obligates himself, his heirs, executors and administrators, to pay a certain sum of money to another at a day appointed.

The *penal* sum, or penalty, attached to the bond for its breach or forfeiture, is usually drawn for double the amount of the bond or money borrowed, in order to cover the principal, interest expense, and damages sustained from non-performance of the covenants, which is all that is now recoverable upon forfeiture of a bond, no matter what the amount of the penal sum, or penalty, inserted. Formerly, the whole penalty was recoverable at law.

A recognizance is an obligation of *record*, entered into before some court of record or magistrate duly authorized, with condition to do some particular act; as to appear at court, to keep the peace, etc.

Another distinction between a recognizance and a bond is, that a *bond* is a creation of a fresh debt or obligation *de novo*, while a *recognizance* is the acknowledgment of a *former* debt, upon record.

A defeasance upon a bond, recognizance, or judgment recovered is a condition which when performed, defeats or undoes it, and discharges the estate of the obligor.

Alienation by matter of record.—These assurances or conveyances are such as do not depend entirely on the act or consent of the parties themselves, but are where the sanction of some court of record is called in, to substantiate and witness the transfer of real property. They are: Private acts of Parliament, the King's Grants, Fines, and Common Recoveries.

Private acts of Parliament, as a *species of assurances,* are such as, by the transcendant authority of Parliament, are calculated to give such reasonable powers of relief as are beyond the reach of the courts, or ordinary course of law.

A fine of lands or tenements, also called an acknowledgment of a feoffment of record, is an amicable composition or agreement of a suit, either actual or fictitious, by leave of the King or his justices, whereby the estate or lands in question are acknowledged to be the right or property of one of the parties.

The force and effect of fines, when levied by such as have themselves any interest in the estate, are to assure the lands in question to the cognizee, by barring the respective rights of parties, privies, and strangers.

Fines are of equal antiquity with the first rudiments of the law, instances having been produced of them even prior to the Norman invasion.

Their origin was founded on an actual suit commenced at law for the recovery of the possession of land or other hereditaments, and the possession gained by composition, which possession thus acquired, was found to be so sure and effectual that fictitious actions were often commenced to obtain the same security.

A fine is so called because it puts an end not only to the suit thus commenced, but also to all other kinds of suits and controversies concerning the same matter.

A common recovery was so far like a Fine that it is a suit, either actual or fictitious, for lands, brought against the tenant of the freehold, who thereupon vouches another, who undertakes to defend the tenant's title, but upon such vouchee's *making default*, the land is recovered by judgment at law against the tenant, who, in return, obtains judgment against the vouchee to recover lands of equal value in recompense. This supposed adjudication of the right binds all persons, and vests a free and absolute title, or fee-simple, in the recoverer.

They were invented by the ecclesiastics, to elude the statutes of *mortmain*, the religious houses setting up a fictitious title to the land, which it was *intended* they should have, and brought an action to recover it against the tenant, who, by fraud and collusion, made no defence, and judgment being thereby given to the religious houses, they "*recovered*" the land, by sentence of law, upon a supposed prior title.

These *common recoveries*, thus originally invented by the ecclesiastics to elude the statutes of *mortmain*, were afterwards encouraged by the finesse of the courts of law of Edward IV, in order to put an end to all fettered inheritances, and bar not only estates-tail, but also remainders and reversions expectant thereon, which was the force and effect of a *recovery*, provided the tenant in tail suffers, or is vouched in, such recovery. For it was found that these *estates-tail* were of such great inconvenience, by tying up the landed property and creating perpetuities, that in order to unfetter them, common recoveries were encouraged by the judges, and by their use all limitation upon *estates-tail* were removed, and an absolute and pure fee-simple passes as the legal effect.

These common recoveries are considered simply in the light of a *conveyance on record*, invented to give a tenant in tail an absolute power to dispose of his estate, as freely as if he was tenant in fee simple. It is the only mode of conveyance by which a tenant in tail can effectually dock the entail; for by *fine* he only *bars his issue,* and not subsequent remainders and reversions.

By statute, *fines* and *common recoveries* are swept away, both in England and in this country.

Alienation by special custom is confined to those conveyances or assurances by special custom that include the transfer of *copyhold* lands, and such customary estates as are holden in ancient demesne, or manors of a similar nature.

This is effected by *Surrender*, which is the giving up of the estate into the hands of the lord for the purposes expressed in the surrender.

Of assurance by surrender, the several parts are: *Surrender* by the tenants into the hands of the lord, to the use of another, according to the custom of the manor; *Presentment* by the tenants, or homage, of such surrender; and *Admittance* of the surrenderee by the lord, according to the uses expressed in such surrender.

Alienation by devise is the method contained in a man's last will and testament of disposing of lands and tenements.

It is also styled a *revocable* assurance, *posthumously* disposing of property or the custody of children.

Before the conquest, lands were devisable by will in England, but upon the introduction of the military tenures, the restraint upon devising lands naturally took place, as a breach of the feudal doctrine of non-alienation without the consent of the lord; and so it stood at common law, until again authorized by the Statute of Wills, 34 Henry VIII; and subsequently made more universal by the statute of tenures, 29 Charles II.

A will is a disposition of real and personal property, to take effect after the death of the testator.

Will and *Devise* are generally considered, and used, as synonymous; but when the Will operates on personal property only, it is called a *testament*, and when upon real estate only, a *devise*. Where the instrument disposes of *both* real and personal property, it is usually denominated "the last will and testament."

Testaments of personal property, or chattels, operate upon whatever the testator dies possessed of; but *Devises* only upon such real property, or lands, as were his at the time of executing and publishing his will.

Wills or devises must be in writing, signed by the testator, or some person in his presence by his direction, and be subscribed by two or more witnesses in his presence and in the presence of each other.

In construing wills or devises, and deeds or common assurances, the general rules and maxims, as laid down by the courts, are as follows:

That the construction be favorable, and as near the minds and apparent intentions of the parties as the rules of law will admit; therefore, the construction must be reasonable, and agreeable to common understanding.

That where the intention is clear, too minute a stress be not laid on the strict and precise signification of words.

That the construction be made upon the entire instrument, and not from disjointed parts of it.

Words bearing two senses to be taken in the sense *agreeable to law.*

Rejecting the *latter* of two totally repugnant clauses in a deed, and the *former* in a will.

Deeds to be taken most strongly against the maker, but *devises* to be most favorably expounded, to pursue, if possible, the will of the devisor, who, for want of advice or learning, may have omitted the legal or proper phrases.

In the contruction or expounding of Wills and Devises, **the intention of the testator is admitted to be the pole-star by which the courts must steer**, yet that intention is liable to be very much controlled by the application of technical rules and the superior force of technical expressions.

THINGS PERSONAL, or chattels.—Under this name are included all sorts of things movable, which may attend a man's person wherever he goes, which includes whatever wants the duration or the immobility attending things real. They also include something more, the whole being comprehended under the general name of *chattels.*

Things personal, or chattels, may be considered with reference to their *distribution,* the *property therein,* and the *title* to them.

AS TO THEIR DISTRIBUTION: Chattels are divided into *chattels real* and *chattels personal.*

Chattels real are such as concern or savor of the realty, and are so styled as being interests issuing out of, or annexed to, *real estate,* and of which they have one quality, viz : *immobility,* which denominates them real, but want a sufficient legal determinate *duration,* which constitutes them *chattels ;* as a lease for a term of years, a mortgage, and the like.

Chattels personal are, properly and strictly speaking, *movables* which may be annexed to, or attend on, the person of the owner wherever he goes.

Property in things personal, or chattels, is either in *possession,* as where a man has not only the right, but the actual enjoyment, of the thing; or in *action,* where a man has only a bare right, without occupation or enjoyment,—called a *thing* or *chose in action,* being recoverable by action at law.

A thing or chose in action is defined to be a thing incorporeal, or *a right*, as an annuity, money due on a bond, etc.

Property in possession is *absolute* or *qualified*.

Absolute property is where a man has such an exclusive right in the thing that it cannot cease to be his without his own act or default.

Qualified property is such as is not in its nature permanent, but may sometimes subsist, and at other times not subsist, which latter may arise where the subject is incapable of absolute ownership, or from the peculiar circumstances of the owners.

Limitations of personal goods and chattels, in remainder, *after* a bequest for life, are allowed in last wills and testaments.

Things personal may belong to their owners not only in severalty, but in joint-tenancy and in common also, as well as real estates, but not in coparcenary, because they do not descend from the ancestor to the heir.

Stock used in a joint-undertaking, as by way of partnership in trade, is always considered as *common*, and not as *joint* property; and there shall be *no* survivorship therein.

Title to things personal may be *acquired* or *lost*, by Occupancy, Prerogative, Forfeiture, Custom, Succession, Marriage, Judgment, Gift or Grant, Contract, Bankruptcy, Testament, and by Administration.

Title by occupancy is that which still gives to the first occupant a *right* to those few things which have no legal owner, or are incapable of permanent ownership, such as *goods captured* from alien enemies, *things found*, the *benefit of the elements, animals wild* by nature, *emblements*, things gained by *accession*, things gained by *confusion, literary property, inventions*, etc.

The right of taking goods of alien enemies is restrained to such captors as are authorized by the public authority of the State.

Movables found upon the earth, or in the sea, unclaimed by any owner, are supposed to be abandoned by the last proprietor, and therefore belong, as originally in a state of nature, to the first occupant or fortunate finder.

The benefit of the elements,—the light, the air, the water, etc.,—thus, too, only can be appropriated.

Animals feræ naturæ, or wild by nature, all mankind has a right to pursue and take, by the original grant of the Creator, which natural right still continues unless where restrained by law.

Emblements must be referred to this principle of occupancy also. They are subject to many, though not all, the incidents attending personal chattels. They are not the object of *larceny* before they are severed from the ground.

Accession, by natural or artificial means, as the *growth* of vegetables, the pregnancy of animals, embroidering of cloth, the conversion of wood or metal into utensils, etc., is a doctrine of property also grounded upon this principle.

Confusion of goods, also,—as where the goods of two persons are indistinguishably intermixed,—the English and Civil law essentially agreeing that, if the mixture be by mutual consent, the proprietors have each an interest in common, in proportion to their respective shares. But where one willfully intermixes his own with that of another, without his knowledge or approbation, the law, to guard against fraud, gives the entire property to him whose original domain is invaded.

A copyright, or patent, is a right or property which a person has in his own original composition or invention, and, being grounded on labor and inventive skill, is properly reducible to this head, *occupancy* itself being supposed to be founded on *personal* labor,—ancient wells being the acknowledged property of the diggers of them, while the land thereabout was still in common.

The *identity* of a literary composition consists entirely of the sentiment and the language.

Title by prerogative is a method of acquiring property in personal chattels, by the *King's prerogative*, whereby a right may accrue, either to the crown itself or to such as claim under the title of the crown,—as by the King's grant, or by prescription, which supposes an ancient grant.

Title by forfeiture is that whereby a title to goods and chattels may be acquired or lost, as a punishment for some crime or misdemeanor, and a compensation for the offense and injury to the party injured,—such as treason, felony, manslaughter and *præmunire*.

Title by custom is that whereby a right vests in some particular persons, either by the local usage of some particular place, or by the almost general and universal usage of the kingdom,—as heriots, mortuaries, and heir-looms.

Heriots are a customary tribute of goods and chattels, payable to the lord of the fee on the decease of the tenant or owner of the lands. It now consists of the best live beast the tenant dies possessed of, or sometimes the best inanimate good, as a jewel or piece of plate, but it is always a personal chattel.

Heriots are of Danish origin, and a relic of villein tenure. They are either *heriot-service* or *heriot custom*.

Heriot-service amounts to little more than a mere *rent*; it is due upon a special reservation in a grant or lease of lands.

Heriot custom depends merely upon immemorial usage and custom, and arises upon no special reservation whatsoever.

Mortuaries are a sort of *ecclesiastical* heriots, being a customary gift claimed by and due to the minister, in many parishes, on the death of his parishoners.

Heir-looms,—*loom*, of Saxon origin, signifying a *limb* or member of the inheritance,—are such goods and chattels as, contrary to the nature of chattels, shall go, by special custom, to the heir, along with the inheritance, and not to the executor of the last proprietor; as crown jewels, charters, deeds, court-rolls, chests containing them, monuments, tombstones, and coats-of-arms.

Heir-looms by special custom are sometimes carriages, utensils, and other household implements, but such custom must be *strictly* proved.

Heir-looms by general custom are whatever is strongly affixed to the freehold or inheritance, and cannot be severed from it without violence or damage.

Title by succession is that by which one set of men may, by succeeding another set, acquire a property in their goods and movables. In strictness of law, this applies to corporations aggregate and such corporations sole as are the heads and representatives of bodies aggregate; for, in judgment of law, a corporation never dies.

Title by marriage is where chattels and personal property belonged *formerly* to the wife, but which, on *marriage*, are, by act of law, vested absolutely in the husband, with the same degree of property and with the same powers as the wife, when sole, had over them *provided* he reduces them to possession.

The paraphernalia of the wife, which consists of her apparel and ornaments, suitable to her rank and degree, she acquires a property in by marriage.

Title by judgment is where, in consequence of some suit at law, a man may in some cases not only *recover*, but originally *acquire*, a right to personal property,—as to *penalties*, recoverable by an action popular; *damages*, given to a man by a jury, as compensation and satisfaction for some injury sustained, and *costs* of suit.

Title by gift or grant is acquired in chattels by the voluntary conveyance of them to another, in writing or by word of mouth, the strongest evidence of which is the *delivery* of them into the possession of the person to whom given. A true or proper gift or grant is always accompanied with delivery of possession, and takes effect immediately.

Gifts are always gratuitous.

Grants are upon some consideration or equivalent.

Under the head of gifts or grants of chattels *real* may be included all leases of lands for years, assignments and surrenders of those leases, and all other methods of conveying an estate less than freehold.

Title by contract *usually* conveys an interest merely in action.

A contract is an agreement, upon sufficient consideration, to do or not to do a particular thing.

Contracts may be either *express* or *implied*, and *executed* or *executory*.

Express contracts are where the terms of the agreement are openly uttered and avowed at the time of the making.

Implied contracts are such as reason and justice dictate, and which, therefore, the law presumes that every man undertakes to perform.

Executed contracts are such in which the right and the possession are transferred *together;* they convey a *chose* in possession.

Executory contracts are such in which the *right only* is transferred; they convey a *chose* in action.

A nudum pactum, or *naked compact*, is an agreement to do or to pay anything on one side, without any compensation or consideration. It is totally void in law.

The most usual species of personal contracts are, Sale or Exchange, Bailment, Hiring, Borrowing, and Debt.

Sale or exchange is a transmutation of property from one man to another, in consideration of some price or recompense in value.

An exchange is where it is a commutation of goods for goods.
A sale is where it is a transfer of goods for money.

There is an *implied* warranty annexed to every sale, that the seller sells them as his own, or has authority to sell them; and if the title proves defective, a purchaser of goods and chattels may have satisfaction from the seller.

BAILMENT,—from the French *bailler*, to deliver,—is a delivery of goods in trust, upon a contract express or implied, that the trust shall be faithfully performed by the bailee.

Bailments are divided into five sorts, viz:

Depositum, or *deposit*, where the property bailed is to be kept by the bailee, for no particular purpose, without recompense. In this case the bailee must exercise *ordinary* care.

Mandatum, or *commission*, is where the bailee undertakes to do something to, or simply carry, the bailment, *without* recompense. Here the bailee must use a degree of diligence and care adequate to the undertaking.

Commodatum, or *loan for use*, is where the property is intrusted to the bailee without pay, to be used by him, for his own benefit. In this case the bailee must use more care than in either of the preceding cases.

Pignori acceptum, or *pawn*, is the bailment of a thing as a security for a debt. This bailee must use the same care as in the preceding cases.

Locatum, or *hiring*, is a bailment for reward, by which the hirer gains a temporary qualified property in the thing hired, and the owner acquires an absolute property in the stipend or price. Here the bailee must use due care and diligence.

Locatum is subdivided into three classes, viz:

Locatio rei, or hiring, by which the hirer gains a temporary use of the thing.

Locatio operis faciendi, where something is to be done to the thing bailed.

Locatio operis mercium vehendarum, where the thing is merely to be carried from one place to another.

Hiring and borrowing are contracts whereby the possession and a transient qualified property in chattels is transferred, for a particular time or use, on condition that the identical goods be restored at the time appointed.

Hiring is always for a price, stipend, or recompense.

Borrowing is merely gratuitous.

This *price*, being calculated to compensate for the *inconvenience*, *risk*, or *hazard* of loaning, gives birth to the doctrine of *interest, usury, bottomry, respondentia,* and *insurance.*

Interest is a moderate and legal profit allowed money-lenders, to recompense them for the *inconvenience* of parting with it.

Usury is an *exorbitant* and *illegal* profit taken by moneylenders.

Sometimes the *hazard* may be greater than the rate of interest allowed by law will compensate, which gives rise to certain practices and *exceptions* to the general rule of law regarding and limiting interest rates, viz:

Bottomry is in the nature of a mortgage of a ship, whereby the owner or master raises money to enable him to carry on his voyage, and pledges the keel or bottom of the ship as security.

If the ship is lost, the lender loses his money; but if it returns, he receives back his principal and also the premium or interest agreed upon, however it exceed the ordinary and legal rate of interest.

If there be more bottomry loans than one upon the ship, then, contrary to the principle of priority in payment of mortgages on land, here the *last* loan is entitled to be paid *first*, on the principle that the latter loans, by preserving the ship, have saved the earlier ones.

Respondentia is where the loan is not upon the vessel, but the goods and merchandise, which must necessarily be sold or exchanged in the course of the voyage. Here only the borrower personally is bound to answer the contract, and therefore said to take up money at *respondentia*.

Insurance is a contract between A and B, that upon A's paying a premium equivalent to the hazard run, B will indemnify or *insure* him against a particular event.

It is founded upon one of the same principles as the doctrine of interest upon loans,—that of *hazard*, but not that of inconvenience.

Debt as a species of personal contract, is any contract whereby a certain sum of money becomes due to the creditor.

Any contract whereby a determinate sum of money becomes due to any person and is not paid, but remains in *action* merely, is a *contract of debt*.

Debt, therefore, is a species of contract whereby a chose in action, or a right to a certain sum of money, is mutually acquired and lost.

Debts are generally divided into debts of *record*, debts by *special contract*, and debts by *simple contract*, which latter includes *paper-credit*.

A debt of record is a sum of money which appears to be due by the evidence of a court of record.

A judgment is a *contract* of the highest nature, being established by the sentence of a court of judicature.

Debts by speciality or *special* contract, are such whereby a sum of money becomes due, or is acknowledged to be due by deed or instrument under seal.

A written agreement, not under seal, is classed as a parol or simple contract, and is usually considered as such, just as much as any agreement by mere word of mouth.

Debts by simple contract are such where the contract upon which the obligation arises is ascertained by mere *oral* evidence, the most simple of any; or by notes unsealed, which are capable of more easy proof, and *therefore, only*, better than verbal promise.

Paper-credit consists of simple contract debts, by bills of exchange, promissory notes, etc.

Bills of exchange or *drafts* are open letters of request from one man to another, desiring him to pay a sum named therein to a third person, on his account.

The writer is called the *drawer;* the person to whom written, the *drawee;* and the party to whom payable, the *payee.*

They are either *foreign* or *inland*, and the law upon both is essentially the same.

Promissory notes, or *notes of hand*, are a plain and direct engagement in writing to pay a sum specified, at the time limited, to a person named, or sometimes to his order, or to the bearer at large.

Paper-credit may be transferred or assigned contrary to the general rule of the common law that no chose in action is assignable, which assignment is the *life* of paper-credit. It is done by the payee writing his name, *in dorso*, or on the back of it, thereby assigning over his whole property in it to another, called the indorsee, who may assign it to another and so on *ad infinitum*.

Acceptance is a contract by the drawee to pay the bill, grounded on an acknowledgment that the drawer has effects in his hands, or at least credit sufficient to warrant the payment;

for, in order to make himself liable, he must *accept* the bill, either verbally or in writing.

Protest is *legal* notice of *dishonor* to prior parties.

The *object* of protest is to fix the responsibility of prior parties, for in the absence of such notification, the loss falls on the holder of the bill. A bill dishonored or refused must be demanded of the *drawer*, as soon as possible, in order to fix his responsibility.

Title by bankruptcy is that method by which a right is acquired to the property of a bankrupt; for, immediately upon the act of bankruptcy, the property of the bankrupt's personal estate is vested, by construction of law, in the assignees, and they, when they have collected the whole or converted it into money, distribute it, by equal proportional dividends, among the creditors.

Assets are whatever goods and chattels of a bankrupt that may be converted into money.

Title by testament is the method of acquiring personal property according to the express directions of the deceased proprietor, which we call a *testament*.

Title by Administration is the method of acquiring personal property also according to the will of the deceased proprietor, not expressed, indeed, but *presumed* by law, which we call *administration*.

A testament or will is the legal declaration of a man's *intentions* which he *wills* to be performed after his death.

They are *written* and *verbal* or *nuncupative*, the latter depending on oral evidence, being declared by the testator *in extremis*, before a sufficient number of witnesses, and afterwards reduced to writing.

Testaments are of very high antiquity, being found among the ancient Hebrews, and have existed in England immemorially, whereby the deceased was at liberty to make this predisposition of his estate, dividing it into three equal parts: one to his wife, and one to his heirs or lineal descendants, called their *reasonable parts;* the other was entirely at his own disposal, and in disposing of which he was bound, by custom, to remember his lord and the church, by leaving them his two best chattels, which was the origin of *heriots* and *mortuaries*.

An intestate is one deceased who has made no such disposition of his goods as were testable.

Generally speaking, all persons may make wills, unless for want of sufficient *discretion:* as those *non compos mentis,* male *infants* under the age of fourteen, and females under twelve, etc.; for want of sufficient *liberty* and *free will,* or on account of *criminal conduct.*

A codicil is a supplement to a will or an addition made to it by the testator.

It annexes to, and must be taken as a part of, the testament, being for its explanation, alteration, or to make some addition to or subtraction from former dispositions of the testator. This may also be either written or nuncupative.

No testament is of any effect till after the death of the testator.

A testament may be avoided if made by a person laboring under any of the *incapacities* before mentioned.

Also, by making another testament of a *later date,* which annuls all former ones; and if the last will is but the republication of a former one, it still annuls everything preceding it, and establishes the original or former one again.

Also, by *cancelling* or *revoking* it, which a testator may always do, no matter how strong or irrevocable the terms he may have formerly used therein; for no one's acts or words can alter the disposition of *law.*

Marriage, or the *birth of a child,* is by law construed to be the revocation of a will.

An executor is he to whom another commits, by will, the execution of his last will and testament.

An executor de son tort is one who acts as executor without just authority. He is liable to all the trouble of an executorship without any of the profits or advantages.

An administrator is in effect an executor appointed by *law;* that is, he is one appointed by the court to administer upon the goods and effects of a person dying *intestate.*

Administration de bonis non is where the course of representation or administration being *interrupted* it is necessary to commit administration afresh of the goods of the deceased not administered by the former executor or administrator.

Administration cum testamento annexo is where there is no executor named in the will, or if any incapable person be named, or a person named refuses to act.

The offices and duties of executors and administrators

are in general much the same, except that the former are *bound* to follow the *will*, which the latter are not; and an executor may do many acts before he proves the will, but an administrator can do nothing till letters of administration are granted.

The interests vested in an executor by the *will* of the deceased may be continued and kept alive by the will of the *executor*, because the power of an executor is founded upon the special confidence and actual appointment of the *deceased;* hence he is allowed to transmit that power to another in whom he has equal confidence; but with an administrator it is otherwise, for he is merely the appointee or officer of the *law*.

The powers and duties of executors and administrators, who are also called *personal representatives*, are: to bury the deceased in a suitable manner, to prove his will, make and swear to an inventory of goods and chattels, whether in possession or *action*, collect the same, pay deceased's debts, next legacies, and then the *residuum* to the residuary legatee, or if none, to next of kin.

Debts of the deceased must be paid in the following order of priority: Funeral charges, expenses of proving will, and the like; debts due to the King or state, on record or specialty; debts preferred by statute; debts of record, as judgments, statutes and recognizances; debts on specialties, as rents, bonds and covenants; debts on simple contracts, as notes unsealed and verbal promises.

A legacy is a bequest or gift of goods and chattels by testament; the assent of the executor is necessary to its perfection, and the person to whom it is given is styled the *legatee*.

Legacies are *vested* or *contingent*.

A contingent legacy, if it be left to one *when* he attains or *if* he attains the age of twenty-one, and he dies before that time, is a *lapsed* legacy.

Vested legacies are legacies to one *to be paid* when he attains the age of twenty-one, and if the legatee dies before that time it goes to his representatives. It is an interest commencing *in præsenti*.

If the legatee dies before the testator the legacy is a lost or *lapsed* legacy, and shall sink into the *residuum*.

A donatio causa mortis is a death-bed gift or disposition of property; that is, when a person in his last sickness, apprehending his dissolution near, delivers or causes to be delivered to another the possession of any personal goods to keep, in case of his decease.

It needs not the assent of his executor, yet it shall not prevail against creditors, and is accompanied with this *implied* trust, that if the donor lives it shall revert to him, being only given in contemplation of death.

ANALYSIS OF BOOK III.

Private wrongs, for which the laws of England have provided redress:

- 1. By the mere act of the parties,
- 2. By the mere operation of law,
- 3. By both together, or suit in courts; wherein
  - 1. Of courts; and therein of
    - 1. Their nature and incidents,
    - 2. Their several species, viz:
      - 1. Of public or general jurisdiction; as
        - 1. The court of common law and equity,
        - 2. Ecclesiastical courts,
        - 3. Military courts, and
        - 4. Maritime courts.
      - 2. Of private or special jurisdiction.
  - 2. Of the cognizance of wrongs; in the courts
    - 1. Ecclesiastical,
    - 2. Military,
    - 3. Maritime, and
    - 4. Of common law, courts; wherein
      - 1. Of the respective remedies and INJURIES affecting
        - 1. The rights of private persons;
          - 1. Absolute, or
          - 2. Relative.
        - 2. The rights of property
          - 1. Personal,
            - 1. In possession; by
              - 1. Dispossession, or
              - 2. Damage.
            - 2. In action; by breach of contracts.
          - 2. Real; by
            - 1. Ouster, or dispossession; of
              - 1. Freeholds, or
              - 2. Chattels real.
            - 2. Trespass,
            - 3. Nuisance,
            - 4. Waste,
            - 5. Subtraction,
            - 6. Disturbance.
        - 3. The rights of the crown.
      - 2. Of the pursuit of remedies; for wrongs and injuries
        - 1. By action at common law, wherein of
          - 1. Original,
          - 2. Process,
          - 3. Pleading,
          - 4. Demurrer and issue,
          - 5. Trial, by
            - 1. Record,
            - 2. Inspection,
            - 3. Witness,
            - 4. Certificate,
            - 5. Wager of battel,
            - 6. Wager of law,
            - 7. Jury.
          - 6. Judgment,
          - 7. Appeal,
          - 8. Execution.
        - 2. By proceedings in the courts of equity.

BOOK III.

PRIVATE WRONGS.—Wrongs are the privation of right, and are divisible into *private* wrongs and *public* wrongs.

Private wrongs are an infringement or privation of the private or civil rights of *individuals*, and are frequently termed *civil injuries*.

Public wrongs are a breach and violation of public rights and duties which affect the whole *community*, and are distinguished by the appellation of *crimes* and *misdemeanors*.

The remedy for private injuries is by application to courts of justice—that is, by civil *suit* or *action*—for which purpose courts of justice are instituted, in order to protect the weak from the insults of the stronger, by expounding and enforcing those laws by which rights are defined and wrongs prohibited.

This *redress* of private wrongs or civil injuries may be effected by the mere act of the *parties*, by mere operation of *law*, or by both together, or *suits* in court.

Redress by act of the parties is of two kinds, viz: that by act of the injured party *only*, and that by joint act of *all* the parties.

Redress by the sole act of the party injured is by *defence* of one's self or relations, by *recaption* of goods, by *entry* on lands and tenements—to oust intruders, by *abatement* of nuisances without riot—by *distress*, for rent, damages, amercements, etc., and by *seizing of heriots*.

Self-defence is justly called the *primary* or *first law of nature*, and is not, nor can it be, taken away by the law of society. It is held as an excuse for breaches of the peace, and even homicide itself.

Recaption happens when any one hath deprived another of his property in goods or chattels, and the owner claims and takes them wherever he happens to find them.

A nuisance is anything that worketh hurt, inconvenience, or damage, or unlawfully annoys another.

Distress is the taking of a personal chattel out of the possession of the wrong-doer into the custody of the party injured, to procure satisfaction for the wrong committed.

A man's tools and utensils of trade cannot be distrained; nor things which cannot be rendered again in as good plight as when distrained.

Replevy—*replegiare*—i. e., to take back the pledge—is when a person distrained upon applies to the sheriff or his officers, and has the distress returned into his own possession upon giving security to try the *right* of taking it.

Redress by joint act of all the parties is by *accord* and *arbitration*.

Accord is a satisfaction *agreed* upon between the party injured and the party injuring; which, when performed, is a bar of all actions on this account.

Arbitration is where the parties submit all matters in dispute to the judgment of two or more arbitrators.

Redress by the mere operation of law is by *retainer* and *remitter*.

Retainer is where a creditor is executor or administrator, and the law permits him to *retain* his own debt before other creditors in equal degree; otherwise he must sue himself, which would be an absurdity, and leave him in a worse condition than other creditors.

Remittitur is where one has the true property in lands, but is out of possession thereof, and has no right to enter without recovering possession in an action—hath afterwards the freehold *cast* upon him by some subsequent and, of course, defective, title: in this case he is *remitted* or sent back by operation of law to his ancient and more certain title.

Redress effected by act of both law and the parties is by *suit* or action in the *courts* of justice, wherein may be considered the *courts themselves*, and the *cognizance of wrongs* or *injuries* therein.

Of courts in general we may consider their *nature* and *incidents*, and their several *species*.

THEIR NATURE AND INCIDENTS.—A court is a place wherein justice is judicially administered.

Incidents or *constituent parts* to all courts are plaintiffs, defendants, judge, attorneys, etc.

Courts are either of *record* or *not of record*.

A court of record is that where the acts and judicial proceedings are enrolled or *recorded* for a perpetual memorial and testimony, which rolls are called the *records* of the court, and are of such high and super-eminent authority that their truth cannot be called in question.

A court not of record is the court of a private man, whom the law will not intrust with any discretionary power, as courts baron, and other inferior jurisdictions.

An attorney is one who is put in the place, stead, or turn of another to manage his matters of law.

It is a general rule that where there is a *legal right* there is also a *legal remedy*, by suit or action at law, whenever that right is invaded.

A suit or action is the lawful demand of one's right.

It is an ordinary *proceeding* in a court of justice, by which a party prosecutes another party for the enforcement or protection of a right, the redress or prevention of a wrong, or the punishment of a public offence.

Fictions *in law* are those things that have no real essence in their own body, but are acknowledged and accepted in law for some special purpose. They are highly beneficial and useful, as the maxim is ever invariably observed that no fiction shall extend to work an injury, its proper operation being to prevent a mischief or remedy an inconvenience that might result from the general rule of law.

AS TO THEIR SPECIES.—Courts are of a *public* or *general* jurisdiction, or of a *private* or *special* jurisdiction.

Courts of a public or general jurisdiction are the Courts of Common Law and Equity, the Ecclesiastical Courts, the Military Courts, and the Maritime Courts.

The courts of common law and equity are the Court of *Piepoudre*, the Court Baron, the Hundred Court, the County Court, the Court of Common Pleas, of King's Bench, of Exchequer, of Chancery, of Exchequer-Chamber, and the House of Peers; to which may be added, as auxiliaries, the Courts of Assize and Nisi Prius.

The court of piepoudre, so called from the dusty feet of the suitors, is a court of record incident to every fair and market. They are instituted to do justice expeditiously among the variety of persons that resort from distant places to a fair or market. It is the lowest court.

The court baron is a court incident to every manor of the kingdom, to be holden by the steward within the said manor.

A hundred court is only a larger court baron, being held for all the inhabitants of a particular hundred instead of a manor.

A county court is a court incident to the jurisdiction of the sheriff.

A court of common pleas is for the trial of all matters of law arising in civil causes, whether real, personal, or mixed and compounded of both.

Pleas, or suits, are of two sorts: *pleas of the crown*, which comprehend all crimes and misdemeanors wherein the King (on behalf of the public) is the plaintiff, and *common pleas*, which include all *civil* actions depending between subject and subject.

In this court only can *real* actions be originally brought, and all other or personal pleas between man and man, this court sitting to hear and determine all matters of *law* arising in *civil* causes, whether *real, personal* or *mixed*.

The court of king's bench, so called because the King used formerly to sit there in person, is the *supreme court of common law* in the kingdom.

The court of exchequer is a court of inferior rank to that of the King's bench or common pleas, and is intended principally to order the revenues and collect the debts and duties of the crown.

The high court of chancery is in matters of civil property the most important of any of the King's superior and original courts of justice, and derives its name from the judge or lord *chancellor*, who presides over it.

The court of exchequer-chamber is only a court of appeal to correct the errors of other jurisdictions.

The house of peers is the *supreme court of judicature* in the kingdom; it has no original jurisdiction, but only upon appeals and writs of error.

The courts of assize and nisi prius are composed of two or more commissioners, who are twice every year sent by the King all over the kingdom to try certain cases by *jury*, etc.

The ecclesiastical courts were various, and exercised jurisdiction over such ecclesiastical matters in which it was supposed the Court of Rome, or the Pope, had proper or rightful preference. They are not courts of record.

The *ecclesiastical* and *lay* courts were first separated by William the Conqueror. In the times of our Saxon ancestors there was no distinction between them.

The military courts are also not courts of record, and the only permanent one is that of *chivalry*, the courts *martial* annually established by act of Parliament being only temporary.

The maritime courts are the courts of admiralty and their courts of appeal. They have power and jurisdiction to determine all maritime injuries arising upon the seas.

Like the ecclesiastical courts, the proceedings in these courts are according to the method of the civil law, and they are not courts of record.

Courts of a private or special jurisdiction are those whose jurisdiction is private and special, confined to *particular* spots, or instituted to redress only *particular injuries.*

These particular jurisdictions, derogating from the general jurisdiction of the courts of common law, are ever strictly restrained, and cannot be extended farther than the express letter of their privileges will most explicitly warrant.

COGNIZANCE OF PRIVATE WRONGS BY THE COURTS.—*All private wrongs* or *civil injuries* are cognizable either in the courts ecclesiastical, military, maritime or those of common law.

In the ecclesiastical courts the injuries cognizable are *pecuniary, matrimonial* and *testamentary.*

The pecuniary injuries are Subtraction of tithes, Non-payment of ecclesiastical dues, Spoliation, Dilapidations, Non-repairs of the church, and the like.

The matrimonial injuries are Jactitation of marriage, i. e., where one boasts that he is married to another, whereby a common reputation of their marriage may ensue, Subtraction of conjugal rights, Inability for the marriage state, and Refusal of decent maintenance to the wife.

The testamentary injuries are Disputing the validity of wills, Obstructing of administrations, and Subtraction of legacies.

The ecclesiastical courts or tribunals subsist and are admitted, in England, not by any right of their own, but upon bare sufferance and toleration from the municipal laws, and they are principally guided by the rules of the civil and canon laws. They must have recourse to the laws of England to be informed how far their jurisdiction extends, or what causes are permitted and what forbidden to be discussed or drawn in question before them, the only uniform rule to determine the jurisdiction of the courts in England being the common law.

The ecclesiastical courts have no other process than that of excommunication to enforce their sentences when pronounced, and the courts of common law will award a prohibition against the proceedings of the spiritual courts when they are manifestly repugnant to the fundamental maxims of the municipal law. Otherwise they lend a supporting hand to their authority.

In the military courts the injuries cognizable are Injuries in point of honor, Encroachments in coat-armor, Precedency, etc.

The proceedings are in a *summary* method, and its jurisdiction is declared by statute to be, "that it hath cognizance of contracts touching deeds of arms or of war, out of the realm, and also of things which touch war within the realm, which cannot be determined or discussed by the common law, together with other usages and customs to the same matters appertaining."

In the maritime courts the injuries cognizable are injuries which, though in their nature of common law cognizance, yet being committed on the high seas, out of the reach of ordinary courts of justice, are therefore to be remedied in a peculiar court of their own.

The proceedings of a court of admiralty much resemble those of the civil law, but are not entirely founded thereon, as they likewise adopt and make use of other laws as occasion requires.

In the common law courts the injuries cognizable are all the possible injuries whatsoever that do not fall within the exclusive cognizance of either the *ecclesiastical, military* or *maritime* tribunals.

IN THE COURTS OF COMMON LAW, in treating of their *cognizance of private wrongs* or *injuries,* may be considered the wrongs or injuries *themselves* and their *remedies;* and the pursuit of those remedies in the several courts.

The plain and natural remedy for every species of wrong or injury cognizable by the courts of common law is, in general, by putting the party injured into possession of that right whereof he is unjustly deprived.

This is effected by delivery or restoration of the *thing* detained, or subject-matter in dispute, to the rightful owner; or, where that remedy is impossible or inadequate, by giving the party injured a satisfaction in *damages.*

The instruments by which these remedies may be ob-

tained are by suits or actions at law, which are distinguished into three kinds: *Real, Personal* and *Mixed.*

Personal actions are such whereby a man claims a debt, or personal duty, or damages in lieu thereof; or damages for some injury done to his person or property.

The former are said to be founded on *contracts* and the latter on *torts.*

Real actions concern real property only, and are such whereby the plaintiff claims title to have any lands or tenements, rents, commons, or other hereditaments, in fee-simple, fee-tail, or for term of life.

Mixed actions are suits partaking of the nature of the other two, whereby some real property is demanded, and also personal damages for a wrong sustained.

All injuries are either with or without *force* or violence.

WRONGS OR INJURIES, and their remedies.—They are either injuries to the *rights of persons,* or injuries to the *rights of property.*

Injuries to the rights of persons are either to their *absolute* or *relative* rights.

Injuries to the absolute rights of individuals are injuries to *personal security,* to *personal liberty* and to *private property.*

Injuries to personal security are against one's Life, Limbs, Body, Health, or Reputation.

Injuries to the limbs and body are Threats, Assaults, Battery, Wounding and Mayhem.

Threats and *Menaces* alone only become an injury or wrong when attended with some consequent *inconvenience.*

Assault is an attempt or offer to beat another, without touching him.

Battery is the unlawful beating of another.

Wounding consists in giving another some dangerous hurt.

Mayhem consists in violently depriving another of the use of a member proper for his defence in fight.

Injuries to health are by any unwholesome practices that effect, or tend to any apparent damage, to a man's vigor or constitution.

Injuries to reputation are Slander and Malicious Words, Libels, and Malicious Prosecutions.

Slander is the malicious defaming of a person in his reputation, profession, or livelihood, by words tending to his damage, or derogation.

Libels are injuries affecting a man's reputation by printing, writing, pictures, signs, or the like, which, by setting a man in an odious or ridiculous light, thereby tend to diminish his reputation.

The action of trespass on the case is a universal *remedy* given for all personal wrongs and injuries *without* force, or where the act is *not immediately* injurious, but only by consequence, and collaterally.

It is so called because the plaintiff's whole *case* or cause of complaint is set forth at length in the original writ.

The action of trespass vi et armis is the remedy for injuries accompanied *with* force or violence, or where the act done is in itself an *immediate* injury to another's person or property.

Injuries to personal liberty are by false imprisonment only, which consists in any kind of confinement or detention of another without sufficient authority.

Habeas corpus (have the body) is the great and efficacious writ in all cases of illegal confinement. It is a writ of *right* which may not be denied, and is directed to the person detaining another, commanding him to produce the *body* of the prisoner, with the day and cause of his caption and detention, before the judge or court awarding the writ, that they may enquire into the cause of the commitment, and ascertain if it be just.

Injuries to the relative rights of persons, or to their rights in their relations to each other in society, are such injuries as affect the rights of Husbands, Parents, Guardians and Masters.

Injuries to a husband are Abduction or taking away his wife, Adultery or criminal conversation with her and Beating or otherwise abusing her.

Injuries to parents and guardians are, Abduction of their children or wards.

Injuries to masters are Retaining his servants, or beating them.

INJURIES TO THE RIGHTS OF PRIVATE PROPERTY are either to those of *personal* or *real* property.

Injuries to personal property may be to property in *possession* or in *action*.

Injuries to personal property in possession are by *Dispossession*, or by *Damage*, while in the owner's possession.

Dispossession may be effected by unlawful *taking*, and by an unlawful *detaining*, though the original taking might be lawful.

The unlawful taking of goods and chattels is remedied by actual *restitution*—obtained by action of replevin, or by satisfaction in *damages*—obtained by action on the case, trespass or trover.

For the unlawful detaining of goods lawfully taken, the remedy is also by actual *restitution*—obtained by action of replevin or detinue, or by satisfaction in *damages*—by action on the case, or trover and conversion.

For damage to personal property while in the owner's possession, the remedy is in *damages;* by action of trespass *vi et armis,* if the act be *immediately* injurious; or by action of trespass on the case, if the act occasions *consequential* damage.

The action of replevin, being founded upon a distress wrongfully taken and without sufficient cause, is a re-delivery of the pledge or thing taken in distress to the owner, upon his giving security to try the right of the distress and to restore it, if the right be adjudged against him; after which the distrainor may keep it till tender made of sufficient amends, but must then re-deliver it to the owner.

The action of detinue is for the recovery of the possession of goods in specie.

It is not much used, having given place to the action of trover.

The action of trover in its origin was an action of *trespass on the case,* for the recovery of damages against such a person as had found another's goods and refused to deliver them on demand, but converted them to his own use.

This action having certain advantages over that of detinue, such as requiring a less degree of certainty in describing the goods, by *fiction of law,* actions of *trover* were at length permitted to be brought; the injury being in the *conversion.*

Injuries to personal property in action arise by breach of *contracts,* express or *implied.*

Breaches of express contracts are by non-payment of *debts,* by non-performance of *covenants,* and by non-performance of *promises* or *assumpsits.*

Breaches of implied contracts are such as arise from the *nature and constitution of government,* as the non-payment of money which the laws have directed to be paid; and such as arise from *reason and construction of law,* as the non-performance of legal **presumptive or implied assumpsits,** viz: of a *quan-*

tum meruit, of a *quantum valebat*, of expending money for another, of receiving money to another's use, of an *insimul computassent* on an account stated, of performing one's duty in any employment with integrity, diligence and skill.

Debt is a sum of money due by certain and express agreement.

A promise is in the nature of a verbal covenant, and wants nothing but the solemnity of writing and sealing to make it absolutely the same.

Qui tam actions, or *popular actions*, are such where, usually, forfeitures created by statute are given at large to any common informer, or any person who will sue for the same. Sometimes part is given to the King, state, poor, or public use, and the other part to the informer or prosecutor.

Express warranty of chattels is that whereby the warrantor covenants or undertakes to *insure* that the thing which is the subject of the contract is as represented.

INJURIES TO REAL PROPERTY are Ouster, Trespass, Nuisance, Waste, Subtraction and Disturbance.

Ouster, or dispossession, is a wrong or injury that carries with it the amotion or deprivation of possession; for thereby the wrong-doer gets into the actual occupation of the land or hereditament, and obliges him that hath a right to seek his legal remedy, in order to gain possession and damages for the injury sustained.

It is either from *freeholds*, or from *chattels real*.

Ouster from freeholds is effected by Abatement, Intrusion, Disseizin, Discontinuance and Deforcement.

Abatement is the entry of a stranger after the death of the ancestor, and before the *heir*.

Intrusion is the entry of a stranger, after a particular estate of freehold is determined, before him in *remainder* or *reversion*.

Disseizin is a wrongful putting out of him that is *seized* of the freehold.

Discontinuance is where a tenant in tail, or husband of a tenant in fee, makes a larger estate of the land than the law alloweth.

Deforcement includes any other wrongful detainer of the freehold, from him who hath the *property*, but who never had the possession.

Ouster from chattels real is from estates by statute-merchant, statute-staple, and *elegit*, or from an estate for years. It is effected by a kind of disseizin or ejectment.

A writ of ejectione firmæ, or *action of trespass in ejectment*, lies where lands, etc., are let for a term of years, and the lessee is ousted from his term; by which he recovers possession of his term and damages.

Ejectment is now the usual method adopted for trying titles to land, instead of an action real.

Trespass is an entry on another man's ground without lawful authority, or cause of justification, and doing some damage, however inconsiderable, to his property.

The *law* always couples the idea of *force* with that of trespass or intrusion upon the property of another.

Nuisance, or annoyance, signifies anything that worketh hurt, inconvenience, or damage.

It may be either a *public* and *common* nuisance, or a *private* nuisance, which latter is anything done to the hurt or annoyance of the corporeal or incorporeal hereditaments of another.

Waste is a spoil and destruction of an estate, either in houses, woods, or lands, by demolishing, not the temporary profits only, but the very substance of the thing, to the injury of him that hath the present interest, or him in remainder or reversion.

It is either *voluntary*, as by actual and designed demolition; or *permissive*, arising from mere negligence and want of care.

Subtraction is where a person who owes any suit, duty, custom, or service to another, withdraws or neglects to perform it; as rent and other services due by tenure, custom, and the like.

It differs from disseizin in that the latter strikes at the very title of the party injured, and amounts to an ouster or actual dispossession; whereas Subtraction is committed without any denial of the right, and consisting merely of non-performance.

Disturbance is usually a wrong done to some incorporeal hereditament, by hindering or disquieting the owners in their regular and lawful enjoyment of it. It may be of franchises, of commons, of ways, of tenure, or of patronages.

The pursuit of remedies in the courts furnished by the laws of England is by *suit* or action in the *Courts of Common Law*, or by proceedings in the *Courts of Equity*.

OF ACTIONS IN THE COURTS OF COMMON LAW.—In an *action* in the court of Common Pleas, (which is the original and proper court for prosecuting *civil* suits,) the general and orderly parts are the original writ, the process, the pleadings, the issue or demurrer, the trial, the judgment and its incidents, the proceedings in the nature of appeals, and the execution.

The original writ, or *præcipe,* is the beginning or foundation of a suit, and is directed to the defendant by the officer of the court, commanding him to do some certain thing, as to *appear* in court, or *show cause* to the contrary.

The process is (or includes) the means of *compelling* the defendant to appear in court, viz: either by summons, attachment, *distringas, capias ad respondendum,* and *testatum capias, alias,* and *pluries* writs, writ of *exigi facias,* proclamations, and outlawry, appearance and common bail, arrest, and special bail.

The summons is a written or verbal warning to appear in court at the return of the original writ.

The writ of attachment issues on the non-appearance of the defendant at the return of the original writ, whereby the sheriff is commanded to *attach* him by seizing some of his goods, which he shall forfeit if he do not appear, or by making him find safe pledges or securities, who shall be amerced in case of his non-appearance.

The writ of distringas, or distress *infinite,* issues after attachment, if the defendant forfeits his security and does not appear.

The writ of capias ad respondendum issues, commanding the sheriff to take the *body* of the defendant who neglects to appear after summons, attachment, and *distringas.*

The writ of testatum capias issues when the sheriff returns that defendant is *non est inventus,* or not to be found, in his bailiwick, and is directed to the sheriff of the county in which the defendant is supposed to be, reciting the former writ, and that it is *testified* that the defendant lurks or wanders in his bailiwick, wherefore he is commanded to take him.

The writ of exigi facias, or *exigent,* required the sheriff to cause the defendants to be proclaimed, required, or exacted, in five county courts successively, to render himself; and if he does, then to take him as in a *capias;* but if he does not appear, he shall then be outlawed.

Outlawry is putting a man out of the protection of the law, so that he is incapable to bring an action for redress of injuries; and is also attended with the forfeiture of all one's goods and chattels.

Appearance is when the defendant answers any of the different writs commanding him to appear in court, by duly presenting himself in person or by attorney.

Bail is security given for one's appearance in court at a future day.

Bail is from the French word *bailler*, to deliver; because the defendant is bailed or delivered to his securities upon their giving security for his appearance, and is supposed to continue in their friendly custody instead of going to jail.

PLEADINGS are the mutual altercations between the plaintiff and defendant reduced to writing.

The general and orderly parts of pleading are the declaration, the defence, the plea, the replication, the rejoinder, the sur-rejoinder, the rebutter, the sur-rebutter, etc.

The declaration *narratio* or count, anciently called the *tale*, is the first pleading in which the plaintiff sets forth his cause of complaint at length.

Local actions are where possession of land is to be recovered, or damages for an actual trespass, or for waste, etc., affecting land.

Transitory actions are for injuries which might happen anywhere; as debt, detinue, slander, and the like.

Venue or *visne* is the *vicinia* or neighborhood in which the injury is declared to be done.

A nonsuit is when the plaintiff neglects to deliver or file a declaration for two terms after the defendant appears; or is guilty of other delays or defaults against the rules of law; or where in any subsequent stage of the action he is adjudged not to follow or pursue his remedy as he ought to do; in which cases a nonsuit, or *non-prosequitur* is entered and he is said to be *non-pros'd*.

A retraxit is an open and voluntary renunciation by the plaintiff of his suit in court, whereby he forever loses his suit.

A discontinuance is when the plaintiff leaves a chasm in the proceeding of his cause, as by not continuing the process regularly from day to day, and from time to time, as he ought to do.

Defence in its true legal sense, signifies, not a justification, protection, or guard, but merely an opposing or denial of the truth of the validity of the complaint.

Claim of cognizance or *conusance* is a claim to have the action tried in some special jurisdiction. It must be claimed before defence made, if at all.

Imparlance is a continuance of the cause, which the defendant is entitled to demand, and may, before he pleads, have granted by court, to see if he can end the matter amicably, without farther suit, by talking with the plaintiff.

Oyer.—The defendant may crave *oyer* of the writ, or of the bond or other specialty, upon which the action is brought; that is to *hear* it read to him.

A plea is the defendant's answer of fact, to the plaintiff's declaration.

Pleas are of two sorts, *dilatory pleas* and *pleas to the action*.

Dilatory pleas are such as tend merely to delay or put off the suit, by questioning the *propriety of the remedy*, rather than by denying the injury.

They are, to the jurisdiction of the court, to the disability of the plaintiff, or in abatement.

Pleas to the action are such as dispute the very *cause* of suit or answer to the merits of the complaint.

They are made by confessing or denying any *cause* of action, and are either *general* or *special*—pleas that totally deny the cause of complaint being either the *general issue* or a *special plea* in *bar*.

The general plea, or *general issue*, is what traverses, thwarts, and denies at once the whole declaration, without offering any special matter whereby to evade it.

An issue is a fact affirmed on one side and denied on the other.

Special pleas are usually in the affirmative, though sometimes in the negative; but they always advance some new fact not mentioned in the declaration; and then they must be averred to be true in the common form—"and this he is ready to verify."

An estoppel is a *special plea* in *bar*, which happens where a man has done some act or executed some deed which *estops* or precludes him from averring anything to the contrary.

The conditions and qualities of a plea are that it be single and contain only one matter; that it be direct and positive, and not argumentative; that it have convenient certainty of time, place and persons; that it answer the plaintiff's allegations in every material point, and that it be so pleaded as to be capable of trial.

A motion is an occasional application to court by the parties or their counsel, in order to obtain some rule or order of court necessary in the progress of a cause.

The replication is when the *plea* is in, if it does not amount to, an issue, but only evades it, the plaintiff may plead again, and reply to the defendant's plea.

The subsequent pleadings are the rejoinder, the sur-rejoinder, the rebutter, the sur-rebutter, etc.

To give color is to suppose one to have an appearance or color of title—bad in deed in point of law.

Departure in pleading consists in varying from the title or defence which the party has once insisted on. This must be carefully avoided; the replication must support the declaration, and the rejoinder the plea.

New or novel assignment is when the plaintiff who has alleged in his declaration a *general* wrong, in his replication, after an *evasive* plea by the defendant, reduces that general wrong to more *particular certainty* by *assigning* the injury afresh in such manner as clearly to ascertain and identify it.

Duplicity in pleading must be avoided by every plea being simple, entire, connected, and confined to one single point.

Issue and demurrer.—Issue is where the parties in the course of pleading, come to a point affirmed on one side, and denied on the other; which, if it be matter of *law*, is called a *demurrer;* but if matter of fact, it still retains the name of an *issue of fact*.

A demurrer confesses the facts to be true, but denies the law arising upon those facts.

Continuance is the detaining of the parties in court from time to time.

Plea of puis darien continuance, or *since the last adjournment*, is where the defendant is permitted to plead some new matter that has arisen since he has pleaded, or even after issue or demurrer.

TRIAL is the examination of the matter of *fact* put in issue.

The several species of trial are by record, by inspection or examination, by certificate, by witnesses, by wager of battel, by wager of law and by *jury*.

Trial by the record is only had when the existence of such record is the point in issue; as where a matter of record is pleaded in any action, as a fine, judgment, etc., and the opposite party pleads "*nul tiel* record."

Trial by inspection, or *examination,* is had by the court, principally when the matter in issue is the evident object of the senses, and where, for the greater expedition of a cause, the judges, upon the testimony of their own senses, decided the point in dispute.

Trial by certificate is where such certificate must have been conclusive to a jury, as where the evidence of the person certifying is the only proper criterion of the point in dispute.

Trial by witnesses, or without the intervention of a jury, (the method in the civil law) is where the judge is left to form his own sentence upon the credit of the witnesses examined.

Trial by wager of battel, or *judiciary duel,* is in the nature of an appeal to Providence, under an apprehension and hope that heaven would give the victory to him who had the right.

Trial by wager of law is only had where the matter in issue had been privately transacted between the parties themselves, without witnesses present, and consisted in the defendant's discharging himself from the claim on his own oath, bringing with him at the same time into court eleven of his neighbors to swear that they believed his statement to be true.

Trial by jury, or *per pais,* (by the country) is of two kinds: *extraordinary,* or that of the grand assise or grand jury, consisting of sixteen jurors, instituted by Henry II to do away with the barbarous custom of duelling, etc.; and *ordinary,* by a jury of twelve free and lawful men of the body of the county.

Juries were either *special,* as where the causes were of too great nicety for the discussion of ordinary freeholders, or where the sheriff was suspected of partiality, or *common,* as one returned by the sheriff according to the directions of statute.

Challenges are exceptions made to jurors, and are either to the *array* or to the *polls.*

Challenges to the array are at once an exception to the *whole* panel.

Challenges to the polls are exceptions to *particular* jurors and are of four kinds, viz:

Propter honoris respectum, as if a lord of parliament be impanelled on a jury, he may be challenged by either party or may challenge himself.

Propter defectum, as for defect in estate sufficient to qualify one to be a juror, etc.

Propter affectum, as for suspicion of bias or partiality.

Propter delictum, as for some crime that affects the credit of the juror.

A tales is a supply of such men as are summoned upon the first panel, in order to make up a deficiency in the same.

Evidence signifies that which demonstrates, makes clear or ascertains the truth of the very fact or point in issue, either on the one side or the other. No evidence ought to be admitted on any other point.

A verdict is the finding of the jury.

A special verdict is where the jurors state the facts as they find them to be proved, and pray the advice of the court thereon.

JUDGMENT is the *sentence of the law* pronounced by the court upon the matter contained in the record.

A judgment is either upon demurrer, upon a verdict, by confession or default, or by nonsuit or retraxit, and may be *interlocutory* or *final.*

Final judgment is such as at once puts an end to the action.

Interlocutory judgments are such as are given in the middle of a cause, upon some plea, proceeding or default, which is only intermediate and does not finally determine or complete the suit.

EXECUTION is putting the sentence of law in force.

The writ of habere facias possessionem is a writ of seizin of the freehold directed to the sheriff, commanding him to give actual possession to the plaintiff of lands recovered by him at law.

The writ of capias ad satisfaciendum is an execution of the highest nature, depriving a man of his liberty till he makes the satisfaction awarded.

The writ of scire facias is a judicial writ, founded upon some record, and requiring the person against whom it is brought to show cause why the party bringing it should not have the advantage of such record.

The writ of fieri facias commands the sheriff to seize and sell the defendant's goods and chattels, sufficient to satisfy the judgment and costs.

The writ of levari facias commands the sheriff to seize certain of the defendant's lands to satisfy the plaintiff's demands.

PROCEEDINGS IN THE COURTS OF EQUITY

differ from those in the Courts of Common Law, principally in three points, viz:

In the mode of proof—by a discovery on the oath of the party, which gives a jurisdiction in matters of account and fraud.

In the mode of trial—by depositions taken in any part of the world.

In the mode of relief—by giving a more specific and extensive remedy than can be had in the courts of common law, by executing agreements, staying waste or other injuries by injunction, directing the sale of incumbered lands, by the true construction of the securities for money, by considering them merely as a pledge, and by the execution of trusts or uses in a manner analogous to the law of legal estates.

Equity, in its true and genuine meaning, is the soul and spirit of all law; *positive* law is construed and *rational* law is made by it.

ANALYSIS OF BOOK IV.

Public Wrongs; in which are considered
 1. The general nature of crimes and punishments,
 2. The persons capable of committing crimes,
 3. Their several degrees of guilt; as
    1. Principals,
    2. Accessories.
 4. The various crimes; more peculiarly offending
    1. God and religion,
    2. The law of nations,
    3. The King and government; viz:
       1. High treason,
       2. Felonies injurious to the prerogative,
       3. Præmunire,
       4. Misprisons and contempts.
    4. The commonwealth; viz: offences against
       1. Public justice,
       2. Public peace,
       3. Public trade,
       4. Public health,
       5. Public economy.
    5. Individuals; being crimes against
       1. Their persons; by
          1. Homicide,
          2. Other corporeal injuries.
       2. Their habitations,
       3. Their property.
 5. The means of prevention; by security for
    1. The peace, or
    2. The good behavior.
 6. The method of punishment; wherein of
    1. The several courts of criminal jurisdiction;
    2. The proceedings therein.
       1. Summary, or
       2. Regular; by
          1. Arrest,
          2. Commitment and bail,
          3. Prosecution; by
             1. Presentment,
             2. Indictment,
             3. Information,
             4. Appeal.
          4. Process,
          5. Arraignment, and its incidents,
          6. Plea, and issue,
          7. Trial and conviction,
          8. Clergy,
          9. Judgment,
             1. Forfeiture,
             2. Corruption of blood,
          10. Avoider of judgment; by
             1. Falsifying, or reversing, the attainder;
             2. Reprieve, or pardon.
          11. Execution.

BOOK IV.

PUBLIC WRONGS being breaches of general and public rights, affect the whole community, and are called **crimes and misdemeanors**, in treating of which may be considered the general *nature* of crimes and punishments; the *persons* capable of committing crimes; their several *degrees of guilt;* the several *species of crimes;* the *means of preventing crime;* and the *method of punishment.*

GENERAL NATURE OF CRIMES AND THEIR PUNISHMENT.—A crime or misdemeanor is an act committed or omitted in violation of a public law either forbidding or commanding it.

A crime, in its *limited* sense, is confined to felony. They are indictable, and are defined and punishable by statute and common law.

A misdemeanor, in its *limited* sense, is a lesser degree of crime, and includes offenses inferior to felony, but still punishable by indictment, and other prescribed proceedings.

Offenses are crimes not indictable, but punishable summarily, or by forfeiture of a penalty.

Misprisons and contempts are all such *high offences* as are under the degree of capital.

Crimes are distinguised from *civil injuries*, in that they are a breach and violation of the public rights, due to the whole community.

In all cases the crime includes an injury.

Every public offense is also a *private* wrong, because it affects the individual as well as the community.

Punishments may be considered with regard to the *power*, the *end,* and the *measure* of their infliction.

The power or *right* of inflicting human punishments, for natural crimes, or such as are *mala in se,* was, by the law of nature, vested in every individual, but, by the fundamental contract of society, is now transferred to the sovereign power, in which is also vested, by the same contract, the right of punishing positive offences, or such as are *mala prohibita*.

The end of human punishment is to prevent future offences—by amending the offender, by deterring others through his example, and by depriving him of the power to do future mischief.

The measure of human punishment must be determined by the wisdom of the sovereign power, and not by any uniform rule; though that wisdom may be regulated and assisted by certain general and equitable principles.

The persons capable of committing crimes are all persons, unless there be in them a *defect of will*; for, to constitute a legal crime, there must be both a vicious *will* and a vicious *act*.

As a vicious will without a vicious act is no civil crime, so, on the other hand, an unwarrantable act, without a vicious will, is no crime at all.

The will is wanting, or does not concur with the act, in three cases, viz:

First.—Where there is a defect of understanding, as infancy, idiocy, lunacy and intoxication,—which last, however, is no excuse.

Second.—Where no will is exerted, as misfortune, or chance, and ignorance or mistake of fact.

Third.—Where the act is constrained by force and violence, as from compulsion or inevitable necessity, which is that of civil subjection, of *duress per minas*, choosing the least of two evils, where one is unavoidable, and want or hunger—which is no legitimate excuse.

Infants under fourteen years of age are *prima facie,* adjudged to be incapable of crime.

If a lunatic has lucid intervals of understanding, he must answer for what he does in those intervals—*ignorantia legis neminem excusat.*

PRINCIPALS AND ACCESSORIES are the different degrees of guilt in criminals.

Principals may be so in two degrees.

A principal in the first degree is he that is the actor or absolute perpetrator of the crime.

A principal in the second degree is he who is present, aiding and abetting the act to be done.

An accessory is he who is not the chief actor in the offence, nor present at its performance, but is some way *concerned* therein, either before or after the fact committed.

An accessory before the fact is one who being *absent* at the time of the crime committed, doth yet procure, counsel, or command *another* to commit a crime.

An accessory after the fact is where a person *knowing* a felony to have been committed, receives, relieves, comforts, or assists the felon.

In all degrees of crime under felony there are no accessories; all are principals.

The several species of crimes are such as offend God and his holy *Religion*, the *Law of Nations*, the King and *Government*, the Public or *Commonwealth* and *Individuals*.

Offences against God and religion are Apostacy, Heresy, Offences against the Established Church, Blasphemy, Profane swearing and cursing, Witchcraft, Religious imposters, Simony, Sabbath-breaking, Drunkenness and Lewdness.

Apostacy is a total renunciation of Christianity.

Heresy is an obstinate and public denial of some of the essential doctrines of Christianity.

Simony is the corrupt presentation of anyone to an ecclesiastical benefice for gifts or reward.

Offences against the law of nations are principally incident to States or nations, but when committed by private subjects are then the objects of the municipal law.

They are Violations of safe-conducts, Infringement of the rights of embassadors and Piracy.

Piracy is committing those acts of robbery and depredation on the high seas which, if committed on land, would have been felony.

Offences against the King and government are Treason, Felonies injurious to the prerogative, Præmunire, and other Misprisons and Contempts.

Treason, treachery, or breach of faith, is an offence against the duty of allegiance, and is the highest known crime, for it aims at the very destruction of the commonwealth.

Præmunire is the offence of adhering to the temporal power of the Pope, in derogation of the regal authority, by introducing a foreign power into the land, in paying that obedience to papal process and authority that constitutionally belongs to the King.

Misprisons and contempts are all such high offences as are under the degree of capital.

Misprison of treason consists in the bare knowledge and concealment of treason, without any degree of assent thereto.

Offences against the public or commonwealth are against Public *Justice*, Public *Peace*, Public *Trade*, Public *Health*, and Public Police or *Economy*.

Offences against public justice are Embezzling or vacating records or falsifying proceedings in court by personating others, etc., Compelling prisoners to become approvers, Obstructing execution of legal process, Escapes from arrest, Breach of prison, Rescue, Returning from transportation, Taking rewards to help one to his stolen goods, Receiving stolen goods, Theft-bote, or compounding a felony, Barretry, Maintenance, Champerty, Compounding prosecutions on penal statutes, Conspiracy and threats of accusation to extort money, Perjury and subornation thereof, Bribery, Embracery, False verdict of jurors, Negligence of public officers, etc., Oppression by magistrates and extortion of officers.

Embezzlement is the act of appropriating to one's self that which is received in trust for another.

Rescue is the forcibly and knowingly freeing another from an arrest and imprisonment.

Theft-bote, or *compounding of Felony*, is the crime of receiving back from a felon one's goods or other amends, upon agreement not to prosecute.

Barretry is the habitual moving, exciting, stirring up and maintaining suits and quarrels, at law, or otherwise.

Maintenance bears a near relation to barretry, being an officious intermeddling in a suit that in no way belongs to one, by *maintaining* or assisting either party, with money or otherwise.

Champerty is a species of maintenance, being a bargain between two that they share the lands sued for between them, if they prevail, the champertor bearing the expenses of the suit.

A conspiracy is an agreement between two or more persons to do an unlawful act, or any of those acts which, by the *combination*, become injurious to others.

Perjury is where a person to whom a lawful oath has been administered in some judicial proceeding, swears willfully, absolutely, and falsely, in a matter material to the issue.

Subornation of perjury is the offence of procuring another to take such false oath as constitutes perjury in the principal.

Bribery is when a judge, or other person, takes any undue reward to influence his behavior in office.

Embracery is an attempt to corrupt or influence a jury, by any means whatever, whether the juror gives a verdict or not, and whether the verdict be true or false.

Offences against the public peace are Riotous assemblies, Armed or hunting in disguise, Threatening or extorting by letters, Destroying turnpikes, flood-gates, etc., Affrays and breaches of the peace, Riots, routs, and unlawful assemblies, Tumultuous petitioning, Forcible entry and detainer, Going unusually armed, Spreading false news, Pretended prophesying, Challenges to fight and Libels.

Disturbance is the hindering or disquieting people in their lawful enjoyment and privileges.

An affray is the fighting of two or more persons in some public place, to the terror of the people.

If it be in private, it is an *assault*.

A riot is where three or more actually do an unlawful act of violence, either with or without a common cause or quarrel.

A rout is where three or more meet to do an unlawful act upon a common quarrel, and only make some *advances* toward it.

Unlawful assemblies are where three or more *assemble* together to do an unlawful act, and part without doing it, or making any motion towards it.

Riots, routs, and *unlawful assemblies,* to constitute them, *must* have at least *three* persons.

Forcible entry and detainer is violently taking or keeping possession of lands and tenements, with menaces, force, and arms, and without the authority of law.

Offences against public trade are Owling, Smuggling, Fraudulent bankruptcy, Usury, Cheating, Forestalling, Regrating, Engrossing, Monopolies, Exercising a trade not having served an apprenticeship, Transporting and enticing our artists to settle abroad.

Owling—so called from being carried on at night—is transporting wool or sheep out of the kingdom, to the detriment of its staple manufacture.

Smuggling is importing goods without paying the duties thereon.

Forestalling is buying or contracting for any merchandise or victual while on its way to market.

Regrating is buying corn, or other dead victual, and selling it again in the same market, which enhances prices.

Engrossing is buying up corn, or other dead victual, in *large* quantities, to sell again.

Monopolies are much the same offence in other branches of trade, that *engrossing* is in provisions.

In another sense, a monopoly is where a right, before common to all, is withdrawn from the mass of the community and vested in one or more individuals, to the exclusion of all others.

Offences against the public health are Irregularities in time of plague or of quarantine, and Selling unwholesome provisions.

Offences against the public police, economy or domestic order are Clandestine and irregular marriages, Bigamy, Idling and wandering of soldiers and mariners, Remaining in England of outlandish persons called Egyptians or Gipsies, common nuisances, idleness, vagrancy, etc., Luxury and extravagance, Gaming, Destroying game, etc.

Common nuisances are Annoyances in highways, bridges and rivers, Offensive trades, *Disorderly houses*, Lotteries, fireworks, Eaves-dropping, Common scolds, etc.

Offences or crimes against individuals are either against their *Persons*, their *Habitations*, or their *Property*.

Offences against the persons of individuals are Homicide or other Corporal injuries.

Homicide is the taking of life, or the killing of any human creature; and it is either *justifiable*, *excusable*, or *felonious*.

The **first** has no share of guilt at all; the **second** very little; but the **third** is the highest crime against the law of nature that man is capable of committing.

Justifiable homicide is either by *command* or *permission* of law.

By command of law, as the execution of criminals.

By permission of law, viz: **First**, for the advancement of public *justice*, as by an officer in discharge of his duty.

Second, to prevent some felony or atrocious crime; as if any person attempts to break open or burn a house in the night-time, or to rob or murder another.

Excusable homicide is by *misadventure*, or in *self-defence*.

Homicide by misadventure is where a man, doing a lawful act, without any intention of hurt, unfortunately kills another.

Homicide in self-defence is upon that principle of self-preservation whereby a man may protect himself when attacked by another; as if violently, or where there is no other means of escape except by slaying his assailant.

Chance-medley is such killing as happens in self-defence upon a sudden rencounter or affray; it is excusable rather than justifiable.

There is one species of homicide in self-defence where the party *slain* is equally innocent as he who occasioned his death, namely: in the case of two persons shipwrecked, struggling for the same plank, and one is pushed off.

Felonious homicide is the killing of a human creature, without justification or excuse, which is by *killing one's self*, or by *killing another*.

Killing one's self, or suicide, is where one deliberately, or by any unlawful malicious act, puts an end to his own life.

Killing another is either *murder*, where it arises from wickedness of the heart, or *manslaughter*, where it does *not*.

Manslaughter is the unlawful killing of another, without malice, either express or implied.

It is either *voluntary* or *involuntary*.

Voluntary manslaughter is upon a sudden heat or quarrel.

Involuntary manslaughter is perpetrated in the commission of some unlawful act.

In every case of homicide upon provocation, if there be sufficient cooling time for passion to subside and reason to interpose, and the person so provoked afterwards kills the other, *this* is deliberate revenge, and not heat of blood, and is murder.

Excusable homicide in self-defence differs from voluntary manslaughter on a sudden provocation, in that, in the one case, there is an *apparent necessity*, for self-preservation, to kill the aggressor; and in the other, no necessity at all, it being only a *sudden act of passion*.

When an involuntary killing happens while in the commission of an unlawful act, in general it will be either *murder* or *manslaughter*, according to the nature of the act which occasioned it. If, in the prosecution of a *felonious* intent, or if in its *consequences* naturally tending to bloodshed, it will be murder; but if no more than a mere civil *trespass* was intended, it will only amount to manslaughter.

Murder is when a person of sound memory and discretion unlawfully killeth any reasonable creature in being and under the King's peace, with malice aforethought, either express or implied.

(By *statute* in Pennsylvania, all murder which shall be perpetrated by means of poison, or by lying in wait, or by any other kind of willful, deliberate, and premeditated killing, or which shall be committed in the perpetration or attempt to perpetrate any arson, rape, robbery, or burglary, shall be deemed murder in the *first degree;* and all other kinds of murder shall be deemed murder of the *second degree*).

Express malice is when one, with a sedate, deliberate mind and formed design, doth kill another.

Implied malice is where, for instance, a man willfully poisons another, or kills another without any, or but little, provocation.

Parricide is the murder of one's parents.

Fratricide, the murder of one's brother.

OTHER CORPORAL INJURIES to the persons of individuals, not amounting to homicide, are Mayhem, Abduction, and marriage or defilement, Seduction, Fornication, Adultery, Rape, Buggery, Assault, Battery, Wounding, False Imprisonment and Kidnapping.

Fornication is the unlawful carnal knowledge of an unmarried person with another.

When either party is married the offence, as to him or to her, is *adultery*.

Adultery, or *criminal conversation*, is the violation of conjugal fidelity.

Seduction is the corruption of women, as by illicit connection with any female of good repute, under twenty-one years of age, and under promise of marriage.

Rape is the carnal knowledge of a woman forcibly, and against her will.

Buggery is the crime against nature, committed with man or beast.

Kidnapping is the forcible stealing away of a person from his own country, and sending him into another.

Offences against the habitations of individuals are Arson and Burglary.

Arson is the malicious and willful burning of the house or out-house of another.

Burglary is the breaking and entering in the night-time the mansion house of another, with intent to commit a felony.

Offences against private property of individuals are Larceny, Malicious Mischief and Forgery.

Larceny is the felonious taking and carrying away of the personal goods of another.

Simple larceny, or plain theft, is unaccompanied with any other atrocious circumstances.

Compound larceny includes the aggravation of a taking from one's house or person.

Robbery, or open larceny from the person, is the felonious and forcible taking from the person of another goods or money of any value, by violence or putting him in fear.

Malicious mischief is the doing of mischievous damage to private property, without any intent to gain by another's loss, but out of a spirit of wanton cruelty or revenge.

Forgery is the fraudulent making or alteration of a writing, to the prejudice of another man's right.

The means of preventing offences or crimes (since *preventive* justice is upon every principle of reason, humanity, and sound policy) is by compelling suspected persons to give *security* to *keep the peace,* or for *good behavior,* and is effected by binding them in *recognizance,* which is an obligation with one or more securities, entered on record, and taken in some court, or by some judicial officer.

The methods of punishment include the *proceedings* in courts, which in criminal courts are *summary* or *regular.*

Summary proceedings are such whereby a man may be convicted of divers offences without any formal process or jury, at the discretion of the judge.

The regular proceedings in the courts of common law are Arrest, Commitment and Bail, Prosecution, Process, Arraignment, Plea and Issue, Trial and Conviction, Clergy, Judgment, Reversal of Judgment, Reprieve or Pardon and Execution.

Arrest is the apprehending or restraining of one's person, in order to be forthcoming to answer an alleged or suspected crime.

Commitment is the confinement of one's person in prison for safe custody, by warrant from proper authority.

Bail is a security given, according to law, to insure the attendance at a future time of a party in court, and taken before a proper tribunal.

Commitment being only for safe custody, whenever *bail* will answer the same intention, it ought to be taken. But in offences of a capital nature, no bail can be a security equal to the actual custody of the person. Such persons have no other sureties but the four walls of the prison. In bailable cases bail must not be refused, insufficient bail must not be taken, nor excessive bail required.

Prosecution, or the manner of accusing and prosecuting offenders, is by *presentment, indictment, information* and *appeal*.

Presentment is the notice taken by a grand jury of any offence, from their *own* knowledge or observation, and upon which an indictment may be framed.

Indictment is a written accusation of one or more persons of a crime or misdemeanor, preferred to and presented upon oath by a grand jury expressing, with sufficient certainty, the person, time, place and offence.

Informations are of two kinds: those at the suit of the King and a subject, upon penal statutes—a sort of *qui tam* action, where part of the penalty goes to the informer; and those at the suit of the King or State only.

Appeal is an accusation or suit brought by one private subject against another, as for larceny, rape, mayhem, arson, homicide, etc., which the King cannot pardon, but the party injured alone can release.

An inquisition is the act of a jury, summoned by the proper officer, to enquire into a matter, upon the evidence laid before them.

Process, or the means of compelling the appearance of the defendant to answer when indicted, in his absence, is, in misdemeanors, by *venire facias*, distress infinite, and *capias;* in capital crimes, by *capias* only; and in both by outlawry.

Arraignment is the calling of the prisoner to the bar of the court, to answer the matter charged upon him in the indictment.

The plea of the prisoner, or defensive matter alleged by him in his arraignment, is either a plea to the jurisdiction, a demurrer in point of law, a plea in abatement, a special plea in bar, as a former acquittal, conviction, attaint, or a pardon, or the general issue, *not guilty*.

A plea to the jurisdiction is when an indictment is before a court that hath no cognizance of the offence, the prisoner may except to the jurisdiction of the court by a plea to the jurisdiction without answering to the crime alleged.

A demurrer in point of law to the indictment is when the fact alleged is allowed to be true, but the prisoner joins issue upon some point of law in the indictment, by which he insists that the fact as stated is no felony, treason, etc., as alleged.

A plea in abatement is principally for a *misnomer*, or wrong name, etc.

A special plea in bar goes to the merits of the indictment, and gives a reason why the prisoner ought not to answer it at all, nor put himself upon trial for the crime alleged.

The plea of a *former acquittal* is founded on the common law maxim, that no man is to be brought into jeopardy of his life, or tried more than once for the same offence.

Trials for offences or crimes were formerly more numerous than at present. The different kinds were by Ordeal—either fire or water, by the Corsned, or morsel of excreation; by Battle or duel—in appeals, etc.; by Parliament, and by *jury*.

Trial by ordeal was principally in use among our Saxon ancestors, as also that of the *corsned;* the former being the most ancient, and was of two kinds—by *fire* and *water;* that by fire being confined to persons of a higher rank.

Trial by fire ordeal was performed by taking up in the hand, unhurt, a piece of red-hot iron of two or three pounds weight, or walking, unhurt, barefoot and blindfolded, over nine red-hot plough-shares, laid at unequal distances.

By this method Queen Emma, the mother of Edward the Confessor, is said to have cleared her character, when suspected of familiarity with Alwyn, Bishop of Winchester.

Trial by water ordeal was performed either by plunging the bare arm up to the elbow in boiling water, unhurt, or casting the suspected person into a river or pond; if he floated without any action of swimming, it was deemed evidence of his guilt, but if he sunk, he was acquitted.

Trial by ordeal was abolished in the reign of Henry III, (about 1250.)

Trial by the corsned, or morsel of excreation, was by swallowing a piece of cheese or bread, about an ounce in weight, consecrated with abjuration, "I will take the sacrament upon it; may this morsel be my last," etc., desiring of the Almighty that it might cause convulsions and paleness, etc., if guilty.

Historians assure us that Goodwin, Earl of Kent, in the reign of Edward the Confessor, abjuring the death of the King's brother, at last appealed to his corsned, which stuck in his throat and killed him.

In trials by jury challenges may be made on the part of the King, or that of the prisoner; and either to the whole array or the separate polls, and for the same reasons made in *civil* cases; but in *criminal* cases the prisoner is allowed to make *peremptory* challenges,—that is, without showing any cause or reason.

Benefit of clergy was an arrest of judgment in criminal cases, and had its origin in the usurped jurisdiction of the popish ecclesiastics, in exempting clergymen or their clerks, which included every one that could read, etc., from criminal process before the secular judges, in certain capital cases only. The defendant was burned with a hot iron in the brawn of his left thumb, to show that he had been admitted to this privilege, which was not allowed twice to the same person.

Judgment follows upon conviction, being the pronouncement of that punishment which is expressly ordained by law.

Judgment is reversed by *falsifying* or *reversing* the attainder or judgment, or by *reprieve* or *pardon*.

Attainder is the stain or corruption of the blood of a criminal capitally condemned; it is the immediate inseparable consequence, by the common law, on sentence of death being pronounced, or of outlawry for a capital offence. Its *consequences* are forfeiture of property and corruption of blood, and the criminal becomes dead in law.

It differs from conviction in that it is *after* judgment, whereas conviction is *before* judgment pronounced, and may be quashed upon some point of law reserved.

Attainder is falsified or reversed for matter *dehors*, or not apparent on the face of the record, by writ of error for mistakes apparent on the face of the record and by act of Parliament.

Outlawry, when reversed, restores the party to the same plight as if he had appeared upon the *capias*.

Reprieve, from *reprendre*—to take back—is a temporary withdrawing or suspension of a sentence or judgment, whereby the execution is delayed.

It is granted by the judges where they are not satisfied with the verdict, the evidence suspicious, the indictment insufficient, where there is doubt, for time to apply for pardon, because of pregnancy, insanity, non-identity, etc.

Pardon is a permanent avoider of the judgment, by the King's mercy, drawn in due form of law, and allowed in open court, thereby making the offender a new man.

The King cannot pardon offenses prosecuted by appeal, common nuisances, or offenses against penal statutes, nor is his pardon pleadable to impeachment by the commons in Parliament.

Penal laws, or *statutes*, are those which prohibit an act and impose a penalty for the commission of it.

Execution is, in criminal cases, the completion of human punishment.

The warrant of execution is sometimes under the hand and seal of the judge, by writ from the King, or by rule of court, but commonly by the judge's signing the calendar of prisoners, with their separate judgments in the margin.

"The student will observe that the knowledge of the law is like a deep well, out of which each man draweth according to the strength of his understanding."—*Coke.*

THE

LAW OF CONTRACTS.

———

ABRIDGED.

ANALYSIS.

Parties to a contract.
    Law of contracts, in its widest sense.
    Miscellaneous definitions.
    Classification of parties.
    Joint parties.
    Agents.
    Factors and brokers.
    Servants.
    Attorneys.
    Trustees.
    Executors and administrators.
    Guardians.
    Corporations.
    Joint stock companies.
    Partnership.
    New parties, by novation.
    New parties, by assignment.
    Gifts.
    New parties, by endorsement.
    Infants.
    Married women.
    Persons of insufficient mind to contract.

Consideration and assent.

Subject-matter of contracts.
    Purchase of real property.
    Hiring of real property.
    Sale of personal property.
    Warranties.
    Stoppage IN TRANSITU.
    Guaranty or surety-ship.
    Hiring of persons.
    Contracts for service.
    Marriage.
    Divorce.
    Bailment.
    Law of shipping.
    Construction and interpretation of contracts.
    Entirety of contracts.
    Law of place.
    Defences.
    Estoppels.
    Statute of frauds.
    Statute of limitations.
    Interest and usury.
    Damages.
    Lien.
    Remedy in equity, or specific performance.
    Bankruptcy and insolvency.

CONTRACTS.

THE LAW OF CONTRACTS, in its widest extent, may be regarded as including nearly all the law which regulates the relations of human life.
Almost the whole procedure of human life implies, or rather is, the continual fulfilment of *contracts*.

A contract, in legal contemplation, is an agreement between two or more parties, upon sufficient consideration, for the doing or the not doing of some particular thing.

The word "contract" is of comparatively recent use as a law term; formerly courts and lawyers spoke only of "obligations," —meaning "bonds,"—"covenants," and "agreements," which last was used as we now use the word "contract."

Contract comprises, in its full and more liberal signification, every description of agreement, obligation, or legal tie, whereby a party binds himself, or becomes bound, expressly or impliedly, to another, to pay a sum of money or perform or omit to do a certain act.

Obligation denotes, in its proper and confined sense, *every legal tie* which imposes a necessity of doing, or abstaining from doing any act. It is distinguished from *imperfect obligations*, as charity, gratitude, etc., which, though imposing a general duty, do not confer a particular right; and from *natural obligations*, which, though having a definite object, and binding in conscience, afford no legal remedy.

Lawyers now generally use the word *obligation* in reference to a particular species of contracts, viz: *bonds*, and adopt the term *contract* when they wish to convey a more extensive idea of a legal remedy.

Agreement, considered in its strict and more critical meaning, clearly imports a reciprocity of obligation. It is a term seldom applied to specialties: and "contract" is generally confined to simple contracts.

Promise is used to denote the engagement of a person, without regard to the consideration for it, or corresponding duty of the other party.

Contracts by specialty are those reduced to writing and attested by a seal, and contracts of record,—as judgments, recognizances, etc.

Simple contracts are all those which are not contracts by specialty.

A contract not under seal is the mutual agreement of two or more persons, competent to contract, founded on a sufficient and legal motive, inducement, or consideration, to perform some legal act, or omit to do anything, the performance whereof is not enjoined by law.

Contracts, whether *written* or only spoken, are, in law, if not sealed, equally and only parol contracts.

The essentials of a legal contract are the *Parties*, the *Consideration*, the *Assent of the Parties* and the *Subject-matter of the Contract*.

PARTIES TO A CONTRACT.

CLASSIFICATION OF PARTIES.—Parties may act independently and severally, or jointly, or jointly and severally.

They may act as representatives of others, as Agents, Factors or Brokers, Servants, Attorneys, Trustees, Executors or Administrators and Guardians.

They may act in a collective capacity,—as Corporations, Joint Stock Companies, and Partnerships.

They may be New Parties,—by Novation, by Assignment and by Endorsement.

They may be Parties disabled in whole or in part,—as Infants, Married Women, Bankrupts or Insolvents, *Non Compos Mentis*, Drunkards, Spendthrifts, Seamen, Aliens, Slaves, Outlaws, Attainted, or Excommunicated.

Joint Parties.—Whenever an obligation is undertaken by two or more, or a right given to two or more, it is the general presumption of law that it is a joint obligation or right. Words of express joinder are not necessary for this purpose.

On the other hand, there should be words of severance, in order to produce a several responsibility or a several right.

Whether the *liability* incurred is joint or several depends upon the terms of the contract, if they are express; otherwise, upon the intention of the parties as gathered from the circumstances of the case.

Where the obligation is joint and several, an ancient and familiar rule of law forbids it to be treated as several as to some of the obligors and joint as to the rest.

Where there are three or more obligees or promisees, the contract, if treated as joint by any, must be treated as joint by all.

In general all contracts, whether express or implied, and resulting from the operation and construction of law, are joint where the interest in them of the parties for whose benefit they are created is joint, and separate where that interest is separate.

The nature, and especially the entireness of the consideration, is of great importance in determining whether the promise be joint or several; for if it moves from many persons jointly, the promise of repayment is joint; if from many persons, but from each severally, there it is several.

Incidents of joinder.—Parties to be considered joint in law must be so connected as to be in some measure identified.

If two or more are jointly bound, or jointly and severally bound, and the obligee releases one of them, all are discharged.

Joint trustees are not necessarily liable for each other, or bound by each others' acts. Each is liable for the acts of others only so far as he concurred in them, or connived at them, actively or negligently.

If one or more of several joint obligees die, the right of action is solely in the survivors, and if all die, the action must be brought by the representatives of the last survivor.

Contribution.—Where two or more persons are jointly, or jointly and severally, bound to pay a sum of money, and one or more of them pay the whole, or more than his or their share, and thereby relieve the others so far from their liability, those paying may recover from those not paying the aliquot proportion which they ought to pay.

AGENTS.—There are two principles in relation to the law of agency, on one of which it is founded, while the other measures the responsibility of the principal for the acts of an agent.

The first is that the agent is but the instrument of the principal, who acts by him; the thing done being the act of the principal.

The second is that as between the principal and a third

party, the principal is responsible and bound by the acts of his agent on two grounds, namely : that he has actually created his agency; and that he has, by acts or words, fully authorized the third party to believe the person to be his agent.

General agent is one authorized to transact all his principal's business, or all his business of some particular kind.

Special or particular agent is one authorized to do one or two special things.

But it is not always easy to find a precise rule which determines with certainty between these two kinds of agency.

The importance of the distinction lies in the rule, that **if a particular agent exceed his authority, the principal is not bound; but if a general agent exceed his authority, the principal is bound,** *provided* the agent acted within the ordinary and usual scope of the business he was authorized to transact, and the party dealing with the agent did not know that he exceeded his authority.

The rule is, as to the public, that the authority of a general agent may be regarded by them as measured by the usual extent of his general employment.

An agent's authority is that which is given by the declared terms of his appointment, notwithstanding secret instructions; or that with which he is clothed by the character in which he is held out to the world, although not within the words of his commission.

It is a fundamental proposition that **one man can be bound only by the authorized acts of another**. He cannot be charged because another holds a commission from him and falsely asserts that his acts are within it.

Where an agent is employed to transact some specific business, and only that, yet he binds his principal by such subordinate acts as are necessary to, or are usually and properly done in connection with, the principal act, or to carry the same into effect.

An authority to sell does not carry with it authority to sell on credit unless such be the usage of the trade; but if there be such usage, then the agent may sell on credit, unless specially instructed and required to sell only for cash.

And if he sells for credit, having no authority to do so, he becomes personally responsible to his principal for the whole debt.

If the power of an agent be given by a written instrument, which instrument is known to the party contracting with him, such instrument must be followed strictly, and the power given by it cannot be varied or enlarged by evidence of usage.

An agent employed to sell, without express power to warrant, cannot give a warranty which shall bind the principal, unless the sale is one which is usually attended with warranty, in which case he may.

The usage of trade or business is of great importance in determining all these questions.

Appointment of agents.—An agent generally may be appointed by parol, and so authorized to do any thing which does not require him to execute a deed for his principal.

He may be authorized by parol to make and sign contracts in writing, and it seems to be now settled that he may be authorized, without writing, to make and sign even those contracts which are not binding upon his principal, unless in writing signed by him.

Subsequent confirmation.—As agency may be presumed from repeated acts of the agent, adopted and confirmed by the principal previously to the contract in which the question is raised, so, also, such agency may be confirmed and established by a subsequent ratification.

If a party does not disavow the acts of his agent as soon as he can after they come to his knowledge, he makes these acts his own.

Adoption of the agency in part, adopts it in whole.

The ratification of the tort of an agent does not, in general, relieve the agent from liability; although, by such ratification in tort as well as in contract, a liability is incurred by the principal.

An agent who has the power to appoint a sub-agent may ratify his act, and thereby make it binding on the agent's principal.

Signatures by an agent.—It has been regarded as an established principle, that no person is held to be the agent of another in making a written contract, unless his agency is stated in the instrument itself, and he therein stipulates for his principal by name.

A person holding some office, sometimes signs his name, adding to it the name of his office, for the purpose of representing himself as an official agent, and preventing his personal liability; but this mere addition seldom has this effect, being usually regarded only as a word of description.

Right of action under a contract made by an agent.—
In contracts by deed no party can have a right of action under them but the party whose name is to them; but in simple contracts an undisclosed principal may show that the apparent party was his agent, and may put himself in the place of his agent, but not so as to affect injuriously the rights of the other party.

Where the name of the principal is disclosed at the time the contract is made by the agent, the former is the proper party to sue upon the contract.

Liability of an agent.—An agent is not personally liable, unless he transcends his agency, or departs from its provisions; or unless he expressly pledges his own liability, in which case he is liable, although he describes himself as agent; or unless he conceals his character of agent; or unless he so conducts as to render his principal inaccessible or irresponsible; or unless he acts in bad faith.

Where an agent transcends his authority, but believes in good faith that he has such authority, if he and the third party with whom he deals are both innocent, yet the loss resulting from his want of authority having to fall somewhere, it seems but just that it should rest on him who has assumed, innocently but yet falsely, that he possessed this authority.

An agent who exceeds his authority, and fails to bind his principal, becomes liable himself.

An agent who exceeds his authority, renders himself liable to the whole extent of the contract, although a part of it was within his authority.

Revocation of authority of an agent.—It is a general principle that an authority is always revocable; and that the principal may at any time put an end to the relation between himself and his agent by withdrawing the authority, unless the authority is coupled with an interest, or given for a valuable consideration.

The death of the principal operates, *per se*, as a revocation of the agency, but not if the agency is coupled with an interest vested in the agent.

Fraud or misconduct of the agent the principal is liable for, and this although the principal be innocent, *provided* the agent acted in the matter as his agent, and distinctly within the line of business intrusted to him.

Notice to the agent, the principal is affected by, respecting any matter distinctly within the scope of his agency, when the notice is given before the transaction begins, or before it is so far completed as to render the notice nugatory,

The notice to the agent may be implied as well as express.—*Knowledge* obtained by the agent in the course of *that very transaction* is notice.

Shipmasters.—A master of a ship has, by the policy of the law merchant, some authority not usually implied in other cases of general agency; thus, he may, if the exigencies and necessities of his position require it, borrow money and make his owner liable, and pledge the ship, where too distant from the owner to consult him without inconvenience or injurious delay. He may even sell the ship or property intrusted to him, in case of extreme necessity.

Mutual rights and obligations of principal and agent as to each other.—An agent with instructions is bound to regard them in every point, nor can he depart from them, without making himself responsible for the consequences.

If loss ensue from his disregard to his instructions, he must sustain it; if profit, he cannot retain it, but it belongs to his principal.

A principal discharges his agent from responsibility for deviation from his instructions when he accepts the benefit of his act.

He may reject the transaction altogether; but he must do so at once, and decisively, as soon as fully acquainted with it.

The principal is generally held by the partial execution of the agent's authority, but would not be where he could show that the things embraced within the authority he gave were *united* in that authority and in his intention, and that it would be a detriment to him to take a part only.

The agent has not the right to make another person the representative of his principal, without authority to do so. The employment and trust are personal.

A substitute appointed by an agent who has the power of substitution, becomes the agent of the original principal, and may bind him by his acts.

An agent is bound to as great diligence and care for

his principal as a reasonable man under similar circumstances would take of his own affairs.

He is also bound to possess and exert the skill and knowledge necessary for the proper performance of the duties which he undertakes.

It is a prevailing principle of law, that an agent must not put himself, during his agency, in a position which is adverse to that of his principal.

The agent of an agent is generally accountable only to his own principal, and not to the principal of the party for whom he acts; and a sub-contractor cannot pass by his immediate employer and sue the principal or proprietor of the work.

Factors and brokers are both and equally agents, but with this difference: the *Factor* is entrusted with the property, which is the subject-matter of the agency; the *Broker* is only employed to make a bargain in relation to it. The compensation to both is usually a commission.

Factors under a commission.—A factor who sells under a *del credere*, or guaranty commission, becomes merely a *surety* to his principal, and is bound to pay only if the buyer does not.

Of the duties and rights of factors and brokers.—They are bound to ordinary care, and are liable for any negligence, error, or default, incompatible with the care and skill properly belonging to the business that they undertake.

They must conform to the usages of the business, and they have the power such usages would give, and can bind the principal only to a usual obligation.

A factor, from the nature of his employment, **is a general agent.**

If he has no *del credere* commission, he may still be personally liable to his principal.

A factor may buy and sell, sue and be sued, collect money, receive payments, give receipts, and the like, in his own name; but a broker, only in the name of his principal.

A factor has a lien on the property in his hands for his commissions, advances, and expenses. Possession is necessary to give a lien, and a broker, therefore, has no lien, nor a right to his commissions, as a general rule, until the whole service for which these commissions are to compensate is performed.

Servants.—The general principle is that a master is responsible for the tortious acts of his servant *which were done in his service*.

The responsibility of the master grows out of, is measured by, and begins and ends with, his *control* of the servant.

ATTORNEYS are made so by letter or power of attorney, or they are attorneys of record.

It is a general rule that **one acting under a power of attorney cannot execute for his principal a sealed instrument, unless the power of attorney be sealed.**

If the grantor has given to A a power of attorney in the ordinary form, authorizing him to execute a deed for him as his attorney, and this person writes the name of the grantor in his absence, without saying "by A, his attorney," or writing his own name, this would not seem to be a sufficient execution of the deed.

In executing a deed by attorney, the power, being delegated to the attorney, is with him, and the deed takes effect from his act; therefore the instrument which gives the power is to be strictly examined and construed.

Attorney of record, more commonly called an *attorney at law*, is one who has been duly admitted by competent authority to practice in the courts. His implied duty to use reasonable skill and care is the same as that of other persons to whose care and skill anything is intrusted. He is not responsible for mistake in a doubtful point of law, or of practice, nor for the fault of counsel retained by him. He is liable for disclosing privileged communications. If discharged by one party, he may act for an *opposite* party, provided he makes no improper use of knowledge obtained by him while acting for the first party, if his discharge was not for misconduct.

The law implies a contract on the part of the client to pay his attorney the legal fees, or statute rate of compensation; and if the client asserts that the services were to be rendered for a less compensation, the burden rests on him to prove this bargain.

An attorney cannot maintain an action for compensation of services, unless he can show that they were *requested*.

An attorney has a lien on the judgment he recovers, and on the papers of the case, for his costs and fees.

TRUSTEES.—*Trusts* in the English law had a fraudulent origin. It was sought, by the intervention of a trustee, to evade the feudal law of tenures, and the prohibition of the statutes of mortmain, and to place property where a creditor could not reach it.

The common law treats trustees in most respects as agents.

Classification of Trusts.—They are *simple* when property is vested in one person *upon trust* for another, without any particular directions, or provisions; and *special,* where the purposes of the trust, and the manner in which they are to be accomplished are especially pointed out and prescribed.

They may be merely *ministerial,* as where one receives money only to pay the debt of the giver, or an estate is vested in him merely that he may convey it to another; or they may be *discretionary,* where much is left to the prudence and judgment of the trustee.

Private Trustees are those to whom property, real or personal, has been given to be held in trust for the benefit of others.

The *legal* estate is in the trustee, and the equitable estate is in the *cestui que trust;* but as the trustee *holds the estate,* although only with the power and for the purpose of managing it, he is bound *personally* by the contracts he makes as trustee, although designating himself as such; and nothing will discharge him but an express agreement of both parties to act upon the responsibility of the funds alone, or some other responsibility *exclusive* of that of the trustee.

Public trustees are those who hold for the benefit of the whole public, as for a town or parish. The important difference between these trustees and private trustees is in respect to their personal responsibility for their contracts.

Where one acts distinctly for the public, and in an official or *quasi* official capacity, although he engages that certain things should be done, he is not liable.

But trustees and other officers are sometimes held personally upon their contracts, as for payment of wages, material supplied, etc., where they have charge of public works and have funds which they may use for these purposes.

The true principle which runs through all these cases, and applies alike to private and public trustees, **is, To whom did the promisee give credit, and to whom did the promisor understand him to give credit?**

Executors and administrators act as the *personal representative* of the deceased, having in their hands his means, for the purpose of discharging his liabilities, or executing his contracts, and of carrying into effect his will.

In general, they are liable only so far as these means, or assets in their hands, are applicable to such purpose; but they may, under certain circumstances, become personally liable.

In general, every right ex contractu, which the deceased possessed at the time of his death, passes to his executor or administrator; and so strong is this rule, that it prevails against special words of limitation in the contract itself.

Executors or administrators may sue either in their individual or representative characters; but should sue in the latter capacity, to avoid a set-off against them of their individual debts.

On the death of one of several executors, either before or after probate, the entire right of representation survives to the others.

But if an administrator dies, or a sole executor dies intestate, no interest and no right of representation is transmitted to his personal representatives.

Guardians of all descriptions are treated by courts as trustees, and, in general, are required to give security for the faithful discharge of their duty, unless appointed by will, and the testator has exercised the power given him by statute, of requiring that the guardian shall not be called upon to give bonds.

Duty and power of a guardian.—A guardian is held in this country to have only a naked authority, not coupled with an interest. His possession of the property of his ward is not such as gives him a personal interest, being only for the purpose of agency. But for the benefit of his ward, he has a very general power over it; he manages and disposes of the personal property at his own discretion, though safer for him to obtain the authority of court for any important measure, which he *must* have in disposing of the real estate.

To secure the proper execution of his trust, he is not only liable to an action by the ward, after the guardianship terminates, but during its pendency the ward may call him to account by his next friend, or guardian *ad litem*.

A guardian cannot, by his own contract, bind the person or estate of his ward; but if he promise, on a sufficient consideration, to pay the debt of his ward, he is personally bound by his promise, although he expressly promises as guardian.

An action will not lie against a guardian on a contract made by the ward, but must be brought against the ward, and may be defended by the guardian.

As trustee, a guardian is held to a strictly honest discharge of his duty, and cannot act in relation to the subject of his trust for his own personal benefit, in any contract whatever.

And if a benefit arises thereby, as in the settlement of a debt due from the ward, this benefit belongs wholly to the ward.

CORPORATIONS.—A corporation aggregate is, in law, a person.

A contract of a corporation, as of an individual, may be implied from the acts of the corporation, or of their authorized agents.

A corporation must execute its deed under its corporate seal, otherwise the deed is void.

A corporation may employ one of its members as its agent, and the same person, while such agent, may also be an agent for the other contracting party, and sign for him the memorandum required by the Statute of Frauds.

Corporations authorized by their charter to act in a prescribed manner, may, by practice and usage, make themselves liable on contracts entered into in a different way.

Officers and directors of a corporate body are trustees of the stockholders, and cannot, without fraud, secure themselves advantages not common to the latter.

Joint stock companies are partnerships whereof the capital is divided or agreed to be divided into shares, and so as to be transferable without the express consent of all the co-partners.

A joint stock company is not a corporation, yet it differs in some respects from a common partnership.

A member of a partnership may assign his interest in the property of a firm, but the assignee does not become a partner unless the other co-partners choose to admit him; but in *joint stock* companies provision is made beforehand for such transfer, which is the principal object and effect of the division into shares.

In other respects, **the law regarding joint stock companies and partnerships is very similar.**

The power of a managing committee to pledge the credit of

the members of a society, depends upon the rules and by-laws of the society.

Such a case is governed by the law of principal and agent, and not that of partnership.

PARTNERSHIP exists when two or more persons combine their property, labor, and skill, or one or more of them, in the transaction of business for their common profit.

A partnership is presumed to be general when there are no stipulations, or no evidence from the course of business to the contrary.

But it may be created for a specific purpose, or be confined by the parties to a particular line of business, or even a single transaction.

Usually, the parties own together both the property and the profits; but there may be a partnership in the profits only.

Real estate of a partnership.—The rule is, that when real estate is purchased with partnership funds, for partnership purposes, it will be treated as partnership property.

All kinds of property may be held in partnership.

The good-will of an establishment is considered, at least for some purposes, as partnership property.

The good-will signifies the advantage or benefit which is acquired by an establishment, beyond the mere value of the capital, stock, funds, or property employed therein, in consequence of the general public patronage and encouragement which it receives from constant or habitual customers, on account of its local position or common celebrity or reputation for skill, or affluence, or punctuality, etc.

Delectus personarum.—The partnership must be voluntary, and therefore no partner and no majority of partners can introduce a new member without the consent of the others.

The *delectus personarum*, that is, the choice of persons, is always preserved; and if one sells out his interest, the partnership is dissolved, and can only be renewed by the agreement of all.

Partnership may be formed by deed, or by parol, and with or without a written agreement.

Partnership, in general, is constituted between individuals, by an agreement to enter together into a general or a particular business and share the profits and the losses thereof; but the mere sharing of profits, without any connection whatever in the business, is not enough to constitute a partnership.

To distinguish between partnership and tenancy in common: if the property owned jointly is so owned for the purpose of a joint business and is so used, and the profits resulting from a common fund, it is partnership property; otherwise not.

Right of action between partners.—Generally, one partner cannot sue a co-partner *at law* in respect to any matter growing out of the transactions of the partnership and involving the examination of the partnership accounts, but resort must be had to courts of equity.

But a partner may sue a co-partner on an *express* agreement, and perhaps on an *implied* one, to do any act not involving a consideration of the partnership accounts.

If partners finally balance all their accounts, or a distinct part thereof is entirely severed by them from the rest, a suit at law is maintainable for the balance.

Sharing of losses.—Partners *inter se*, may make what bargain they will about losses, but no such agreement will prevent such partner from being liable for the debts of the partnership, unless the creditors knew of this bargain between the partners, and with this knowledge gave credit to the other partners only.

Secret and dormant partners.—A *secret* partner is one not openly and generally declared to be a partner; and a *dormant* partner is strictly one who takes no share in the transaction or control of the partnership business.

Dormant partner is often held to mean one whose name is not publicly mentioned, and the phrases *secret* and *dormant* partners are sometimes, but inaccurately, used as synonymous.

A dormant partner is liable when discovered, and he cannot join as plaintiff in an action, because there is no sufficient privity of contract between him and the party who contracted with the firm; but he may be sued and joined as defendant.

Retiring partners, who receive thereafter a share of the profits, are still liable; but not when receiving an annuity or definite sum, no way dependent on the profits.

A partner is not responsible for credit given to the firm after retirement, with proper notice of the fact.

Nominal partner is one held out to the world as such without actual participation of profit and loss. He is held generally as responsible for the debts of the partnership.

CONTRACTS. 133

Joint liability.—Persons are not to be held jointly liable upon a contract as partners, unless they have a joint interest existing at the time of the formation of the contract.

The liability of a partner springs *either* from his holding himself out to the world *as such, or* from his participation in the business, and its profit or loss.

Authority of each partner.—It is a general rule that the whole firm and all the members of a co-partnership are bound by the acts and contracts of one partner with reference to the partnership business and affairs—such act or contract being in law the act or contract of all.

One partner may sell the whole stock in trade by a single contract, if the sale be free from fraud.

A purchase or sale, by one partner, binds all the others.

The act of each partner is considered as the act of the whole partnership, or of all the partners, only so far as that act was within the scope of the business of the firm.

In general, notice to one partner is binding upon all.

A release by one partner is a release by all, both in law and in equity; and a release to one partner is a release to all, but fraud or collusion destroys the effect of such release.

Generally, a partner cannot bind his co-partners by *deed* without express authority, except in the presence of his co-partner, and with his consent.

No particular mode of holding one's self out as a partner is necessary to make one liable as such; but it must be a voluntary act.

The liability of an incoming partner for old debts is not to be presumed.

The authority of a partner to bind his firm rests, indeed, upon a necessity bounded and measured by this—that **the partnership is not bound by the acts or contracts of any partner, not within the legitimate scope of the partnership business.**

A partner has no implied authority, except so far as is necessary to carry on the business of the firm.

Power of a majority.—Whether a majority of the partners of a firm can bind the minority is not yet quite determined by authority.

Dissolution of a partnership does not affect the liability of the partners for *former* debts, but, in general, it prevents the incurring of a new joint liability.

However dissolution takes place, the former partners are partners no longer, but tenants in common.

Where a partnership is not to endure for a time certain by the articles of co-partnership, or where that time has expired, it may be dissolved, at the pleasure of any partner.

Assignment of a co-partner's interest in the partnership funds operates, *ipso facto*, a dissolution; and an assignment by one partner of his share of the future profits to another partner is a dissolution of the partnership, because the essence of that is a participation of the profits.

Bankruptcy of the firm, or of one partner, operates an immediate dissolution.

Insolvency, under the statutes, would have the same effect.

So, also, death of a partner; or mutual consent.

Proper notice should be given of a dissolution.

Rights of creditors in respect to partnership funds.— The property of a partnership is bound to the payment of the partnership debts, and the right of a private creditor of one co-partner to that partner's interest in the property of the firm, is postponed to the right of the partnership creditor.

Whether the *private* property of a partner is equally preserved for his private creditors is not, perhaps, certain.

A levy of execution does not give the creditor a separate possession of the goods, for the indebted partner had no such possession himself.

The sheriff takes and can sell only the right and interest of the indebted partner to and in the whole fund.

Limited partnership, or special partnership is where a person puts into the stock of a firm a definite sum of money, and assumes a responsibility and share of the profits, which shall be in proportion to the money thus contributed, and no more.

Partnerships of this kind, being wholly unknown to the common law, are authorized and regulated only by statute; and the provisions are generally as follows: *first,* there must be one or more who are *general* partners, and one or more who are *special* partners; *secondly,* the names of the special partners do not appear in the firm, nor have they all the powers and duties of active members; *thirdly,* the sum proposed to be contributed by the special partners must be actually paid in; *fourthly,* the arrangement must be in writing, specifying the names of the partners, the amount paid in, etc., which is to be acknowledged before a magistrate, recorded and advertised.

NEW PARTIES BY NOVATION, or substitution.—*Novation* is a transaction whereby a debtor is discharged from his liability to his original creditor by contracting a new obligation in favor of a new creditor, by the order of his original creditor.

In principle, this would seem to be in contradiction or exception to the ancient rule that a personal contract cannot be assigned so as to give the assignee a right of action in his own name.

To give the transaction its full legal efficacy, the original liabilities must be extinguished; and the mutual assent of all the three parties is necessary to make it an effectual novation, or substitution.

The debtor does not undertake to pay the debt of another, but contracts an entirely new debt of his own, the consideration of which is the absolute discharge of the old debt.

New parties by assignment.—ASSIGNMENTS OF CHOSES IN ACTION. The term *choses in action* is used in contradistinction to *chose in possession;* it includes all rights to personal property not in possession which may be enforced by action.

Any right under the contract, either express or implied, which has not been reduced to *possession*, is a chose in *action;* and is so called because it can be enforced against an adverse party only by an action at law.

At common law, the transfer of such a chose in action was entirely forbidden, because by such a transfer **the only thing which passes is a right to go to law,** the ancient law abhorring litigation. But probably the stronger and better reason was that no debtor shall have a new creditor substituted for the original one without his consent; for he may have substantial reasons for choosing whom he should owe. Courts of equity have, for a long time, disregarded this rule, and, as a general rule, permit the assignee of a chose in action to sustain an action in his own name; but they will also prevent the debtor from being oppressed or injured.

It is not to be understood that the assignee of a *chose in action* may always enforce his claim in a court of equity, but simply that he may proceed in equity in *his own name*, whenever he is entitled to go into a court of equity at all. It is well settled that the *mere fact* of one's being the assignee of a *chose in action* will not entitle him to go into a court of equity. His remedy is generally complete at law, by a suit *in the name of the assignor*, and to that he will be left. It is only when the legal remedy is in some manner obstructed, or rendered insufficient, that a court of equity will interpose.

Courts of law also permit and protect assignments of choses in action to a certain extent.

If the debtor assent to the assignment, and promise to pay the assignee, an action may be brought by the assignee in his own name; but otherwise he must bring it in the name of the assignor; and this rule applies to the assignment of a negotiable bill or note, unless it be endorsed by the assignor.

Formerly, courts of law did not take notice of an equity or trust, for trusts are within the original jurisdiction of a court of equity; but of late years it has been found productive of great expense to send the parties to the other side of the Hall: so wherever courts of law have seen that the justice of the case is clearly with the plaintiff, they have not turned him round upon this objection, but will take notice of a trust, and consider who is beneficially interested. So, if courts of law will take notice of a trust, why should they not of an equity?

There are assignments of choses in action which will not be sustained either in equity or at law, as being against public policy; as by an officer in the army or navy of his pay, salaries of a judge, right of action of a tort, etc.

The death of an assignor will not defeat the assignment, but the assignee may bring the action in the name of the executor or administrator of the deceased.

Manner of assignment.—The equitable interest in a chose in action may be assigned for a valuable consideration by a mere delivery of the evidence of the contract, and it is not necessary that the assignment be in writing. So the equitable interest in a judgment may be assigned by a delivery of execution. But a mere agreement to assign, without any delivery, actual or symbolical, of the writing evidencing the debt, does not constitute a sufficient assignment.

Equitable defences.—An assignee of a chose in action takes it subject to all the equities of defence which exist between the assignor and the debtor.

The assignee does not take a legal interest nor hold what he takes by a legal title; but he holds by an equitable title an equitable interest. This interest courts of law will protect only so far as the equities of the case permit, and any subsequent assignee is subject to the same equities as his assignor.

In some States the assignee of a chose in action may now bring an action upon it in his own name, by statutory provision; but this change is only in the form of the action, and not in its effect. The assignee is still subject to the same equities of defence as before.

Covenants annexed to land.—A covenant affecting real property, made with a covenantee who possesses a transferable interest therein, is annexed to the estate, and is transferable at law, passing with the interest in the realty to which it is annexed, and often called a "covenant running with the land."

Covenants between landlord and tenant, lessee and reversioner, run with the land.

Such are covenants to repair, to grant estovers for repair or for firewood, quiet enjoyment, and the like.

Gifts, or voluntary assignments of chattels.—Gifts by persons competent to give, and which are completed by transfer of possession, however voluntary they may have been, are regarded by the law as executed contracts, founded upon mutual consent.

Gifts inter vivos.—It is essential to a gift that it goes into effect at once and completely. If it regards the future it is but a promise, and being a promise without a consideration, cannot be enforced and has no legal validity.

Hence *delivery* is essential to the validity of every gift; nor will transfer by writing alone satisfy the requirement of delivery. The delivery may be *constructive*, as the nature of the thing and its actual position require.

A gift by a competent party, made perfect by delivery and acceptance, is then irrevocable by the donor; but if prejudicial to existing creditors, it is void as to them.

Gifts causa mortis.—Much that was said of gifts *inter vivos* applies equally to these gifts.

The law watches, however, this kind of transfer jealously, and is unwilling that it should take the place of wills, because of uncertainty, which the law seeks to avoid in reference to wills by its precautions and provisions as to their execution.

NEW PARTIES BY ENDORSEMENT.—Negotiable bills and notes.—Bills of exchange and promissory notes made *payable to order*, are called *negotiable* paper, and they may be transferred by endorsement, and the holder can sue in his own name, and the equitable defences which might have existed between the promisor and the original promisee are cut off.

By the ancient rules of law we have seen that the transfer of *simple* contracts was entirely forbidden. It is generally said that the law of bills and notes is exceptional; that they are choses in action, which by the policy of the law merchant, and to satisfy the necessities of trade and business, are permitted to be assigned as other choses in action cannot be.

By the practice of merchants the transfer of negotiable paper is made by endorsement.

The endorsement of a blank note binds the endorser to any terms as to amount and time of payment which the party to whom he intrusts the paper inserts.

If the note be originally made payable to "bearer," it is negotiated or transferred by delivery merely.

The holder of negotiable paper, endorsed in blank or made payable to bearer, is presumed to be the owner for consideration.

If circumstances cast suspicion on his ownership, then he must prove that he gave value for it.

From general principles, if any one, not the payee of a negotiable note, or in case of a note not negotiable, if any party writes his name on the back of the note at the time it is made, his signature binds him in the same way as if it was on the face of the note and below that of the maker; that is to say, he is held as a joint maker, or as a joint and several maker, according to the form of the note.

One who endorses a note in blank at any time before it is endorsed by the payee, may be held as an original promisor.

Bills and notes are usually considered together, the law respecting them being in most respects the same.

Essentials of negotiable bills and notes.—A note made payable to the maker's own order is a negotiable note.

A certificate of deposit in a bank has been held negotiable by our highest authority.

The word "negotiable," however, does not make a note negotiable.

It is sufficient in law if the makers name appears *in* the note, as, "I, John Doe, promise," etc. But signature at the bottom is so usual that the want of it would taint the note with suspicion.

As a negotiable bill or note is intended to represent and take the place of money, it must be payable in money and not in goods.

The payment must not rest upon any contingency or uncertain event.

If the amount be expressed both in writing and in figures, the written words prevail over the figures.

If the words " for value received," be not expressed they will be implied by law.

As with a note, so with a bill of exchange, the payee must be sufficiently certain at the time the instrument is drawn.

Where instruments are not negotiable, third parties may become interested; but if they are to be regarded as new parties at all, it is only with much qualification.

Endorsement.—The endorsement of a bill or note passes no property unless the endorser had at the time a legal property in the note.

If a note is once endorsed in blank, it is thereafter transferable by mere delivery so long as the endorsement continues blank, and its negotiability cannot be restricted by subsequent special endorsements.

Any person may accept or endorse a bill, or sign or endorse a note, as agent for another; and the principal is held, and not the agent, if there was sufficient authority for the act, and the act itself was properly done.

Endorsement after maturity.—Bills and notes are usually transferred by endorsement before they are due; but they *may* be so transferred after they are due, and before they are paid.

The bona fide holder of a bill by endorsement before maturity, takes it subject to no equities existing between his assignor and the promisor which are not indicated on the face of the note, and to none which do not exist at the time of the transfer.

The law is otherwise, however, if the bill or note were transferred to him when overdue; and, although he pays a full consideration for it, he receives nothing but the title and rights of his assignor, and it is said that any defence which might be made against the assignor may be made available against the assignee.

Although paper negotiable when overdue is subject to equitable defences, yet a demand must be made on the acceptor or maker within a reasonable time, and reasonable notice must be given to an endorser, or he will be discharged.

As between the original parties to negotiable paper, the consideration may always be enquired into; and so it may as between endorser and endorsee.

In general, accommodation notes or bills are governed by the same rules as negotiable paper for consideration.

Notes on demand.—Bills and notes payable on demand are in one sense always overdue; they are not, however, so treated until payment has been demanded and refused; then they become like bills on time which have been dishonored.

A note payable generally, but not specifying any time of payment, is due immediately.

Checks on bankers should be presented at once; and the rule as to overdue notes is applied with more strictness to them.

A check on a broker, payable to bearer, is a negotiable instrument, and may pass by endorsement so to entitle the holder to sue the endorser, as in the case of a bill of exchange.

Transfer of bills and notes—A bill once paid by the acceptor can no longer be negotiated.

The holder of a bill or note payable to bearer, or of one payable to some payee or order and endorsed in blank, may transfer the same by mere delivery, and is not liable upon it.

It is a general principle that one who pays money without consideration, may recover it back.

If a note be payable on its face, or by endorsement, to a party or his order, that party can transfer the note in full property only by his endorsement; and when he endorses it, he makes himself liable to pay it, if those who ought to have paid it to him, had he continued to hold it, fail to pay it to the party to whom he orders it to be paid.

The endorser may guard against this by endorsing it with the words "without recourse," which mean, by usage, that the holder is not to have, in any event, recourse to the endorser.

By acceptance and by each endorsement a new contract is formed.

The liability of an endorser may be considered, first, as depending on the demand of payment, and then as to notice of non-payment, and the proceedings necessary thereon.

Presentment for acceptance should be made by the holder or his authorized agent, to the drawee or his authorized agent, during the usual hours of business.

The drawee has until the next day to determine whether he will accept, but may answer at once

The usual way of accepting is by writing the word "accepted" on the face of the bill, and signing the acceptor's name; but there is no precise formula or method, it seeming to be enough if it is substantially a promise to pay, whether in writing upon the bill, or a separate paper, or by parol.

Presentment for payment.—A bill or note must be presented for payment at its maturity, or the endorsers are not held; they guarantee its payment, not by express words, but by operation of law.

Each endorser transfers by endorsement a debt due to himself, and if by the guaranty which springs from his endorsement, he has to pay this debt to another, he is entitled to all such prompt knowledge of the failure of the party whom he guarantees, and of his own consequent liability, as will enable him to secure a payment of this debt to himself, if that be possible.

Generally the question of reasonable time, reasonable diligence, and reasonable notice, is open to the circumstances of every case, and is determined by a reference to them; but in regard to bills and notes, the law merchant has defined all of these with great exactness.

The general rule is, that the drawer and endorsers of a bill and the endorsers of a note are discharged from their liability, unless payment of the bill or note be demanded from the party previously bound to pay it, on the day on which it falls due.

If the party who should pay the note has absconded or has no domicil or regular place of business, and cannot be found by reasonable endeavors, payment need not be demanded of him, because it would be of no utility to a subsequent party; but still, **notice of the facts should be given.**

Neither a bill or note drawn payable at a place certain, nor a bill drawn payable generally, but accepted payable at a specified place, need be presented at that place, in order to sustain an action against the maker or acceptor; but he may show, by way of defence, that he was ready there with funds, and thus escape all damages and interest.

The drawers and endorsers are certainly discharged by a neglect to demand payment at the specified place.

Of whom, when, and where the demand or presentment for payment should be made.—Demand of payment should be made by the holder, or his authorized agent, of the party bound to pay, or his authorized agent; and at his usual place of business, or residence.

Usually, all bills and notes on time, when grace is not expressly excluded, are entitled to grace.

But notes payable on demand are not entitled to grace, nor are checks on banks, though payable on time.

The days of grace constitute part of the original contract on negotiable notes.

Whenever the maker of a note is entitled to grace, the endorser has the same privilege.

Notice of non-payment.—Where a bill is not accepted, or a bill or note is not paid at maturity by the party bound then to pay it, all subsequent parties must have immediate notice of this fact.

The omission to give such notice may, however, be excused by circumstances which rendered it impossible, or nearly so.

In general, the notice must be given within a reasonable time; which is a question of law for the court.

A bill or note, although overdue, does not cease to be negotiable, and if endorsed after overdue, there may still be a demand and notice of default in order to charge the endorser.

Notice is sometimes waived by writing on the note the words, "I waive demand and notice," etc., which is sufficient.

Notice should be given as soon as on the day following that on which payment has been refused.

If Sunday or any other day intervene, which, by law or by established usage, is not a day of business, then it is not counted, and the obligation as to notice is the same as if it fell on the succeeding day.

But if the last day of grace falls upon such a day, then it is payable on the day before.

The purpose of notice is that the party receiving it may obtain security from the party liable to him for the sum for which he is liable to other parties.

The holder may leave without notice whom he will, and hold by due notice those whom he will; and the endorser, having due notice, must himself notify prior parties to whom he would look.

Protest.—If a foreign bill be not accepted, or not paid at maturity, it must be protested at once. Inland bills are generally, and promissory notes very often, protested in like manner, but this is not required by the law merchant.

Notarial protest is generally admissible, but not conclusive evidence of the facts therein stated, which properly belong to the act of protest.

INFANTS.—Their disability to contract rests in general on the ground of want, immaturity or incapacity of mind.

All persons are denominated infants by common law until the age of twenty-one.

As a general rule, the contract of an infant is said to be not void, but voidable; that is, he may, either during his minority or within a reasonable time after he becomes of age, avoid the contract, if he will.

But the contract of the infant for *necessaries* is neither void nor voidable. It is permitted for his own sake that he may make a valid contract for these things. The word "necessaries," in relation to an infant, is not used in a strict sense; but the social position of an infant, his means and those of his parents, are taken into consideration.

Obligations of parents in respect to infant children. The obligation of the father to maintain the child is and always has been recognized, in some way and in some degree, in all civilized countries.

Where goods are supplied to an infant which are not necessaries, the father's authority must be proved to make him liable; but where they are necessaries, the father's authority is presumed, unless he supplies them himself, or was ready to supply them.

Where he has been deserted by the father, or driven away from him, either by command or by cruel treatment, there the infant carries with him the credit and authority of the father for necessaries.

A father may, by an agreement with his minor child, relinquish to the child the right which he would otherwise have to his services, and may authorize those who employ him to pay him his wages, and will then have no right to demand those wages, either from the employer or from the child. Such an agreement may be *inferred* from circumstances.

A father is not liable for the willful tort of his infant child.

An infant is protected against his contracts, but not against his frauds or other torts.

CONTRACTS OF MARRIED WOMEN—General effect of marriage on the rights of the parties.—At common law the disability of a married woman is almost entire, her personal existence being merged, for most purposes, in that of her husband. This was not so among the Anglo-Saxons, nor with the earlier Teutonic races, but is one of the effects of the feudal system, the principal object of which was to make the whole strength of the state available as a military force.

The contracts of a married woman, made before her marriage, enure to the benefit of her husband, but do not vest in him absolutely. They are choses in action which he *may* reduce to his own possession during her life.

A married woman can make no valid contract; hence the husband cannot be bound by any contract which she may attempt to make, but he is responsible for her torts.

In general, whatever she earns, she earns as his servant and for him, for in law her time and labor, as well as her money, are his property.

She may be the agent of the husband, and in that character make contracts which bind him; and this agency need not be expressed, but is raised by law from a variety of circumstances, as to hire servants, or to purchase articles necessary for the family use, for herself, etc.

If the wife separates from the husband by his fault, she carries with her all her rights to necessaries, and he who supplies them may hold the husband for their price.

Where they live together, there is a presumption of law, arising from cohabitation, that the husband assents to contracts made by the wife for the supply of articles suitable to their station, means and way of life.

If the wife leave the husband without just cause, and refuses to cohabit with him, she loses all right to maintenance from him.

A liability very similar to that which falls upon one who is legally a husband, rests also upon him who lives with a woman as his wife, who is not so.

Persons of insufficient mind to contract.—If one enters

CONTRACTS. 145

into a contract while deprived of reason, and afterwards recover his reason, he may repudiate that contract, and this, although a temporary insanity was produced by his own act, as by intoxication.

Courts of law as well as equity afford protection to those who are of unsound mind.

Persons under duress.—A contract made by a party under compulsion is void, because there is no *consent*, and also from being founded in *wrong*.

CONSIDERATION AND ASSENT.

CONSIDERATION.—A promise for which there is no consideration cannot be enforced at law.

A contract *under seal* is, in general, valid, without reference to the consideration, because, it is said, the seal implies a consideration.

In some of the States by *usage,* and in others by *statute*, the want or failure of consideration may be a good defence against an action on a sealed contract.

A consideration must be proved where the contract is in writing but not under seal, as much as if the contract were oral only.

It is said that the difference between sealed and unsealed instruments is now a mere unmeaning and arbitrary distinction, made by technical law and not sustained by reason.

The kinds of consideration at common law are two: *good* and *valuable*.

A good consideration, such as that of blood or natural love and affection, as when a man grants an estate to a near relation.

A valuable consideration, such as money, marriage, or the like, which the law esteems an equivalent given for the grant.

An equitable consideration is sufficient as between the parties, although it be not valuable. It is sufficient in all conveyances by deed, and in transfers not by deed, but accompanied by immediate possession.

Consideration means something which is of some value in the eye of the law, moving from the plaintiff; it may be some benefit to the defendant, or some detriment to the plaintiff; but at all events it must be moving from the plaintiff.

Adequacy of consideration.—If the consideration is valuable, it need not be *adequate;* that is, the court will not enquire into the exact proportion between the value of the consideration and that of the thing to be done for it: but it must have *some* real value.

Where one through mistake of the law acknowledges himself under an obligation which the law does not impose, he is not bound by such promise, although, in general, ignorance of the law is no excuse or defence, for if it were, a " premium would be held out to ignorance."

Prevention of litigation is a valid and sufficient consideration, for the law favors the settlement of disputes.

An agreement to *forbear* for a time proceedings at law or in equity, to enforce a well-founded claim, is a valid consideration for a promise.

In general, a waiver of any legal right, at the request of another party, is a sufficient consideration for a promise, or a waiver of any equitable right.

An assignment of a debt or a right is a good consideration for a promise by the assignee.

Work and service are a very common consideration for a promise, and always sufficient, if rendered at the request of the party promising.

Trust and confidence in another often form a sufficient consideration to hold that other to his undertaking.

If a person makes a mere gratuitous promise, and then enters upon the performance of it, he is held to a full execution of all he has undertaken.

A promise for a promise is a good consideration, but there must be an absolute mutuality of agreement, so that each party has the right at once to hold the other to a positive agreement.

Where several promise to contribute to a common object, desired by all, the promise of each may be a good consideration for the promise of the others.

In general, *subscriptions* on certain conditions, in favor of the party subscribing, are binding when the acts stipulated as conditions are performed.

Considerations void in part.—Where the consideration is entire and incapable of severance, then it must be wholly good or wholly bad.

If the promise be entire, and not in writing, and a part of it relate to a matter which by the statute of frauds should be promised in writing, such part being void, avoids the whole contract; but if of a nature *divisible*, and the part not required to be in writing by statute may be enforced without injustice to the promisor, *that* portion of the agreement will be binding.

Illegality of consideration.—In general, if any part of the entire consideration for a promise, or any part of an entire promise, be illegal, whether by statute or at common law, the whole contract is void.

But if one gives a good and valid consideration, and thereupon another promises to do two things, one legal and the other illegal, he shall be held to do that which is legal, *unless* the two are so mingled and bound together that they cannot be separated, in which case the whole promise is void.

Impossible considerations are wholly bad and insufficient.

A consideration which one cannot perform without a breach of the law is bad, and so is one which cannot be performed at all.

But a promise is not void merely because it is difficult or even improbable.

In order to found a consideration for a promise it is necessary that the party by whom the promise is made should have the power of carrying it into effect; and that the thing to be done should in itself be legal.

Failure of consideration.—When the consideration appears to be valuable and sufficient, but turns out to be *wholly* false or a mere nullity, a promise resting on this consideration is no longer obligatory.

If a diminution or failure of the consideration were such as in effect and really to take away *all* the value of the consideration, it would be regarded as one that had wholly failed.

Where a consideration fails only in part, if there be a substantial consideration left, although much diminished, it would still sustain the contract.

While it is true that a failure of consideration is a good ground for the recovery of the money paid, it must be remembered that it is a familiar and well settled principle of law that where a person, with full knowledge of all the circumstances, pays money voluntarily and without compulsion or duress of person or goods, he shall not afterwards recover back the money so paid.

Rights of a stranger to the consideration.—By an ancient rule of law, recognized and enforced in modern times, no stranger to the consideration of an agreement could have an action on such agreement, although it were made expressly for his benefit; but it seems to be held, in recent cases, that, while the rule itself is not denied, it would generally be held inapplicable where the beneficiary has any concern whatever in the transaction.

But where the promise is made under seal, and the action must be debt or covenant, then it must be brought in the name of the party to the instrument; and a third party, for whose benefit the promise is made, cannot sue upon it.

The time of the consideration may be of the past, of the present, or of the future.

The general rule is that a past or executed consideration is not sufficient to sustain a promise founded upon it, unless there was a request for the consideration *previous* to its being done or made.

But this previous request need not always be express, or proved, because it is often implied,—as, *first*, where one accepts or retains the beneficial result of voluntary service; *secondly*, where one is compelled to do for another what that other should do, and was compellable to do; and, *thirdly*, where one does voluntarily, and without request, that which he is not compellable to do, for another who is compellable to do it.

Where the law implies both the previous request and also a subsequent promise, there no other promise than that which is so implied can be enforced, if the consideration for the promise be an executed one.

Where the consideration is wholly executed, the law implies in some cases a previous request, provided a promise be proved; but will not imply a request and thence imply a promise.

On the other hand, wherever the law implies the promise, there it will also imply a request; and hence it may be said that express request is unnecessary where the law implies a promise.

ASSENT OF THE PARTIES.—There is no contract unless the parties thereto assent, and they must assent to the same thing, in the same sense.

The assent must comprehend the whole of the proposition; it must be exactly equal to its extent and provisions, and it must not qualify them by any new matter.

At a sale by auction, every bid by any one present is an offer by him. It becomes a contract as soon as the hammer falls or the bid is otherwise accepted; but until accepted, may be withdrawn.

Contracts on time.—Strictly speaking, all offers are on time. Nor can it be necessary that the acceptance should follow the offer instantaneously. A reasonable time is allowable, and what this is must be determined by the circumstances of the case.

If the offerer gives a day for acceptance, without consideration for the delay, he may, at any time within that day, before acceptance, recall his offer. So he may if he gives no time. If he makes an offer, and instantly recalls it before acceptance, although the other party was prepared to accept it the next instant, the offer is effectually withdrawn; but acceptance before withdrawal binds the parties, if made while the offer continues; and the offer does continue in all cases, either a reasonable time or the time fixed by the party himself.

An offer by letter is a continuing offer until the letter be received, and for a reasonable time thereafter, during which the party to whom it is addressed may accept the offer.

It is held that this offer may be withdrawn by the maker at any moment; and that it is withdrawn as soon as a notice of such withdrawal reaches the party to whom the offer is made, and not before.

If the party accepts the offer before such withdrawal, the bargain is completed; there is then a contract founded upon mutual assent.

These letters are supposed to be properly addressed and mailed and to reach the proper party at a proper time.

Cases of delay and hindrance form exceptions to the principle above stated, and must be decided on their own facts and merits.

If the party receiving an offer by letter put his answer of acceptance into the mail, he has done all that he could do, and is in no way responsible for the casualties of the mail service.

SUBJECT-MATTER OF CONTRACTS.

THE SUBJECT-MATTER OF EVERY CONTRACT is something which is to be done, or which is to be omitted. Where the thing to be done is the payment of money, the remedy is adequate and perfect. But where the thing to be done is anything else than the payment of money, there the common law can only give a remedy which may be entirely inadequate; for it can only give a money remedy. The foundation of the common law of contracts may be said to be the giving of damages for the breach of a contract. And where the contract is specifically for the payment of money, and for nothing else, still the law does not generally, in form, decree an execution of the contract, but *damages* for the breach of it.

This inability of the common law was among the earlier and most potent causes which gave rise to courts of equity, which have a very complete jurisdiction over this class of cases.

Purchase and sale of real property.—Simple contracts are often made for the purchase of real estate, and the specific performance of these contracts may be enforced in equity, or actions may be brought on them at common law.

But neither equity nor law will enforce such contract, if it be founded upon fraud, or gross misrepresentation, etc.; but mere inadequacy of price—not gross, and not attended by circumstances indicating fraud or oppression—is not sufficient to avoid it.

Auction sales.—Estates are frequently sold at auction; and in that case, the plans and descriptions should be such as will give true information; for if they are deceptive or materially erroneous, the purchaser is not bound to take the estate.

The weight of authority seems in favor of permitting an owner in person to bid, or to employ a person to bid for him, if he does this with no purpose of "puffing," but merely to prevent a sacrifice of the property under a given price.

An auctioneer has no authority to rescind the sale for either party without specific orders, although the purchase money be not yet paid.

If an auctioneer does not disclose the name of the owner of the property which he sells, he is himself liable to an action by the buyer for the completion of the contract.

So, also, if he sold or warranted without authority.

An auctioneer has such a special property in the goods, that he may bring an action for the price, even if the goods be sold in the house of the owner and were known to be his. But the buyer may set off a debt due to him from the owner.

After the sale is finished the auctioneer is no longer the agent of the owner, and a payment to him of the price is not a payment to the owner, unless by usage or on other evidence he can be shown to have authority to receive the money.

The rules of law applicable to auction sales of personal and of real property are the same, except so far as they are necessarily distinguished by the nature of the property sold.

HIRING OF REAL PROPERTY.—Of lease—the *means* by which it is usually affected.

A lease is a contract whereby one party (the tenant) has the possession and profits of the land, and the other party (the landlord) reserves a rent which the tenant pays him by way of compensation.

Any general description will suffice to pass the demised premises, if it be capable of distinct ascertainment and identification.

Liabilities of the lessor.—There is an implied covenant on the part of the lessor to put the lessee into possession, and that he shall quietly enjoy, etc.

Liability and obligation of the tenant.—He is liable to an action either for non-payment of rent or for refusing to take possession.

He is not bound to pay taxes unless he agree to.

A tenant is not bound to make general repairs, but he must make such as are made necessary by his use of the house and are required to keep the premises in tenantable condition, and outgoing tenants must leave the premises wind and water tight.

A lessee may assign over the whole or a part of his term in the premises.

A tenant may not dispute his landlord's title, for he is estopped from changing by his own act the character and effect of his tenure.

If the lessee proves an interference with his beneficial enjoyment of the premises which is material and intentional, this would be a defence against an action for rent; but the interference must be deliberate, and by the landlord himself, and not by another tenant or other person.

Surrender of leases by operation of law.—Surrender takes place when the lessee does something incompatible with the lease, and the lessor assents or co-operates, as if the lessor gives and the lessee accepts a new valid lease.

Away-going crops.—A tenant whose estate is terminated by an uncertain event, which he could neither foresee nor control, is entitled to the annual crop which

he sowed while his estate continued, by the law of *emblements*.

Otherwise, in case of a tenant for years, for he knows when his lease will expire; but still he has usually some right to the crop he sowed, according to usage, agreement, etc.

Fixtures.—The tenant may annex some things to the freehold and yet retain the right to remove them.

In general, he may remove whatever he has added, if he can do so without any injury to the premises, unless he has actually built it in, so as to make it an integral part of what was there originally.

Notice to quit.—A tenant whose tenancy may be determined by the will of the landlord is entitled to notice of that determination, nor can he be dispossessed by process of law, without that previous notice.

A notice to quit is necessary in all those cases in which the implication of law creates a tenancy from year to year, or one determinable by the landlord. No particular form is necessary.

It should be served upon the tenant personally, or by leaving it with the tenant's wife or servant, at the usual place of abode of the tenant, and if so left it is sufficient, although it never reached the tenant.

A valid notice properly served vests the premises in the landlord, and absolutely terminates the tenant's right of possession at the time stated.

Apportionment of rent arises where the lessor sells his right to the land to different purchasers.

It is now settled that the *apportionment* must be in proportion to the *value*, and not quantity, and this is a question of fact for the jury to settle upon the evidence offered them.

The remedy for non-payment of rent due and unpaid, provided by the common law, is the summary and somewhat perilous authority of *distress*.

The distress must be reasonable in amount, and the property distrained cannot be carried out of the county; and the distress must not be made at night.

The goods may be replevied by the owner at any time within a certain number of days, and the question of indebtedness, or any other which affects the right of distress, may be tried; but if not replevied, they may be sold, and the proceeds applied to the payment of the rent due.

CONTRACTS. 153

The landlord is punishable for unlawful distress, and the tenant for unlawful rescue of the goods or prevention of distress.

SALE OF PERSONAL PROPERTY.—The **essential of a sale**, at common law, is the agreement of the parties that the property in the subject-matter should pass from the vendor to the vendee, for a consideration given, or promised to be given, by the vendee.

There is a presumption that every sale is to be consummated at once; that the chattel is to be delivered and the price paid without delay.

Original owners may reclaim their property wherever it may be, and take it without any payment to the holder.

Absolute sale of chattels.—For a sale to be valid in law there must be parties, a consideration, and a thing to be sold.

A sale may be good in part and void as to the residue; good as between the parties, but void as to creditors; good as to some of the creditors, but void as to others.

The price to be paid must be certain, or so referred to a definite standard that it may be made certain; and the thing sold must be specific, and capable of certain identification.

The effect of a sale is, that if the sale be complete, the property in the thing sold passes to the purchaser, and if not complete, it remains with the original owner.

The property does not pass absolutely unless the sale be completed, and it is not completed until the happening of any event expressly provided for, or so long as anything remains to be done to the thing sold, to put it into a condition for sale, or to identify it, or discriminate it from other things, or to determine its quantity, if the price depends on this, etc.

And even if an earnest, or part of the price, be paid, the sale is not complete under these circumstances, and if it finally fail, the money paid may be recovered back.

If it be sold for cash and the price be not paid, or if it be sold on credit, but by the terms of the bargain is to remain in the hands of the vendor, the vendor has a lien on it for the price, and only payment or tender gives the vendee a right to possession.

If sold on credit and the buyer, by the terms of the bargain, has the right of immediate possession without payment, but the thing sold actually remains in the possession of the seller until the credit has expired, and the price is still unpaid, it seems that the seller then has a lien for the price.

If it be sold on credit, and there is no agreement in respect to the delivery or possession of the goods, the prevailing, but not quite universal, rule, gives to the purchaser at once a complete right not only of property, but of possession, subject only to defeasance under the law of stoppage *in transitu*.

Possession and delivery.—While as between the parties, the property passes by a sale without delivery, it is not valid, in general, as against a third party without notice, without delivery.

If no time be appointed for delivery, or for payment, these acts must be done within a reasonable time; and if neither party does anything within that period, the contract is deemed to be dissolved.

Conditional sales.—In every sale, unless otherwise expressed, there is an implied condition that the price shall be paid before the buyer has a right to possession; and this is a condition precedent.

Any misstatement, made fraudulently, and capable of having any effect on the sale, will avoid it; for a buyer is discharged from a purchase made under "catching conditions."

It is a well recognized principle that courts will not make a contract for the parties which they have not made themselves.

Warranties.—Accompanying a sale of chattels. There are two kinds in respect to their *subject-matter*, viz: warranty of *title*, and warranty of *quality*. There are also two kinds with respect to their form, as they may be *express* or *implied*.

The seller of a chattel, if *in possession*, warrants by implication that it is his own, and is answerable to the purchaser if it be taken from him by one who has a better title than the seller, whether the seller knew the defect in his title or not.

But if the seller is out of possession, and no affirmation of title is made, then it may be said that the purchaser buys at his peril.

It is the fault of the buyer who asks for or receives a warranty if it does not cover as much ground and give him as effectual protection as he intended.

If there be no express warranty, the law, in general, implies none; the rule is, *caveat emptor*,—let the purchaser

CONTRACTS. 155

beware, or take care of his own interests,—for it is always in the power of a purchaser to demand a warranty.

The rule, however, never applies to cases of fraud, never proposes to protect a seller against his own fraud, nor to disarm a purchaser from a defence or remedy against a seller's fraud.

The seller may let the buyer cheat himself *ad libitum*, but must not actively assist him in cheating himself.

As mere silence implies no warranty, neither do remarks which should be construed as simple praise or commendation.

If goods be sold by sample, there is an implied warranty that the goods correspond to the sample.

Where a contract of sale is in writing, and contains no warranty, there parol evidence is not admissible to add a warranty.

It is fraud, if the seller conceals existing faults, and draws the attention of the buyer away so as to prevent his discovering them, or places the property in such circumstances that discovery is impossible, or made very difficult.

The buyer may bring his action at once, founding it upon the breach of warranty, without returning the goods; but his continued possession of the goods and their actual value would be considered in estimating the damages.

Or, he may return the goods forthwith, and if he does so without unreasonable delay, this will be a rescission of the sale, and he may sue for the price, if he has paid it, or defend against an action for the price if one be brought by the seller.

But if he has sold a part before his discovery of the breach, and therefore cannot return them, he may still rescind the sale, and will be liable for the market value of what he does not return.

In general, when a buyer asserts that the goods he purchased are not what they were warranted to be, he must forthwith return the goods, if he would rescind and avoid the sale.

Delay in doing so would be construed into an admission that there was no such deficiency, or into a waiver of his right to rescind the sale because of such deficiency.

In general, there is no implied warranty whatever arising from judicial sale.

STOPPAGE IN TRANSITU.—If a vendor, who has sent goods to a purchaser at a distance, finds that the purchaser is insolvent, he may stop the goods at any

time before they reach the purchaser, which right is called the right of stoppage *in transitu*.

To effect this, notice of the consignor's claim and purpose given to the carrier before delivery, is sufficient.

The prevailing authority and reason are in favor of this *stoppage in transitu*, being an exercise of a lien by the seller, and not a rescission of the sale.

When and how the right may be exercised.—The general rule is, that this right exists as long as the goods are *in transitu*.

They are *in transitu* until they pass into the possession of the vendee.

Guaranty or suretyship is the contract by which one person is bound to another for the due fulfillment of a promise or engagement of a third party. Warranty is applied to a contract as to the title, quality, or quantity of a thing sold.

No special words or form are necessary to constitute a guaranty.

Unless the conditions of a guaranty are strictly complied with by the party to whom it was given, the guarantor will not be bound.

It often happens that what appears to be a promise to pay the debt of another is not in writing, but is nevertheless enforced by the courts on the ground that it is an original promise, and not a collateral one, and therefore not within the requirements of the statute of frauds.

Where the promise to pay the debt of another is founded upon a new consideration, and this consideration passes between the parties to this promise, and gives to the promisor a benefit which he did not enjoy before, and would not have possessed but for the promise, then it will be regarded as an original promise, and will be enforced, although not in writing.

Whether a contract is collateral or original, may be a question of *construction*, and then it is for the court; but it is often regarded as a question of fact, and then it is for the jury.

Consideration.—Although the promise to pay the debt of another be in writing, it is nevertheless of no force unless founded upon a consideration.

Wherever any fraud exists in the consideration of the contract of guaranty, or in the circumstances which induced it, the contract is entirely null.

Agreement and acceptance.—A contract of guaranty, or a promise to pay the debt of another, is not valid unless it is accepted by the promisee.

Where the proposition of guaranty, or letter of credit, is future in its application, and uncertain in its amount, the guarantor must have notice that his guaranty is accepted.

The reason of this is that the guarantor may know distinctly his liability, and have the means of arranging his relations as he would with the party in whose favor the guaranty is given, and take from him security or indemnity.

Change of liability.—The guarantor cannot be held to any greater extent than the original debtor, either in point of amount or of time. Nor can this liability be extended or enlarged by operation of law without his consent.

Anything which operates as a novation, discharges the surety. But the guarantor may assent to the change, and waive his right of claiming a discharge because of it.

A surety is discharged where the creditor, after notice and request, has been guilty of a delay which amounts to gross negligence, and by this negligence the surety has lost his security or indemnity.

The guarantor promises only to pay the debt of another, in case that other does not pay it; hence the creditor must first diligently endeavor to secure the debt from the principal debtor.

Notice to the guarantor.—**A guaranty may be extinguished** or discharged by the fact that the guarantee gives no notice to the guarantor of the failure of the principal debtor, and of the intention of the guarantee to enforce the guaranty. For a guarantor is entitled to reasonable notice of this.

A demand on the principal debtor, and a failure on his part to do that which he was bound to do, are requisite to found any claim against the guarantor; and notice of the failure must be given to him.

Revocation of guaranty.—A promise of guaranty is always revocable at the pleasure of the guarantor by sufficient notice, unless it be made to cover some specific transaction which is not yet exhausted, or unless it be founded upon a continuing consideration, the benefit of which the guarantor cannot or does not renounce.

HIRING OF PERSONS.—Servants.—Where the contract is for a certain time, if the master discharge the servant before the time, he is still liable, unless the servant has given cause, by showing himself unable or unwilling to do what he has undertaken to do.

A promise by the servant to obey the lawful and reasonable orders of his master, within the scope of his contract, as implied by law, and a breach of this promise, in a material matter, justifies the master in discharging him.

If the contract be for a time certain, and the servant leave without cause before the time expires, it is a general rule that he has no claim for the services he has rendered.

But if prevented from performing the stipulated amount of labor by sickness, or similar inability, he may recover pay for what he has done on a *quantum meruit*.

On the same principle of entirety of contract, it is held that if a servant is discharged for misconduct during the currency of a quarter, he is entitled to no wages from the beginning of that quarter.

If the contract be dissolved by mutual consent, he may recover wages *pro rata*, without any express contract to that effect.

Where wrongfully dismissed he may recover for the whole term.

In general, whatever service is rendered and received, a contract of hiring, or an obligation to pay will be presumed.

The statute of frauds requires that a promise not to be fulfilled or performed within one year from the making shall be in writing.

Contracts for service generally.—There is in all such contracts a promise, implied if not expressed, that the party employing will pay for the service rendered; and on the other hand, that the party employed will use due care and diligence, and have and exercise the skill and knowledge requisite for the employment undertaken.

It is on this ground that physicians and surgeons are liable for any injury caused by their want of due skill or care.

Where there is a contract for a piece of work for a definite sum, and, as often happens, *extra* work is done by the party employed, he cannot recover for such extra work, or even for better materials used, if he had not the authority of the other party therefor; but this authority may be implied.

MARRIAGE.—Contracts to marry are as valid and effectual in law as any, and in actions upon them damages may be recovered, not only for pecuniary loss, but for suffering and injury to condition and prospects.

The promises must be reciprocal, but they need not be made at the same time; for if an offer be made, though retractable until acceptance, yet if not retracted, it remains open for acceptance for a reasonable time, and when accepted, the contract is complete.

The very words, or time, or manner of the promise need not be proved, for it may be inferred from circumstances.

A promise to marry at the end of five years has been held in this country to be within that clause of the statute of frauds which requires that a promise not to be performed within one year from the making shall be in writing.

A contract to marry, without specification of time, is a contract to marry within a reasonable time, each party having a right to reasonable delay.

Contracts to marry, like most others, may be on condition; and if the condition be legal and reasonable, the liability of the parties under it attaches as soon as the condition is satisfied.

If the promise is to marry on request, a request should be alleged and proved.

The defences which may be urged against an action to enforce a promise to marry are very numerous: Consanguinity within those degrees within which marriage is prohibited by the statutes of the several States; bad character of the plaintiff, or his or her lascivious conduct; false and injurious language used by plaintiff concerning defendant; bad health, if such as to incapacitate for marriage, or render it unsafe or improper; entire deafness or blindness, or other important physical incapacity, occurring after the promise; so if a widow conceals her previous marriage and betroths herself as a virgin, which would be a fraud; all of these being good defences.

A dissolution of the contract by mutual consent would of course be a sufficient defence, but it must be a real and honest consent. But a pre-engagement by the defendant is no sufficient defence.

Damages are peculiarly within the power of the jury in cases of this kind, and courts are very unwilling to set aside a verdict in these cases on the ground of excessive damages.

Promises in relation to settlements or advances.—A promise to give to a woman, or settle upon her, a specific sum or estate, on her marriage, is valid.

But such promises are certainly within the statute of frauds, as made "in consideration of marriage," although a promise to marry is not. They must therefore be in writing in those of our States which have enacted this clause of that statute.

Contracts in restraint of marriage are wholly void.

Contracts of marriage, in most governments, are held to be valid and binding, notwithstanding it is entered into with no rites or ceremonies.

Evidence of marriage, from cohabitation, acknowledgment by the parties, reception by the family, connection as man and wife, and general reputation, is receivable in nearly all civil cases.

Consent is the essence of this contract, as of all others, or it is void.

Divorce a vinculo annuls the marriage altogether, and it restores the parties to all the rights of unmarried persons. It is granted for adultery, desertion, cruelty, long imprisonment, etc. The law and practice in this respect differ in the different States, being precisely alike in no two of them.

A divorce a mensa et thoro was once the most common, but most of the causes which formerly only sufficed for this are now very generally made sufficient for a divorce *a vinculo.*

BAILMENT is a delivery of goods in trust upon a contract, express or implied, that the trust shall be faithfully executed on the part of the bailee.

A bailee is always responsible, in some degree or measure, for the property delivered to him; he is bound to take care of it.

Courts have established three kinds or degrees of care.

Frst.—Slight care, or that degree of care which every man of common sense, though very absent and inattentive, applies to his own affairs.

Secondly.—Ordinary care, or that degree of care which every person of ordinary and common prudence takes of his own concerns.

Thirdly.—Great care, or the degree of care that a man remarkably exact and thoughtful gives to the securing of his own property.

There are, therefore, three degrees of negligence.

CONTRACTS.

First.—Gross negligence, or the absence of slight care.

Secondly.—Ordinary negligence, or the absence of ordinary care.

Thirdly.—Slight negligence, or the absence of great care.

The classification of bailments is into *depositum,* or deposit without compensation or reward; *mandatum,* or gratuitous commission, wherein the mandatary agrees to do something with or about the thing bailed; *commodatum,* or loan, where the thing bailed is lent for use, without pay, and is to be itself returned; *pignus,* or pledge, when the thing bailed is security for debt; and *locatio,* or hiring, for a reward or compensation.

Depositum is where a thing is placed with a depositary to be kept for a time, and returned when called for, the depositary to have no compensation; the benefit of the transaction being wholly on the side of the bailor, the bailee is liable only for *gross* negligence.

The depositary is bound to deliver the thing as it was, and with it all its increase or profit.

But one cannot be made a depositary against his will; he must consent, but the consent may be implied or inferred.

Mandatum is where the commission is gratuitous; and here, also, the transaction is for the exclusive benefit of the bailor, and the bailee is held only for *gross* negligence.

In deposit, the *safe-keeping* is the principal matter; in mandate, the *work* to be done with or about the thing; hence the first is said to be in *custody,* and the second in *feasance.*

Mandates and deposits may be considered as contracts, and the obligations growing out of them may be enforced by action of assumpsit, as it is well settled by the authorities that the delivery and acceptance of the goods constitute a sufficient consideration.

Gratuitous bailees being thus liable *ex-contractu,* may also be made liable *ex-delicto* if they have committed a tort upon the property intrusted to them.

Commodatum is when a thing is borrowed to be used by the borrower without any reward or compensation to be received by the owner from him. This transaction resembles the two former,—in so far as it is *gratuitous,* but unlike them in that the benefit belongs exclusively to the *bailee,* and he is therefore bound to *great* care, and liable for *slight* negligence.

Pignus, or pledge, is a bailment for the mutual benefit of both parties, for while the pledgee obtains security for his debt, the pledgor obtains credit, or delay, or other indulgence. The bailee is therefore bound only to ordinary care, and is liable only for ordinary neglect.

In the power of disposal a mortgagee differs greatly from a pledgee, in that he may sell his mortgage and by his sale transfer the right of property from himself to the purchaser, subject to the redemption of the mortgagor; but the pledgee, having only the possession and not the property, cannot transfer the property or thing pledged, nor sell until the debt becomes due and is unpaid.

Locatio, or hiring, **is usually classified as follows**: *Locatio rei*, where a thing is hired and the hirer acquires a temporary use of the thing bailed; *Locatio operis faciendi*, where the bailee is hired to do some work or bestow some care on the things bailed; *Locatio operis mercium vehendarum*, where the bailee is hired to carry the goods for the bailor from one place to another This form of *locatio* embraces also the carrying of passengers.

Locatio rei.—When the owner of a thing lets it to another, who is to have the use of the thing and pay a compensation therefor, the contract between the parties is for their mutual benefit. The bailee is bound to take ordinary care of the thing bailed.

The hirer is equally responsible for the negligence of his servants as for his own, provided that this negligence occurred when the servant was in the discharge of his duty, or obeying the commands or instructions of his master, express or implied.

If the loss occur through theft or robbery, or the injury result from violence, the hirer is only answerable when his imprudence or negligence caused or facilitated the injurious act.

When the thing bailed is lost or injured, the hirer is bound to account for such loss or injury.

The proof of negligence or want of due care is thrown upon the bailor, and the hirer is not bound to prove affirmatively that he used reasonable care.

On the part of the hirer there is an implied obligation to use the thing only for the purpose and in the manner for which it was hired, and he must in no way abuse the thing hired.

The hirer must surrender the property at the time appointed, and if no time be specified in the contract, then whenever called upon after a reasonable time.

Locatio operis faciendi.—The cases in which the bailee is to do some work or bestow some care upon or about the thing bailed, may be divided into *Mechanics,* who are employed in the manufacture or repair of the article bailed to them; *Warehousemen* or *Wharfingers,* who are charged with the custody of the thing bailed; *Postmasters,* who receive letters, etc., to be sent as directed, and *Innkeepers,* who receive guests and the goods of guests.

Mechanics, where employed to make up materials furnished, or to alter or repair a specific thing, there the contract becomes one of mutual benefit, and only ordinary care is required: but it may vary much in different cases.

A workman employed to make up materials, or to alter or repair a specific article, has a lien upon the materials of the things for his pay.

Warehousemen are also held only to ordinary diligence, as in their case also the contract is for mutual benefit.

These men also have a lien on the goods which they store, for their charges.

Postmasters, and persons employed as deputies or in the post-offices, are answerable for any injury sustained by their misconduct or neglect of duty.

Innkeepers are insurers of the property committed to their care, against everything but the act of God, public enemies, or the neglect or fraud of the owner of the property.

An inn has been judicially defined as "a house where the traveler is furnished with everything which he has occasion for whilst upon his way." There need not be a sign to make it an inn.

An innkeeper may require of his guest to place his goods in a particular place, and under lock and key, or he will not be answerable.

No special delivery or direction of the goods to the innkeeper is necessary to charge him, for it is enough if they are fairly according to common practice, within his custody.

He cannot refuse to receive a guest, unless his house is full, and he is actually unable to receive him, and if on false pretences he refuses, he is liable to an action.

He may refuse to receive a disorderly guest, or require him to leave his house.

A guest may leave an inn for a time and still leave his property under the safeguard of the landlord's liability, but not for an indefinite period.

Locatio operis mercium vehendarum.—The owner of goods may cause them to be carried by a *private carrier, gratuitously,* or by a private carrier *for hire,* or by a *common carrier.*

Any one who carries goods for another is a *private* carrier, unless he comes within the definition of the common carrier.

The private carrier for hire is bound to ordinary diligence and liable for ordinary negligence, because this bailment is for the benefit of both bailor and bailee.

Common carriers may be carriers of goods or of passengers, or of both. They are not only responsible for any loss of or injury to the goods they carry which is caused by their negligence, but the law raises an absolute and conclusive presumption of negligence whenever the loss occurs from any other cause than "the act of God," or "the public enemy."

"**The act of God**" is a cause which operates without any aid or interference from man.

A common carrier is one who undertakes for hire to transport the goods of such as choose to employ him from place to place.

A private carrier may or may not carry for another, as he prefers; but a common carrier is bound to receive and carry all the goods offered for transportation, subject to all the responsibilities incident to his employment, and is liable to an action in case of refusal.

All carriers are held to act by their agents, and to be responsible for the acts of their servants and agents, under the common rules of agency.

As soon as the goods are delivered and received they are at the risk of the carrier.

The responsibility of the carrier is fixed by his acceptance of the goods without objection, whatever be the manner of the delivery.

Delivery to a carrier must be known to the carrier, in order to create a responsibility on his part.

As the liability of the carrier begins with a delivery of the goods to him, so it continues until the delivery of the goods by him.

He is bound not only to carry them to their destined place,

but to deliver them there to the bailor, or as the bailor may direct.

If the consignee refuse to receive the goods, or cannot receive them, or is dead, or absent, this will excuse delay in delivery, but will not absolve the carrier from all duty or responsibility.

In general, the delivery of the goods must be to the owner or consignee himself, or to his agent.

One of the distinctions between the private carrier and the common carrier is that the first has no lien on the goods for his freight, while the latter has.

Common carriers of passengers are liable only where the injury has arisen from their own negligence; and they are liable for injuries resulting from the *slightest* negligence on their part.

The peculiar responsibility of a common carrier may be destroyed by express contract between himself and one who sends goods or takes them with him.

Although a common carrier cannot, by a mere notice, extinguish his peculiar liability, yet he can in this way materially modify and qualify it.

So, too, he has a right to say he will not carry goods beyond a certain value; or that, if he does, he must be paid for it by a premium on the increased risk; and this is reasonable, as tending to give the carrier exact knowledge of what he carries and of what risk he runs.

If the carrier's notice be public, and only a limited and qualified one, and in itself reasonable, the sender is bound thereby.

It has been held that a railroad company is bound to introduce improvements which are ascertained to be practicable and conducive to safety, and are therefore liable for an injury caused by neglect in not introducing them.

Fraud or willful misrepresentation, or intentional concealment, on the part of the sender of goods, or of the passenger, extinguishes the liability of the common carrier, so far as it is affected by such misconduct.

The principle that the carrier is bound only by a responsibility which he knows and can provide for, seems to be the principal cause of recent modifications of his liability in respect to the baggage of a passenger.

The word "baggage" is held not to include a trunk containing valuable merchandise, and nothing else; and it does not embrace samples of merchandise carried by a passenger in a trunk, with a view of enabling him to make bargains for the sale of goods.

The plaintiff is a competent witness, *ex necessitate*, to prove the contents of his trunk and their value.

LAW OF SHIPPING.—Any person may become an owner of a ship in the same way as of any other chattel, unless some peculiar means or process is required by law.

Part-owners of ships are those who own definite parts or proportions of the whole ship; and they are always tenants in common.

A part-owner may sell his share to whom he will.

The majority of part-owners, and more certainly a majority in interest and in number, may, generally, control and employ a ship at their pleasure.

Sale of ships. The rules of the common law as to evidence, agency, and warranty, applicable to sales of chattels, apply here; for a ship is a personal chattel, although one of a peculiar character.

The universal rule in regard to the sale of chattels is that the want or delay of possession by the purchaser is a badge of fraud which may defeat the sale; and this applies to a ship, with some modifications, arising from the peculiar character and use of the chattel.

Transfer by bottomry.—*Originally* this contract was made and the bond executed by the master in a foreign port, to raise funds to enable the ship to return to her home port.

Bottomry bonds are maritime contracts which transfer the ship to the bottomry creditor, as a security for advances made by him; in which respect it is similar to a mortgage, or pledge; but differs from a pledge in that possession is not transferred to the creditor.

The debt is paid and the bond discharged by the loss of the ship.

A later bond takes precedence of an earlier one, because the later bond saves the ship for the earlier; thus reversing the rule applied to mortgages.

An owner may make a bottomry bond anywhere or for any reason; but the master of the ship may lawfully make this bond *abroad* only, and from absolute *necessity*.

Respondentia.—A respondentia bond is nearly the same thing in respect to the cargo, which the bottomry bond is in respect to the ship; it is another resource which the master has of raising funds, in cases of necessity, by hypothecating the whole, or part of the cargo; which, if lost, the lender has no claim for repayment.

An owner of a ship lets it to others to use by an instrument called a charter party.

Salvage is the compensation earned by persons who have voluntarily assisted in saving a ship or cargo from destruction.

The ground upon which the liberal compensation usually granted in salvage cases rests is a marine peril, voluntary service, and success.

Salvage is never merely pay, or in the nature of wages; it is always a reward: the amount being determined by the danger incurred, the skill manifested, the difficulty and duration of the service; but it is much influenced by the numerous precedents in adjudged cases.

General average.—The rule is that where maritime property is in peril, and the sacrifice of a part is made for, and causes the safety of the rest, that which is saved contributes to make up the loss of that which is sacrificed; but the sacrifice must be voluntary and successful.

Seamen have a lien for their wages on the ship and freight, and it prevails even over a bottomry bond.

CONSTRUCTION AND INTERPRETATION OF CONTRACTS.—What a contract means is a question of law; the court, therefore, determines the construction of a contract.

The principles of construction are much the same at law and in equity.

So, too, whether the instrument to be construed has a seal or not, the same rules and principles of construction will be applied to it.

The intention, or to ascertain what the parties themselves meant or understood, is the first point. Courts will construe as near to this as rules of law will permit, but cannot adopt a construction of a legal instrument which shall do violence to the rules of language, or to the rules of law.

A contract which the parties intended to make, but did not make, cannot be set up in the place of one

which they did make, but did not intend to make.

The same intention must be collected from the same words of a contract in writing, whether with or without a seal.

General rules of construction.—The subject-matter of the contract is to be fully considered.

A party will be held to that meaning which he knew the other party supposed the words to bear, if this can be done without making a new contract for the parties.

A construction which would make the contract legal is preferred to one which would have an opposite effect.

It is a rule that the whole contract should be considered in determining the meaning of any or of all its parts.

Another rule requires that the contract should be supported rather than defeated.

A further rule requires that all instruments should be construed "*contra proferentum*"—that is, against him who gives or undertakes, or enters into an obligation—unless in the case of the sovereign.

No precise form of words is necessary, even in a specialty. Even a bond may be made without the words "held and firmly obliged," etc., although they are technical and usual.

In general, **where clauses are repugnant and incompatible**, the earlier prevails in deeds and other instruments *inter vivos*, if the inconsistency be not so great as to avoid the instrument for uncertainty; but in the construction of wills the latter clause prevails, as it is presumed to be a subsequent thought, and the last will of the testator.

The law frequently supplies by its implications the wants of express agreements between the parties; but it never overcomes by its implications the express provisions of parties.

If the whole contract can be construed *together* so that the written words and those printed make an intelligible contract, this construction should be adopted; but if not, in general, preference should be given to the *written* part.

Entirety of contracts.—Whether a contract is entire or separable is often of great importance.

Like most other questions of construction, it depends upon the intention of the parties, and this must be discovered in each case by considering the language employed and the subject-matter of the contract.

If the part to be performed by one party consists of several distinct and separate items, and the price to be paid by the other is apportioned to each item to be performed, or is left to be implied by law, such a contract will generally be held to be severable.

So, where the price to be paid is clearly and distinctly apportioned to different parts of what is to be performed, although the latter is in its nature single and entire.

If the consideration to be paid is single and entire, the contract must be held to be entire, although the subject of the contract may consist of several distinct and wholly independent items.

Apportionment of contracts.—A contract is said to be apportionable when the amount of consideration to be paid by the one party depends upon the extent of performance by the other.

When parties enter into a contract by which the amount to be performed by the one, and the consideration to be paid by the other, are made certain and fixed, such a contract cannot be apportioned.

Courts of justice can only carry into effect such contracts as parties have made. They cannot make contracts for them, or alter or vary those made by them.

Conditional contracts.—Whether a contract be conditional or not depends not on any formal arrangement of the words, but on the reason and sense of the thing as it is to be collected from the whole contract.

No precise words are requisite to constitute a condition.

Presumptions of law.—There are some general ones which may be considered as affecting the construction of contracts.

Thus, it is a presumption of law that parties to a simple contract intended to bind not only themselves, but their personal representatives, and such parties may sue on the contract, although not named therein.

It is also a legal presumption that every grant carries with it whatever is essential to the use and enjoyment of the grant.

Where anything is to be done, as goods to be delivered, or the like, and no time is specified in the contract, it is then a presumption of law that the parties intended and agreed that the thing should be done in a reasonable time; but what is a reasonable time is a question of law for the court.

The effect of custom or usage is that an established custom may add to a contract stipulations not contained in it; or may control or vary the meaning of the words.

The common law is every day adopting as rules and principles the mere usages of the community, for ancient, universal, and perfectly established custom is in fact *law*.

A custom is applicable or has a bearing on a contract, when it is *so far* established, and so far known to the parties, that it must be supposed that their contract was made in reference to it.

For this purpose the custom must be established and not casual; uniform and not varying; general and not personal, and known to the parties.

Custom and usage are not the same thing; custom is the thing to be proved, and usage is the evidence of the custom.

Whether a custom exists, is a question of *fact*; but in the proof of this fact, questions of law of two kinds may arise: *first*—whether the evidence is admissible; and *secondly*—whether the facts stated are legally sufficient to prove a custom.

As a general rule, the knowledge of a custom must be brought home to a party who is to be affected by it.

But no custom, however universal, old or known, unless it has actually passed into law, has any force over parties against their will.

Hence, in the interpretation of contracts, **it is an established rule that no custom can be admitted which the parties have seen fit expressly to exclude**, for a custom can no more be set up against the clear intention of the parties than against their express agreement; and no usage can be incorporated into a contract which is inconsistent with the terms of the contract.

Where the terms of a contract are *plain*, usage, even under that very contract, cannot be permitted to affect materially the construction to be placed upon it; but when it is *ambiguous*, usage for a long time may influence the judgment of the court, by showing how it was understood by the original parties to it.

Admissibility of extrinsic evidence in the interpretation of written contracts.—It is very common for parties to offer evidence external to the contract, in *aid* of the *interpretation of its language*.

The general rule is that such evidence cannot be ad-

mitted to contradict or vary the terms of a valid, written contract; or, as the Scotch law expresses it, "writing cannot be cut down or taken away by the testimony of witnesses."

When parties, after whatever conversation or preparation, at last reduce their agreement to writing, this may be looked upon as the final consummation of their negotiation and the exact expression of their purpose.

Where the agreement between the parties is one and entire, and only a part of this is reduced to writing, it would seem that the residue may be proved by extrinsic evidence.

If there are contemporaneous writings between the same parties, so far in relation to the same subject-matter that they may be deemed part and parcel of the contract, although not referred to in it, they may be read in connection with it.

It is nevertheless certain that some evidence from without must be admissible in the *explanation* or *interpretation* of every contract.

As to the parties or the subject-matter of a contract, the general rule is that extrinsic evidence may and must be received and used to make them certain, if necessary for that purpose.

But as to the terms, conditions, and limitations of the agreement, the written contract must speak exclusively for itself.

Where the language of an instrument has a settled legal meaning, its construction is not open to evidence.

An instrument may be shown to be void and without legal existence or efficacy, as for want of consideration, or for fraud, or duress, or any incapacity of the parties, or any illegality in the agreement.

If no consideration be named, one may be proved.

A receipt for money is peculiarly open to evidence, as it is only *prima facie* evidence that the sum has been paid.

Experts are persons possessing peculiar knowledge and skill requisite for the interpretation of contracts.

A *patent* ambiguity of words is that which appears to be ambiguous upon the deed or instrument; a *latent* ambiguity is that which seems certain, and without ambiguity, for anything that appears upon the deed or instrument, but there is some collateral matter out of the deed that breeds the ambiguity.

If a contract be intelligible, and evidence shows an uncertainty, not in the contract, but in its subject-matter or its application, other evidence which will remove this uncertainty is admissible; but if a contract is not certainly intelligible by itself, it may be said that evidence which makes it so must make a new contract; and, therefore, such evidence is not admissible; but this is subject to some qualification.

The law will not make, nor permit to be made, for parties, a contract other than that which they have made for themselves.

If the contract which the parties have made is *incurably uncertain*, the law will not, or rather cannot, enforce it; and will not, on the pretence of enforcing it, set up a different but valid one in its stead; it will only declare such a supposed contract no contract at all.

Evidence may explain, but cannot vary or contradict, written language.

THE LAW OF PLACE treats of the *lex loci contractus*, the *lex domicillii*, the *lex loci rei sitæ*, and the *lex fori*.

General principles.—Laws have no force by their own proper vigor, beyond the territory of the State by which they are made.

All laws duly made and published by any State bind all persons and things within that State.

Foreign laws may have a qualified force, or some effect, within a State, either by the comity of nations, or by special agreement, as by treaty, or by constitutional requirements, as in case of our own country.

It is a general principle, founded in the necessities of national intercourse, that a contract which is valid where made, is to be held valid everywhere; and if void or illegal by the law of the place where made, it is void everywhere.

The rule is that personal property follows the person, and it is not in any respect to be regulated by the *situs*.

Wherever the domicile of the proprietor is, there the property is to be considered as situated.

The general rule as to the construction of contracts relating to movables is, they are to be construed according to the law of the place where they are made, or the lex loci contractus, and if they relate to immovables, or real property, they are to be construed according to the law of the place where the property is situated, or the *lex loci rei sitæ.*

All *personal* contracts are to be construed and applied according to the law of the place where they were made.

Domicile.—Every person has in law a home, or domicile; and every domicile, whether the original or subsequent one, continues until a new one is acquired; for no person can have more than one domicile at the same time.

One's domicile, or home, is in the country in which he permanently resides.

Both fact and intent are necessary to constitute a domicile.

Of the place of the contract.—If the contract is made in one place to be performed in another, generally speaking, the place of performance is the place of the contract; the most common instance of which is that of a promissory note.

But *debts* have no *locus* or *situs;* they accompany the creditor everywhere, and authorize a demand upon the debtor anywhere.

But on the *trial,* and in respect to all questions as to the forms, or method, or conduct of process, or remedy, the law of the place of the forum is applied.

A marriage which is valid in the place where it is contracted, is valid everywhere.

A *divorce* granted in a State in which both parties had their actual domicile, *and also* were married, is valid everywhere.

Generally, every state recognizes the validity of a divorce granted where both parties have their actual domicile, if granted according to the law of that place.

The principle that questions which have been distinctly settled by litigation shall not be again litigated, has been in many cases extended to foreign judgments.

DEFENCES.—Payment to an agent in the ordinary course of business binds the principal, unless the latter has previously notified the debtor to pay to himself only.

So, payment to one's attorney is as effectual as if made to the principal; or payment to one's partner.

Payment to a creditor's wife will not be a good payment unless she was his agent, either expressly or by course of business.

One may be justified in making payments to a party who is

sitting in the creditor's counting-room, *apparently* intrusted with the transaction of the business, and authorized to receive money, although he be not so in fact.

Payment by letter, and its risk, depends upon circumstances; but in general, the debtor is discharged, although the money do not reach the creditor, if he was directed or expressly authorized by the creditor so to send it, or if he can distinctly derive such authority from its being the usual course of business; but not otherwise.

Payment in good bank-bills, not objected to at the time, is a good payment; and so is a tender of such bills; but the creditor may object and demand specie.

Payment by check is not presumed to be received as an absolute payment, even if the drawer has funds in the bank.

The holder of the check is not bound by receiving it, but may treat it as a nullity if he derives no benefit from it, provided he has been guilty of no negligence which has caused an injury to the drawer.

A negotiable promissory note is not payment, unless circumstances show that such was the intention of the parties.

A debtor who owes his creditor money on distinct accounts, may direct his payments to be applied to either, as he pleases.

If the debtor makes no appropriation, the creditor may apply the money as he pleases.

If neither party makes a specific appropriation of the money, the law will appropriate it as the justice and equity of the case require.

A general payment must be applied to a prior legal debt, in preference to a subsequent equitable claim.

In cases of payments which are not made by the debtor voluntarily, the creditor has no right of appropriation, but must apply the money towards the discharge of all the debts in proportion.

The method of computing interest that generally prevails in the case of partial payments is to compute the interest on the principal sum from the time when interest became payable to the first time when a payment, alone, or in conjunction with preceding payments with interest cast on them, shall equal or exceed the interest due on the principal. Deduct this sum, and cast interest on the balance, as before. In this way payments are applied first to keep down the interest, and then to diminish the principal of the debt, and the creditor does not receive compound interest.

Performance.—If it be *tender* of the money, it can be a defence only when made before the action is brought, and when the demand is of money, and is definite in amount, or capable of being made so.

It need not be made by the defendant personally; if made by a third person, at his request, it is sufficient.

So it need not be made to a creditor personally; but it must be made to an agent actually authorized to receive the money.

The whole sum due must be tendered, as the creditor is not bound to receive a part of his debt.

To make a tender valid, the money must be actually produced and proffered, and in money made lawful by the State in which offered.

The general rule is that the performance must be such as is required by the true spirit and meaning of the contract, and the intention of the parties as expressed therein.

A partial performance may be a defence *pro tanto*, or it may sustain an action *pro tanto;* but this can be only in cases where the duty to be done consists of parts which are distinct and severable in their own nature, and are not bound together by expressions giving entirety to the contract.

If the contract specifies no time, the law implies that it shall be performed within a reasonable time, and will not permit this implication to be rebutted by extrinsic testimony going to fix a definite time, because this varies the contract.

What is a reasonable time is generally a question of law.

That is a reasonable time which preserves to each party the rights and advantages he possesses, and protects each party from losses that he ought not to suffer.

Computation of time shall always conform to the intention of the parties, so far as that can be ascertained from the contract, aided by admissible evidence.

If there is nothing in the language or subject-matter of the contract, which clearly indicates the intention of the parties, time should be computed exclusive of the day when the contract was made.

If the performance of a contract becomes impossible by contingencies which should have been foreseen and provided against in the contract, and still more, if they might have been prevented, the promisor should be held answerable.

Defences resting upon the acts of the plaintiff.—It is a good defence to an action on a contract, that the obligation to perform the act required was dependent upon some other thing which the other party was to do, and has failed to do.

In all cases a promisor will be discharged from all liability, when the non-performance of his obligation is caused by the act, or the fault, of the other contracting party.

Generally, no contract can be rescinded by one of the parties, unless both can be restored to the condition in which they were before the contract was made.

Accord and satisfaction is another defence, and is substantially another agreement between the parties in satisfaction of the former one; and also an execution of the latter agreement.

It must be advantageous to the creditor; he must receive from it a distinct benefit, which otherwise he would not have had.

Arbitrament and award is a somewhat analogous defence. By accord and satisfaction, the parties have agreed as to what shall be done by one to satisfy the claim of the other; by arbitrament and award, they have agreed to submit the question to third persons.

This agreement may be made by the parties directly, or through their agency.

If the award embraces matter not included in the submission, it is fatal.

An award must be certain, possible, reasonable and final, or conclusive.

Generally, in the construction of awards, they are favored and enforced, whenever this can properly be done.

No special form of an award is necessary in this country.

An award is *prima facie* binding upon the parties, and the burden of proof is upon the party who would avoid it.

In general, arbitrators, have full power to decide upon questions of law and fact, embraced in the submission. They have power to decide all questions as to the admission and and rejection of evidence. Their decision upon matters of fact and law, when acting within the scope of their authority, is conclusive, for they are judges of the parties' own choosing.

They have not only all the powers of equity, as well as of

law, but may do what no court could do in giving relief or doing justice.

A release is a good defence, whether it be made by the creditor himself, or result from the operation of law.

Alteration, if it does not vary the meaning of the instrument, or does not affect its operation, is no good reason why it should make the instrument void.

Generally, no immaterial alteration would avoid an instrument.

In the absence of explanation, evident alteration of any instrument is generally presumed to have been made *after* the execution of it; and consequently it must be explained by the party who seeks to take advantage from it.

The pendency of another suit, for the same cause, and between the same parties, is a good cause of abatement of an action.

The general rule of law forbids that a defendant should be harassed by two suits for the same cause at the same time.

The current of authorities is to the effect that the pendency of an action in a *foreign* tribunal, although of competent jurisdiction, is not good cause of abatement.

A former judgment on the same matter in issue is a conclusive bar; for the whole purpose of the law being to settle questions and terminate disputes, it will not permit a question which has been settled to be tried again.

Set-off is a mode of defence by which the defendant acknowledges the justice of the plaintiff's demand, but sets up a demand of his own against the plaintiff, to counterbalance it in whole or in part; so the balance only is the debt, and he to whom it is due should sue for that only.

Set-off is in the nature of a cross-action, and is substituted for that for the purpose of preventing unnecessary litigation.

The demand must be *due* to the party, or the claim must be possessed by him *in his own right*.

It must be reasonably certain. In general, demands may be set off which are for liquidated damages; that is, when their amount is specific, or is directly and distinctly ascertainable by calculation; and also all those which usually may be sued for and recovered under the common counts.

Illegal contracts.—All contracts which provide that anything shall be done which is distinctly prohibited by law, or morality, or public policy are void.

Contracts resting on *maintenance,* or *champerty,* are void.

Fraud, which is the *intentional* and *successful* employment of any cunning, deception, or artifice, used to circumvent, cheat, or deceive another, voids every contract, and annuls every transaction.

But the fraud must be *material* to the contract or transaction, which is to be avoided because of it.

If the fraud be such that, had it not been practiced, the contract would not have been made, or the transaction completed, then it is material to it.

The fraud must be such as to work an actual injury.

Though the law cannot lay hold of a merely intended fraud, yet it will recognize as a fraud a statement which is literally true, but substantially false; for the purpose and effect of the thing will prevail over its form; as if one asserts that another whom he recommends has property to a certain amount, knowing all the while that, although he possesses this property, he owes for it more than it is worth.

It must appear that the injured party not only did in fact rely upon the fraudulent statement, but had a right to rely upon it, in the full belief of its truth.

If one injures another by statements which he knows to be false, he shall be held answerable, although there be no evidence of gain to himself, or of any interest in the question, or of malice, or intended mischief.

But if the statement be false in fact, and injurious because false, if it were believed to be true by the party making it, it is not a fraud on his part.

A party may rescind a contract on the ground of fraud, but if he would do so he must do it at once on discovering the fraud, or a delay would be regarded as a waiver of his right.

The law never presumes fraud.

Material misrepresentations, which go to the substance of a contract, avoid that contract, whether they are caused by mistake, and occur wholly without fault, or are designed and fraudulent.

ESTOPPELS.—In general, an estoppel is an admission or declaration, which the law does not permit him who has made it to deny or disprove for his own benefit, and to the injury of another.

Estoppel by record.—The general rule is that no man shall be permitted to make any averment which contradicts the record of that wherein he was a party.

Estoppel by deed.—The general rule is a party to a bond, or to an indenture, or to a deed of conveyance, can deny nothing which the bond in its condition or the indenture or deed of conveyance in their recitals aver.

But the seal has no longer the solemnity or force which it once had.

In most American courts the recital in a deed of the payment of money, or consideration clause, may be denied, the object of the deed being to transfer the title, and not to state the terms of the purchase.

The general operation of the deed being untouched, evidence varying the consideration may be received.

There is no estoppel which shall prevent a party from saying that a deed is inoperative and void.

Estoppel in pais, or an estoppel in fact, is one which does not spring from a record, or from a deed, but is made to appear to the jury (who are "the country") by competent evidence.

The rule that the consideration of negotiable paper cannot be inquired into, excepting as between immediate parties, is founded upon this principle of estoppel.

Another estoppel *in pais*, of an analogous character, is that when a man has made a declaration or representation, or caused, or, in some cases, not prevented, a false impression, or done some significant act, with intent that others should rely and act thereon, and upon which others *have* honestly relied and acted, he shall not be permitted to prove that the representation was false, or the act unauthorized or ineffectual, if injury would occur to the innocent party who had acted in full faith in its truth or validity.

The whole law of estoppel may seem to rest only on the ground that the law will not permit a party to profit by his own fraud; and upon fraud, actual or constructive, most of the cases do certainly rest.

The whole doctrine of estoppels *in pais* originated in courts of equity, and passed from them into courts of law.

THE STATUTE OF FRAUDS passed in the twenty-ninth year of Charles II, was intended as an effectual prevention of all the more common frauds practiced in society.

The fourth and seventeenth sections affect the law of contracts.

By the fourth section it is enacted that "no action shall be brought whereby to charge any executor or administrator, upon any special promise, to answer damages out of his own estate; or whereby to charge the defendant upon any special promise to answer for the debt, default, or miscarriages of another person; or to charge any person upon any agreement made upon consideration of marriage; or upon any contract for the sale of lands, tenements, or hereditaments, or any interest in or concerning them, or upon any agreement that is not to be performed within the space of one year from the making thereof, unless the agreement upon which such action shall be brought, or some memorandum or note thereof shall be in writing, and signed by the party to be charged therewith, or some other person thereunto by him lawfully authorized."

The seventeenth section enacts that "no contract for the sale of any goods, wares, or merchandise, for the price of ten pounds sterling, or upwards, shall be allowed to be good, except the buyer shall accept part of the goods so sold, and actually receive the same, or give something in earnest to bind the bargain, or in part payment, or that some note or memorandum in writing of the said bargain be made and signed by the parties to be charged by such contract, or their agents thereunto lawfully authorized."

If the agreement be not itself signed, but a letter alluding to and ackowledging the agreement is signed, this is sufficient.

Where one is in the habit of using instruments with his name printed in them, this will be his signature.

And so if he writes it in pencil.

The agreement need not be signed by both parties, but only by him who is to be charged by it.

By the early decisions of the English courts, since abundantly confirmed, it was settled in that country the consideration must be expressed, but in this country in some of the States the judicial decisions have not only denied this, but the statutes have expressly declared the statement of the consideration unnecessary.

Of the form of the agreement, it need only be said that it must be adequately expressive of the intent and obligation of the parties.

If a contract be in its nature entire, and in one part it satisfies the statute, and in others does not, then it is altogether void; but if these parts are severable, then it may be good in part and void in part.

STATUTE OF LIMITATIONS.—The statute 21 James I. c. 16, enacted, among other things, that all actions of account, and upon the case, other than such accounts as concern the trade of merchandise between merchant and merchant, their factors or servants, all actions of debt grounded upon any lending, or contract without specialty, actions of debt for arrearages of rent, should be commenced and sued within six years next after the cause of such actions or suit, and not after.

Any tribunal which enquires into the validity of a claim must admit that its *age* is among the elements which determine the probabity of its having a legal existence and obligation.

The statute proceeds upon the expediency of refusing to enforce a stale claim, whether paid or not, and not merely on the probability that a stale claim has been paid; and this expediency is the actual basis of the law of limitations.

The natural presumption is that claims which have been long neglected are unfounded, or at least are no longer subsisting demands; and this presumption the statute has erected into a positive bar.

New promise.—The law is not entirely settled as to what constitutes a *new* promise, which removes the bar of the statute.

Without taking into consideration the act requiring the new promise to be in writing, we may draw from the decisions on the subject, the following conclusions as established by law, the most general of which are that there must be either an express promise, or an acknowledgment expressed in such words, and attended by such circumstances as give to it the meaning, and therefore the force and effect of a new promise.

It is not necessary that the acknowledgment should be of any precise amount, but if there be an admission of any debt, and of legal liability to pay it, evidence may be connected with this admission, to show the amount; and even if the parties differ as to the amount, an admission of the debt may remove the bar of the statute.

But the acknowledgment must not be of a mere general indebtedness.

An acknowledgment to revive a debt should in fact amount to, or imply, a promise to pay it.

Part payment of a debt has always been held to take it out of the statute, the six years being counted from such payment.

If a debtor owes his creditor several debts, some of which are barred by the statute of limitations, and some are not, and pays a sum without appropriating it to any particular debt, although the creditor can appropriate the sum so paid to the debts that are barred, he cannot thereby take them out of the operation of the statute.

Payment cannot revive the debt unless it be made by one who had authority to bind the debtor; thus, a payment by a wife, without specific authority from the husband, does not revive the debt as to him.

If the debt consists of principal and interest, a payment on account of either will take the whole residue of both out of the statute.

And if there be mutual accounts, and a balance be struck, it has been held that this converts the items allowed into a part payment, to take the case out of the statute.

The authorities are against the power of one to bind others who were formerly partners with him, by his acknowledgment of a barred partnership debt.

The period of limitation begins to run, in general, from the period when the creditor could have commenced his action.

Thus, if a credit is given, the six years begin when the credit expires; and if the money be payable on the happening of a certain event, the six years begin from the happening of the event.

If a demand be necessary to sustain an action, only after it is made does the statute begin.

But a note, payable "on demand," is due always, and the statute begins as soon as the note is made.

The statute begins to run whenever the creditor or plaintiff *could* bring his action, and not when he knew he could; thus it is said that if one promises to pay when able, as soon as he is able, the statute runs, although the creditor did not know it.

If the action rests on a breach of contract, it accrues as soon as the contract is broken, although no injury result from the breach till afterwards.

If money be payable by instalments, the statute begins to run as to each instalment from the time when it becomes due.

Exceptions.—The statute of James provides that if the plaintiff, at the time when the cause of action accrues, is within the age of twenty-one years, *feme covert, non compos mentis,* imprisoned, or beyond seas, he may bring his action at any time within six years after the disability ceases or is removed; hence the statute does not begin to run in such cases until after the disability is removed.

In general, if the statute begins to run, its operation can not afterwards be arrested. Thus, if the disability should not exist when the cause of action arose, but should begin one month afterwards, and remain, as if the creditor should go abroad and not return, the statute runs in the same way as if the disability never existed.

In cases of fraud, the prevailing rule prevents the six years from beginning to run, even at law, until the fraud is discovered by the plaintiff.

The statute affects the remedy only, and not the debt; for it only declares that " no action shall be maintained," and not that the cause of action is made void.

Hence, although the remedy by action is lost, a lien is not lost; therefore, if one hold a note, against which the statute has run, and also a mortgage or pledge of real or personal property, to secure it, he cannot sue the note, but he can take or hold possession of the property and sell it, if it be personal, with proper precautions; or have a bill in equity to foreclose his mortgage.

INTEREST AND USURY.—Usury is the taking of more interest for the use of money than the law allows.

The law affects a usurious contract with two consequences; one is the avoidance of the contract; the other is the penalty for the breach of the law.

The penalty is not incurred until usurious interest be in some way paid or received, although the contract may be avoided for this cause at any time.

If a contract is accidentally usurious, that is, made so by some mistake in calculation, or other error in fact, against the intention of the parties, the mistake may be corrected and the contract saved.

Contracts for compound interest are sometimes said to be usurious, but courts do not generally declare such contracts usurious; the extent to which they have gone is that of refusing to enforce a contract to pay interest thereafter to grow due, unless upon a promise of the debtor made *after* the interest, upon which interest is demanded has accrued.

Of late years, the aversion of law to allow money to *beget* money, has very much diminished; and probably a bargain in advance for the payment of compound interest, in all its facts reasonable and free from suspicion of oppression, would be enforced in court.

And it is now held that interest may be charged upon interest from the time it is payable.

DAMAGES.—The common law does not aim at preventing a breach of duty, or compelling fulfillment of a contract by direct means. This equity does.

As a general rule, the common law contents itself with requiring him who has done an injury to another to pay the injured party damages.

The principle which measures damages, at common law, is that of giving compensation for the injury sustained—a compensation which shall put the injured party in the same position in which he would have stood had he not been injured.

Liquidated damages.—The law will permit parties to determine, by an agreement which enters into the contract, what shall be the damages which he who violates the contract shall pay to the other; but it does not always sanction or enforce the bargain they may make on this subject.

Damages thus agreed upon beforehand, when sanctioned by the law, are called *liquidated damages.*

Where the parties make this agreement, but not in such wise that the law adopts it, then the damages thus agreed upon are a penalty, or in the nature of a penalty.

Where parties agree upon the damages to be paid for a breach of contract, whatever name they give it, they do substantially the same thing which is done by a bond, with penalty. And there is no more reason why the courts should regard the agreement, if it opposes reason and justice, in the one case than in the other.

It is, therefore, a rule that the action of the court shall not be defined and determined by the terms which the parties have seen fit to apply to the sum fixed upon. Though they call it a penalty, or give it no name at all, it will be treated as liquidated damages—that is, it will be recognized and enforced as the measure of damages, if, from the nature of the agreement and the surrounding circumstances, and in reason and justice, it ought to be.

And, although they call it liquidated damages, it will be treated as a penalty, if, from a consideration of the whole contract, it appears that the parties intended it as such.

Courts, then, are generally guided by the intentions of the parties in determining whether the sum contracted to be paid upon the non-performance of a covenant is to be considered as liquidated damages, to be enforced according to the terms of the agreement, or as a penalty to be controlled by an assessment of damages by a jury.

The principle of compensation is that which lies at the foundation of the common-law measurement of damages.

And this is not the less true, although there are difficulties in the application of this principle, and exact and adequate compensation is seldom the result of a law suit. Thus, the expenses of reaching this result, as counsel fees and the like, and the labor and anxiety even of successful litigation, are not often compensated.

The bodily pain resulting from an injury is always to be considered in estimating damages.

Exemplary or vindictive damages are such where, after a jury have gone to the full length of adequate compensation for the whole injury sustained by the plaintiff, the law authorizes them to begin anew, and add to these damages something more, by way of punishment to the defendant; hence, such damages *exceed* the measure of legal *compensation*.

"Vindictive" has been used as descriptive of these damages; but "exemplary" is much better.

Exemplary damages are such as go beyond a compensation or satisfaction for the plaintiff's injury.

From all injuries the law implies that damages are sustained.

Exemplary damages are generally confined to actions ex-delicto.

The court must state, as matter of law, in what kinds or classes of cases such damages may be given; the jury may then decide whether the case before them is of that kind or class.

Direct or remote consequences.—Damages will not, in

general, be given for the consequences of wrong-doing, which are not the natural consequences, because it is only for them that the defendant is held liable.

It is an ancient and universal rule, resting upon obvious reason and justice, that **a wrong-doer shall be held responsible only for the proximate, and not for the remote consequences of his actions**—the maxim being, *In jure, non remota causa sed proxima spectatur.*

It is a general principle, that **every defendant shall be held liable for all of those consequences which might have been foreseen and expected as the result of his conduct**, but not for those which he could not have foreseen, and was therefore under no moral obligation to take into consideration.

No action for damages will lie, unless an actual injury is either sustained, or inevitable; damages being a compensation for some actual injury sustained.

Nominal damages are given where a wrong is done, but no actual injury sustained.

In an action for a breach of contract, the breach, but not actual damage, being proved, nominal damages will be awarded.

If no actual injury has been sustained beyond that which the verdict and judgment will themselves correct, and the case does not call for exemplary damages, the jury would then be directed to give nominal damages, that is, a sum of insignificant value, but called damages.

LIEN is a right to hold possession of another's property, for the satisfaction of some charge attached to it.

The essence of this right is possession.

Lien is neither a *jus ad rem* nor a *jus in re*, but a simple right of retainer.

It is a universal rule that a prior lien gives a prior claim, which is entitled to prior satisfaction out of the subject it binds.

Liens exist by common law, or are created either by usage, by statute, or by express agreement of parties.

Continuance of possession being indispensable to the existence of liens at law, an abandonment of the custody of the property over which the right extends divests the lien.

In general, a lien confers no power to sell, even where the keeping would be attended with expense; but where the deposit is by way of security for a loan, the lender, it seems, may sell upon default of payment.

Taking other security for the debt will discharge a lien upon personal property. Security, however, may be received under such special circumstances as not to operate as a waiver of the lien.

As a general proposition, there can be no lien where credit is given.

Under ordinary circumstances, a lien is merged in a purchase of the property by the person holding possession under his lien.

No tortious possession can give a lien.

The usual cases in which the law creates a lien are where the person performing services would have no other sure remedy.

An attachment on mesne process does not exactly correspond to a lien; it is only a contingent conditional charge until the judgment and levy. The goods attached are in the custody of the law for the benefit of all parties concerned, and the plaintiff has not a lien on them.

Equitable liens are such which exist only in equity, as vendor's and vendee's lien in sales of real estate, lien by deposit of deeds, partnership liens and liens *pendente lite*.

A vendor's lien on land holds for any part of the purchase money which remains unpaid, against all persons except a purchaser for a valuable consideration without notice.

REMEDY IN EQUITY, OR SPECIFIC PERFORMANCE.—Courts of law can give no other remedy for breach of contract than damages, but courts of *equity* compel the party in fault to a specific performance of his undertaking.

The true purpose of equity is not to violate the law, but to fulfill its purpose by supplying those wants which render its administration of its own principles imperfect.

Equity has always preferred and professed to follow the law

In decreeing specific performance equity does but carry out the principles of the common law, giving that remedy which the courts of common law would give if their mode of administering justice were adapted to the case.

The most general rule which lies at the foundation of an

equitable decree for specific performance, and to which all other rules are or should be subordinate, is that **this equity arises whenever a contract is broken which was binding at law, and the remedy at law is plainly inadequate.**

It is only where the legal remedy is inadequate or defective that it becomes necessary for courts of equity to interfere.

In general, all the rules of construction and of evidence in equity are the same as at law, although they may be applied with greater freedom to the special merits of each case.

A rule of frequent occurrence in equity applies to many cases in which specific performance is sought: viz, that equity will consider that as done which ought to have been done.

The general purpose of equity is to moderate the rigor of law and supply its deficiencies, and bring it into harmony with conscience and moral justice.

Equity fully adopts the rule that no contract shall be enforced which does not rest upon a valuable consideration, but construes and applies it somewhat more rationally and less technically.

Generally, equity affords relief by enforcing the specific performance of *any* written contract, without reference to its subject-matter.

Effect of the statute of frauds in equity upon contracts.—In this country it is the prevailing rule that a part performance of an oral contract takes it out of the operation of the statute of frauds.

Law gives no relief where the mistake is one of law, or one arising from ignorance of law.

It was once intimated that the maxim "*Ignorantia legis neminem excusat*" applied only to crimes and public offences, but it is now agreed that it is of equal force in civil cases at law. Whether this rule has equal force in equity may not be quite so certain. It seems that equity gives relief in mistakes of law, where law would not, for courts generally may be regarded as having conclusively established the rules, subject, perhaps, to some qualifications in particular cases.

A contract cannot, in general, be rescinded for an innocent mistake, if the rescission will work an injustice to either party, or, in other words, if both parties cannot be replaced substantially in their former condition.

BANKRUPTCY AND INSOLVENCY.—It is settled

that the United States and the several States have a concurrent power to enact a bankrupt law or an insolvent law.

The several states may pass laws on this subject when there is no national law.

But a national law of this kind supersedes and suspends every state law.

In bankruptcy and insolvency, although the word "assignee" is used, it is inaccurate, as the property is transferred by the *law* and not by the owner, who is the only party who can assign.

It is the purpose of the insolvent laws to give to the creditors all they could take by attachment or levy, so it gives them nothing more.

Contracts, considered in relation to their substance, are either *commutative* or *independent, principal* or *accessory*.

Commutative contracts are those in which what is done, given or promised by one party is considered as equivalent to, or in consideration of, what is done, given or promised by the other.

Independent contracts are those in which the mutual acts or promises have no relation to each other, either as equivalents or as considerations.

A principal contract is one entered into by both parties, on their accounts, or in the several qualities they assume.

An accessory contract is made for assuring the performance of a prior contract, either by the same parties or by others, such as suretyship, mortgage, and pledges.

Eminent domain.—The law or right of eminent domain is the right reserved by a State or the government to resume the possession of property, or any part of it, whenever it shall be wanted for the use of the State; payment or compensation being made, or adequately provided for by law, for all that is thus resumed.

This is then a right reserved and possessed by the public, and a right which extends over all property.

If there be no public necessity, there is no public right; and land taken by the sovereign without such necessity, although for compensation, is unlawfully taken.

Whatever a citizen of this country owns, he holds in the same way as if he could trace his title back to an original grant from the sovereign or State.

PLEADINGS:

INCLUDING

PARTIES TO ACTIONS,

AND

FORMS OF ACTIONS.

ABRIDGED.

ANALYSIS.

Parties to actions.
 In form ex contractu.
  Plaintiffs.
  Defendants.
 In form ex delicto.
  Plaintiffs.
  Defendants.

Forms of action, in general, viz: real, personal, and mixed.
 In form ex contractu.
  Action of Assumpsit.
  " " Debt.
  " " Covenant.
  " " Detinue.
 In form ex delicto.
  Action on the Case.
  " of Trover.
  " " Replevin.
  " " Trespass.
  Action of Ejectment.
  Action for mesne profits.
  Mistake in form of action.
  Joinder of actions.
  Election of actions.

Pleading, in general.
  The facts necessary to be stated.
  Mode of stating facts.
  Rules for construing pleadings.
  Division of pleadings.
  General requisites or qualities of a plea.
 The declaration.
  General requisites or qualities of.
  Parts and particular requisites of.
  Conusance or cognizance of a suit.
  Oyer.
  Imparlance.
 Pleas Dilatory and Peremptory.
  Pleas in abatement.
  Pleas in bar.
  Defences to actions on contracts not under seal.
  Pleas by several defendants.
  Pleas of set-off.
 Replications.
  Parts of, viz: commencement, body, and conclusion.
  Denying a particular fact.
  New Assignment.
  Qualities of.
   Departure.
 Rejoinder, sur-rejoinder, rebutter, etc.
  Issue.
 Repleaders.
 Demurrers.
 Defects in pleading.
  Intendment.
  Cured by **verdict**.

PLEADINGS.

PLEADING is the statement, in a logical and legal form, of the facts which constitute the plaintiff's cause of action, or the defendant's ground of defence.—*Chitty.*

Pleadings are the mutual altercations between the plaintiff and defendant, reduced to writing.—*Blackstone.*

Pleadings are the proceedings, from the declaration to the issue joined.—*Wharton.*

PARTIES TO ACTIONS.

The general rule is, that **the action should be brought in the name of the party whose legal right has been affected**, against the party who committed or caused the injury, or by or against his personal representative.

In general, courts of law do not directly recognize *mere equitable* rights, but leave them to the protection of courts of *equity.* That rule, however, prevails more strictly as regards *real property* than with respect to injuries to the *person* or *personal property.*

ACTIONS IN FORM EX CONTRACTU.—Plaintiffs. In general, the action on a *contract*, whether express or implied, or whether by parol, or under seal, or of record, must be brought in the *name* of the party in whom the *legal interest* in such contract was vested, and, in general, with his *knowledge and concurrence*, or at least a sufficient indemnity must be tendered before his name can properly be used by the party beneficially interested.

The right of action at law has been vested solely in the party having the strict *legal* title and interest, in exclusion of the mere equitable claim.

In simple contracts, or instruments *not under seal*, it seems to be a general principle that the party for whose sole benefit it is evidently made may sue thereon in his own name, although the engagement be not directly to or with him.

In the case of bills of exchange and promissory notes there is an *option* of plaintiff that might be considered *an exception* to the general peremptory rule that the right of suing can only be in *one* person or set of persons: viz, that a party to a bill may, by arrangement between the parties, be the plaintiff, although the bill at the time be in the rightful possession of another party to the bill.

The action against a carrier for loss of goods sent by a vendor to a vendee must, in general, be brought in the name of the *latter*, and not of the consignor, because the law implies that by the delivery to the carrier, the goods became the property of the consignee, and at his risk, subject, of course, to the unpaid vendor's right of stoppage *in transitu.*

A mere servant or agent with whom a contract is expressly made on behalf of another, and who has no direct beneficial interest in the transaction, cannot, in general, support an action thereon.

But when an *agent* has any *beneficial interest* in the performance of the contract, as for commissions, etc., or a special property or interest in the subject-matter of the agreement, he may support an action in his own name upon the contract, as in the case of a factor, broker, warehouseman, carrier, auctioneer, etc.

When the contract was made with several persons, whether it were under seal, or in writing but not under seal, or by parol, *if their legal interest were joint,* they must all, if living, join in an action, in form *ex contractu,* for the breach of it, though the covenant or contract with them was in terms joint and several.

The reason assigned why all should join is that when the interest is joint, if several were permitted to bring several actions for one and the same cause, the court would be in doubt for which of them to give judgment.

But when the legal interest and cause of action of the covenantees are several, each *may* and *should* sue *separately* for the particular damages resulting to him individually, although the covenant be in its terms joint.

It is improper, as well in *equity* as at *law*, for a party to be joined in a suit who has neither legal nor beneficial interest in its subject-matter.

Where a covenant is made with two or more parties to pay them money for themselves or for the use of another, it is not correct to use the name of one only of the covenantees, although the others have omitted to execute the deed. Where joint covenantees *may* join, they must do so.

In the case of partners it is a general rule that all the members of the firm should be the plaintiffs in an action upon a contract made with the firm, nor can any private arrangement by the firm, that one only of the partners shall bring the action, give him a right to sue alone.

In the case of **dormant partners**, not privy to the contract, it seems that the other members of the firm *may omit* their names in an action.

If **tenants in common** (who hold by distinct titles) *jointly* demise premises, reserving an entire rent, they may, and perhaps should, join in an *action* to recover it; but if the rent be reserved to them separately in distinct parts, they must sue separately.

Joint tenants, unlike tenants in common, have a unity of title and interest, in respect of which they *must jointly* sue upon a contract relating to the estate, which is made by or enures to the benefit of all.

Parceners, for the same reason, must join in an action *ex contractu* which relates to their tenements.

The consequences of a mistake in *omitting* to join a party who ought to have been made a plaintiff in an action *ex contractu*, or in *adding* a party improperly in such an action, are extremely serious.

The general rule is that the omission of proper parties as plaintiffs in cases of contract may be taken advantage of at the trial under the general issue; and if it appear on the face of the pleadings, it is fatal on demurrer, or on motion in arrest of judgment, or on error; and though the objection may not appear on the face of the pleadings, the defendant may avail himself of it, either by a *plea in abatement* or as a ground of nonsuit.

If there be a legal ground for omitting to use the name of one of several covenantees as a plaintiff, as his death, etc., it is necessary to show such excuse for the nonjoinder in the declaration.

Where a party with whom a bond, simple contract, or other mere *personal* contract was made, has assigned his interest therein to a third person, the latter cannot, in general, sue in his own name, the interest in and remedy upon *personal* contracts being *choses in action*, which are not in general assignable at law, so as to give the assignee a right of action in his own name, but he must proceed in that of the assignor, or, if he be dead, in the name of his personal representative.

There are many instances in which, by express legislative provision, the assignee of a chose in action may sue in his own name to enforce the recovery of the demand. The operation of the bankrupt and insolvent act is to this effect.

By the custom of merchants the assignee or transferee of a bill of exchange or check on a banker may sue thereon in his own name.

When one or more of several obligees, covenantees, partners, or others having a *joint legal* interest in the contract, dies, the action must be brought in the name of the survivor, and the executor or administrator of the deceased must not be joined, nor can he sue separately, though the deceased alone might be entitled to the *beneficial* interest in the contract, and the executor must resort to a court of equity to obtain from the survivor the testator's share of the sum recovered; but if the interest of the covenantees were *several*, the executor of one of them may sue, though the other be living.

In the case of a mere *personal* contract, or of *a covenant not running with the land*, if it were made only with *one* person, and he be dead, the action for the breach of it must be brought in the name of his executor or administrator in whom the legal interest in such contract is vested.

But on a covenant relating to *realty*, as for good title on a deed of conveyance, an *executor* cannot sue even for a breach in the lifetime of his testator without showing some special damage to the *personal estate of the latter*, but the action must be brought in the name of the *heir* or *devisee*.

If an executrix or administratrix marry, she and her husband should join for the breach of any *personal* contract made with the deceased; but if she sue alone, the defendant cannot avail himself of the nonjoinder except by a plea in abatement; and when a bond or other contract is made to husband and wife as executrix, he may sue alone.

When an executor dies after he has proved the will, his executor, or the executor of such executor, is the party to sue on the contract made with the original testator, provided the money to be recovered would be the assets of the representative of the original testator himself; and the same rule applies in the case of the death of an administrator of the intestate. If the money to be recovered would be assets of the original testator, then, in case of the death of his first representative, administration *de bonis non* must be obtained, and the defendant sued accordingly.

In the case of bankruptcy, the *legal* rights of the bankrupt, arising from contracts made with him, and in the performance whereof the bankrupt is beneficially interested, are, by the express provisions of the Bankrupt Act, transferred to and vested in his assignees, who may recover the same *in their own names*. There are cases, however, in which the bankrupt may sue as trustee for his creditors.

In the case of insolvency, the Insolvent Debtor's Act directs that the prisoner shall, at the time of petitioning for relief, assign all the estate and effects he is then possessed of, and all future effects which may come to him, before he shall become entitled to his discharge, to the provisional assignee of the court; and that it shall be lawful for the provisional assignee to sue in his own name, *if the court shall so order,* for the recovering, obtaining and enforcing of any estate, debts, effects, or rights of any such prisoner.

The effect of marriage, at least in courts of *law,* is to deprive the wife of all separate legal existence, her husband and herself being in law but one person.

It is therefore a general rule, that she cannot, during the marriage, maintain an action without her husband; either upon contracts made by her before or after marriage, although they may be living apart under the provisions of a formal deed of separation, or by virtue of a divorce *a mensa et thoro* for adultery.

The exceptions are in the instance of a divorce *a vinculo matrimonii,* or where the husband is dead in law.

All chattels personal of the wife in possession are by marriage absolutely given to the husband, and for the recovery of them he may sue alone; and it is a general principle "that *that* which the husband may discharge alone, and of which he may make disposition to his own use, for the recovery of this he may sue without his wife."

As mere *choses in action* of the wife do not by the marriage vest absolutely in the husband until he reduce them in possession, and if not reduced into possession, she would take them by survivorship. In general, he cannot sue alone, but must join his wife in all actions upon bonds, and other personal contracts made with the wife *before* the marriage, whether the breach were before or during coverture; and also for rent or any other cause of action accruing before the marriage, in respect of the real estate of the wife.

When the wife is executrix or administratrix, as her interest is in *autre droit*, the husband must, in general, join in an action.

In general, the wife cannot join in an action upon a contract made during the marriage, as for her work and labor, goods sold, or money lent by her during that time; for the husband is entitled to her earnings, and they shall not survive to her, but go to the personal representatives of the husband, and she could have no property in the money lent or the goods sold.

But when the wife can be considered as the *meritorious* cause of action, as of a bond or other contract under seal, or a promissory note, be made to her separately, or with her husband, or if she bestow her personal labor and skill in curing a wound etc., she may join with the husband, or he may sue alone.

Where the wife is joined in the action, in these cases, the declaration must distinctly disclose her interest, and show in what respect she is the meritorious cause of action, and there is no intendment to this effect.

For rent, or other cause of action, accruing during the marriage, or a lease or demise, or other contract, relating to the land or other real property of the wife, whether such contract were made before or during the coverture, the husband and wife may *join*, or *he may sue alone*.

If the husband survive, there is a material distinction between chattels real and *choses in action*. The husband is entitled to the chattel real by survivorship, and to all rent, etc., accruing during the coverture; and also to all chattels given to the wife during the coverture, in her *own* right.

But mere *choses in action*, or contracts made with the wife before coverture, do not survive to the husband, and he must, to recover the same, sue as administrator of his wife.

If the wife survive, she is entitled to all chattels real which her husband had in her right, and which he did not dispose of in his life-time, and to arrears of *rent*, etc., which became due during the coverture, upon her antecedent demise, or upon their joint demise, during the coverture to which she assents after his death, and to all arrears of rent and other *choses in action* to which she was entitled before the covertures, and which the husband did not reduce into actual possession.

The consequences of a mistake in the proper parties, in the case of *baron* and *feme*, are, that when a married woman might be joined in the action with her husband, but sues alone, the objection can only be pleaded in abatement, and not in bar, though the husband might sustain a writ of error, and if she marry after writ, and before plea, her coverture must be pleaded in abatement, and cannot be given in evidence under the general issue.

But when a *feme* improperly sues alone, having no legal right of action, she will be nonsuited; and if she improperly join in an action with her husband, who ought to sue alone, the defendant may demur, or the judgment will be arrested, or reversed on a writ of error.

And if the husband sue alone, when the wife ought to be joined, either in her own right, or in *autre droit*, he will be nonsuited; or if the objection appear on the record, it will be fatal in arrest of judgment, or on error.

DEFENDANTS.—In general, the action upon an *express* contract, whether it be by deed or merely in writing, or by parol, must be brought against *the party who made it*, either in person or by agent.

A party who expressly contracts, and permits credit to be given to him, is liable, although he were not the strict *legal owner* of the property in respect of which the contract is made, nor *beneficially* interested.

Difficulties frequently occur in deciding who should be made the defendant in an action upon a promise created or *implied by law* from a particular state of facts. **In this case it must be ascertained who is the party subject to the legal liability, for he is the person who should be sued.**

A mere equitable or moral obligation to pay a demand

is, in the absence of an express promise, insufficient to support an action.

A contract made by an agent, as such, is, in law, the contract of the principal; the general rule, therefore, is that when a person has contracted, in the capacity of an *agent*, and that circumstance is known at the time to the person with whom he contracts, such agent is not liable to an action for non-performance of the contract, even for a deceitful warranty, if he had authority from his principal to make the contract.

If an agent covenant under seal for the act of another, though he describe himself in the deed as contracting for and on the part and behalf of such other person; or if he accept or draw a bill of exchange generally and not as agent, he is personally liable, unless in the case of an agent on behalf of government.

In general, where an agent enters into a written agreement as if he were the principal, and the credit is given to him, he is personally liable; but this liability must be collected from the instrument upon a reasonable exposition of the whole of its terms.

Where the agent does not, at the time the contract is made, disclose that he is acting merely as an agent, and the principal is unknown, the latter may, when discovered, be sued upon the agreement.

But the principal is not liable upon the contract of his agent, if the other party to the agreement, with full knowledge of the facts, and the power and means of deciding to whom he will give credit, elect to give credit to the agent only, in his individual character.

At law, one partner or tenant in common cannot in general sue his co-partner, or co-tenant, in any action in form *ex contractu*; but must proceed by action of account, or by bill in equity.

It is an answer to an action that a party is *legally interested in each side of the question.* A party cannot be both plaintiff and defendant in an action. If, therefore, one of the plaintiffs be also a member of the firm against which the action is brought, upon a contract entered into by the firm, the action shall fail, although the other partners only be sued.

A lunatic is liable for goods suitable to his rank, supplied to him upon a contract which a person, not aware of his infirmity, *bona fide* enters into with him.

The rule is, that several persons contracting together with the same party, for one and the same act, shall be regarded as jointly and not individually or separately liable, in the absence of any express words to show that a distinct as well as entire liability was intended to fasten upon the promisers. This rule is more particularly obvious in the case of promises *implied* by law.

Where there are several parties, **if their contract be joint**, they must all be made defendants, although they subsequently arrange amongst themselves that one only of them shall perform the contract.

Where the covenant or promise is so framed that it does not confer upon the plaintiff a remedy against the contractors jointly, but each is only *separately* responsible for his own act, it is essential to sue them distinctly; but where it appears upon an instrument that a promise by two contractors was *intended* to be *joint*, it may be treated as such, although the promise be *in terms* several only.

When the contract is several as well as joint, the plaintiff is at liberty to proceed against the parties jointly or each separately, though their interest be joint. But if there be more than two parties to a joint and several contract, as where three obligors are jointly and severally bound, the plaintiff must either sue them all jointly or each of them separately.

In general, when a contract is joint and several, if the debt be considerable, it is most advisable to proceed separately, so that the creditor may thereby retain his legal remedies against each, in case of death of one or more of the parties.

Courts of law, as well as equity, will not take cognizance of distinct and separate claims or liabilities of different persons in suit, though standing in the same relative situations; therefore, in an action *ex contractu* against several, it must appear on the face of the pleadings that their contract was joint, and that fact must also be proved on the trial.

Mis-joinder in an action founded on a contract. **If too many persons be made defendants**, and the objection appear on the pleadings, either of the defendants may demur, move in arrest of judgment, or support a writ of error; and even if the objection do not appear upon the pleadings, the plaintiff may be nonsuited upon the trial if he fail in proving a joint contract.

The consequences of the joinder of too many defendants in an action founded on a *contract* are in general so important, it is advisable in cases where it is doubtful how many parties are liable, to proceed only against those defendants who are certainly liable; in which case *non-joinder* can only be taken advantage of by a plea in abatement.

In general, in the case of a mere personal contract, the action for the breach of it cannot be brought against a person to whom the contracting party has assigned his interest, and the original party alone can be sued.

There may, however, in some cases be a *change of credit*, by agreement between the parties, so as to transfer the liability from the original contracting party to another, or to one only of the original parties.

In the case of a *joint* contractor, if one of the parties die, his executor or administrator is *at law* discharged from liability, and the survivor alone can be sued; and if the executor be sued, he may either plead the survivorship in bar, or give it in evidence under the general issue; but in equity the executor of the deceased party is liable, unless in some instances of a surety.

If the contract were several, or joint and several, the executor of the deceased may be sued at law in a separate action; but he cannot be sued jointly with the survivor, because one is to be charged *de bonis testatoris*, and the other *de bonis propriis*.

When the contracting party is dead, his executor or administrator, or in case of a joint contract, the executor or administrator of the survivor, is the party to be made defendant, and is liable, though not expressly named in the covenant or contract.

If the contract is under seal (or of record), the *heir* of the party contracting is liable to an action for the breach of an *express* covenant therein; provided the ancestor expressly bound himself "and his heir," by the deed or obligation; and provided the heir have *legal* assets by descent from the obligor.

When the contracting party has become bankrupt, and has obtained his certificate, he is in general no longer liable to be sued in respect of any debt due from him when he became bankrupt, or of any claim or demand which the creditor might have proved under the commission.

By the insolvent act an insolvent complying with the requisitions of the act is to be discharged by the court from his liabilities.

In general, a feme covert cannot be sued alone at law; and when a *feme sole*, who has entered into a contract, marries, the husband and wife must be jointly sued.

When the husband survives, he is not liable to be sued in that character for any contract of the *feme* made before coverture, unless judgment had been obtained against him and his wife before her death; if she die before judgment, the suit will abate.

But if the husband neglects, during her life, to reduce her *choses in action* into possession, the creditor may sue the person who administers thereto, for debts due before her marriage, and for rent accruing during the coverture; or for money due upon a judgment obtained against husband and wife he may be sued alone as the survivor.

In case the wife survive, she may be sued upon all her unsatisfied contracts made before coverture.

If the husband be sued alone upon the contract of his wife before coverture, and the objection appear upon the face of the declaration, the defendant may demur, move in arrest of judgment, or bring a writ of error. If the contract were misdescribed as being that of the husband, the plaintiff would be nonsuited under the general issue at the trial, upon the ground of variance between the contract stated in the declaration and that proved. But if the wife be sued alone upon her contract before marriage, she must plead her coverture in abatement, or a writ of *error coram nobis* must be brought; and the coverture in such case cannot be pleaded in bar, or given in evidence upon the trial as a ground of nonsuit; and if she marry pending an action against her, it will not abate, but the plaintiff may proceed to execution without noticing the husband. But if a *feme covert* be sued upon her supposed contract made during coverture, she may in general plead the coverture in bar, or give it in evidence under the general issue, or under *non est factum*, in the case of a deed. And if the husband and wife be improperly sued jointly on a contract after marriage, the action will fail as to both.

ACTIONS IN FORM EX-DELICTO.—Plaintiffs.—The action for a tort must, in general, be brought in the name of the person whose *legal* right has been affected, and who was *legally* interested in the property at the time the injury was committed.

A *cestui que trust*, or other person, having only an *equitable* interest, cannot, in general, sue in the courts of common law against his trustee, or even a third person, unless in cases where the action is against a mere wrong-doer, and for an injury to the actual possession of the *cestui que trust*.

Many of the rules and instances which have been stated in respect to the person to be made the plaintiff in actions in form *ex-contractu*, here also govern and are applicable.

Actions in form *ex-delicto*, are for injuries to the *absolute* or *relative* rights of *persons*, or to *personal* or *real property*.

With respect to injuries to the relative rights of persons, in the case of *master and servant*, the master may sue alone for the battery of, or for debauching, his servant, although they are not related, where there is evidence to prove a consequent loss of service; and a father may sue for the seduction of his daughter, although she was married, provided some loss of service can be proved.

The wife, the child, and the servant, having no legal interest in the person or property of the husband, or parent, or master, cannot support an action for an injury to them.

The action for an injury to the absolute rights of persons, as for assaults, batteries, wounding, injuries to the health, liberty, and reputation, can only be brought in the name of the party immediately injured; and if he die, the remedy determines.

The *absolute* or *general* owner of *personal* property, having also the right of immediate possession, may, in general, support an action for any injury thereto, although he never had the actual possession.

An action for an injury to personalty may also be brought in the name of the person having only a *special* property or interest of a limited or temporary nature therein. But in this case, the general rule seems to be that the party should have had the actual possession.

There are cases in which a party having the *bare possession* of goods, which is *prima facie* evidence of property, may sue a mere wrong-doer who takes or injures them, although it should appear that the plaintiff has not the strict legal title, there being no claim by the real owner, and the defendant having no right or authority from him.

The person in possession of real property *corporeal*, whether lawfully or not, may sue for an injury committed by a stranger, or by any person who cannot establish a better title; and in trespass to land, the person actually in possession, though he be only a *cestui que trust*, should be the plaintiff and not the trustee. But the rule is otherwise in ejectment, which is an action to try the right; and the fictitious demise must be in the name of the party legally entitled to the possession, although the beneficial interest may be in another, and according to the strict nature of the right; thus, tenants in common *cannot* join but must *sever*, in separate demises, in a declaration in ejectment.

When two or more persons are jointly entitled, or have a *joint legal interest* in the property affected, they must, in general, join in the action, or the defendant may plead in *abatement*.

Several parties cannot, in general, sue jointly for injuries to the *person*—as for slander, battery, or false imprisonment of both—but each must bring a separate action.

In actions for injuries to *personal property*, joint tenants and tenants in common must join, or the defendant may plead in abatement; but parties having several and distinct interests cannot, in general, join.

In actions for injuries to *real* property, joint tenants and parceners must join in real as well as personal actions, or the non-joinder may be pleaded in abatement.

Of the consequences of non-joinder in actions, in form *ex delicto* which are not for the breach of a contract, the rule is that if a party who ought to be joined be omitted, the objection can only be taken by plea in abatement, or by way of apportionment of the damages on the trial; and the defendant cannot, as in actions in form *ex contractu*, give in evidence the non-joinder, as a ground of non suit, on the plea of a general issue, or demur, or move in arrest of judgment, or support a writ of error, although it appear upon the face of the declaration or other pleading of the plaintiff that there is another party who ought to have joined.

The consequences of mis-joinder.—If *too many* persons be made co-plaintiffs the objection, if it appear on the record, may be taken advantage of, either by demurrer, in arrest of judgment, or by writ of error; or if the objection do not appear on the face of the pleadings, it would be a ground of nonsuit on the trial.

We have seen that *choses in action ex contractu* are not in general assignable at law, so as to enable the assignee to sue in his own name; the same rule prevails in case of injuries *ex delicto*, either to the person or to personal or real property.

When one or more of several parties jointly interested in the property at the time the injury was committed, is dead, the action should be in the name of the survivor, and the executor or administrator of the deceased cannot be joined, nor can he sue separately. But if the parties had separate interests in respect of which they might have severed in suing, the personal representative of the deceased may maintain a separate action, provided the *tort* was not of such a nature that it died with the person.

We have seen that the right of action for the breach of a *contract* upon the *death* of either party, in general, survives to and against the executor and administrator of each; but in the case of *torts*, when the action must be in form *ex delicto*, for the recovery of damages, and the plea not guilty, the rule at common law was otherwise; it being a maxim that *actio personalis moritur cum persona*. By statute this rule has been altered in relation to *personal property*, and in favor of the personal representative of the *party injured;* but if the action can be framed in form *ex contractu*, this rule does not apply.

In the case of injuries to the person, whether by assault, battery, false imprisonment, slander, or otherwise, if either party who received or committed the injury die, no action can be supported, either by or against the executors or other personal representatives.

So, also, with respect to injuries to *real* property, if either party die, no action in form *ex delicto* could be supported either by or against his personal representatives. But statutes have introduced a material alteration in the common law doctrine, as well *in favor* of executors and administrators of the party injured, as *against* the personal representatives of the party injured, but respects only injuries to *personal* and *real property*, and subject to certain *restrictions* as regards the commencement of an action for such injury within a *short time after the death*, and declaring that the damages to be recovered from an executor or administrator shall be ranked or classed with *simple contract debts*.

In case of bankruptcy, when the injury consists in the unlawful detention of any part of the bankrupt's *real* or *personal* property, the assignees may bring actions for the purpose of recovering the possession or value thereof; but for mere *personal torts* to the *bankrupt*, no right of action passes to the assignee.

In case of insolvency, the rules upon this subject appear to be analogous to those in case of bankruptcy.

In the case of marriage, the wife having no legal interest in the person or property of her husband, cannot, in general, join with him in any action for an injury to them, except in an action for a joint malicious prosecution of both, in which they may join in respect of an injury to both, or the husband may sue alone for the injury to himself and expenses of defense.

For injuries to the person, or to the personal or real property of the wife, committed *before* the marriage, when the cause of action would survive to the wife, she *must* join in the action, and if she die before judgment therein, it will abate.

But in detinue to recover personal chattels of the wife, in the possession of the defendant before the marriage, perhaps the husband must sue alone, because the law transfers the property to him.

When an injury is committed to the *person* of the wife, *during coverture,* the wife cannot sue alone in any case; and the husband and wife *must* join if the action be brought for the personal suffering or injury to the wife, and in such case the declaration ought to conclude to their damage, and not that of the husband alone; for the damages will survive to the wife if the husband die before they are recovered.

With respect to personal property, when the cause of action had only its inception before the marriage but its completion afterwards; as in case of trover before marriage and conversion during it, or of rent due before marriage, and a rescue afterwards, the husband and wife may join, or they may sever in trover or trespass. In detinue, it seems the husband should sue alone.

When the cause of action has its inception, as well as completion, after the marriage, the husband must sue alone.

In *real* actions for the recovery of the land of the wife, and in a writ of waste thereto, the husband and wife must join; but for damages or a tort, the husband may sue alone.

If the husband survive, he may maintain an action of trespass, etc., for any injury in regard to the person or property of the wife, for which he might have sued alone during the coverture.

If the wife survive, any action for a *tort* committed to her personally, or to her goods or real property before marriage, or to her personal or real property during coverture, will survive to her.

The consequences of a mistake in the proper parties in the case of husband and wife, seem to be nearly the same in actions in form *ex delicto*, as in those *ex contractu*.

DEFENDANTS.—In *personal* or *mixed* actions, in form *ex delicto*, the person committing the injury, either by himself or his agent, is, in general, to be made the defendant; but *real* actions can only be supported against the claimant of the freehold.

The general rule is, that all persons are liable to be sued for their own tortious acts, unconnected with, or in disaffirmance of, a contract.

It is a clear general rule that *corporations* are liable to be sued as such, in case or trover for any *torts* they may cause to be committed; and corporations and incorporated companies may be sued in that character, for damages arising from the breach by them of a duty imposed by law.

An action cannot be maintained against a judge or justice of the peace, acting *judicially* in a matter within the scope of his jurisdiction, although he may decide erroneously; nor against a juryman, attorney-general, or a superior military or naval officer, for an act done in the execution of their respective offices.

With regard to joint tenants and tenants in common of realty, the general rule appears to be that ejectment will lie by one against the other only in the case of an *actual* ouster; and after a recovery in such action, trespass for mesne profits may be brought. So, trespass will lie where there has been a total destruction of the subject-matter of the tenancy in common.

With respect to a tenancy in common of a chattel, the rule is that one tenant in common cannot sue his co-tenant if he merely take the chattel away; for in law the possession of one is the possession of both, and each has equally a right to take and retain such possession. But if one of the tenants in common destroy, misuse, or spoil the chattel, the other may maintain an action at law.

If a *third* person collude with one partner in a firm to injure the other partners in their joint trade, the latter may maintain a joint action against the person so colluding.

All persons who direct or order the commission of a trespass, or the conversion of personal property, or assist upon the occasion, are in general liable *as principals,* though not benefited by the act.

On principles of public policy a *sheriff* is liable *civilly* for the tortious acts of his under-sheriff, in the course of the execution of their duties.

The distinctions with regard to the liabilities of the owners of *animals,* are important, particularly as they affect the form of the action.

The owner of domestic or other animals, not naturally inclined to commit mischief, as dogs, horses, oxen, etc., is not liable for any injury committed by them to the person or personal property, unless it can be shown that he had previous notice of the animal's mischievous propensities, or that the injury was attributable to some other neglect on his part; and though notice can be proved, the action must be *case,* and not *trespass.*

The liability to an action in respect of *real* property may be for misfeasance, or malfeasance, or for nonfeasance. In these cases the action should, in general, be against the party who did the act complained of, or against the occupier, and not against the owner, if the premises were in possession of his tenant, unless he be covenanted to repair.

An agent, or servant, though acting *bona fide* under the directions and for the benefit of his employer, is personally liable to third persons for any tort or trespass he may commit in the execution of the orders he has received.

An attorney, acting *bona fide* and professionally, may not be personally liable in cases where he does not exceed the line of his duty.

It is an established rule that an action does not lie against a steward, manager, or agent, for damage done by the negligence of those employed by him in the service of his principal, but the principal, or those actually employed, alone can be sued.

There are some torts which in legal consideration may be committed by several, and for which a joint action may be supported against all the parties. Thus a *joint* action may be brought against several for a malicious prosecution, assault and battery, publishing a libel, etc.; but if in legal consideration the act complained of *could not have been committed by several persons*, and can only be considered the tort of the actual aggressor, or the distinct tort of each, a separate action against the actual wrong-doer only, or against each, must be brought. Therefore a joint action cannot be supported against two for verbal slander, etc.

The consequences of mis-joinder or non-joinder.—If several persons be made defendants jointly, where the tort *could not*, in point of law, be joint, they may demur, and if verdict be taken against all, the judgment may be arrested or reversed on a writ of error; but the objection may be aided by the plaintiffs taking a verdict against only one; or if several damages be assessed against each by entering a *nolle prosequi* as to one after verdict and before judgment.

In other cases where in point of fact and of law several persons *might have been jointly guilty of the same offence*, the joinder of more persons than were liable in a personal or mixed action in *form ex delicto*, constitutes no objection to a partial recovery, and one of them may be acquitted, and a verdict taken against the others.

On the other hand, if several persons jointly commit a tort, the plaintiff in general has his election to sue all or some of the parties jointly, or one of them separately, because a *tort is in its nature a separate act* of each individual.

In actions in form ex delicto, against one only, for a tort committed by several, he cannot plead the non-joinder of the others in abatement or bar, or give it in evidence under the general issue; for a plea in abatement can only be adopted in those cases where regularly all the parties *must* be joined, and not where the plaintiff *may* join them all, or not, at his election.

This rule applies only in actions for torts, strictly unconnected with contract.

A recovery against one of several parties who *jointly* committed a tort, precludes the plaintiff from proceeding against any other party not included in such action.

As in the case of a breach of a covenant, so in that of torts, the *assignee* of the estate is not liable for an injury resulting from any nuisance, or wrongful act, committed thereon before he came to the estate; but if he *continue* the nuisance, he may be sued for such continuance.

At common law, upon the death of the wrong-doer, the remedy for torts unconnected with contracts in general, determines; and, until statutory provision, no action could be supported against the executor or administrator of the party who committed the injury. Many of the preceding observations on the rule *actio personalis moritur cum persona,* in its relation to the death of *plaintiffs* are equally applicable to the case of the death of the wrong-doer.

For injuries to the person, if the wrong-doer die before judgment, the remedy determines, and there is no instance of an action having been supported for such injuries against his personal representatives.

In general, also, no action in form *ex delicto* could, before statutory provision, be supported against an executor for an injury to *personal property* committed by his testator.

For injuries to *real* property no action in form *ex delicto* could, in general, be supported against the personal representatives of the wrong-doer; but a court of equity will frequently afford relief against the executor of the wrong-doer.

The bankrupt act does not contain any provision enabling a person injured by any personal tort, committed by the bankrupt before his bankruptcy, to obtain remuneration from the funds of the bankrupt, which become vested in the assignees for the benefit of the creditors.

The same rule holds in the case of an insolvent, as in the instance of a bankrupt, with regard to a claim for *damages* for a *tort* committed by the insolvent.

In case of marriage, action for torts committed by a woman, before her marriage, must be brought against the husband and wife jointly. So also for torts committed by the wife *during* coverture. But the plaintiff cannot in the same action proceed also for slander or other tort committed by the husband alone; nor can the husband and wife be sued jointly for slander by both.

The consequences of mistake, in the cases of *baron* and *feme* are if the wife be sued alone for her tort before or after marriage, she must plead her coverture in abatement, and cannot otherwise take advantage of it; but if the husband and wife be sued jointly for torts, of which they could not in law be jointly guilty, as for slander by both, if the objection appear on the face of the declaration, the defendant may demur, move in arrest of judgment, or support a writ of error.

FORMS OF ACTIONS.

It is no longer necessary, as formerly, to state the whole cause of action and form of complaint **in the writ**, yet it is still necessary for the practitioner to decide on the proper *form of action* to be adopted, and to state it, though very concisely, in the writ, and which form of action must afterwards be adhered to in the declaration, or the latter will be set aside for irregularity.

Actions are, from their subject-matter, distinguished into *real, personal,* and *mixed.*

Real actions are for the specific recovery of real property only, and in which the plaintiff, then called the defendant, claims title to lands, tenements, or hereditaments, in fee-simple, fee-tail, or term for life—such as writs of right, formedon, dower, etc.

Personal actions are for the recovery of a debt or damages, for the breach of a contract, or a specific personal chattel, or a satisfaction in damages for some injury to the person, personal or real property.

Mixed actions partake of the nature of the other two, the plaintiff proceeding for the specific recovery of some real property, and also for damages for an injury thereto.

Personal actions are in form *ex contractu*—in other words, for breach of *contract;* or, *ex delicto,* for *wrongs* unconnected with contract.

Actions ex contractu, or upon *contracts,* are principally *assumpsit, debt, covenant,* and *detinue.*

Actions ex delicto, or for *wrongs* or *torts,* are *case, trover, replevin,* and *trespass, vi et armis.*

ACTIONS IN FORM EX CONTRACTU.—Assumpsit is an action for the recovery of damages for the non-performance of a parol or simple contract, or, in other words, a contract not under seal, nor of record. It is not sustainable, however, unless there has been an *express contract,* or unless the law will *imply* a contract.

It is not judicious to adopt this form of action where the plaintiff may declare in tort in cases where, by suing *ex contractu,* the right of set-off may attach.

The general issue or most general plea in this action, is *non-assumpsit.*

Debt is an action so-called because it **is in legal consideration for the recovery of a debt eo nomine and in numero**, and though *damages* are in general awarded for the detention of the debt, in most instances they are merely nominal.

It is a more extensive remedy for the recovery of money than assumpsit or covenant, for *assumpsit* is not sustainable upon a specialty, and *covenant* does not lie upon a contract not under seal; whereas *debt* lies to recover money due upon legal liabilities, or upon simple contracts, express or implied, written or verbal, and upon contracts under seal, or of record, on statutes by a party grieved, or by common informer; and **whenever the demand is for a sum certain, or capable of being reduced to a certainty.**

Though debt lies, as a general rule, for a sum certain, yet it is the proper remedy for a penalty imposed by statute, though the amount is uncertain, and is to be fixed by the court between certain sums.

The action of debt cannot be supported for a debt payable by installments till the whole of them be due, though for rent payable quarterly, or otherwise, or for an annuity, or on stipulation to pay a certain amount on one day, and a certain amount on another, debt lies on each default, and even where one sum is payable by installments, if the payment be secured by a penalty, debt is sustainable for such penalty.

Formerly the *plea* of the general issue in this action was *nil debet*. But now in actions of debt on simple contract, other than on bills of exchange and promissory notes, the defendant pleads "that he *never was* indebted in manner and form as in the declaration alleged," etc.; in debt on specialty, the plea denying the execution of the deed set out in the declaration, is *non est factum*; and to debt on record, *nul tiel record*.

Covenant is an action and remedy provided by law for the recovery of damages for the breach of a covenant or contract under seal.

Covenant and debt are concurrent remedies for the recovery of any *money* demand, where there is an express or implied contract in an instrument under seal to pay it; but in general, debt is the preferable remedy, as in that form of action the judgment is final in the first instance, if the defendant do not plea

Covenant is the *peculiar* remedy for the non-performance of a contract made under seal, where the damages are unliquidated, and depend in amount on the opinion of the jury, in which case neither debt nor *assumpsit* can be supported.

The usual plea in this action is *performance with leave*, etc.

Detinue is the action and only remedy by suit at law for the recovery of a personal chattel in specie, except in those instances where the party can obtain possession by replevying the same, and by action of replevin.

This action is somewhat peculiar in its nature, and it may be difficult to decide whether it should be classed amongst forms of action *ex contractu*, or should be ranked with actions *ex delicto*.

The right to join detinue with debt, and to sue in detinue for not delivering goods in pursuance of the terms of a bailment to the defendant, seem to afford ground for considering it rather as an action *ex contractu*, than an action of tort.

On the other hand, it seems that detinue lies, although the defendant wrongfully became the possessor thereof in the first instance, without any relation to any contract.

This action is only sustainable for the recovery of a specific chattel, and not for real property. The goods for which it is brought must be distinguishable from other property, and their identity ascertainable by some certain means, so that if the plaintiff recover, the sheriff may be able to deliver the goods to him.

It seems to be a general rule that the plaintiff must have a general or special property in the goods, *at the time the action was commenced*, in order to maintain detinue.

The gist or main point of this action is the wrongful detainer, and not the original taking.

In pleading it is usual to state that the defendant acquired the goods by *finding*, except where he is declared against as a bailee; —yet that allegation is not traversable; and it was observed in a case, that, if detinue could not be supported because the original taking was tortious, a person might be greatly injured, and have no adequate remedy; for in trover damages only can be recovered, and the thing detained may be of such a description that a judgment merely for damages would be an inadequate satisfaction.

With respect to the *pleadings* in this action, *more certainty* is necessary in the *description* of the chattels than in an action of trover or replevin.

The plea of the general issue in this action is *non detinet*. This action is now not much used, having given place to that of trover in practice.

ACTIONS IN FORM EX DELICTO.—Personal actions in form *ex delicto*, and which are principally for the redress of wrongs unconnected with contract, are case, trover, replevin, and trespass *vi et armis*.

Mixed actions are ejectment, waste, etc.

If the injury be *forcible*, and occasioned *immediately* by the act of the defendant, trespass *vi et armis* is the proper remedy; but if the injury be not in legal contemplation *forcible*, or *not direct* and *immediate* on the act done, but only *consequential*, then the remedy is by *action on the case*.

Injuries ex delicto are in legal consideration committed *with force*, as assaults, batteries, etc., or *without force*, as slander, etc. They are also either *immediate and direct* or *mediate and consequential*.

Force is in legal consideration either *implied* by law or *actual;* force is implied in every trespass, *quare clausum fregit*.

The distinction is material; an injury is considered *immediate* when the act complained of *itself*, and not merely a consequence of that act, occasions the injury.

But where the damage or injury ensued not directly from the act complained of, it is termed *consequential* or mediate, and cannot amount to a *trespass*.

Where the act occasioning an injury is unlawful, the intent of the wrong-doer is immaterial.

It is a general rule that if a party be in the prosecution of a legal act **an action does not lie for an injury resulting from an inevitable or unavoidable accident** which occurs without *any* blame or default on his part.

Action on the case lies generally to recover damages for torts not committed with force, actual or implied; or having been occasioned by force, where the matter affected was not tangible, or the injury was not immediate, but consequential, in which cases trespass is not sustainable.

Case is the proper remedy for an injury to the *absolute rights of persons* not immediate, but consequential, also for injuries to the *relative* rights of persons, except where really committed with force, when *trespass* is the proper remedy.

For injuries to personal property, not committed with

force or not immediate, or where the plaintiff's right thereto is in reversion, *case* is also the proper remedy.

Where there is an express promise and a legal obligation results from it, then the plaintiff's cause of action is most accurately described in *assumpsit*, in which the promise is stated as the gist of the action.

But where from a given state of facts the law raises a legal obligation and a consequential damage, there, although *assumpsit* may be maintainable upon a promise implied by law to do the act, still **an action on the case founded in tort** is the more proper form of action, in which the plaintiff in his declaration states the facts out of which the legal obligation arises, the obligation itself, the breach of it, and damage resulting from that breach.

Where injuries to *real property corporeal* are immediate and committed on the land, etc., in the possession of the plaintiff, the remedy is trespass; but where the injury is not immediate, but consequential, or where the plaintiff's property is only in reversion, and not in possession, the action should be in case.

The *plea* in this action is principally the general issue, *not guilty*.

Action of trover, or *conversion*, was in its origin an action of trespass, on the case for the recovery of damages against a person who had *found* goods and refused to deliver them on demand to the owner, but *converted* them to his own use, from which word *finding* (trover) the remedy is called an action of trover.

The injury lies in the conversion and deprivation of the plaintiff's property, which is the *gist* of the action, which action is for the recovery of *damages* to the extent of the value of the thing converted.

The object and result of the suit are not the recovery of the thing itself, which can only be recovered by action of detinue or replevin.

Lord Mansfield thus defines this action: "In *form* it (i. e. the trover) is a fiction; in *substance* it is a remedy to recover the value of personal chattels wrongfully converted by another to his own use."

The action is confined to the conversion of goods or personal chattels.

To support this action the plaintiff must, at the time of the conversion, have had a complete *property*, either *general* or *special*, in the chattel, and also *actual possession*, or the *right* to the *immediate possession* of it.

In the case of a conversion by wrongfully taking, it is not necessary to prove a demand and refusal; proof of the wrongful act is sufficient to establish the conversion; but a demand and refusal are necessary in *some* cases, as where the defendant became, in the first instance, lawfully possessed of the goods, etc.

For a wrongful taking of goods, trover is, in general, a concurrent remedy with trespass; but the converse does not hold, for trover may often be brought where trespass cannot.

The general issue in this action is, *not guilty*.

Action of replevin is that whereby the owner of goods unjustly taken and detained from him may regain possession thereof through the medium of and upon application to the sheriff, upon giving him security to prosecute an action against the person who seized. It is principally used in cases of distress, but it seems that it may be brought in any case where the owner has goods taken from him by another.

This action is of two sorts, in the **detinet**, where goods are still detained by the person who took them, to recover the value thereof and damages; and in the **detinuit,** for the recovery of *damages* only, for the taking of the goods, and for the detention till the time of the replevy, and not the value of the goods themselves. The former is now obsolete.

Replevin can only be supported for taking personal chattels, and not for taking things attached to the freehold, and which are in law considered fixtures, and cannot be delivered to the distrainor upon a writ of *retorno habendo*.

To support replevin the plaintiff must, at the time of the caption, have had either the general property in the goods taken, or a special property therein.

If the plaintiff has not the immediate right of possession, replevin cannot be supported, but the party must proceed by an action on the case.

In order to maintain replevin the plaintiff must prove either a tortious taking or a tortious detention of the property replevied.

The general issue in this action is, *non-cepit;* but under this the defendant cannot dispute the plaintiff's property, which must be denied by a special plea.

Action of trespass only lies for injuries committed with force, and generally only for such as are *immediate*, and the intention of the wrong-doer is in general immaterial in this action.

The term trespass, in its most extensive signification, includes every description of *wrong* on which account an action on the case has been usually called "trespass on the case;" but technically it signifies an injury committed *vi et armis.*

The difference between an action of *trespass* and an action on the case is, that in the former the plaintiff complains of an immediate wrong, and in the latter, of a wrong that is the consequence of another act.

The gist of this action is the injury to the possession, and the general rule is that unless at the time the injury was committed the plaintiff was in actual possession, trespass cannot be supported, and though the title may come in question, yet it is not essential to the action that it should.

Actual and exclusive possession, without a legal title, is sufficient against a wrong-doer, or a person who cannot make out a title, *prima facie,* entitling him to the possession, or show any right or authority from the real owner.

No action will lie against a judge for what he does *judicially,* though it were done maliciously; at least he would not be liable in trespass in such case. But when an inferior court is guilty of an *excess* of jurisdiction, or has *no jurisdiction* over the subject-matter, *trespass* may be supported for anything done under such proceeding.

The want of jurisdiction in a court rendering a judgment, renders the judgment *coram non judice* and void, and the magistrate and all others concerned in enforcing the judgment would be trespassers.

The general issue in this action is, *not guilty.*

Action of ejectment lies for the recovery of the possession of *real* property, in which the lessor of the plaintiff has the *legal* interest and a *possessory right,* not barred by the statute of limitation. It is not a *real* action, nor a mere *personal* action, but is what is termed a *mixed* action, partly for the recovery of the thing or property itself, and partly to recover damages, which in general are merely nominal; but in some cases between landlord and tenant such damages are in effect the full amount of the mesne profits up to the time of trial.

Ejectment is an action founded in fiction, being brought in the name of a nominal plaintiff whose supposed right to the possession is founded on a supposed demise made to him by the party or parties really entitled to the possession of the property.

The action cannot be commenced until the real plaintiff's *right of entry* has accrued.

Mere nominal damages and costs only being recoverable in this action, in order to complete the remedy for damages when the possession has been long detained, an action of trespass for the *mesne profits* must, in general, be brought after the recovery in ejectment.

With respect to the title, a party having a right of entry, whether his title be in fee-simple, fee-tail, or in copy-hold, or for life, or years, may support an action of ejectment; but the right of possession must be of some duration, and exclusive; hence it cannot be supported where a party has merely a license to use land, or for a standing place, etc.

The general rule governing this action is that the lessor of the plaintiff must recover upon the *strength of his own title*, and of course he cannot in general found his claim upon the insufficiency of the defendant's, for possession gives the defendant a right against every person who cannot show a sufficient and better title, and the party who would change the possession must therefore first establish a legal title.

This action is only sustainable for what, in fact, or in point of law, amounted to an ouster or dispossession of the lessor of the plaintiff. But such *ouster* may, and usually is, by merely *holding over;* and an immediate tenant may be sued for the holding over by his under-tenant, though against his will.

If a tenant under-let, and at the end of his term his sub-tenant refuse to quit, the original lessor may support ejectment against *both*, and both are liable to pay mesne profits.

Action for mesne profit is in *form* an action of trespass *vi et armis*, but in *effect* to recover the rents and profits of an estate, as a satisfaction to the real plaintiff for the injury he has sustained by being kept out of possession, and the mesne profits, which in general not being included in the verdict in the ejectment, the law has provided this remedy for that injury; the action of ejectment, as at present conducted, though nominally a *mixed* action, being altogether a mere fiction, it being brought by a *nominal* plaintiff against a *nominal* defendant for a *supposed* ouster, merely *nominal* damages are given.

In general, any person found in possession, after a recovery in ejectment, is liable to the action; and it is no defence that he was on the premises merely as an agent, and under the license of the defendant in ejectment, for no man can license another to do an illegal act; but generally the person against whom the judgment in ejectment has been given ought to be made the defendant in this action.

Mistake in the form of action.—When the objection to the *form* of the action is substantial, and appears *upon the face of the declaration*, without regard to *extrinsic facts*, it may be taken advantage of by demurrer, or by motion in arrest of judgment, or by writ of error.

When the objection to the form of action *does not appear on the face of the pleadings*, it can only be taken as a ground of non-suit, in which case the defendant will be entitled to his costs.

If by either of these means the plaintiff fail in his action, and judgment be given against him for that reason, and not upon the merits, he is at liberty to commence a fresh action, and the defendant cannot plead in bar the proceedings in the first ineffectual suit.

Joinder of actions.—Where the plaintiff has two *causes of action* which may be joined in one action, he ought to bring one action only, and if he commence two actions, he may be compelled to consolidate them and to pay the costs of the application.

The joinder in action often depends on the form of the action, rather than on the *subject-matter* or *cause of action;* thus, in an action against a carrier for the loss of goods, if the plaintiff declare in *assumpsit* he cannot join a count in trover, as he may, if he declare against him in case; for the joinder depends on the *form* of the action.

When the *same plea* may be pleaded, and the *same judgment* given on all the counts of the declaration, *or* whenever the *counts* are of the *same nature*, and the *same judgment* is to be given on them all, though the pleas be different, as in the case of debt upon bond and on simple contract, they may be joined. Perhaps the latter, that is, the *nature* of the cause of action, is the best test or criterion by which to decide as to the joinder of counts. By this rule we may decide, in general, what forms of action may be joined in the same declaration.

It is a general rule that actions in form ex contractu cannot be joined with those in form ex delicto.

A person cannot in the same action join a demand in *his own right*, and a demand as *representative* of another, or *autre droit;* nor demands against a person on his *own* liability, and on his liability in his *representative* capacity.

Election of actions.—The party injured frequently has an election of several remedies for the same injury, and the due exercise of this election being of great importance, it may be useful to state the principal points which direct the choice of several remedies.

A strict legal title is essential to the support of some remedies, but in others the plaintiff's bare possession of the property affected is sufficient. Where the title of the plaintiff may be doubtful, it is in general advisable to adopt the latter description of remedy.

Of bail and process in actions in form *ex delicto*.—In *case, trover, detinue,* and *trespass,* the defendant cannot be arrested without a special order of the court or judge, and it is not usual to grant such order, except where there has been an outrageous battery, or the defendant is about to quit the kingdom; therefore in cases where it may be material to have the security of *bail,* the action should, if possible, be framed in *assumpsit* for money had and received, etc. Where, however, the defendant has been already arrested, the form of action must correspond with the affidavit to hold to bail and the form of action stated in the *capias,* or other process.

The number of parties.—We have seen that in an action in form *ex contractu,* if a person who ought to be made *co-plaintiff* be omitted, it is a ground of nonsuit, etc., except in the case of executors and administrators, whereas in actions in forms *ex delicto,* the non-joinder of a party who should have been a co-plaintiff can only be pleaded in abatement; hence the latter form of action is preferable, if it can be adopted, where there is reason to doubt who should be joined as a plaintiff.

Number of the causes in action.—Where the plaintiff has several demands of a similar kind, recoverable in different forms of action, he frequently may, and then he ought, to proceed for the whole in that form of action which will embrace his various claims.

Of the defence.—By a judicious choice of the remedy, the defendant may be frequently precluded from availing himself of a defence which he might otherwise establish.

The venue.—In some cases there may be two or more actions in effect for the same injury, the one *local* and the other *transitory;* consequently the latter form of action should be adopted where it may be advisable to try the cause out of the county where the estate is situated.

As to the evidence, it is frequently more convenient that the action should be trespass than case, because if laid in, trespass, no nice points can arise upon the evidence by which the plaintiff may be defeated upon the form of the action, as there may in many instances if case be brought. Very often the form of action, by driving the defendant to plead more specially, may narrow the plaintiff's evidence.

Of costs.—In actions in form *ex contractu*, the plaintiff is in general entitled to *full costs.*

The judgment and execution.—The action of debt is frequently preferable to *assumpsit* or covenant, because the judgment in debt by *nil dicit*, etc., is, in general, final, and execution may be issued immediately without the expense and delay of a writ of enquiry. Replevin, or detinue, is preferable to trover, when it is important to obtain the goods themselves.

The circumstance of a party having elected one of several remedies by *action*, will not in general preclude him from abandoning such suit, and after having duly discontinued it, he may adopt any other remedy.

The plaintiff cannot in general bring a fresh species of action, for the same cause, whilst the former is depending, or after it has been determined by a verdict.

PLEADING IN GENERAL.

Pleading is the statement in a logical and *legal form* of the *facts* which constitute the plaintiff's cause of action, or the defendant's ground of defence.

The grand object contemplated by the system is the production of a certain and material issue between the parties, upon some important part of the subject-matter of dispute between them.

THE FACTS NECESSARY TO BE STATED.—In general, **whatever circumstances are necessary to constitute the cause of complaint, or the ground of defence, must be stated** in the pleadings, and **all beyond is**

surplusage; *facts* only are to be stated, and not arguments or inferences, or matters of law; in which respect, the pleadings at law differ materially from those in equity.

There are *some facts* of such a *public* or *general* nature, that the courts *ex-officio* take notice of them, and which consequently ought not to be unnecessarily stated in pleading; such are public matters relating to the King and to Parliament; public statutes, and the facts which they recite; ecclesiastical, civil, and marine laws; common law rights and duties, and general customs; days of the week, etc., on which particular days fall; the divisions of the country into counties, etc.; the meaning of English words and terms of art, according to their ordinary acceptation; of their own course of proceedings; the privileges they confer on their officers, etc.

Where the law presumes a fact, or it is necessarily implied, it need not be stated.

Where the law presumes the affirmative of any fact, the negative of such fact must be proved by the party averring it in pleading.

Illegality in a transaction is never presumed; on the contrary, everything is presumed to have been legally done till the contrary is proved.

It is a general rule of pleading, that **matter which should come more properly from the other side need not be stated**; i. e.—it is enough for each party to make out his own case or defence.

Although any particular fact may be the gist of a party's case, and the statement of it indispensable, it is still a most important principle of the law of pleading that in alleging the fact, it is unnecessary to state such circumstances as *merely tend to prove the truth* of it. **The dry allegation of the fact, without detailing a variety of minute circumstances which constitute the evidence of it, will suffice.**

The object of the pleadings is to arrive at a specific issue upon a given and material fact; and this is attained, although the *evidence* of such fact, to be laid before the jury, be not specifically developed in the pleading.

Though the general rule is that facts only are to be stated, yet there are some instances in which the statement in the pleading is valid, though it does not accord with the real facts, **the law allowing a fiction;** as in the action of ejectment, in which the statement of the demise to the nominal plaintiff is fictitious. So in trover and detinue, the usual allegation that the defendant *found* the goods, rarely accords with the fact; and where the number, quantity, species or value of a thing, need not be proved precisely as laid, it is usual to state a greater number than really was the case, in order to admit of greater latitude in evidence; but except in these and a few other well known instances, established and recognized in pleading, for the convenience of justice, the pleading matter known to the party to be untrue, is censurable.

The rule relating to duplicity, or doubleness, tends more than any other, to the production of a *single* issue upon the *same* subject-matter of dispute—the real object of the science of pleading. It precludes both parties from stating or relying upon more than one *matter*, constituting a sufficient ground of action in respect of the same demand, or a sufficient defence to the same claim, or an adequate answer to the precedent pleading of the opponent.

The plaintiff cannot, by the common law rule, in order to sustain a single demand, rely upon two or more distinct grounds or matters, each of which, independently of the other, amounts to a good cause of action in respect of such demand. And the same count must not contain two promises in respect of the same subject-matter.

The defendant could not, in answer to a single claim, rely on several distinct answers, nor can he now do so in one plan.

At common law the declaration may comprise several counts upon different distinct demands of the same nature, or distinct counts upon the same claim.

And several distinct facts or allegations, however numerous, may be comprised in the same plea or other pleading, without amounting to the fault of duplicity, if one fact, or some of the facts, be but dependent upon, or be mere inducement or introduction to, the others, or if the different facts form together but one connected proposition or entire matter or point.

To avoid any unnecessary statement of facts, as well as prolixity in the statement of those which may be necessary, is of the greatest importance in pleading, as the statement of immaterial or irrelevant matter or allegations, is not only censurable, as creating unnecessary expense, but also frequently affords an advantage to the opposite party, either by affording

PLEADINGS. 225

him matter of objection on the ground of variance, or as rendering it incumbent on the party pleading to adduce more evidence than would otherwise have been necessary.

If the matter unnecessarily stated be wholly foreign and irrelevant to the cause, so that no allegation whatever on the subject was necessary, it will be rejected as surplusage, and it need not be proved; nor will it vitiate even on a special demurrer, it being a maxim that *utile per inutile non vitiatur*.

But if the very ground of the action be mis-stated, that will be fatal, for then the case declared on is different from that which is proved, and the plaintiff must recover *secundum allegata et probata*.

The introduction of unnecessary words of form will not vitiate the rest of a replication which is good.

Surplusage is never assignable as cause of demurrer; but surplusage in tendering an *issue* or in *other part* of *pleading*, tending to embarrass the opponent, may be assigned specially as cause of demurrer.

The general rule is that a pleading inconsistent with itself, or repugnant, is objectionable.

Mode of stating facts.—The principal rule is that they must be set forth with *certainty*.

Less certainty is requisite when the law presumes that the knowledge of the facts is more *properly* or *peculiarly* in the opposite party.

Where a subject comprehends multiplicity of matter, and a great variety of facts, there, in order to avoid prolixity, **the law allows general pleading.**

In general, *pleadings* must not be insensible or repugnant, nor ambiguous or doubtful in meaning; not argumentative, nor in the alternative.

Rules for construing pleadings.—It is a maxim that everything shall be taken most strongly against the party pleading, where the meaning of the words is equivocal.

But the maxim must be received with this qualification: that the language of the pleading is to have a reasonable intendment and construction; and where an expression is capable of different meanings, that shall be taken which will *support* the declaration.

The division of pleadings, or the *parts* of pleadings are arrangeable under two heads: the *regular parts* being those which occur in the ordinary course of a suit; and the *irregular or collateral parts* being those which are occasioned by mistakes in the pleadings on either side.

The regular parts of pleading are: first—the *declaration*, or count; second—the *plea*; third—the *replication*; fourth—the *rejoinder*; fifth—the *sur-rejoinder*; sixth—the *rebutter*; seventh—the *sur-rebutter*; eighth—*pleas puis darien continuance*—where the matter of defence arises *pending* the suit.

The irregular or collateral parts of pleading are first—*demurrers* to any part of the pleadings above mentioned; second—*demurrers to evidence* given at trials; third—*bills of exception*; fourth—*pleas* in *scire facias*; fifth—*pleas in error*.

The general requisites or qualities of a plea are first—it must be *single*, and *avoid duplicity*; second—it must be *direct* and *positive*, not argumentative; third—it must have convenient *certainty* of *time, place* and *persons*; fourth—it must answer the plaintiff's *allegations* in everything *material*; fifth—it must be pleaded so as to be *capable of trial*.

The declaration is a specification in a methodical and legal form of the circumstances which constitute the plaintiff's *cause of action*; which necessarily consists of the statement of a legal *right*, or, in other words, a right recognized in courts of law, not merely in a court of equity; and of an *injury* to such right remediable at law by action, as distinguished from the remedy by bill in equity.

The general requisites or qualities of a declaration, are: I. **That it correspond with the process, and in bailable actions, with the affidavit to hold to bail**—with respect to, first, the *names* of the parties to the action. Secondly, the *number* of such parties. Thirdly, the *character* or *right* in which they sue or are sued. Fourthly, the *cause* and *form* of action. II. **That it contains a statement of all the facts necessary in point of law to sustain the action,** and no more. III. **That these circumstances be set forth with certainty and truth**—that is, first, who are the *parties* to the suit. Secondly, a *time* when every material or traversable fact happened, in personal actions. Thirdly, a *place* should be alleged where every material and traversable fact occurred. Fourthly, it is still more material that certainty and accuracy be observed in the *more substantial parts* of the declaration, which state *the cause of action itself.*

The several parts and particular requisites of declarations are first, The title of the Declaration as to the *Court*. Secondly, The title of the Declaration as to the *Time* when it is filed or delivered. Thirdly, The *Venue* in the *margin*. Fourthly, The *Commencement*. Fifthly, The *Body*, according to the form of action: e. g. in *assumpsit*, six points are principally to be attended, to, namely, the *inducement, consideration, promise, averments, breach*, and *damages*. Sixthly, The *Conclusion*. Seventhly, The *Profert* of Deeds, Probates, Letters of Administration, etc. Eighthly, The Statement of *Pledges* to be discontinued. Ninthly, Other *miscellaneous* points.

The cause of action in every case consists of three different points—the *right*, the *injury*, and the consequent *damages*.

The inducement in an action of *assumpsit* is in the nature of a preamble stating the circumstances under which the contract was made or to which the consideration has reference.

The consideration stated should appear to be *legally sufficient* to support the promise for the breach of which the action is brought.

In declaring upon *bills of exchange* and *promissory notes* and some other legal liabilities, the mere statement of the liability which constitutes the consideration is sufficient; but in other cases of simple contracts, it is necessary that the declaration should disclose a consideration, which may consist of either benefit to the defendant, or detriment to the plaintiff, or the promise will appear to be *nudum pactum*, and the declaration will be insufficient.

An executed consideration consists of something *past* or *done* before the making of the promise.

Executory considerations are those to be yet performed; the *promise* having been made, or the thing done.

Concurrent considerations occur in the case of mutual promises, and partake of the nature of the preceding two. The plaintiff's *promise* is *executed*, but the *thing* which he has engaged to perform is *executory*, as in promises to marry, etc.

Continuing considerations are such as are executed in part only.

The three last classes are sufficient to support a contract not void for other reasons.

Great accuracy is required in the statement of the *consideration*, which in an action of *assumpsit* forms the basis of the contract, and if any error appear to have been made in describing it, the consequence will be that the whole contract is mis-described.

When *no consideration* is stated in the declaration, or when that which is stated is *clearly insufficient* or *illegal*, the defendant may either demur or move in arrest of judgment, or support a writ of error.

The perfection of pleading consists in combining brevity with the requisite certainty and precision.

The contract must be stated correctly, and if the *evidence differ from the statement*, the whole foundation of the action fails; because the contract is entire in its nature, and must be proved as laid. In this respect there is a material distinction between the statement of *torts* and of contracts, the former being divisible in their nature, and the proof of part of the tort or injury being, in general, sufficient to support the declaration.

A contract or written instrument should be stated according to its legal effect. The party is not *compelled* to follow the precise form of words in which the contract was made; it suffices if he state its true legal effect and operation.

Averment signifies a positive statement of facts, in opposition to argument or inference.

Variance is a disagreement or difference between two points of the same legal proceeding, which ought to agree. It is between the Writ and Declaration, or the Allegation and the Proof.

The common counts in assumpsit are the *indebitatus* count, the *quantum meruit*, the *quantum valebat*, and the *account stated*.

In actions for torts or *wrongs*, the declaration should state the *matter* or *thing* affected; the plaintiff's *right* thereto; the *injury*; and the *damages* sustained by the plaintiff.

In actions brought for *injuries* to *real property*, the *quality* of the realty, as whether it consists of houses, lands, or other *corporeal* hereditaments, should be shown.

In actions for injuries or taking away *goods or chattels*, it is, in general, necessary that their *quality*, *quantity* or *number*, and *value* or *price* be stated.

In trover, trespass and case, *damages* only being recoverable, less particularity is required than in detinue and replevin, for by these latter forms of action the plaintiff can claim or recover *the goods themselves*.

In personal actions, damages are the gist of the suit;

PLEADINGS.

in *real* actions, *the right* or *title* forms the prominent subject of enquiry.

In an action on the *case*, founded on an express or implied *contract*, the declaration must *correctly state the contract*, or the particular duty or consideration from which the liability results, and on which it is founded; and a variance in the description of a *contract*, though in an action *ex delicto*, may be as fatal as in an action in form *ex contractu*.

Injuries ex delicto are either committed with or without *force*, and are immediate or *consequential;* they may also arise from malfeasance, misfeasance, or non-feasance.

In some actions, the *scienter*, i. e. the intent, being material, must be *alleged* and *proved*.

In general, when the act occasioning damage is in itself unlawful, without any other extrinsic circumstance, the intent of the wrong-doer is immaterial in point of law, though it may enhance the damages.

In an action *ex delicto*, upon *proof of part only of the injury charged*, the plaintiff will be entitled to recover *pro tanto*, provided the part which is proved afford, *per se*, a sufficient cause of action; for *torts* are, generally speaking, divisible.

The statement of the *time* of committing injuries *ex delicto* is seldom material; it may be proved to have been committed either on a day anterior or subsequent to that stated in the declaration.

The *place* is only material in *local* actions, or where the precise *situation*, or rather *description* of the land, houses, etc., is particularly stated, as in trespass and replevin.

Damages are either general or special. General damages are such as the law *implies* or presumes to have accrued from the wrong complained of. **Special damages** are such as *really* took place and are not implied by law.

Presumptions of law are not, in general, to be pleaded or averred as facts.

In the case of libel or slander, great care must be taken in setting out the *particular libellous matters* or *words complained of.* The libel itself, or slanderous words, must be set out in *hæc verba*, or as uttered.

The claim of conusance or **cognizance of a suit** is defined to be an intervention by a *third person*, demanding judicature in the cause against the plaintiff, who has chosen to commence his action out of the claimant's court.

It is in form a question of jurisdiction between the two courts, and not between the plaintiff and defendant, as in the case of a plea to the jurisdiction, and therefore it must be demanded by the party entitled to conusance, or by his representative.

A plea to the jurisdiction must be pleaded in person, but a claim of conusance may be made by attorney.

Defence is defined to be the *denial* of the truth or validity of the complaint, and does not merely signify a *justification*.

Oyer is a prayer or petition recited or entered into in pleading, that the party may *hear* read to him the deed, etc., stated in the pleadings of the opposite party, and which deed is by intendment of law in court when it is pleaded with a a profert.

Imparlance, in its most general signification, means *time* given by the court to either party to answer the pleading of his opponent, as either to plead, reply, rejoin, etc., and is said to be nothing else but the continuance of the cause till a further day.

PLEAS DILATORY AND PLEAS PEREMPTORY constitute the general division of *pleas*.

Dilatory pleas are to the *jurisdiction*, to the *disability of the person*, to the *count or declaration*, and to the *writ*, the three last being generally termed *pleas in abatement*.

Pleas to the jurisdiction.—Where the court has no jurisdiction at common law, or it has been taken away by act of Parliament, such want of jurisdiction may, in general, be pleaded in *bar*, or given in evidence under the general issue, and is not properly the subject of a plea in abatement.

In all pleas to the jurisdiction of the *superior* courts, it must be shown that there is another court in which justice may be effectually administered, for if there be no other mode of trial, that alone would give the superior court jurisdiction.

Peremptory pleas are those which lead to an issue which settles the dispute, and are called *pleas in bar* of the action.

Pleas in abatement.—Whenever the subject-matter of the plea of the defence is that the plaintiff cannot maintain *any* action *at any time*, whether present or future, in respect of the supposed cause of action, it may, and usually must, be pleaded in *bar;* but the matter which merely defeats the *present* proceeding, and does not show that the plaintiff is *forever* concluded, should in general be pleaded in *abatement*.

PLEADINGS. 231

Pleas in abatement are divided into those relating—

- I. To the disability of the person suing or being sued, as
  - 1st. Of the plaintiff;
  - 2dly. Of the defendant.
- II. To the count or declaration.
- III. To the writ, viz:
  - 1st. To the form of the writ, viz:
    - 1st. Matter apparent on the face of it;
    - 2dly. Matter DEHORS.
  - 2dly. To the action of the writ.

As pleas in abatement do not deny and yet tend to delay the trial of the merits of the action, great accuracy and precision are required in framing them. They should be certain to every intent, and be pleaded without any repugnance.

As dilatory pleas rarely affect the merits of the suit, and object mere matter of form, they constitute an exception to the general principle of pleading, that *a plea* must either traverse or confess and avoid the alleged cause of action.

Pleas in bar go to the *merits* of the case, and deny that the plaintiff has *any* cause of action.

They are of *two* kinds, as well in action on contracts as for torts, viz: **first**—they *deny* that the plaintiff *ever* had the cause of action complained of, or, **secondly**—they *admit* that he *once had* a cause of action, but insist that it *no longer subsists*, having been determined by some *subsequent* matter. They are also either to a whole or to a part of the declaration.

The true object of pleading is to apprise the adverse party of the ground of defence, in order that he may be prepared to contest it, and not be taken by surprise.

It is well settled, that in an action for a libel or slanderous words, the defendant cannot *under the general issue* give in evidence the *truth* of the matter, or any part of it, *even in mitigation of damages*, but *must* justify *specially*.

It is a matter of prudence, depending on the facts of each case, whether or not to plead a justification.

Pleas in bar must either deny or confess and avoid the matter alleged in the plaintiff's declaration.

It is a general rule at common law, that matters in mitigation of damages, etc., which cannot be specially pleaded, may be given in evidence under the general issue.

The general issue, or general plea, is what denies at once the whole declaration, without offering *special* matter.

Analytical table of the defences to actions on contracts not under seal, the sub-divisions being nearly the same in each form of action.

I. Deny that there ever was cause for action.
  1. Deny that a sufficient contract was ever made.
    1. That no contract was in fact made.
    2. Incompetency of plaintiff to be contracted with.
      Plaintiff an alien enemy at time of contract.
    3. Defendant incapable of contract.
      1. Infancy.
      2. Lunacy, Drunkenness, etc.
      3. Coverture.
      4. Duress.
    4. Insufficiency of consideration.
      1. Inadequacy of consideration.
      2. Illegality of consideration, viz:
        At common law, and
        By different statutes.
    5. Contract obtained by fraud.
    6. The act to be done illegal or impossible
    7. The form of contract insufficient.
      1. At common law.
      2. By statute.
        As statute against frauds.
    8. No sufficient stamp.
  2. Admit a sufficient contract, but show that before breach there was
    1. A release.
    2. Parol discharge.
    3. Alteration in terms of contract by consent. [ation, etc.
    4. Non-performance by plaintiff of a condition precedent, alter-
    5. Performance, payment, etc.
    6. Contract became illegal or impossible to perform.

II. Admit that there was cause of action, but avoid it by showing subsequent or other matter.
  1. Plaintiff no longer entitled to sue.
    1. An alien enemy.
    2. Attainted
    3. Outlaw.
    4. A bankrupt, insolvent debtor, etc.
  2. Defendant no longer liable to be sued.
    1. A certified bankrupt.
    2. An insolvent debtor.
  3. Debt recoverable only in a court of conscience.
  4. Cause of action discharged.
    1. By payment.
    2. Accord and satisfaction.
    3. Foreign attachment.
    4. Tender.
    5. Account stated and negotiable security taken by plaintiff.
    6. Arbitrament.
    7. Former recovery.
    8. Higher security given.
    9. A release.
    10. Statute of limitations.
    11. Set-off.
  5. Plea by executor, etc.

Matter of *estoppel* must be specially pleaded as such.

PLEADINGS.

In framing a special plea, it is also necessary to consider whether the defendant is under terms of pleading *issuably*.

An issuable plea is a plea in chief to the merits upon which the plaintiff may take issue and go to trial, on a general demurrer for some defect in substance.

A plea in abatement is not an issuable plea.

In every species of *assumpsit* all *matters in confession and avoidance* shall be *specially* pleaded.

The general qualities of a plea in bar are

First.—That it be adapted to the nature and form of the action, and also be conformable to the count.

Secondly.—That it answer all which it assumes to answer, and no more.

Thirdly.—That it deny or admit and avoid the facts; and herein of giving color, and of pleas amounting to the general issue.

Fourthly.—That it be single.

Fifthly.—Certain.

Sixthly.—Direct and positive and not argumentative

Seventhly.—Capable of trial.

Eighthly.—True; and herein of *sham* pleas.

Pleas in bar, unlike pleas in abatement, offer matter which is a conclusive answer or defence to the action upon the merits. They are divisible into pleas of *traverse* or *denial*, and pleas by way of *confession* and *avoidance;* as all pleas in bar must *deny* or *confess and avoid* the facts stated in the declaration.

Pleas in denial are either the general issue in those actions in which so general a traverse is admissible, or they occur in instances in which, there being no general issue, as in covenant, etc., some specific fact is specially disputed.

The *principles* of pleading and express rules require, in general, that **matter in confession and avoidance should be specially pleaded** and not be given in evidence under the general issue or traverse.

A special plea amounting to the general issue or general plea is bad.

A plea in confession and avoidance must give *color* to the plaintiff.

To give color is to give credit for an apparent or *prima facie* right of action.

Pleading is a statement of *facts*, and not a statement of argument; it is therefore a rule that a plea should be direct and positive, and advance its position of fact in an absolute form, and not by way of rehearsal, reasoning, or argument.

Every plea should be so pleaded as to be *capable of trial,* and therefore must consist of matter of *fact,* the *existence* of which may be tried by a jury on an issue, or the *sufficiency* of which as a defence may be determined by the *court* upon *demurrer,* or of matter of *record* which is triable by the record itself.

Every plea should be true and capable of proof, for, as it has been quaintly said, "Truth is the goodness and virtue of pleading, as certainty is the grace and beauty of it."

Sham pleading, that is, the pleading of matter known by the party to be false, for the purpose of delay or other unworthy object, has always been considered a very culpable abuse of justice, and has often been censured and set aside with costs.

The rules which prevail in the construction and allowance of a plea in bar are first—That it is to be construed most strongly against the defendant; secondly—That a general plea, if bad in part, is bad for the whole; thirdly—That surplusage will not in general vitiate.

If an allegation is *capable* of two meanings, that exposition shall be adopted which will support, not that which will destroy, the pleading.

Pleas by several defendants.—In general, when the defence is in its nature joint, *several defendants* may join in the same plea, or they may sever without committing fault of duplicity in pleading, and one defendant may plead in abatement, another in bar, and the other may demur.

A plea which is bad in part is bad in toto.

The plaintiff may, in an action in form *ex delicto,* against several defendants enter a *nolle prosequi* as to one of them; but in actions in form *ex contractu,* unless the defence be merely in the *personal* discharge of one of the defendants, a *nolle prosequi* cannot be entered as to one defendant without discharging the others, for the cause of action is entire and indivisible.

Pleas of set-off.—In actions upon *simple contracts* or *specialties* for the payment of *money,* the defence frequently is a cross-demand for a *debt* due from the plaintiff to the defendant. At *common law,* and independently of the statutes of set-off, a defendant is in general entitled to retain or claim by way of *deduction,* all just allowances or demands accruing to him, or **payments** made by him, in respect of the *same* transaction or account, which forms the ground of action; but before the statutes of set-off, where there were *cross-demands unconnected with each other*, a defendant could not in a court of law defeat the action by establishing that the plaintiff was indebted to him even in a larger sum than that sought to be recovered, and relief could only be obtained in a court of equity.

Some of the principal rules upon the subject of set-off are that the debt sued for and that sought to be set off should be *mutual* debts, and due to each of the parties respectively in the *same right* or *character*.

The statutes speak only of mutual *debts*, consequently the demand of each party must be in the nature of a *debt;* so that a set-off is excluded in all actions *ex delicto*, and it cannot be admitted even in actions *ex contractu*, if the claim of either party be for uncertain or unliquidated *damages*.

It has been held that a debt of *inferior degree* cannot be set off against one of *higher degree*.

The debt attempted to be set off must be *completely due* and in *arrear* at the time the action *was commenced;* and a legal and *subsisting* debt, not barred by the statute of limitations.

REPLICATIONS.—Before the plaintiff *replies* or *demurs* to the plea, he should consider whether or not he *may* treat it as a nullity, and sign judgment.

If the plea does not profess to answer the whole action, and leaves a part unanswered, the plaintiff should sign judgment *pro tanto*.

If the plea properly conclude "to the country," etc., *in assumpsit*, as well as in other actions, the replication may add the common *similiter*, i. e. "doth the like," etc.; *or* if the plea conclude with a verification, may deny the alleged matter of defence, or may confess and avoid it by applying *new matter*.

The conclusion to a special plea may be to the *country*, as thus, "and this the plaintiff prays may be inquired of by the country," etc., or with a verification; thus, "and this the plaintiff is ready to verify."

When the plea concludes to the *country*, the replication consists either of the common or special *similiter*.

The *common similiter* is "and the plaintiff doth the like."

The *special similiter* is "and the plaintiff, and as to the said pleas of the defendant, by him first and secondly above pleaded, and whereof he hath put himself upon the country, doth the like."

The parts of a replication to a plea containing new matter are first, the *commencement;* secondly, the *body;* and thirdly, its *conclusion.*

The commencement in such case professes wholly to deny the effect of the defendant's plea.

The body shows the ground on which that denial is founded.

The conclusion is either to the country or to the record, if it merely deny the plea; but if the replication contain *new matter,* it should *conclude* with a *verification,* and a prayer that judgment be awarded in the plaintiff's favor.

The *body* of the replication contains matter of *estoppel;* a *traverse* or *denial* of the plea; a *confession and avoidance* of it; or, in the case of an *evasive* plea, a *new assignment.*

There is no real distinction between traverses and denials; they are the same in substance.

Any pleading by which the truth of the opponent's allegation is disputed is termed a pleading by way of traverse or denial.

The first object of pleading being to bring the point in dispute between the parties, at as early a stage of the cause as possible, to an *issue* or point which is *not multifarious or complex,* the issue must in general be single; but this *single point* may consist of *several facts* if they be dependent and connected.

A party may traverse and deny any *material* and issuable allegation in his opponent's pleading.

But if an allegation in the opposite pleading be altogether *immaterial,* it cannot be traversed; otherwise the object of pleading, viz: the bringing the parties to an issue upon a matter or point decisive of the merits, would be defeated.

It is also a most material rule upon this subject that a traverse should be taken on *matter of fact,* not mere matter of conclusion of *law.*

The traverse should also be on some *affirmative matter,* and not put in issue a negative allegation; nor too *large;* nor yet too *narrow,* so as to prejudice the defence.

In general, a traverse, denial, or allegation should be so framed as to be *divisible,* and entitle the party pleading to recover *pro tanto,* if he prove part of the allegation.

Replications denying a particular fact or facts, are, in point of *form,* of *three* descriptions; *first,* the plaintiff protests some fact or facts, and denies the other, concluding to the

PLEADINGS.

country; or, *secondly*, he at once denies the particular fact intended to be put in issue, and concludes to the country; or, *thirdly*, formally traverses a particular fact, and concludes with a verification.

It is a rule that every pleading is taken to confess such traversable matter of *fact* alleged on the other side as it does not traverse.

It is a general rule that there cannot be a traverse after a traverse where the first was material, and of matter necessarily alleged.

The general rule is that *a replication must confess and avoid, or traverse the matter stated in the plea;* and in this respect a replication resembles a plea.

New assignment is *a more minute* and *circumstantial* manner of *re-stating* the cause of action, or some part thereof, alleged in the declaration, in consequence of the defendant having, through mistake or design, omitted to answer it in his plea. It is a kind of replication in the *nature* of a new declaration.

The object of a new assignment is to correct an error in the plea, and to aver that the defendant has omitted to answer the whole or a part of the true ground of complaint.

New assignments are principally confined to the action of trespass, as it rarely becomes necessary to new-assign in any other form of action.

The conclusion of a new assignment must be with a verification, in order that the defendant may have an opportunity of answering it.

A new assignment being in the nature of a new declaration, and dismissing the previous pleading from consideration, so far as respects the matter newly assigned, the defendant should plead to it precisely as to a declaration, either by denying the matter newly assigned, by the plea of not guilty, etc., or by answering it by a special plea of matter of justification; and he may plead several pleas.

To the plea or pleas to the new assignment the plaintiff should *reply* precisely as to pleas to a declaration, and if the plea be such as would require a new assignment, if pleaded to a declaration, the plaintiff should again new-assign to such plea.

The conclusions of replications, in point of *form*, should either be to the *country*, or *with a verification.*

It is an established rule, applicable to every part of pleading, subsequent to the declaration, that when there is an affirmative on one side and a negative on the other, or *vice versa*, the conclusion should be to the country, although the affirmative and negative be not in express words, but only tantamount thereto.

It is a general rule that when *new matter* is alleged in a replication, it should conclude with an averment or verification, in order to give the defendant an opportunity of answering it.

The qualities of a replication in a great measure resemble those of a plea, viz: *First*—that it must answer so much of the plea as it professes to answer, and that if bad in part, it is bad for the whole. *Secondly*—that it must be conformable to, and not depart from, the count. *Thirdly*—that it must present matter of *estoppel*, or must *traverse* or *confess and avoid* the plea. *Fourthly*—that, like a plea, it should be certain, direct, positive and not argumentative, and also that it be triable. *Fifthly*—that it must be single.

It is a settled rule that the replication must not *depart* from the allegations in the declaration in any *material* matter.

A departure in pleading is said to be when a party quits or departs from the case or defence which he has first made, and has recourse to another; it occurs when the replication or rejoinder, etc., contains matter not pursuant to the declaration or plea, etc., and which does not support and fortify it.

The only mode of taking advantage of a *departure* is by demurrer, which may be either general or special; and if the defendant or the plaintiff, instead of demurring, take issue upon the replication or the rejoinder containing a departure, and it be found against him, the court will not arrest the judgment.

If the plaintiff do not dispute and cannot avoid the *facts* stated in the plea, but contends that their legal operation is insufficient to defeat the action, he must *demur* to the plea.

The replication must not be double, that is, contain two answers to the same plea.

When a replication, or a plea in bar in replevin, concludes *to the country*, the defendant can only demur, or add the common *similiter*, which is, "and the defendant doth the like;" and it is material that the defendant should take care that the *similiter* be added, for otherwise he cannot move for judgment, as in case of a nonsuit.

A rejoinder is the defendant's answer to a replication, and is in general governed by the same rules as those which affect pleas, with this additional quality, that it must *support* and not *depart* from the plea.

Sur-rejoinders, rebutters and sur-rebutters seldom occur in pleading, and are governed by the same rules as those to which the previous pleading of the party adopting them is subject.

Issue is defined to be a single, certain and material point issuing out of the allegations or pleadings of the plaintiff and defendant, though in common acceptation it signifies the *entry* of the pleadings themselves.

An issue is either in *law*, upon a demurrer, or in *fact*, when the matter is triable by the court upon *nul tiel record*, or a jury upon pleadings concluding to the country. The term "issue" is proper where only one plea has been pleaded, and though it be applied to several counts, and issue is joined upon such plea. An issue should, in general, be upon an *affirmative and a negative*, and not upon two affirmatives. It should also be upon *a single and a certain point*, and its principal quality is, that it must be upon a *material* point.

An informal issue is where a *material* allegation is traversed in an *improper* or *artificial manner*.

Repleader.—When the issue is *immaterial*, the court will award a *repleader*, if it will be the means of effecting substantial justice between the parties, but not otherwise.

In repleader—i. e. to plead again—the parties must begin again at the first fault which occasioned the immaterial issue: thus, if the declaration be insufficient, and the bar and replication are also bad, the parties must begin *de novo;* but if the bar be good, and the replication ill, at the replication.

Where the plea is good in form, though not in fact, or, in other words, if it contain a defective title, or ground of defence by which it is apparent to the court by the defendant's own showing, that in *any* way of putting it, he can have *no merits*, and the issue joined thereon be found for him, there, as the rewarding of a repleader could not mend the case, the court, for the sake of the plaintiff, will at once give judgment *non obstante veredicto*.

But where the defect is not so much in the title as in the manner of stating it, and the issue joined thereon is immaterial, so that the court knew not for whom to give judgment, whether for the plaintiff or defendant, then, for the more satisfactory administration of justice, they will award a repleader.

A judgment *non obstante veredicto* is always upon the *merits*, and never granted but in a very clear case; a repleader is upon the *form* and *manner* of pleading.

When matter of defence had arisen after the commencement of the suit, it could not be pleaded in bar of the action *generally*, but must, when it had arisen *before plea* or continuance, be pleaded as to the *further* maintenance of the suit; and when it had arisen after plea, and before replication, or *after issue joined*, then *puis darien continuance*.

If any matter of defence has arisen after an *issue in fact* has been joined, or after a joinder in demurrer, it may be pleaded by the defendant; as that the plaintiff has given him a release, or that the plaintiff is a bankrupt, etc. And if the defendant became bankrupt, and obtained his certificate after issue joined, he should plead this defence *puis darien continuance*.

So it may be pleaded in abatement that a *feme sole* plaintiff has married; or in an action by an administrator, that the plaintiff's letters of administration had been revoked, *puis darien continuance*, etc.

Pleas of this kind are either in abatement or in bar.

A plea *puis darien continuance* is not a departure from, but is a waiver of the first plea, and no advantage can afterwards be taken of it, nor can even the plaintiff afterwards proceed thereon.

The courts will sometimes set aside a plea *puis darien continuance* when it is manifestly fraudulent, and against the justice of the case.

DEMURRERS.—When the declaration, plea, or replication, etc., appears on the *face of it* and without reference to *extrinsic* matter, to be defective, either in substance or form, the opposite party may, in general, *demur*.

Demurrer has been defined to be a declaration that the party demurring will "go no further," because the other has not shown sufficient matter against him that he is bound to answer.

Where the pleading is defective in *substance* it is advisable, in general, to demur, because the party succeeding thereon is entitled to costs; but where the judgment is reversed in error, no costs are recoverable.

A demurrer admits the *facts* pleaded, and merely refers the question of their *legal* sufficiency to the decision of the court.

Demurrers are either general or special; general, where no particular cause is alleged; **special,** when the particular imperfection is pointed out and insisted upon as the ground of demurrer; the former will suffice when the pleading is defective in *substance,* and the latter is requisite where the objection is only to the *form* of pleading.

A demurrer is either to *the whole,* or to *a part only,* of a *declaration.*

In point of form, no precise words are necessary in a demurrer, and a plea which is in substance a demurrer, though very informal, will be considered as such; and it is a general rule that there cannot be a demurrer to a demurrer.

A party should not demur unless he be certain that his own previous pleading is substantially correct, for it is an established rule that upon the argument of a demurrer, the court will, notwithstanding the defect of the pleading demurred to, give judgment against the party whose pleading was first defective in *substance;* for on demurrer the court will consider the *whole* record, and give judgment for the party who thereon appears to be entitled to it.

DEFECTS IN PLEADING are aided or cured without any actual *amendment,* viz: First—by *pleading over.* Secondly—by *intendment,* or *presumption, after verdict;* and, thirdly—by the *Statutes of Jeofails.*

Pleading over is to answer the defective pleading in such a manner that an omission or informality therein is *expressly* or *impliedly* supplied, or rendered formal or intelligible.

Intendment, *after verdict,* is a doctrine founded on the *common law,* independent of any statutory enactments; the general principle upon which it depends appears to be that where there is any defect or omission in pleading, whether in *substance* or *form,* which would have been a fatal objection upon demurrer, yet if the issue joined be such as necessarily required, on the trial, proof of the facts so defectively stated or omitted, and without which it is not to be presumed that either the judge would direct the jury to give, or the jury would have given the verdict, such defect or omission is *cured by the verdict.*

The main rule on the subject of intendment is that a verdict will aid a *defective statement* of title, but will never assist a statement of a *defective title* or cause of action.

Cured by verdict is an expression signifying that the court will, *after* a verdict, presume or intend that the particular thing which appears to be defectively stated or omitted in the pleading *was duly proved* at the trial.

THE SCIENCE OF PLEADING was no doubt derived from Normandy. The use of stated forms of pleading is not to be traced among the Anglo-Saxons. Pleading was cultivated as a science in the reign of Edward I. The object of pleading is to ascertain by the production of an issue the subject for decision.

I. The rules which tend simply to the production of an issue are:

(a.) That after declaration the parties must at each stage demur or plead, either by way of traverse, or by way of confession and avoidance; and as to the nature and property of pleadings in general, without reference to their being by traverse or by confession and avoidance, the properties are:

That every pleading must be an answer to the whole of what it adversely alleged.

That every pleading is taken to confess such traversable matters alleged on the other side as it does not traverse, but dilatory pleas and pleas by estoppel are exceptions, as also a new assignment.

(b.) That upon a traverse issue must be tendered.

(c.) That an issue well tendered must be accepted.

II. The rule which tends to secure the materiality of the issue is:

(a.) That all pleadings must contain matters pertinent and material; for a traverse must not be taken of an immaterial point, and a traverse must be neither too large nor too narrow.

III. The rules which tend to produce singleness or unity in the issue are:

(a.) That pleadings must not be double.

(b.) But it is allowable both to plead and to demur to the same matter by leave of the courts or a judge.

IV. The rules which tend to produce certainty or particularity in the issue are:

(a.) That the pleadings must have certainty of place.

(b.) That the pleadings must have certainty of time.

(c.) That the pleadings must specify quality, quantity, and value.

(d.) That the pleadings must specify the names of persons,

whether parties to the suit or parties of whom mention is made in the pleading.

(e.) That the pleadings must show title.

(f.) That the pleadings must show authority.

(g.) That, in general, whatever is alleged in pleadings must be alleged with *certainty*.

The rules which tend to certainty are limited and restricted by the following subordinate rules:

It is not necessary in pleading to state that which is merely matter of evidence.

It is not necessary in pleading to state that matter of which the court takes notice *ex officio*.

It is not necessary to state matter which should come more properly from the other side.

It is not necessary to allege circumstances necessarily implied.

It is not necessary to allege what the law will presume.

A general mode of pleading is allowed where great prolixity is thereby avoided.

A general mode of pleading is often sufficient where the allegation on the other side must reduce the matter to certainty.

No greater particularity is required than the nature of the thing pleaded will conveniently admit.

Less particularity is required when the facts lie more in the knowledge of the opposite party than of the party pleading.

Less particularity is necessary in the statement of the matters of inducement or aggravation than in the main allegations.

With respect to acts valid at common law, but regulated as to the mode of performance, by statute, it is sufficient to use such certainty of allegation as was sufficient before the statute.

V. The rules which tend to prevent obscurity and confusion in pleading are:

(a.) That the pleading must not be insensible or repugnant.

(b.) That the pleadings must not be ambiguous or doubtful in meaning; and when two different meanings present themselves, that construction shall be adopted which is the more unfavorable to the party pleading.

(c.) That the pleadings must not be argumentative.

(d.) That the pleadings must not be hypothetical or in the alternative.

(e.) That the pleadings must not be by way of recital, but must be positive in their form.

(f.) That things are to be pleaded according to their legal effect or operation.

(g.) That the pleading should observe the ancient and known forms of expression as contained in approved precedents.

(h.) But formal commencements and conclusions are dispensed with.

(i.) That a pleading which is bad in part is bad altogether.

VI. The rules which tend to prevent prolixity and delay in pleading are:

(a.) That there must be no departure in pleading.

(b.) That where a plea amounts to the general issue it should be so pleaded.

(c.) That surplusage is to be avoided.

VII. The other miscellaneous rules are:

(a.) That the declaration must be conformable to the writ.

(b.) That the declaration shall have its proper commencement, and should in conclusion lay damages and allege production of suit.

(c.) That pleas must be pleaded in due order.

(d.) That pleas in abatement must give the plaintiff a better writ or declaration.

(e.) That dilatory pleas must be pleaded at a preliminary stage of the suit.

(f.) But pleadings do no longer conclude to the country or with a verification.

(g.) And profert of a deed is dispensed with.

(h.) That all pleadings must be properly entitled.

(i.) That all pleadings ought to be true.

The order of pleadings at common law in all actions, except replevin, is as follows:

(1.) Declaration.
(2.) Plea.
(3.) Replication.
(4.) Rejoinder.
(5.) Sur-rejoinder.
(6.) Rebutter.

PLEADINGS.

(7.) Sur-rebutter; after which the pleadings have no distinctive names, for beyond this stage they are very seldom found to extend.

The pleadings 1, 3, 5, and 7 emanate from the plaintiff, the remainder from the defendant.

The pleadings in replevin are as follows:
(1.) Plaint or declaration.
(2.) Avowry, cognizance, or plea of *non cepit*.
(3.) Plea in bar.
(4.) Replication, etc., the ordinary name of each pleading being postponed by one step.

The pleadings in equity are thus arranged:
(1.) Bill of information.
(2.) Answer, plea, demurrer, or disclaimer.
(3.) Replication.

The pleadings in criminal law are:
(1.) Indictment or information.
(2.) Plea or demurrer.
(3.) *Similiter* or joinder.

The pleadings in ecclesiastical causes are:
(I.) In criminal causes.
(a.) The articles.
(II.) The plenary causes, not criminal.
(a.) The libel.
(III.) In testamentary causes.
(a.) The allegation.

Every subsequent plea, in all causes and by whatever party given, is termed
(b.) An allegation.

THE

LAW OF EVIDENCE.

ABRIDGED.

ANALYSIS.

Nature and principles of evidence.
   Preliminary observations.
   Things judicially taken notice of without proof.
   Grounds of belief.
   Evidence—Definition of.
      Direct or positive,
      Circumstantial,
      Presumptive.
         Presumptions of law,
           Conclusive,
           Disputable,
         Presumptions of fact.

Object of Evidence, and Rules governing the production of testimony.
   Relevancy of evidence.
      Rules governing production to the jury.
      Variance.
   Primary and secondary evidence.
   Hearsay evidence.
      Original evidence—often wrongfully called hearsay.
      Exceptions to the rule rejecting hearsay evidence.
   Admissions.
   Confessions.
   Evidence excluded from public policy.
   Number of witnesses.
   Admissibility of parol evidence, to affect writings.

Means of proof, or the Instruments of evidence.
   Witnesses and means of procuring their attendance.
   Competency of witnesses.
      In regard to parties.
      To persons deficient in understanding.
      Those insensible to the obligations of an oath.
      Persons interested.
   Examination of witnesses.
      Direct examination.
      Cross-examination.
   Written evidence.
      Public documents.
         Mode of proof.
      Records and judicial writings.
      Private writings.

EVIDENCE.

NATURE AND PRINCIPLES OF EVIDENCE.

PRELIMINARY OBSERVATIONS.—Evidence, in legal acceptation, includes all the means by which any alleged matter of fact, the truth of which is submitted to investigation, is established or disproved.

Proof is that which establishes a thing by competent and satisfactory evidence.

Demonstration is that high degree of evidence of which none but mathematical truth is susceptible.

Moral evidence is that which alone proves matters of fact, and also includes all the evidence not obtained, either from intuition or from demonstration.

Competent evidence is that which the very nature of the thing to be proved requires as the fit and appropriate proof in the particular case; as the production of a writing, where its contents are the subject of the enquiry.

Satisfactory evidence—sometimes called *sufficient evidence*—is that amount of proof which ordinarily satisfies an unprejudiced mind, beyond reasonable doubt.

Cumulative evidence is evidence of the same kind, to the same point.

Corroborative evidence is that which tends to strengthen and confirm.

Things judicially taken notice of without proof by the courts, are whatever ought to be generally known, within the limits of their jurisdiction.

THE GROUNDS OF BELIEF in evidence are:

First—The uniform habits and necessities of mankind lead us to consider the disposition to believe upon the evidence of extraneous testimony as a fundamental principle of our moral nature. They constitute the general *basis* upon which all evidence may be said to rest.

Secondly—A basis of evidence subordinate to this paramount and original principle, rests upon our faith in human testimony, as sanctioned by experience.

Thirdly—Another basis of evidence is the known and experienced connection subsisting between collateral facts or circumstances, satisfactorily proved, and the fact in controversy.

Fourthly—Another basis claimed by some writers is the effect of coincidences in testimony, which, if collusion be excluded, cannot be accounted for upon any other hypothesis than that it is true.

It is said that "the wise and beneficent Author of Nature intended us to be social creatures, and, as a consequence, that we should receive the greater part of our knowledge from others; hence he implanted in our nature a principle or propensity to speak the truth. This principle has a powerful operation even in the greatest liars, for where they lie once they speak the truth a hundred times. *Truth* is always at the door of our lips, and goes forth spontaneously, if not held back. It is always uppermost, and the natural issue of the mind, and requires no art, training, inducement, or temptation, but only that we yield to a natural impulse. *Lying*, on the contrary, is doing violence to our nature, and is never practiced, even by the worst men, without some temptation."

EVIDENCE is direct or *positive*, and indirect or *circumstantial*.

Direct or positive evidence is such where the *factum probandum*, or fact to be proved, is directly attested by those who speak from their own actual and personal knowledge; the proof applying immediately to the fact to be proved, without any intervening process. It rests upon the second basis of evidence.

Circumstantial evidence is such where the fact to be proved is *inferred* from other facts satisfactorily proved, the proof applying immediately to *collateral* facts, supposed to have a connection, near or remote, with the fact in controversy. It rests upon the third basis of evidence.

Circumstantial evidence is of two kinds, viz: *certain*, or that from which the conclusion necessarily follows, and *uncertain*, or that from which the conclusion does not necessarily follow, but is probable only, and is obtained by a process of reasoning.

A verdict may be well founded on circumstances alone, and these often lead to a conclusion far more satisfactory than direct evidence can produce.

EVIDENCE.

Presumptive evidence is circumstantial evidence, or the evidence afforded by circumstances, with the additional *presumption* of inference, founded on the known usual connection between the facts proved and the guilt of the party implicated; hence it is a more complex and difficult operation of the mind than in circumstantial evidence, though, in truth, the operation of the mind is similar in both. Presumptive evidence is divided into *presumptions of law* and *presumptions of fact.*

Presumptions of law consist of those rules which in certain cases either forbid or dispense with any ulterior enquiry. They are founded upon the first principles of justice, the laws of nature, or the connection usually found to exist between certain things in the experienced course of human conduct and affairs. They are of two kinds: *conclusive* and *disputable.*

Conclusive presumptions of law—also called *imperative* or *absolute* presumptions—are rules determining the quantity of evidence requisite for the support of any particular averment, which is not permitted to be overcome by any proof that the fact is otherwise.

Thus a *sane* man is conclusively presumed to contemplate the natural and probable *consequences* of his own acts, therefore the intent to murder is conclusively inferred from the deliberate use of a deadly weapon.

The *records* of a court of justice are presumed to have been correctly made. A party to the record is presumed to have been interested in the suit.

A *bond*, or other *specialty*, is presumed to have been made upon good *consideration*, as long as the instrument remains unimpeached.

Ancient deeds and *wills*, more than thirty years old, unblemished by any alterations, are said to prove themselves, being presumed valid and the subscribing witness dead.

Estoppels may be ranked in this class of presumptions. A man is said to be estopped when he has done some act which the policy of the law will not permit him to gainsay or deny.

Recitals in deeds, by the general rule, bind all the parties thereto, and operate as an estoppel against them, binding both parties and privies—privies in blood, in estate, and in law. Between such parties and privies the deed, or other matter recited, need not at any time be otherwise proved, the recital of it in the subsequent deed being conclusive.

An infant, under the age of seven years, is conclusively presumed to be incapable of committing any felony, for want of discretion. A female under the age of ten years is presumed incapable of consenting to sexual intercourse.

A married woman, acting in company with her husband, in the commission of a felony other than treason and homicide, is conclusively presumed to act under his coercion, and consequently without any guilty intent.

Where the husband and wife have cohabited together *as such,* and no impotency is proved, the issue is conclusively presumed to be legitimate, though the wife may have been guilty of infidelity.

In the cases of conclusive presumptions, the rule of law merely attaches itself to the circumstances when proved; it is not deduced from them. It is not a rule of inference from testimony, but a rule of protection, as expedient and for the general good.

Disputable presumptions of law are such as are *liable* to be rebutted by proof to the contrary. Here, also, the law itself, without the aid of a jury, infers the one fact from its known and experienced connection with the proved existence of the other, in the *absence* of all opposing evidence.

E. g.—As men do not generally violate the penal code, the law presumes every man *innocent;* but some men do transgress it, and therefore evidence is receivable to repel this presumption.

On the other hand, as men seldom do unlawful acts with innocent intentions, the law presumes every act in itself unlawful to have been criminally intended, until the contrary appears.

On the same principle, where a debt by *specialty* has been unclaimed and without recognition for *twenty years,* in the absence of any explanatory evidence, it is presumed to have been paid.

Presumptions of fact differ from presumptions of law in this, that while those are reduced to fixed rules, these merely natural presumptions are derived wholly and directly from the circumstances of the particular case, without the aid of any rules of law.

Long acquiescence in any adverse claim of right is good ground on which a jury may presume that the claim had a legal commencement.

EVIDENCE. 253.

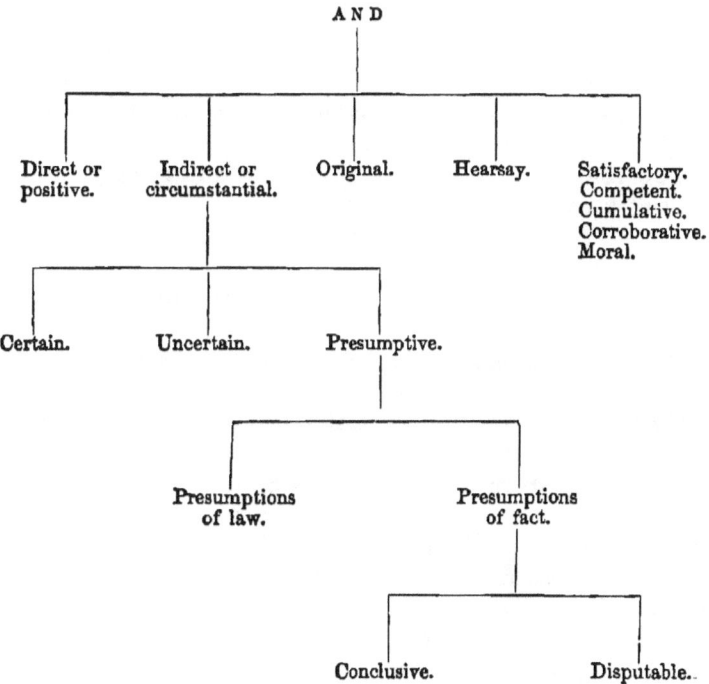

Presumptions of fact fall within the exclusive province of the jury to decide, by themselves, according to the convictions of their own understanding.

OBJECT OF EVIDENCE, AND RULES GOVERNING THE PRODUCTION OF TESTIMONY.

RELEVANCY OF EVIDENCE.—Whether there be any evidence or not, is a question for the judge; whether it is sufficient evidence, a question for the jury.

Where the question is mixed, consisting of both law and fact, so intimately blended, as not to be easily susceptible of separate decision, it is submitted to the jury, who are first instructed by the judge in the principles and rules of law, by which they are to be governed in finding a verdict, and these instructions they are bound to follow.

Questions of interpretation, as well as of construction of written instruments, are for the court alone.

The general rules or principles governing the production of testimony to the jury are:

First—The evidence must *correspond with the allegations* and be confined to the *point in issue.*

Secondly—It is sufficient if the *substance* only of the issue be proved.

Thirdly—The *burden* of proving a proposition, or issue, lies on the party holding the affirmative.

Fourthly—The *best* evidence of which the case, in its nature, is susceptible, *must always be produced.*

Of the first rule in general.—*Surplusage* comprehends whatever may be stricken from the record without destroying the plaintiff's right of action.

It is not necessary that the evidence should bear *directly* upon the issue; it is admissible if it *tends* to prove the issue or constitutes a link in the chain of proof.

Nor is it necessary that its relevancy should appear at the time when it is offered; but if it does not subsequently become connected with the issue, it is to be laid out of the case.

This rule excludes all evidence of collateral facts, for the reason that it tends to draw away the minds of jurors from the point in issue; to excite prejudice, and mislead them;

EVIDENCE. 255

moreover, the adverse party, having had no notice of such a course of evidence, is not prepared to rebut it.

Under this rule, also, evidence of the *general character* of the parties is not admissible in civil cases, unless the nature of the action involves the general character of the party, or goes directly to affect it. In all cases where evidence is admitted touching the general character of the party, it ought manifestly to bear reference to the nature of the charge against him.

Of the substance of the issue.—In the application of the second rule a distinction is made between allegations of matter of *substance* and allegations of matter of *essential description.* The former may be substantially proved; but the latter must be proved with a degree of strictness, extending in some cases even to literal precision.

In general, the allegations of *time, place, quantity, quality* and *value*, when not descriptive of the identity of the subject of the action, need not be proved strictly as alleged.

Variance is a disagreement between the allegation and the proof in some matter in point of law essential to the charge or claim. It being necessary to prove the substance of the issue, any departure from the substance, in the evidence adduced, is fatal, constituting a variance.

Where the matter, whether introductory or otherwise, is descriptive, it must be proved as laid, or the variance will be fatal.

In *actions upon contract*, if any part of the contract proved should vary materially from that which is stated in the pleadings, it will be fatal, for a contract is an entire thing, and indivisible.

The *gravamen* is the substantial grievance, or complaint. In breaches of contracts it is that certain act which the defendant engaged to do, yet has not done.

The *gist* of an action is the cause for which it lies; the ground or foundation of a suit, without which it is not maintainable.

In almost every case, the consequences of a variance between the allegation in the pleadings and the state of facts proved may now be avoided by *amendment* of the record.

The burden of proof, or the third rule, has some exceptions, one of which includes those cases in which the plaintiff *grounds his right of action upon a negative allegation*, and where, of course, the establishment of this negative is an essential element in his case.

The best evidence, or the fourth rule, excludes only that evidence which itself indicates the existence of more original sources of information.

This rule naturally leads to the division of evidence into *primary* and *secondary*.

Primary evidence is that denominated the *best* evidence, or that which affords the greatest certainty of the fact in question.

Secondary evidence is all evidence falling short of this in its degree.

Oral evidence cannot be substituted for any instrument which the law requires to be in writing.

Oral proof cannot be substituted for the *written* evidence of any contract which the parties have put in writing.

A writing, in the possession of the adverse party, is still primary evidence of the contract, and its absence must be accounted for by notice to the other party to produce it, before secondary evidence of its contents can be received.

Oral evidence cannot be substituted for *any writing, the existence of which is disputed*, and which is *material*, either to the *issue* or to the *credit of the witnesses*, and is not merely the memorandum of some other fact.

Where the writing does not fall within either of the three classes already described, there is no ground for its excluding oral evidence.

HEARSAY EVIDENCE is that kind of evidence which does not derive its value solely from the credit to be given to the witness himself, but rests also in part on the veracity and competency of some other person.

The term *hearsay* is used with reference to that which is written, as well as to that which is spoken.

Original evidence.—There are *four classes of declarations*, which, though in truth original evidence, are usually treated under the head of *hearsay*, viz:

First—Where the fact that the declaration *was made*, and not its truth or falsity, is the point in question.

Secondly—Expressions of bodily or mental feelings, where the *existence* or *nature* of such feelings is the subject of enquiry.

Thirdly—Cases of *pedigree*, including the declarations of those nearly related to the party whose pedigree is in question.

Fourthly—All other cases where the declaration offered in evidence may be regarded as part of the *res gestæ*, or surrounding circumstances.

All these classes are involved in the principle of the last.

The general rule of law *rejects all hearsay reports* of transactions, whether written or verbal, given by persons not produced as witnesses.

The principle of this rule is that such evidence requires credit to be given to a statement made by a person who is not subject to the ordinary tests enjoined by law, viz: the sanction of an oath, and want of opportunity for cross-examination.

The surrounding circumstances, constituting parts of the *res gestæ*, or transaction, may always be shown to the jury, along with the principal fact.

The exceptions to the rule of law, rejecting hearsay evidence, are allowed only on the ground of the absence of better evidence, and from the nature and necessity of the case. They are as follows:

First—Those declarations relating to matters of *public* and *general* interest.

Secondly—Declarations relating to *ancient* possessions.

Thirdly—Declarations *against* interest.

Fourthly—*Dying* declarations, and some others of a miscellaneous nature.

Fifthly—Testimony of *deceased* witnesses, given in a former action between the same parties.

On the first exception.—Evidence of common reputation is received in regard to public facts—as a claim of highway or a right of ferry—on somewhat similar ground to that on which public documents, not judicial, are admitted, viz: the interest which all have in their truth, and the consequent probability that they are true.

The value of general reputation, as evidence of the true state of facts, depends upon its being the concurrent belief of minds unbiased, and in a situation favorable to a knowledge of the truth, and referring to a period when this foundation of evidence was not rendered turbid by agitation.

Declarations made after the controversy has originated are excluded, even though proof is offered that the existence of the controversy was not known to the declarant.

Where evidence of reputation is admitted, in cases of public or general interest, it is not necessary that the witness should be able to specify *from whom* he heard the declarations.

The second exception to the rule is allowed in cases of ancient possession, and in favor of the admission of ancient documents in support of it.

The third exception is allowed in the case of declarations and entries made by persons since deceased, and against the interest of the persons making them, at the time they were made, on the *ground* of the *extreme improbability of their falsehood.*

The fourth exception is allowed in the case of dying declarations, on the general principle that they are declarations made *in extremity*, when the party is at the point of death, and when every hope of this world is gone; when every motive to falsehood is silenced, and the mind is induced, by the most powerful considerations, to speak the truth.

They are now only admissible in cases of homicide, where the death of the deceased is the subject of the charge, and the circumstances of the death are the subject of the dying declarations. These declarations are received solely on the ground that they were made *in extremis;* for where they constitute part of the *res gestæ,* or come within the exception of the declarations against interest, or the like, they are admissible as in other cases irrespective of the fact that the declarant was under apprehension of death.

The declarations of the deceased are admissible *only* to those things to which he would have been *competent to testify,* if sworn in the cause.

The *circumstances* under which the declarations were made are to be shown to the *judge,* it being his province, and not that of the jury, to determine whether they are admissible.

If the statement of the deceased was committed to *writing* and *signed* by him, at the time it was made, the writing should be produced, if existing, and neither a copy nor parol evidence admitted in its place.

It has also been held that the *substance* of the declarations may be given in evidence, if the witness is not able to state the precise language used.

The fifth exception includes the testimony of *witnesses,* given in a former action between the same parties, subsequently dead, absent, or disqualified.

What the deceased witness testified may be proved by any

person who will swear from his own memory, or by notes taken by any one who will swear to their accuracy.

Admissions.—Under the head of exceptions to the rule rejecting hearsay evidence, it has been usual to treat of *admissions* and *confessions* by the party, considering them as declarations against his interest, and therefore probably true.

Admission is a term usually applied to *civil transactions* and those matters of fact, in criminal cases, which do not involve criminal intent.

Confession is a term generally restricted to *acknowledgments of guilt.*

The general doctrine is that the declarations of a *party to the record,* or of one *identified in interest with him,* are, as against such party, admissible in evidence.

In the absence of fraud, if the parties have a joint interest in the matter in suit, whether as plaintiffs or defendants, an admission made by one is, in general, evidence against all.

It is a *joint interest,* and not a mere *community of interest,* that renders such admissions receivable.

An *apparent* joint interest is not sufficient to render the admissions of one party receivable against his companions, where the *reality* of that interest is the point in controversy

The law gives the admissions of persons who are not parties to the record, but yet are *interested* in the *subject-matter* of the suit, the same weight as though they were parties to the record. But an admission made after other persons have acquired separate rights in the same subject-matter, cannot be received to disparage their title, however it may affect the declarant himself.

In some cases the admissions of *third* persons, *strangers* to the suit, are receivable, as when the issue is substantially upon the mutual rights of such persons at a particular time; in which case the practice is to let in such evidence in general as would be legally admissible in an action between the parties themselves.

The admissions of a third person are also receivable in evidence against the party who has *expressly referred* another *to him* for information in regard to an uncertain or disputed matter. Whether the answer of a person thus referred to is *conclusive* against the party, does not seem to have been settled.

The *admissions of the wife* will bind the husband only where she has authority to make them.

Admissions of *Attorneys of Record* bind their clients in all matters relating to the progress and trial of the cause. But they must be distinct and formal.

Privity is a term denoting mutual or successive relationship to the same rights of property, and is distributed into classes according to the manner of this relationship, viz: privies in *estate*, as donor and donee, lessor and lessee, and joint-tenants; privies in *blood*, as heir and ancestor, and coparceners; privies in *representation*, as executors and testator, administrators and intestate; and privies in *law*, where the law, without privity of blood or estate, casts the land upon another, as by escheat.

The admissions of one person are evidence against another, in respect of *privity* between them. The ground upon which admissions bind those in privity with the party making them is that they are indentified in interest.

Admissions by third persons, as they derive their value and legal force from the relation of the party making them to the property in question, are taken as parts of the *res gestæ*, and may be *proved* by *any competent witness* who *heard* them, without calling the party by whom they were made.

Admissions may be *implied* from *assumed character, language,* and *conduct*.

Verbal admissions ought to be received with great *caution*. The evidence, consisting as it does in the mere repetition of oral statements, is subject to much imperfection and mistake.

Of the effect of admissions when proved, the rule is that the *whole admission is to be taken together*.

Admissions which have been *acted upon* by others, are conclusive against the party making them, in all cases between him and the person whose conduct he has thus influenced. It makes no difference whether they were made in express language, or are implied from the open and general conduct of the party. In such cases the party is estopped, on the grounds of public policy and good faith, from repudiating his own representations; as illustrated by the case of a man cohabiting with a woman, and treating her in the face of the world as his wife, to whom in fact he is not married.

It makes *no difference*, in the operation of the rule, whether the thing admitted was *true* or *false*; it being the fact that it was acted upon that renders it conclusive.

CONFESSIONS of guilt in criminal prosecutions.

This branch of evidence is divided into two classes, viz: *direct* confessions of guilt; and *indirect* confessions, or those which, in civil cases, are usually termed implied admissions.

Here, also, as before remarked in regard to admissions, the evidence of verbal confessions of guilt is to be received with *great caution*.

It is generally agreed that *deliberate confessions of guilt* are among the most effectual proofs in the law.

Confessions are also divided into *judicial* confessions, or those made before the magistrate, or in court in the due course of legal proceedings; and *extrajudicial* confessions, or those made by the party elsewhere than before a magistrate or in court.

Extrajudicial confessions, *uncorroborated* by any other proof of the *corpus delicti*, are of themselves insufficient to convict.

The *whole* of what the prisoner said at the time of making the confession should be taken together.

Before any confession can be received in evidence in a criminal case it must be shown that it was *voluntary*.

If the confession has been obtained by the influence of *hope*, or *fear*, applied by a third person to the prisoner's mind, it must be excluded.

Evidence excluded from public policy is such as the law dispenses with because greater mischiefs would probably result from requiring or permitting its admission than from wholly rejecting it.

Of this class are communications between *husband and wife*, *professional* communications, *awards, secrets of State,* proceedings of grand and traverse *jurors,* and that which is *indecent* or offensive to public morals or injurious to the feelings or interest of third persons.

Exceptions to the rule are communications made to *clergymen and physicians;* and *grand jurors* may also be asked whether *twelve* of their number actually concurred in the finding of a bill, the certificate of the foreman not being conclusive evidence of that fact.

Number of witnesses, and the nature and quantity of proof required in particular cases.—*Two* witnesses are necessary to convict of high *treason*.

Perjury is a crime sufficiently established by *one* witness, *with corroborating* circumstances.

If the evidence adduced in proof of the crime of perjury consists of *two opposing statements* of the prisoner, and nothing more, he cannot be convicted. For there are cases in which a person might very honestly and conscientiously swear to a particular fact, from the best of his recollection and belief, and from other circumstances subsequently be convinced that he was wrong, and swear to the reverse, without meaning to swear falsely either time.

The evidence arising from circumstances alone may be stronger than the testimony of any single witness.

The statute of frauds, passed in the reign of Charles II, the provisions of which have been enacted, generally in the same words, in nearly all the United States, universally requires all *conveyances* of land, or *interests* in *lands,* for more than three years, to be evidenced by *writing.* All interests in lands, of whatever nature, created by *parol* without writing, being allowed only the force and effect of estates at will, except leases, not exceeding three years, for which term a parol lease is good; but if it is to commence *in futuro,* yet if the term is not to exceed three years, it is good. A parol lease for a longer period than the statute admits is void for the excess.

By the same statute, written evidence, signed by the party to be charged therewith, or by his agent, is required in every case of contract by an executor or administrator, to answer damages out of *his own* estate; in every promise of one person to answer for the debt, default, or miscarriage of another; in every agreement made in consideration of marriage; in every agreement which is not to be performed within a year from the time of making it; in every contract for the sale of lands, tenements, hereditaments, or any interest in or concerning them; also in every case of contract for the sale of goods, unless the buyer shall receive part of the goods at the time of sale, or give something in earnest, to bind the bargain or in part payment.

Devises of lands and tenements are also required to be in writing, signed by the testator and attested by competent witnesses.

Admissibility of parol or verbal evidence, to affect that which is written.—By *written evidence* is here meant not everything in writing, but that only containing the terms of a contract between the parties, and designed to be the repository and evidence of their final intentions.

EVIDENCE.

The rule is that **parol contemporaneous evidence is inadmissible to contradict or vary the terms of a valid written instrument.**

But written instruments may be read by the light of surrounding circumstances, in order to more perfectly understand the intent and meaning of the parties, but *no other words* are to be added to it, or substituted in their stead.

The duty of the court is to ascertain, not what the party secretly intended, but what is the *meaning* of the *words* they have used; and where the language of an instrument has a settled legal construction, parol evidence is not admissible to contradict that construction.

The terms of every written instrument are to be understood in their *plain, ordinary,* and *popular sense* unless by the known usage of trade, or the like, they have acquired a peculiar sense.

The rule under consideration is applied *only* in suits between the *parties to the instrument,* as they alone are to blame if the writing contains what was not intended, or omits that which it should have contained.

The rule excludes *only parol evidence of the language* of the parties, contradicting, varying, or adding to that which is contained in the written instrument.

But where the agreement in writing is expressed in short and incomplete terms, parol evidence is admissible to explain that which is, *per se,* unintelligible, such explanation not being inconsistent with the written terms.

The rule does not restrict the court to the perusal of a single paper or instrument; for, while the controversy is between the original parties, or their representatives, all their *contemporaneous writings,* relating to the same subject-matter, are admissible in evidence.

Neither is the rule infringed by the admission of parol evidence, showing that the instrument is altogether *void,* or that it *never* had any legal existence or binding force, either by reason of fraud, or for want of due execution and delivery, or for the illegality of the subject-matter. And this qualification applies to all contracts, whether under seal or not.

The want of a consideration may also be proved, to show that the agreement is not binding; unless it is under seal, which is generally conclusive evidence of a sufficient consideration, or is a negotiable instrument in the hands of an innocent endorsee.

Fraud, practiced by the party seeking the remedy, upon him against whom it is sought, and in that which is the subject-matter of the action or claim, is universally held fatal to his title.

Parol evidence may also be offered to show that the contract was made for the furtherance of objects *forbidden by law;* or that the writing was obtained by *felony,* or by duress; or that the party was *incapable* of binding himself, by reason of some legal impediment, such as infancy, coverture, want of reason, drunkenness, etc., or that the instrument came into the hands of the plaintiff without any absolute and final *delivery,* by the obligor or party charged.

Nor does the rule apply in cases where the original contract was verbal and entire, and a *part only* of it was reduced to *writing.*

Neither is the rule infringed by the introduction of parol evidence, *contradicting* or *explaining* the instrument in some of its *recitals of facts,* where such recitals do not, on other principles, estop the party to deny them; as, to show that the lands described in the deed as in one parish were in fact situated in another. So, also, parol evidence is admissible to show when a written promise, without date, was in fact made.

As it is a leading rule that written instruments are to be interpreted according to their subject-matter, parol or verbal testimony must be resorted to, in order to ascertain the nature and qualities of the subject to which the instrument refers. Evidence which is calculated to *explain* the subject of an instrument is essentially different in its character from evidence of verbal communications respecting it.

There is *no material difference* of principle in the rules of interpretation between *wills* and *contracts,* except what naturally arises from the different circumstances of the parties. The *object* in both cases is the same, namely: to discover the *intention.* And to do this the court may, in either case, *put themselves in the place of the party,* and then see how the terms of the instrument affect the property or subject-matter. With this view, evidence must be admissible of all the circumstances surrounding the author of the instrument; and if the court, by these means, cannot ascertain the meaning and intention of the author, from the language of the instrument thus illustrated, it is a case of incurable and hopeless uncertainty, and the instrument, therefore, is so far inoperative and void.

Evidence of known and established usage respecting

the subject to which the contract relates also does not infringe the rule which forbids the admission of parol evidence to contradict or vary a written contract. But, though usage *may* be admissible to explain what is *doubtful*, it is not admissible to contradict what is plain.

Neither is the rule infringed by the admission of oral evidence to prove a *new and distinct agreement,* upon a *new consideration,* whether it be as a substitute for the old, or in addition to and beyond it.

Oral evidence is also admissible to show that, by a subsequent agreement, the *time* of performance, in the case of a simple contract, was *enlarged,* or the *place* of performance changed; or that the *damages* for non-performance were waived; or that it was founded upon an insufficient or unlawful *consideration;* or without consideration; or that the agreement itself was *waived.*

Receipts, so far as they go to acknowledge only payment or delivery, are merely *prima facie* evidence of the fact, and not conclusive; therefore, they may be contradicted by oral testimony. But in so far as they are evidence of a contract between the parties, they stand on the footing of all other contracts in writing and cannot be contradicted or varied by parol.

MEANS OF PROOF, OR THE INSTRUMENTS OF EVIDENCE.

WITNESSES, AND THE MEANS OF PROCURING THEIR ATTENDANCE.

The instruments of evidence are divided into two general classes, namely: *written* and *unwritten.*

By *unwritten* or *oral evidence* is meant the testimony given by witnesses *viva voce,* either in open court or before a magistrate acting under its commission or the authority of law.

The attendance of witnesses is procured by a summons called a writ of *subpœna,* every court having power definitely to hear and determine any suit having, by the Common Law, inherent power to call for all adequate proofs of the facts in controversy, and to that end to summon and compel the attendance of witnesses before it. The writ of *subpœna* suffices for only one sitting or term of court; the witness must be summoned anew to each term.

EVIDENCE.

Subpœna, or the ordinary summons, is a judicial writ, directed to the witness, commanding him to appear at court, to testify what he knows in the cause therein described, pending in such court, under a certain penalty mentioned in the writ.

Subpœna duces tecum is the ordinary *subpœna*, containing a *clause* commanding the witness to bring with him also certain books or papers in his possession.

If the witness is in custody, or is in the military or naval service, and therefore not at liberty to attend without leave of his superior officer, which he cannot obtain, he may be brought into court to testify by a writ of *habeus corpus ad testificandum*.

By recognizance is another method by which the attendance of witnesses, in criminal cases, is enforced, which is the usual course upon all examinations where the party accused is committed or bound over for trial.

The service of a subpœna upon a witness ought always to be made in a *reasonable time* before trial. The time is generally fixed by statute, according to the distance, but at *least* one day's notice is necessary, however inconsiderable the distance.

The manner of service should be *personal,* otherwise the witness cannot be chargeable with contempt, for non-appearance.

Witnesses, as well as parties, are protected from arrest while going to the place of trial, while attending there for the purpose of testifying, and while returning home.

Where the witness has been duly summoned, and his fees paid or tendered, or the payment or tender waived, if he willfully neglects to appear, he is guilty of a *contempt* of the process of court, and may be proceeded against by an *attachment*, on motion.

If the witness resides abroad, out of the jurisdiction of the court, and refuses to attend, or is *sick* and *unable* to attend, his testimony can be obtained only by taking his *deposition*.

OF THE COMPETENCY OF WITNESSES.—The Common Law rejects the testimony of *parties*, of persons *deficient in understanding*, of persons *insensible* to the *obligations* of an *oath*, and of persons whose *pecuniary interest is* directly *involved* in the matter in issue.

First.—In regard to parties—The general rule of the Common Law is that *a party to the record,* in a civil suit, *cannot be a witness* either for himself or for a co-suitor in the cause.

This rule of the Common Law is founded not solely in the consideration of interest, but partly, also, in the general **expediency** of avoiding temptations to perjury.

But by statutory provision, parties may now testify in most cases.

The principles which govern in the admission or exclusion of parties as witnesses in *civil* cases are, in general, applicable, with the like force, to *criminal prosecutions*, except so far as they are effected by particular legislation or by considerations of public policy.

The record in a criminal prosecution cannot be used as evidence in a civil suit, either at law or in equity, except to prove the mere fact of the adjudication, or a judicial confession of guilt, by the party indicted.

Where the facts are personally known by the judge, it seems now agreed that the same person cannot be *both witness and judge;* nor can a judge, on the grounds of public interest and convenience, be called to testify to what took place before him in the trial of another cause, though he may testify to foreign and collateral matters.

It has been held in England a very objectionable proceeding on the part of an attorney to give evidence when the acting advocate in a cause, and a sufficient ground for a new trial; but in the United States no case has been found to proceed to that extent, and the fact is hardly ever known to occur.

Secondly.—As to persons deficient in understanding being incompetent to testify; while the deficiency of understanding exists, be the cause of what nature soever, the person is not admissible to be sworn as a witness; but if the cause be temporary, and a lucid interval should occur, or a cure be effected, the competency is restored.

Persons deaf and dumb, though in presumption of law idiots, if proved by the party offering them as witnesses to be persons of *sufficient understanding*, may be sworn and give evidence by an interpreter, writing, or by means of signs.

In respect to children, there is no precise age within which they are absolutely excluded, on the presumption that they have not sufficient understanding. At the age of fourteen every person is presumed to have common discretion and understanding, until the contrary appears; but under that age it is not so presumed, and therefore enquiry is made as to the degree of understanding of the child; and if he appears to have sufficient natural intelligence, and to have been so instructed as to comprehend the nature and effect of an oath, he is admitted to testify, whatever his age may be, the examination being made by the judge, at his discretion.

Thirdly.—Those who are insensible to the obligations of an oath, from defect of religious sentiment and belief, constitute another class of persons incompetent to testify as witnesses, as *atheists, infidels*, etc.

An oath is an outward pledge, given by the witness, that his attestation or promise is made under an immediate sense of his responsibility to God.

As to the degree of religious faith necessary or required in a witness, the rule of law is that the person is competent to testify, if he believes in the being of God, and a future state of rewards and punishments; that is, that Divine punishment will be the certain consequence of perjury.

Persons infamous—that is, who have been legally adjudged guilty of those heinous crimes which men generally are not found to commit unless so depraved as to be unworthy of credit for truth—are included under this general head of exclusion, because of insensibility to the obligation of an oath, the basis of this rule being that such a person is morally too corrupt to be trusted to testify.

No person is deemed infamous in law until he has been legally found guilty of an infamous crime; the mere *verdict* of the jury is not sufficient; *judgment* only is the legal and conclusive evidence of the party's guilt, for the purpose of rendering him incompetent to testify.

Accomplices.—*A particeps criminis*, notwithstanding the turpitude of his conduct, is a competent witness so long as he remains not convicted and sentenced for an infamous crime.

The admission of accomplices as witnesses for the government is justified by the necessity of the case; it often being otherwise impossible to bring the principals to justice. The usual course is to leave out of the indictment those who are to be called as witnesses. When already indicted, whether the accomplice shall be admitted as a witness for the government, or not, is determined by the judges, as in their discretion may best serve the purposes of justice.

The *degree of credit*, however, to be given to an accomplice is a matter exclusively within the province of the jury; and it has become the settled practice, under advice from the bench, *not* to convict a prisoner in any case of felony upon the sole and uncorroborated testimony of an accomplice.

EVIDENCE.

Fourthly.—Those interested in the results of a cause constitute another class of persons incompetent to testify, on the same principle that excludes parties themselves, viz: the temptations and danger of perjury, and the little credit generally found due to such testimony in judicial investigations.

EXAMINATION OF WITNESSES.—This subject lies chiefly in the discretion of the judge, it being from its very nature susceptible of but few positive and stringent rules.

Whatever is left to the discretion of one judge, his decision is not subject to be reversed or revised by another.

If the judge deems it essential to the discovery of truth that the witnesses should be examined *out of the hearing of each other*, he will so order it.

When a witness has been duly sworn, and his competency settled, if objected to, he is first examined by the party producing him, which is called his *direct examination*. He is afterwards examined to the same matters by the adverse party, which is called his *cross-examination*.

In the direct examination of a witness, it is not allowed to put to him what are termed *leading questions*—that is, questions which suggest to the witness the answer desired.

Questions are also objectionable, as leading, which, embodying a material fact, admit of an answer by a simple negative or affirmative. An argumentative or pregnant course of interrogation is as faulty as the like course in pleading.

In some cases leading questions are permitted, even in a direct examination, viz: where the witness appears to be *hostile* to the party producing him, or in the *interest* of the other party, or *unwilling* to give evidence, or where an omission in his testimony is evidently caused by *want of recollection*, which a suggestion may assist.

Indeed, when and under what circumstances a leading question may be put, is a matter resting in the sound discretion of the court, and not a matter which can be assigned for error.

Though a witness can testify only to such facts as are within his own knowledge and recollection, yet he is permitted to refresh and assist his memory by the use of a written instrument, memorandum, or entry in a book, and may be compelled to do so if the writing is present in court.

The cases in which writings are permitted to be used

for this purpose are where used only for assisting the memory of the witness; where he recollects having seen the writing before, and, though he has now no independent recollection of the facts mentioned in it, yet he remembers that, at the time he saw it, he knew the contents to be correct; and where, never having seen the writing, nor recollecting anything contained in it, but knowing the writing to be genuine, his mind is so convinced that he is on that ground enabled to swear positively to the fact. The *time* when the writing, thus used to restore the recollection of facts *should have been made* is generally at the time of the fact in question, or recently afterwards.

In general, though a witness must depose to such facts only as are within his own knowledge, yet there is no rule that requires him to speak with such expression of certainty as to exclude all doubt in his mind.

Though the opinions of witnesses are in general not evidence, yet on certain subjects some classes of witnesses may deliver their own opinions, and on certain other subjects any competent witness may express his *opinion or belief*, thus: as of the identity of a person or of handwriting, etc., and if he testifies falsely as to his belief he may be convicted of perjury. On questions of science, skill, or trade, or others of the like kind, persons of skill, or *experts*, may not only testify to facts, but are permitted to give their opinions in evidence.

Experts, in the strict sense of the word, are persons instructed by experience; but more generally speaking the term includes all men of science, or persons professionally acquainted with the science or practice in question, or conversant with the subject-matter, on questions of science, skill, trade, and others of the like kind.

The law will not permit parties to impeach the general reputation of their witnesses for truth, *after* they have testified, or been produced in court, though there are some exceptions to this rule; as where the witness is not one of the party's own selection, but is one whom the law *obliges* him to call, as the subscribing witness to a deed, etc.

But a party calling a witness is not precluded from proving the truth of any *particular fact*, by any other competent testimony in direct *contradiction* to what such witness may have testified.

Where the witness testifying had previously stated the facts in a *different* manner, the weight of authority seems in favor of admitting the party to show that the evidence has taken him by surprise, and is contrary to the examination of the witness, preparatory to the trial, this being necessary for his protection againt the contrivance of an artful witness.

When a witness has been examined in chief, the other party has a right to *cross-examine* him; but no right to cross-examine, except as to facts and circumstances connected with the matters stated in his direct examination; and if he wishes to examine him as to other matters, he must do so by making the witness his own, and calling him as such, in the subsequent progress of the cause.

Cross-examination is one of the most efficacious tests which the law has devised for the discovery of truth; its object being that the jury, by means of it, may the better understand the character of the witness they are called upon to believe; his situation with respect to the parties, and to the subject of litigation; his interest, motives, inclination, and prejudices; means of correct and certain knowledge of the facts, etc.—by this opportunity of observing his demeanor, and of determining the just weight and value of his testimony.

Where the witness is evidently prevaricating, or concealing the truth, it is seldom by intimidation or sternness of manner that he can be brought to let out the truth; the most effectual method is to examine rapidly and minutely as to a number of subordinate and apparently trivial points in his evidence, concerning which there is little likelihood of his being prepared with falsehood ready made; and where such a course of interrogation is skillfully laid, it is rarely that it fails in exposing perjury or contradiction in some parts of the testimony which it is desired to overturn.

Except in cross-examination, the rule that the evidence offered must correspond with the allegations, and be confined to the point in issue, excludes all evidence of *collateral* facts.

Evidence not being to a material point, the witness can not be punished for perjury, if it were *false.*

A witness cannot be cross-examined as to any fact which is collateral and irrelevant to the issue, *merely* for the purpose of *contradicting* him by other evidence, if he should deny it, thereby to discredit his testimony.

The *privilege* of a witness in *not being compelled to answer* is his own, and not that of the party; counsel, therefore, will not be allowed to make the objection; but where the witness, after being *advised* of his privilege, chooses to answer, he is bound to answer everything relative to the transaction.

Where it reasonably appears that the answer will have a tendency to expose the witness to a penal liability, or any kind of punishment, or to a criminal charge, he is not bound to answer.

If the prosecution, to which he *might* be exposed, is barred by lapse of time, the privilege ceases, and the witness must answer.

When a witness takes advantage of his privilege, and declines answering, no inference of the truth of the fact is permitted to be drawn from that circumstance.

Where by answering, the witness may subject himself to a *civil* action, or *pecuniary* loss, or charge himself with a *debt*, he is bound to answer.

Where the answer of the witness will *not directly and certainly* show his infamy, but will *only tend* to disgrace him, he may be compelled to answer. In criminal offences the rule is different.

But the court must see for itself that the answer will directly show his infamy before it will excuse him from testifying to the fact.

Where the question involves the fact of a previous conviction it ought not to be asked, because there is higher and better evidence which ought to be offered.

In those matters of privilege from answering, *greater* latitude is allowed in making enquiry in the *cross-examination*, that the jury may better understand the character of the witness whom they are asked to believe, *in order* that his evidence may not pass for more than it is worth. Enquiries, therefore, having no tendency to this end, are clearly impertinent.

Where the question goes clearly to the credit of the witness for veracity it is not easy to perceive why he should be privileged from answering, notwithstanding it may disgrace him.

After a witness has been examined in chief his credit may be impeached in various ways besides that of exhibiting the improbabilities of a story by a cross-examination; viz: by *disproving the facts* stated by him, by the testimony of others; by general evidence affecting his *credit for veracity*, and by proof that he has made *statements out of court contrary* to what he has

EVIDENCE.

testified at the trial; but this is only in matters relevant to the issue.

In impeaching the credit of a witness, the examination must be confined to his *general reputation,* and not be permitted as to particular facts. The witness must be able to state what is *generally said* of the person by those among whom the person dwells, or with whom he is chiefly conversant.

A witness cannot be cross-examined as to the contents of a letter, by asking him whether he wrote such, etc., without first showing him the letter, and asking him whether he wrote it; for the contents of every written paper are to be proved by the paper itself, if in existence; and if *lost,* proof of the fact being offered, he may be cross-examined as to its contents; after which he may be contradicted by secondary evidence of its contents.

Nor can he be asked, on cross-examination, *whether he has written such a thing,* stating its particular nature or purport; the proper course being to put the writing into his hands, and to ask him whether it is in his writing.

If the memory of a witness is refreshed by a paper put into his hands, the adverse party may cross-examine the witness upon that paper, without making it his evidence in the cause.

But if the paper is shown to the witness merely to prove the handwriting, this alone does not give the opposite party a right to inspect it, or to cross-examine as to its contents.

After a witness has been cross-examined respecting a former statement made by him, *the party who called him* has a right to *re-examine* him as to the same matter, and to ask all questions which may be proper to draw forth an explanation of the sense and meaning of the expressions used by the witness on the cross-examination, and also of the motive by which the witness was induced to use those expressions.

WRITTEN EVIDENCE.—Writings are divisible into two classes, viz: *Public* and *Private;* the former being either judicial or not judicial; and with respect to the means and mode of proving them—*of record,* or *not of record.*

Public documents.—It has been admitted, from a very early period, that the *inspection* and exemplification of the records of the King's courts is the common right of the subject.

Any person interested in the proceedings has the right to a copy of a judicial record or paper, on applying for it.

18

274   EVIDENCE.

Some records partake both of a public and private character, and are treated as to the one or the other, according to the relation in which the applicant stands to them; *thus:* the books of a corporation are public with respect to its members, but private with respect to strangers.

If an inspection is wanted by a stranger, in a case not within the rule of the Common Law, it can only be obtained by a bill of discovery, through the aid of a court of equity.

Inspection of the books of public officers is subject to the same restriction as in the case of corporation books.

The motion for rule to inspect and take copies of books and writings, when an action is pending, may be made at any stage of the cause, and is founded on an *affidavit*, stating the circumstances under which the inspection is claimed, and that an application therefor has been made to the proper quarter, and refused.

But *when no action is pending*, the proper course is to move for a rule to show cause why a *mandamus* should not issue, commanding the officer having custody of the books to permit the applicant to inspect them, and take copies.

Mode of proof of public documents. Courts take notice judicially of the political constitution, or frame of the government of their own country, its essential and political agents or officers, and its essential, ordinary, and regular operation.

The great seal of the state and the seals of its judicial tribunals require no proof other than inspection. So also seals of state of other nations, recognized by their own sovereign seals of foreign courts of admiralty, and of notaries public.

Public statutes also need no proof, being supposed to exist in the memories of all; but for certainty of recollection reference is had either to a copy from the legislative rolls, or to the book printed by public authority.

Acts of state may be proved by production of the original printed document, from a press authorized by government.

Proclamations, and other acts and orders of the executive of the like character, may be proved by production of the government gazette in which they were authorized to be printed.

Printed copies of public documents, transmitted to Congress by the President of the United States, and printed by the printer

EVIDENCE. 275

to Congress, are evidence of these documents; and in all cases of a proof by a copy, if the copy has been taken by a machine, worked by the witness who produced it, it is sufficient.

As to legislative acts in the United States generally, the printed copies of the laws and resolves of the legislature, published by its authority, are held competent evidence; and it is sufficient, *prima facie,* that the book purports to have been so printed.

The journals of the legislature, and all other *public records* and *documents,* may, from their immovable nature, be proved by examined copies, and it is a *general rule* that, whenever the thing to be proved would require no collateral proof upon its production, it is provable by a copy.

Public writings, such as *official registers,* or *books* kept by persons in *public office,* are entitled to an extraordinary degree of confidence, and are generally admissible in evidence without the ordinary and necessary tests of truth, being so recognized by law, because they are required by law to be kept, the entries in them being of public interest and notoriety, and because they are made under the sanction of an oath of office, or official duty.

All documents of a public nature, which there would be an inconvenience in removing, and which the party has a right to inspect, may be proved by a duly authenticated *copy.*

When the books themselves are produced, they are received as evidence, without further attestation; but they must be accompanied by proof that they come from the *proper repository.*

In regard to foreign laws—the courts do not take judicial notice of them, but they must be proved as facts.

Generally, authenticated copies of the written laws, or of other public instruments of a foreign government, are expected to be produced.

The court *may* proceed on its own knowledge of foreign laws, without the aid of other proof; but in general, foreign laws are required to be verified by the sanction of an oath, unless verified by some high authority, such as the law respects, not less than it respects the oath of an individual.

The usual mode of authenticating foreign laws and judgments is by an exemplification of a copy under the great seal of state, or by a copy proved to be a true copy by a witness who has examined and compared it with the original; or by a certificate of an officer, properly authorized by law to give the copy, which certificate must itself be also duly authenticated.

Foreign unwritten laws, customs and usages are proved by parol evidence.—Sometimes, however, certificates of persons in high authority are allowed, without other proof.

The reciprocal relations between the *national government* and the several *States* composing the *United States*, are not foreign, but **domestic**: hence the courts of the United States take judicial notice of all the public laws of the respective States, and the courts of the several States take judicial notice of all public acts of Congress; but private statutes must be proved in the ordinary way.

A printed volume, purporting on the face of it to contain the laws of a sister State, is admissible as *prima facie* evidence, to prove the statute laws of that State. The *seal* of a State is a sufficient authentication, without the attestation of any officer, or any other proof; and it will be presumed *prima facie* that the seal was affixed by the proper officer.

To entitle a book to the character of official register it is not necessary that it be required by an express statute to be kept, nor that the nature of the office should render the book indispensable; it is sufficient that it be *directed by proper authority to be kept*, and that it be kept according to such directions.

Any approved public and general history is admissible to prove ancient facts of a public nature, and the general usages and customs of the country.

RECORDS AND JUDICIAL WRITINGS.—As to the proof of records, this is done either by mere *production* of the records, or by a copy.

Copies of records are exemplifications, copies by an authorized officer and sworn copies.

Exemplifications are copies under the seal of the court where the record remains.

The record itself is produced only when the cause is in the same court whose record it is; or when it is the subject of proceedings in a superior court.

Copies of records and judicial proceedings, under seal, are deemed of higher credit than sworn copies, as having passed under a more exact critical examination.

The records and judicial proceedings of the courts of any State are proved or admitted in any other court, within the United States, by the attestation of the clerk and the seal of the court annexed, together with a certificate of the judge that the attestation is in due form.

The attestation of the copy must be according to the form used in the State from which the record comes.

An office copy of a record is a copy authenticated by an officer intrusted for that purpose, and is admitted in evidence upon the credit of the officer, without proof that it has been actually examined.

The proof of records, by an *examined copy*, is by producing a witness who has compared the copy with the original, or with what the officer of the court or any other person read, as the contents of the record.

If the record is lost and is ancient, its existence and contents may sometimes be presumed; but after proof of loss, its contents may be proved, like any other document, by any secondary evidence, where the case admits of no better.

The judgments of inferior courts are usually proved by producing from the proper custody the book containing the proceedings, or by examined copies, if perfect.

Depositions taken upon interrogatories, *under a special commission*, cannot be read without proof of the commission under which they were taken.

Testaments are proved by due form of law, *per testes*, upon due notice and hearing of all parties concerned.

Examinations of prisoners in criminal cases are usually proved by the magistrate or clerk who wrote them down.

The proof of writs, whether by production of the writ itself, or by a copy, depends on its having been returned or not. After being returned, it has become matter of record, and is to be proved by a copy from the record. If not returned, it may be proved by producing it; if it cannot be found, after diligent search, it may be proved by secondary evidence, as in other cases.

Justice requires that every cause be once fairly and impartially tried; but having been once so tried, public tranquility demands that all litigation of that question, and *between those parties*, should be forever closed.

Privity denotes mutual or successive relationship to the same rights of property. Persons standing in this relation to the litigating party, being identified with him in interest, are bound by the proceedings, and hence *all privies*, whether in estate, in blood, or in law, are estopped from litigating that which is conclusive upon him with whom they are in privity.

A record may also be admitted in evidence in favor of a stranger, against one of the parties, as containing a *solemn admission*, or judicial declaration by such party, in regard to a certain fact.

The principle upon which judgments are held conclusive upon the parties requires that the rule should apply only to that which was *directly in issue*, and not to everything which was incidentally brought into the controversy.

A record, therefore, is not held conclusive, as to the truth of any allegations which were not material nor traversable; but as to things material and traversable, it is conclusive and final.

The general rules upon the subject of judgments being given in evidence in civil suits seems to be, **first**—that the judgment of a court of concurrent jurisdiction, directly upon the point, is, as a plea, a bar; or as evidence, conclusive, between the same parties, upon the same matter, directly in question, in another court; and **secondly**—that the judgment of a court of exclusive jurisdiction, directly upon the point, is, in like manner, conclusive upon the same matter, between the same parties, coming incidentally in question in another court, for a different purpose. But neither the judgment of a concurrent nor exclusive jurisdiction is evidence of any matter which came collaterally in question, though within their jurisdiction; nor of any matter incidentally cognizable; nor of any matter to be inferred by argument from the judgment.

It is only where the point in issue has been determined that the judgment is a bar.

So, also, to constitute a judgment a complete bar, it must appear to have been a *decision upon the merits*.

As a general rule, a verdict and judgment in a *criminal case* cannot be given in evidence in a civil action, to establish the *facts* on which it was rendered, and a judgment in a *civil action* is inadmissible as evidence in a criminal prosecution.

But the verdict and judgment in any case are always admissible to prove the fact that the judgment was rendered, or the verdict given.

By the constitution and statutes of the United States **judgments of other states, authenticated as the statutes provide, are put upon the same footing as domestic judgments**; but no execution can issue upon such judgments without a new suit in the tribunals of other States.

Depositions are but secondary evidence, and to be admissible as evidence, it is essential that they be regularly taken, under legal proceedings duly pending, and in a manner provided by law.

In regard to the admissibility of a former *judgment* in evidence. It is generally necessary that there be a perfect *mutuality* between the parties, neither being concluded unless both are alike bound; but with respect to *depositions*, though this rule is admitted in its general principle, yet it is applied with more latitude of discretion, and complete mutuality, or identity of all the parties is not required.

As to inquisitions.—The general rule in regard to these documents is, that they are admissible in evidence, but they are not conclusive except against the parties immediately concerned, and their privies.

PRIVATE WRITINGS.—In general, all such produced in evidence must be proved to be genuine.

Solemn obligations and instruments, under the hand of the party, purporting to be evidence of title, such as deeds, bills and notes, must be produced, and the execution of them generally proved, or their absence duly accounted for, and their loss supplied by secondary evidence.

If the instrument is lost, evidence is required that such a paper once existed, slight evidence being sufficient, and that a *bona fide* and diligent search has been unsuccessfully made for it, after which his own affidavit is admissible to the fact of its loss.

The same rule prevails where the instrument is destroyed.

The production of private writings, in which another person has an interest, may be had either by a bill of discovery in proper cases, or, in trials at law, by a writ of *subpœna duces tecum*, directed to the person who has them in his possession.

The courts of common law may also make an *order for the inspection of writings* in the possession of one party to a suit, in favor of the other.

Application for this should be supported by the *affidavit* of the party.

When the instrument is in the hands or power of the adverse party there are, in general, except in the cases mentioned, no other means at law of compelling him to produce it, but the practice in such cases is to give him or his attorney a regular *notice to produce* the original, in order to lay the foundation for the introduction of secondary evidence of the contents of the document or writing, by showing that the party has done all in his power to produce the original.

There are three cases in which such notice to produce is not necessary ; first—where the instrument to be produced and that to be proved are *duplicate originals ;* **secondly**—where the instrument to be proved is *itself a notice*, such as a notice to quit, or a notice of the dishonor of a bill of exchange; **thirdly**—where, from the *nature of an action*, the defendant has notice that the plaintiff intends to charge him with possession of the instrument, as in trover for a bill of exchange.

The principle of the rule does not require notice to the adverse party to produce a paper belonging to a third person, of which he has fraudulently obtained possession, as where, after service of a *subpœna duces tecum*, the adverse party had received the paper from the witness, in fraud of the *subpœna*.

The notice *may be directed* to the party or his attorney, and may be *served on either*, and it must describe the writing demanded, so as to leave no doubt that the party was aware of the particular instrument intended to be called for.

The regular time for calling for the production of papers is not until the party who requires them has entered upon his case, until which time the other party may refuse to produce them, and no cross-examination as to their contents until then is usually permitted.

If, on the production of the instrument, it *appears to have been altered*, **it is incumbent on the party offering it in evidence to explain this appearance.** Every alteration on the face of a written instrument detracts from its credit, and renders it suspicious; and this suspicion the party claiming under it is ordinarily held bound to remove.

If the alteration is noted in the *attestation clause,* as having been made *before* the execution of the instrument, it is sufficiently accounted for, and the instrument is relieved from that suspicion.

Generally speaking, **if nothing appears to the contrary, the alteration will be presumed to be contemporaneous with the execution of the instrument**; but if any ground of suspicion is apparent upon the face of the instrument, the law presumes nothing, but leaves the question of when it was done

EVIDENCE.

by whom, and with what intent, as matters of fact for the jury.

Written instruments which are *altered,* in the legal sense of that term, are *thereby made void,* and **any alteration causing it to speak a language different in legal effect from that which it originally spoke is a material alteration.**

A distinction is to be observed between the *alteration* and the *spoliation* of an instrument as to its legal consequences.

Alteration is an act done upon the instrument **by which its meaning or language is changed, and if what is written upon or erased from the instrument has no tendency to produce this result, or to mislead any person, it is not an alteration.** This term is usually applied to the act of the party entitled under the instrument, and imports some improper design on his part to change its effect.

Spoliation is the act of a stranger, without the participation of the party interested, and is a mere mutilation of the instrument, not changing its legal operation, so long as the original writing remains legible, or, if it be a deed, any trace remains of the seal.

Mutilated portions may be admitted as secondary evidence of so much of the original instrument.

If the alteration is made by the *consent of parties,* such as by filling up of blanks or the like, it is valid.

The instrument, being produced and freed from suspicion, must be proved by the subscribing witnesses, if there be any, or at least by one of them.

A written instrument, not attested by a subscribing witness, is sufficiently proved, to authorize its introduction, by competent proof that the signature of the person whose name is undersigned is genuine.

A subscribing witness is one who was present when the instrument was executed, and who, at that time, at the request or with the assent of the party, subscribed his name to it, as a witness of the execution.

But it is not necessary that he should have actually seen the party sign, nor have been present at the very moment of signing; for if he is called in immediately afterwards, and the party acknowledges his signature to the witness, and requests him to attest it, this is sufficient.

To the rule requiring the production of the subscribing witnesses there are several classes of *exceptions,* viz:

First, where the instrument is *thirty years old*, it is said to prove itself.

Secondly, where the instrument *is produced by the adverse party* pursuant to notice, the party producing it *claiming an interest* under the instrument; for, by so claiming under it, he has admitted its execution.

Thirdly, where, from the circumstances of the witnesses themselves, the party, either from *physical* or *legal obstacles*, being *unable to adduce them;* as if the witness be dead, or cannot be found, or is out of the jurisdiction, or is a fictitious person, or insane, etc.; in all such cases the execution of the instrument may be proved by other evidence.

Fourthly, *office bonds*, required by law to be taken in the name of some public functionary, which documents, *it is said*, have a high character of authenticity and need not be verified by the ordinary tests of truth applied to merely private instruments.

Fifthly, a further exception to the rule has been admitted in the case of letters received in reply to others proved to have been sent to the party.

The degree of diligence in the search for the subscribing witness is the same which is required in the search for a lost paper, the principle being the same in both cases; it must be a strict, diligent and honest enquiry and search, satisfactory to the court, under the circumstances.

When secondary evidence of the execution of the instrument is thus rendered admissible, it will not be necessary to prove the *hand-writing* of more than one witness.

As to the subject of the *comparison* of hands, if the witness has the proper knowledge of the party's handwriting, he *may declare his belief* in regard to the genuineness of the writing in question.

There are two modes of acquiring this knowledge of the handwriting of another, either of which is universally admitted to be sufficient to enable a witness to testify as to its genuineness: **first**, from having *seen him write;* **second**, from having *seen letters*, or other documents, purporting to be the handwriting of the party, and having afterwards *personally communicated* with him *respecting them* or *acted upon them* as his, the party having known and acquiesced in such acts, etc.

This rule requiring personal knowledge on the part of the

witness has been *relaxed in two cases: first*, where the writings are of such *antiquity* that living witnesses cannot be had, and yet are not so old as to prove themselves; here *experts* are called to compare them with other writings admitted to be genuine, or proved to have been respected and treated and acted upon as such by all parties, and to give their opinion concerning the genuineness of the instrument in question, from thus comparing them; *secondly,* where *other writings*, admitted to be genuine, are *already in the case;* here the comparison may be made by the jury, without the aid of experts.

Where the sources of primary evidence of a written instrument are exhausted, secondary evidence is admissible; but whether, in this species of evidence, any degrees are recognized as of binding force is not perfectly agreed, but the better opinion seems to be that, generally speaking, there are none.

The student will not fail to observe the symmetry and beauty of this branch of the law, and will rise from the study of its principles, convinced, with Lord Erskine, that "they are founded in the charities of religion, in the philosophy of nature, in the truths of history, and in the experience of common life."

EQUITY

JURISPRUDENCE

ABRIDGED.

ANALYSIS.

Nature and Character of Equity Jurisprudence.
Origin and History.
General View and Maxims.
Jurisdiction in Cases of Accident.
Mistake.
Actual or Positive Fraud.
Constructive Fraud.
Account.
Partnership.
Discovery.
Cancellation and Delivery of Instruments.
Specific Performance.
Compensation and Damages.
Interpleader.
Bills Quia Timet.
Bills of Peace.
Injunctions.
Trusts.
Mortgages.
Assignments.
Wills.
Election.
Satisfaction.
Charities.
Implied Trusts.
Penalties and Forfeitures.
Infants.
Married Women.
Bills of Discovery.
Bills to Perpetuate Testimony.
Peculiar Defences and Proofs.
Estoppel in Equity.

EQUITY.

NATURE AND CHARACTER OF EQUITY JURISPRUDENCE.

EQUITY, in its true and genuine meaning, is the soul and spirit of all law; positive law is construed, and rational law is made by it.

Aristotle has defined the very nature of equity to be **the correction of the law, wherein it is defective by reason of its universality.**

Equity jurisprudence may properly be said to be **that portion of remedial justice which is exclusively administered by a court of equity,** as contra-distinguished from that portion of remedial justice which is exclusively administered by a court of Common Law.

In the most general sense, we are accustomed to call that equity which, in human transactions, is **founded in natural justice,** in honesty and right, and which properly arises *ex æquo et bono.* In this sense it answers precisely to the definition of justice, or natural law, as given by Justinian in the Pandects.

Taken broadly and philosophically, equity means to do to all men as we would they should do unto us.

This is Natural Equity, which, being derived from the principles of universal truth and justice, prescribes piety and reverence towards God, the Maker and Disposer of us all; honesty and benevolence to one another, by doing good and eschewing evil.

It is clear that human tribunals cannot cope with so wide a range of duties as natural equity comprehends. Taken in a less universal sense, equity is used in contra-distinction to strict law. This is **Moral Equity, which should be the genius of every kind of human jurisprudence,** since it expounds and limits the language of the positive laws, and construes them not according to their strict letter, but rather in their reasonable and benignant spirit.

But it is in neither of these senses that equity is to be understood as the substantial justice which is expounded by our courts of chancery. It is here accepted in a more limited and technical sense, and may be called **Municipal Equity**, and described as **the system of supplemental law administered in chancery, and founded upon defined rules, recorded precedents and established principles to which it closely adheres.**

The grand characteristic of Municipal Equity is displayed in the nature and extent of its redress.

The essential difference between law and equity principally consists in the different modes of administering justice in each, in the mode of *proof*, the mode of *trial* and the mode of *relief*.

The system of our courts of equity is a labored, connected system, governed by established rules, and bound down by precedents from which they do not depart, although the reason of some of them may perhaps be liable to objection. Sometimes a precedent is so strictly followed that a particular judgment, founded upon special circumstances, gives rise to a general rule.

Courts of equity adhere as closely to general rules as courts of law. Each expounds its rules to meet new cases; but each is equally reluctant to depart from them upon slight inconveniences and mischiefs.

One of the most common maxims upon which a court of equity daily acts is **that equity follows the law, and seeks out and guides itself by the analogies of the law.**

Courts of equity **decide new cases, as they arise, by the principles on which former cases have been decided;** and may thus illustrate, or enlarge, the operation of those principles. But **the principles are as fixed and certain as the principles on which the courts of common law proceed.**

One of the most striking and distinctive features of courts of equity is that **they can adapt their decrees to all the varieties of circumstances which may arise**, and adjust them to all the peculiar rights of all the parties in interest; whereas courts of common law are bound down to a fixed and invariable form of judgment in general terms, altogether absolute, for the plaintiff or for the defendant.

Courts of **equity can administer remedies for rights,**

which rights courts of common law do not recognize at all; or, if they do recognize them, they leave them wholly to the conscience and good-will of the parties. Thus, what are technically called Trusts, that is, **estates vested in persons upon particular trusts and confidences**, are wholly without any cognizance at the Common Law; and the abuses of such trusts and confidences are beyond the reach of any legal process.

The remedies in courts of equity are often very different in their nature, mode, and degree, from those of courts of common law, even when each has a jurisdiction over the same subject-matter. Thus, a court of equity, if a contract is broken, will often compel the party specifically to perform the contract; whereas courts of law can only give damages for the breach of it. So, courts of **equity will interfere by way of injunction to prevent wrongs; whereas courts of common law can grant redress only when the wrong is done.**

The most general, if not the most precise, description of a court of equity is that **it has jurisdiction in cases of rights, recognized and protected by the municipal jurisprudence, when a plain, adequate and complete remedy cannot be had in the courts of common law.**

The remedy must be plain; for, if it be doubtful and obscure at law, equity will assert a jurisdiction.

It must be adequate; for if at law it falls short of what the party is entitled to, that founds a jurisdiction in equity.

It must be complete; that is, it must attain the full end and justice of the case.

It must reach the whole mischief, and secure the whole right of the party in a perfect manner, at the present time and in future; otherwise equity will interfere and give relief.

The jurisdiction of a court of equity is, therefore, **sometimes concurrent** with the jurisdiction of a court of law; it is **sometimes exclusive** of it, and it is **sometimes auxiliary** to it.

Equity jurisdiction is distributable into three subdivisions, namely.

(I.) **The assistant,** being auxiliary to the Common Law, and under which range matter of—

1. Discovery for the promotion of substantive justice at Common Law.

2. Preservation of testimony relating to a question at law, from persons not being the litigants.

3. Removal of improper impediments, and prevention of unconscientious defences, at Common Law.

4. Giving effect to, and relieving from, the consequences of Common Law judgments.

(II.) **The concurrent** with the Common Law, comprehending—

1. The remedial correction of fraud.
2. The prevention of fraud by injunction.
3. Accident.
4. Mistake.
5. Account.
6. Dower.
7. Interpleader.
8. The delivery up of documents and specific chattels.
9. The specific performance of agreements.

(III.) **The exclusive**, relating to—

1. Trusts.
2. Infancy.
3. The equitable rights of wives.
4. Legal and equitable mortgages.
5. The assignment of choses in action.
6. Partition.
7. The appointment of receivers.
8. Charities and public trusts.

Equity claims an **exclusive jurisdiction in all matters of trust and confidence**; and wherever, upon the principles of universal justice, the interference of a court of judicature is necessary to prevent a wrong, and the positive law is silent.

ORIGIN AND HISTORY.

The **present equitable jurisdiction of the courts of chancery** seems to have grown up, like most of the other institutions of the English Common Law, from the exigencies of the times and of judicial administration.

Its date may reach back, dimly, into the earliest times, immediately succeeding the **Norman Conquest**; but the well-defined development of the distinct exercise of equitable jurisdiction, for the most part, dates from the time of Edward I; and

EQUITY.

its character is but crude and imperfect until the time of Sir Thomas More and Cardinal Wolsey, under Henry VIII.

Lord Nottingham **laid the foundation of modern equity jurisprudence**, and Lord Hardwicke measurably matured its several departments.

In this country, equity jurisprudence has grown up chiefly since the formation of our national government. Both in the national and State courts **it follows the model of the English court of chancery, except in some of the States, and in the national tribunals it is administered by the common law courts.** In some of the States the equity jurisdiction is very imperfect, and in some it is scarcely known.

The office and name of chancellor was known to the courts of the Roman Emperors, where it originally seems to have signified a chief scribe, or secretary, who was afterwards invested with several judicial powers, and a general superintendency over the rest of the officers of the prince.

The equity jurisprudence at present exercised in this country is founded upon, co-extensive with, and, in most respects conformable to, that of England. It approaches nearer to the latter than the jurisdiction exercised by the courts of Common Law in America approaches to the Common Law as administered in England. The Common Law was not in many particulars applicable to the situation of our country when it was first introduced.

In some of the States of the Union distinct courts of equity are established; in others, the powers are exercised concurrently with the Common-law jurisdiction by the same tribunal, being at once a court of law and a court of equity. **In others, again, no general equity powers exist**; but a few specified heads of equity jurisprudence are confided to the ordinary courts of law, and constitute a limited statutable jurisdiction.

But the *general* features and leading principles of the law of equity are essentially alike *in all the States*, and in all civilized countries.

GENERAL VIEW AND MAXIMS.

Courts of equity are established to detect latent frauds and concealments which the process of the

courts of law is not adapted to reach; to enforce the execution of such matters of trust and confidence as are binding in conscience, though not cognizable in a court of law; **to deliver from such dangers as are owing to misfortune or oversight**; and to give a more specific relief and more adapted to the circumstances of the case than can always be obtained by the generality of the rules of the positive or Common Law.

Although fraud, accident and trust are proper objects of courts of equity, it is by no means true that they are exclusively cognizable therein. On the contrary, **fraud is in many cases cognizable in a court of law.**

Many cases of accident are remediable at law, such as losses of deeds, mistakes in accounts and receipts, impossibilities in the strict performance of conditions, and other like cases.

Trusts, though in general of a peculiar and exclusive jurisdiction in equity, **are sometimes cognizable at law**; as, for instance, cases of bailments, and that larger class of cases where the action for money had and received for another's use is maintained *ex æquo et bono*.

Cases of trusts may exist in which the parties must abide by their own false confidence in others, without any aid from courts of justice.

Thus in cases of illegal contracts, or those in which one party has placed property in the hands of another for illegal purposes, as for smuggling, if the latter refuses to account for the proceeds, and fraudulently or unjustly withholds them, the former must abide by his loss, for, *In pari delicto melior est conditio possidentis, et defendentis*, is a maxim of public policy equally respected in courts of law and courts of equity.

It is a common maxim, that equity follows the law, *Æquitas sequitur legem*. **This maxim is susceptible of various interpretations** It may mean that equity adopts and follows the rules of law in all cases to which those rules may, in terms, be applicable; or it may mean that equity, in dealing with cases of an equitable nature, adopts and follows the analogies furnished by the rules of law.

The maxim is true in both of these senses, as applied to different cases and different circumstances.

When a rule, either of the common or the statute law, is direct, and governs the case with all its circumstances, or the particular point, a court of equity is as much bound by it as a court of law, and can as little justify a departure from it.

If the law commands or prohibits a thing to be done, equity cannot enjoin the contrary, or dispense with the obligation.

In many cases equity acts by analogy to the rules of law in relation to equitable titles and estates. Thus, although **the statutes of limitations are in their terms applicable to courts of law only, yet equity, by analogy, acts upon them,** and refuses relief under like circumstances.

Equity always discountenances laches; and holds that laches is presumable in cases where it is positively declared at law.

In general, in courts of equity, the same construction and effect are given to perfect or execute trust estates as are given by courts of law to legal estates. The incidents, properties and consequences of the estates are the same.

In short, **the maxim that equity follows the law is a maxim liable to many exceptions**; and it cannot be generally affirmed that, when there is no remedy at law in the given case, there is none in equity; or, on the other hand, that equity, in the administration of its own principles, is utterly regardless of the rules of law.

Another maxim is that **where there is equal equity, the law must prevail.**

In such a case, the defendant has an equal claim to the protection of a court of equity for his title, as the plaintiff has to the assistance of the court to assert his title; and then the court will not interpose on either side, **the equities being equal** between persons who have been equally innocent and equally diligent.

A maxim of no small extent is that **he who seeks equity must do equity.**

This maxim principally applies to the party who is seeking relief, in the character of a plaintiff in the court.

Another maxim of general use is that **equality is equity**; or, as it is sometimes expressed, equity delighteth in equality.

It is variously applied; as, for example, to cases of contribution between co-contractors, sureties, and others.

Equity looks upon that as done which ought to have been done, is another maxim in use in our courts of equity.

The true meaning of this maxim is that equity will treat the subject-matter, as to collateral consequences and incidents, in the same manner as if the final acts contemplated by the parties had been **executed exactly as they ought to have been**; not as the parties might have executed them.

The most common cases of the application of the rule are under agreement.

All agreements are considered as performed which are made for a valuable consideration, in favor of persons entitled to insist upon their performance. **They are to be considered as done at the time** when, according to the tenor thereof, they ought to have been performed.

As to the jurisdiction of courts of equity, one rule is that if, originally, the jurisdiction has properly attached in equity in any case, on account of the supposed defect of remedy at law, that jurisdiction is not changed or obliterated by the courts of law now entertaining jurisdiction in such cases, when they formerly rejected it.

The jurisdiction of equity, like that of law, **must be of a permanent and fixed character. There can be no ebb or flow of jurisdiction, dependent upon external changes.** Being once vested legitimately in the court, it must remain there until the legislature shall abolish or limit it.

The jurisdiction having once rightfully attached, it shall be made effectual for the purposes of complete relief.

The court, having acquired cognizance of the suit for the purposes of discovery, will entertain it for the purpose of relief, in most cases of fraud, account, accident and mistake. The ground is stated to be the propriety of preventing a multiplicity of suits.

Where the jurisdiction once attaches for discovery, and the discovery is actually obtained, **the court will further entertain the bill for relief, if the plaintiff prays it.** But this rule is not to be deemed of universal application, for it is laid down in some of our courts that under some circumstances, where the verdict of a jury is necessary to ascertain the extent of the relief, the plaintiff should be left to his action at law, after the discovery is obtained.

JURISDICTION IN CASES OF ACCIDENT.

The concurrent jurisdiction of equity **has its true origin in one of two sources:** either the courts of law, although they have general jurisdiction in the matter, cannot give adequate, specific and perfect relief; or, under the actual circumstances of the case, they cannot give any relief at all.

The jurisdiction of the court, arising from accident in the general sense, is a very old head in equity, and probably coeval with its existence.

By the term **accident** is here intended not merely inevitable casualty, or the act of Providence, or irresistible force; but **such unforeseen events, misfortunes, losses, acts or omissions as are not the result of any negligence or misconduct in the party.**

It is not every case of accident which will justify the interposition of a court of equity. The jurisdiction being concurrent, will be maintained only, **first**—when a court of law cannot grant suitable relief; and, **secondly**—when the party has a conscientious title to relief. Both grounds must concur in the given case, otherwise equity is bound to withhold its aid.

In cases of the loss of sealed instruments, equity will entertain a suit for relief, as well as for discovery, upon the party's making an affidavit of the loss of the instrument and offering indemnity.

Courts of equity often interfere where the party, **from long possession or exercise of a right over property**, may fairly be presumed to have had a legal title to it, and yet has lost the legal evidence of it, or is now unable to produce it.

It may be stated generally that where an inequitable loss or injury will otherwise fall upon a party from circumstances beyond his own control, or from his own acts done in entire good faith, and in the performance of a supposed duty, without negligence, courts of equity will interfere to grant him relief.

Courts of equity will also interfere and grant relief where there has been by accident a **confusion of the boundaries between two estates.**

There are cases of accident in which no relief will be granted in courts of equity. Thus in matters of positive contract, (for it is different in obligations or duties created by law,) it is no ground for the interference of equity that the party has been prevented from fulfilling them by accident; or, that he has been in no default, or, that he has been prevented by accident from deriving the full benefit of the contract on his own side.

The reason is that he might have provided for such contingencies by his contract, if he had so chosen; and the law will presume an intentional general liability, where he has made no exception.

Equity will not afford relief to a party upon the ground of accident, where the accident has arisen from his own gross negligence or fault; for in such case the party has no claim to come into a court of justice to ask to be saved from his own culpable misconduct.

No relief will be granted on account of accident, where the other party stands upon an equal equity, and is entitled to equal protection.

Upon a general survey of the grounds of equitable jurisdiction in cases of accident, it will be found that they resolve themselves into the following: that the party seeking relief has a clear right, which cannot otherwise be enforced in a suitable manner; or, that he will be subjected to an unjustifiable loss, without any blame or misconduct on his own part; or, that he has a superior equity to the party from whom he seeks the relief.

MISTAKE.

We may next consider the jurisdiction of equity, as founded upon the ground of mistake.

This is sometimes the result of accident in its large sense; but as contra-distinguished from it, it is some unintentional act, or omission, or error, arising from ignorance, surprise, imposition, or misplaced confidence.

Mistakes are ordinarily divided into two sorts: mistakes in matter of law, and mistakes in matter of fact.

As to mistakes in matter of law.—It is a well-known maxim that ignorance of law will not furnish an excuse for any person, either for a breach, or for an omission of duty; *ignorantia legis neminem excusat;* and this maxim is equally as much respected in equity as in law.

It probably belongs to some of the earliest rudiments of English jurisprudence, and is certainly so old as to have been long laid up among its settled elements.

If, upon the mere ground of ignorance of the law, men were admitted to overhaul or extinguish their most solemn contracts, and especially those which have been executed by a complete performance, there would be much embarrassing litigation in all judicial tribunals, and no small danger of injustice, from the nature and difficulty of the proper proofs.

The presumption is that every person is acquainted with his own rights, provided he has had a reasonable opportunity to know them. And nothing can be more liable to abuse, than to permit a person to reclaim his property upon the mere pretense that at the time of parting with it he was ignorant of the law acting on his title.

It is accordingly laid down as a general proposition, that in courts of equity **ignorance of the law shall not affect agreements, nor excuse from the legal consequences of particular acts.**

Equity may compel parties to execute their agreements; **but it has no authority to make agreements for them, or to substitute one for another.**

The general rule is that a mistake of the law is not a ground for reforming a deed, founded on such a mistake.

Courts of equity will not grant relief sought **upon the sole ground of mistake of law**; and whatever exceptions there may be to this rule, they are not only few in number, but they will be found to have something peculiar in their characters.

In contemplation of law, all its rules and principles are deemed certain, although they have not, as yet, been recognized by public adjudications. This doctrine proceeds upon the theoretical ground, that *Id certum est, quod certum reddi potest;* and that **decisions do not make the law, but only promulgate it.**

There is ground for a distinction between cases where a party acts or agrees **in ignorance of any title in him,** or upon the supposition of a clear title in another, and cases where there is **a doubt in controversy,** or litigation between the parties as to their respective rights. In the former cases the party seems to labor in some sort under **a mistake of fact, as well as of law.** He supposes, as **a matter of fact,** that he has no title to the property. He does not intend to surrender or release his title, but the act or agreement proceeds upon the supposition that he has none.

But the **distinction between mistakes of law and of**

fact, so far as equitable relief is concerned, is one of policy rather than of principle.

As to compromises, it is said, if they are otherwise unobjectionable, they will be binding, and **the right will not prevail against the agreement of the parties**; for the right must always be on one side or the other, and there would be an end of compromises if they might be overthrown upon any subsequent ascertainment of rights contrary thereto.

Where compromises are fairly entered into, where the uncertainty rests upon **a doubt of fact, or a doubt in point of law,** if both parties are in the same ignorance, the compromise is equally binding, and cannot be affected by any subsequent investigation and result. **But if the parties are not mutually ignorant,** the case admits of a very different consideration, whether the ignorance be of **a matter of fact or of law.**

Cases of surprise, mixed up with a mistake of law, stand upon a ground peculiar to themselves and independent of the general doctrine. In such cases the agreements or acts are unadvised and improvident, and without deliberation; and are held invalid upon the common principle adopted by courts of equity to protect those who are unable to protect themselves, and of whom an undue advantage is taken.

Contracts made in mutual error, under circumstances material to their character and consequences, seem, upon general principles, invalid.

There are few contradictions of, or exceptions to, the general rule that **ignorance of the law, with a full knowledge of the facts,** furnishes no ground to rescind agreements, or to set aside solemn acts of the parties. Ignorance of the law will not avail; innocent mistake of fact will.

The general rule governing courts of equity upon this subject should be, to deny relief sought upon the mere ground of ignorance or mistake of law; and that the exceptions allowed must be of marked character, both in regard to proof, and the degree of injustice consequent upon a denial of relief.

In relation to contracts, it must always be assumed, in regard to both of these classes of mistakes, that the parties impliedly stipulate that they will, each for himself, run his own risk. **That is the implied condition of all contracts.** And the parties cannot properly ask to be relieved from any merely in-

EQUITY.

cidental hardship, resulting from being under **mistake, either as to the true state of the facts or of the law.**

But where the mistake is of so fundamental a character that **the minds of the parties have never in fact met,** or where an **unconscionable advantage has been gained** by mere mistake or misapprehension, and there was no gross negligence on the part of the plaintiff, either in falling into the error or in not sooner claiming redress, **and no intervening rights have accrued,** and the parties may still be placed *in statu quo,* equity will interfere, in its discretion, in order to prevent intolerable injustice.

It must appear that the contract is different from the understanding of both parties to justify the court in reforming it.

As to mistake of fact, the general rule is that an act done, or contract made, under a mistake or ignorance of a material fact, is voidable and relievable in equity.

The ground of this distinction between ignorance of law and ignorance of fact seems to be, that, as every man of reasonable understanding is presumed to know the law, and to act upon the rights which it confers or supports, when he knows all the facts, it is culpable negligence in him to do an act or to make a contract and then to set up his ignorance of law as his defence.

The rule applies not only to cases where there has been a studied suppression or concealment of the facts by the other side, which would amount to a fraud, but also to many cases of innocent ignorance and *mistake on both sides.*

The fact must be material to the act or contract; that is, it must be essential to its character, and an efficient cause of its concoction. For though there may be an accidental ignorance or mistake of fact, yet, if the act or contract is not materially affected by it, the party claiming relief will be denied it.

It is not sufficient in all cases to give the party relief, that the fact is material; but it must be such as he could not by reasonable diligence get knowledge of when he was put upon enquiry.

For if by such reasonable diligence he could have obtained knowledge of the fact, equity will not relieve him; since that would be to encourage culpable negligence. **Equity gives relief to the vigilant, and not to the negligent.**

There must always be shown either the mistake of both

parties, or the mistake of one, with the fraudulent concealment of the other, to justify a court of equity in reforming a contract.

It is essential, in order to set aside such a transaction, not only that an advantage should be taken; but **it must arise from some obligation in the party to make the discovery**, not from an obligation in point of morals only, *but of legal duty*. In such a case the court will not correct the contract, merely because a man of nice morals and honor would not have entered into it. **It must fall within some definition of fraud or surprise.**

The policy of equity is to administer relief to the vigilant, and to put all parties upon the exercise of a searching diligence. **Where confidence is reposed**, or the party is intentionally misled, relief may be granted; but in such a case there is the ingredient of what the law deems a fraud.

Where the means of information are open to both parties, and where each is presumed to exercise his own skill, diligence, and judgment in regard to all extrinsic circumstances, a like principle applies.

Also where the fact is equally known to both parties; or where the fact is doubtful from its own nature; in every such case, if the parties have acted with entire good faith, a court of equity will not interpose. For in such cases the equity is deemed equal between the parties; and when it is so, a court of equity is passive.

Equity has jurisdiction to relieve in respect of a plain mistake in contracts in writing, as well as against frauds in contracts; so that, if reduced into writing **contrary to the intent of the parties**, on proper proof that would be rectified.

Courts of equity have not hesitated to **entertain jurisdiction to reform all contracts**, where a fraudulent suppression, or omission, or insertion of a material stipulation exists, notwithstanding to some extent it breaks in upon the uniformity of the rule as to the **exclusion of parol evidence to vary or control contracts.**

Where there has been an innocent omission or insertion of a material stipulation, contrary to the intention of both parties, and under a mutual mistake, equity will relieve.

We must treat the cases in which equity affords relief, and **allows parol evidence, to vary and reform written contracts and instruments**, upon the ground of accident and mistake, as properly forming, like cases of fraud, exceptions to the general rule, which excludes parol evidence, and as standing upon the same policy as the rule itself.

Relief will be granted in cases of written instruments only where there is a **plain mistake clearly made out by satisfactory proofs.**

A court of equity is not, like a court of law, bound to enforce a written contract; but it may exercise its discretion when a specific performance is sought, and may leave the party to his remedy at law.

Equity may reform a written agreement, **and direct the specific performance of it, when so reformed.**

Relief will be granted in equity in cases of mistake in written contracts, not only when the fact of the mistake is expressly established, but also when it is **fairly implied** from the nature of the transaction.

The courts of equity will not rectify a voluntary deed, unless all the parties consent. If any object, the deed must take its chances as it stands.

In all cases of mistakes in written instruments, equity will interfere only as between the original parties, or those claiming under them in privity; such as personal representatives, heirs, devisees, legatees, assignees, voluntary grantees, or judgment creditors, or purchasers from them, with notice of the facts.

As against *bona fide* **purchasers for a valuable consideration without notice,** courts of equity will grant no relief; because they have, at least, an equal equity to the protection of the court.

Relief will be granted in cases of mistake in written instruments, to prevent manifest injustice and wrong, and to suppress fraud; **it will also be granted to supply defects,** where, by mistake, the parties have omitted any acts or circumstances necessary to give due validity and effect to written instruments.

The same principle applies to cases **where an instrument has been delivered up, or cancelled, under a mistake of the party,** and in ignorance of the facts material to the rights derived under it.

In all cases of relief by aiding and correcting defects or mistakes in the execution of instruments and powers, the party asking relief **must stand upon some equity** superior to that of the party against whom he asks it.

In regard to mistakes in wills, it is said that courts of equity have jurisdiction to correct them, when they are apparent upon the face of the will, or may be made out by a due construction of its terms; for in the cases of wills **the intention will prevail over the words.**

ACTUAL OR POSITIVE FRAUD.

It may be laid down as a general rule, subject to but few exceptions, **that courts of equity exercise a general jurisdiction in cases of fraud,** sometimes concurrent with, and sometimes exclusive of, other courts.

In a great variety of cases fraud is remediable, and effectually remediable at law.

It is not easy to give a definition of fraud in the extensive signification in which that term is used in courts of equity; and it has been said that these courts have, very wisely, **never laid down as a general proposition what shall constitute fraud,** or any general rule beyond which they will not go upon the ground of fraud, lest other means of avoiding the equity of the courts should be found out.

Pothier says that the term *fraud* is applied to every artifice made use of by one person for the purpose of deceiving another.

Labeo defines *fraud* to be any cunning, deception, or artifice, used to circumvent, cheat, or deceive another.

Fraud, in the sense of a court of equity, **properly includes all acts, omissions and concealments which involve a breach of legal or equitable duty, trust, or confidence, justly reposed, and are injurious to another, or by which an undue and unconscientious advantage is taken of another.**

It is equally a rule in courts of law and courts of equity that **fraud is not to be presumed; but it must be established by proofs.**

Equity will grant relief upon the ground of fraud, **established by presumptive evidence,** which evidence courts of law would not always deem sufficient proof to justify a verdict at law.

One of the largest classes of cases in which courts of equity are accustomed to grant relief is where there has been a misrepresentation, or *suggestio falsi.*

If the misrepresentation was of a trifling or immaterial thing; or if the other party did not trust to it, or was not misled by it; or if it was vague and inconclusive in its own nature; or if it was upon a matter of opinion or fact, equally open to the enquiries of both parties, and in regard to which **neither could be presumed to trust the other**; in these and the like cases there is no reason for a court of equity to grant relief upon the ground of fraud.

Whether the party thus misrepresenting a material fact, **knew it to be false, or made the assertion without knowing whether it were true or false,** is wholly immaterial; for the affirmation of what one does not know or believe to be true is equally, in morals and law, as unjustifiable as the affirmation of what is known to be positively false.

It is immaterial whether the fraud was originally concocted by the principal or by the agent; the principal will be held implicated to the fullest extent, if he adopts the acts of his agent.

In civil tribunals a person cannot be allowed to complain of **trifling deviations from good faith** in the party with whom he has contracted. Nothing but what is plainly injurious to good faith ought to be there considered as a fraud sufficient to impeach a contract.

Ordinarily matters of opinion between parties, dealing upon equal terms, though falsely stated, are not relieved against because they are not presumed to mislead, or influence the other party, when each has equal means of information.

Nor is it every willful misrepresentation, even of a fact, which will avoid a contract upon the ground of fraud, if it be of such a nature that the other party had no right to place reliance on it, and it was his own folly to give credence to it; for **courts of equity, like courts of law, do not aid parties who will not use their own sense and discretion upon matters of this sort.**

The defrauded party may, by his subsequent acts, with full knowledge of the fraud, **deprive himself of all right to relief,** as well in equity as at law. Thus, if he knew all the facts, and with such full information, he continued to deal with the party.

Another class of cases for relief in equity is **where there is an undue concealment**, or *suppressio veri*, to the injury or prejudice of another.

It is not every concealment, even of facts material to the interests of a party, which will entitle him to the interposition of a court of equity. The case must amount to the suppression of facts which one party, under the circumstances, is bound in conscience and duty to disclose to the other party, and in respect to which he cannot innocently be silent.

Equity will not correct or avoid a contract merely because a man of nice honor would not have entered into it. **The case must fall within some definition of fraud**; and the rule must be drawn so as not to affect the general transactions of mankind.

It is a rule in equity that all the material facts must be known to both parties to render the agreement fair and just in all its parts; and it is against all the principles of equity that one party, knowing a material ingredient in an agreement, should be permitted to surpress it, and still call for specific performance.

The definition of undue concealment, which amounts to fraud in the sense of a court of equity, and for which it will grant relief, **is the non-disclosure** of those facts and circumstances which one party is under some legal or equitable obligation to communicate to the other; and which the latter has a right, not merely *in foro conscientiæ*, but *juris et de jure*, to know.

At the common law, in the cases of sales of goods, the maxim *caveat emptor* is applied; and unless there be some misrepresentation or artifice, to disguise the thing sold, or some warranty, as to its character or quality, the vendee is bound by the sale, notwithstanding there may be intrinsic defects and vices in it, materially affecting its value. However questionable such a doctrine may be, courts of equity, as well as courts of law, abstain from any interference with it.

The most comprehensive class of cases of undue concealment arises from some peculiar relation, or fiduciary character between parties.

In such cases, if there is any misrepresentation, or any concealment of a material fact, or any just suspicion of artifice or undue influence, **courts of equity will interpose and pronounce the transaction void**, and as far as possible restore the parties to their original rights.

Equity will relieve from all unconscientious advantages or bargains obtained over persons disabled by weakness, infirmity, age, lunacy, idiocy, drunkenness, coverture, or other incapacity.

The general theory of the law, in regard to acts done and contracts made by parties affecting their rights and interests, is that in all such cases **there must be a free and full consent to bind the parties.**

Consent is an act of reason, accompanied with deliberation, the mind weighing, as in a balance, the good and evil on each side.

It is upon this general ground, that there is a want of rational and deliberate consent, that the contracts and other acts of idiots, lunatics, and other persons *non compos mentis*, are generally deemed to be invalid in courts of equity

It is a general principle that contracts made by persons in liquor, even though their drunkenness be voluntary, are utterly void; because they are incapable of any deliberate consent, in like manner as persons who are insane, or *non compos mentis*.

But to set aside any act or contract on account of drunkenness, it is not sufficient that the party is under undue excitement from liquor. It must rise to that degree which may be called excessive drunkenness, where the party is utterly deprived of the use of his reason and understanding.

It may be stated as generally true that the **acts and contracts of persons who are of weak understanding**, and who are thereby liable to imposition, will be held void in courts of equity, if the nature of the act or contract justify the conclusion that the party has not exercised a deliberate judgment, but that he has been imposed upon, circumvented, or overcome by cunning or artifice, or undue influence.

The protection of courts of equity is not to be extended to every person of a weak understanding unless there be some fraud or surprise; for courts of equity would have enough to do if they were to examine into the wisdom and prudence of men in disposing of their estates.

The constant rule in equity is that where the party is not a free agent, and is not equal to protecting himself, the court will protect him

Circumstances, also, of **extreme necessity and distress of the party**, although not accompanied by any direct restraint or duress, may, in like manner, so entirely overcome his free agency as to justify the court in setting aside a contract made by him, on account of some oppression, or fraudulent advantage, or imposition attendant upon it.

Mere inadequacy of price, or any other inequality in the bargain, is not to be understood as constituting *per se,* a ground to avoid a bargain in equity.

But where there are other ingredients in the case of a suspicious nature, or peculiar relations between the parties, gross inadequacy of price must necessarily furnish the most vehement presumption of fraud.

Equity will not relieve in all cases, even of very gross inadequacy, attended with circumstances which might otherwise induce them to act, if the parties cannot be placed *in statu quo.*

Cases of surprise and sudden action without due deliberation may properly be referred to the same head of fraud or imposition.

The surprise here intended must be accompanied with fraud and circumvention, or at least by such circumstances as demonstrate that the party had no opportunity to use suitable deliberation or that there was some influence or management to mislead him.

Gifts and legacies are often bestowed upon persons upon condition that they shall not marry without the consent of parents, guardians, or other confidential persons; and equity will not suffer the manifest object of the condition to be defeated by the *fraud* or dishonest, corrupt, or *unreasonable refusal* of the party whose consent is required to the marriage.

In general, a contract which contemplates a fraud upon third parties is regarded as so far illegal between the immediate parties, that neither will be entitled to claim the aid of equity in its enforcement.

CONSTRUCTIVE FRAUD.

Having considered the subject of **actual or meditated and intentional fraud,** we may now pass to another class of frauds, which, as contradistinguished from the former, are treated as **legal or constructive frauds.**

By constructive frauds are meant such acts or contracts as, although not originating in any actual evil design, or contrivance to perpetrate a positive fraud or injury upon other persons, or to violate private or public confidence, or to impair or injure the public interests, are prohibited at law, as within the same reason, and mischief, as acts and contracts done *malo animo*.

Some cases of construtive frauds are so denominated because they are **contrary to some general public policy,** or artificial policy of the law.

Among these may properly be placed contracts and agreements respecting marriage (commonly called marriage brokerage contracts), by which a party engages to give another a compensation, if he will negotiate an advantageous marriage for him. Such contracts are utterly void, as *against public policy.*

It is upon the same ground of public policy that **contracts in restraint of marriage** are held void.

Conditions annexed to gifts, legacies and devises, in restraint of marriage, are not void, if they are reasonable in themselves, and do not directly or virtually operate as an undue restraint upon the marriage freedom. If the **condition is in restraint of marriage generally,** then, as a condition against public policy, it will be held utterly void.

Courts of equity are not generally inclined to lend an indulgent consideration to **conditions in restraint of marriage.**

Conditions annexed to devises, both of real and personal estate to a widow, that they shall become inoperative in the event of the marriage of the devisee, have been generally recognized and sustained.

Bargains and contracts made in restraint of trade constitute another class of constructive frauds, and are so deemed because inconsistent with the general policy of the law.

Here the known and established distinction is between such bargains and contracts as are in general restraint of trade, and such as are in restraint of it only as to particular places or persons. The latter, if founded upon a good and valuable consideration, are valid. The former are universally prohibited.

In like manner, agreements which are founded upon violations of public trust or confidence, or of the rules adopted by courts in furtherance of the administration of public justice, are held void.

Another extensive class of cases, falling under this head of constructive fraud, respects **contracts for the buying, selling, or procuring of public offices.**

In regard to gaming contracts, courts of equity ought not to interfere in their favor, but ought to afford aid to suppress them; since they are not only prohibited by statute, but may be justly pronounced to be immoral, as the practice tends to idleness and the ruin of families.

It has been argued that the higher and wiser policy in regard to all illegal contracts would be to allow money paid in their furtherance to be recovered back. But the opposite rule prevails, with few exceptions.

Generally, where the parties stand upon equal footing, and the contract is illegal, they cannot expect aid either from the courts of law or equity.

The general rule is that wherever any contract or conveyance is void, either by a positive law, or upon principles of public policy, it is deemed incapable of confirmation upon the maxim, *Quod ab initio non valet, in tractu temporis non convalescit*. But where it is merely voidable, or turns upon circumstances of undue advantage, surprise, or imposition, there, if it is deliberately, and upon full examination, confirmed by the parties, such confirmation will avail to give it an *ex post facto* validity.

Let us pass to the consideration of the second head of constructive frauds, namely: of those which arise from **some peculiar confidential or fiduciary relation between the parties.** In this class of cases there is often to be found some intermixture of deceit, imposition, overreaching, unconscionable advantage, or other mark of direct and positive fraud.

The general principle which governs in all cases of this sort is, that **if a confidence is reposed, and that confidence is abused, courts of equity will grant relief.**

As to the relation of client and attorney or solicitor; it is obvious that this relation must give rise to great confidence between the parties, and to very strong influences over the actions and rights and interests of the client.

The burden of establishing perfect fairness, adequacy, and equity is thrown upon the attorney, upon the **general rule** that he who bargains in a matter of advantage with a person, placing a confidence in him, is bound to show that a reasonable use has been made of that confidence; **a rule applying equally to all** persons standing in confidential relations with each other.

The relation of principal and agent is affected by the same considerations, founded upon the same enlightened public policy. Upon these principles if an agent, employed to purchase for another, purchases for himself, he will be considered as the trustee of his employer.

In all cases of purchases and bargains respecting property, directly and openly made between principals and agents, **the utmost good faith is required.**

The question in all such cases does not turn upon the point whether there is any intention to cheat or not, but upon the obligation from the fiduciary relation of the parties to make a frank and full disclosure.

It is a general rule that a trustee is bound not to do anything which can place him in a position inconsistent with the interests of the trust, or which has a tendency to interfere with his duty in discharging it.

Executors and administrators will not be permitted, under any circumstances, to derive a personal benefit from the manner in which they transact the business, or manage the assets of the estate.

It may be generally stated that wherever confidence is reposed, and one party has it in his power, in a secret manner, for his own advantage, to sacrifice those interests which he is bound to protect, he will not be permitted to hold any such advantage.

The case of principal and surety may be mentioned as an illustration of this doctrine.

The contract of surety imports entire good faith and confidence between the parties in regard to the whole transaction. Any concealment of material facts, or any express or implied misrepresentation of such facts, or any undue advantage taken of the surety by the creditor, either by surprise, or by withholding proper information, will furnish sufficient grounds to invalidate the contract.

There must be something which amounts to fraud to enable the surety to say that he is released from his contract on account of misrepresentation or concealment.

If a creditor, without any communication with the surety and assent on his part, should afterwards enter into any new contract with the principal, inconsistent with the former contract, or should stipulate in a binding manner, upon a sufficient consideration, for further delay and postponement of the day of payment of the debt, that will operate in equity as a discharge of the surety.

Also, if the creditor has any security from the debtor, and he parts with it, without communication with the surety, or by his gross negligence it is lost, that will operate, at least to the value of the security, to discharge the surety.

The surety has a right, upon paying the debt to the principal, to be substituted in the place of the creditor, as to all securities held by the latter for the debt, and to have the same benefit that he would have therein.

Contracts of suretyship limited by time are usually construed strictly, and not to extend beyond the period fixed.

The Statute of Frauds requires certain contracts to be in writing in order to give them validity. In the construction of that statute, a general principle has been adopted, that, as it is designed as a protection against fraud, it shall never be allowed to be set up as a protection and support of fraud. Hence in a variety of cases, where from fraud, imposition or mistake, a contract of this sort has not been reduced to writing, but has been suffered to rest in confidence, or in parol communications between the parties, equity will enforce it against the party guilty of a breach of confidence who attempts to shelter himself behind the provisions of the statute.

In regard to voluntary conveyances, they are protected in all cases where they do not break in upon the legal rights of creditors.

If there is any design of fraud, or collusion, or intent to deceive third persons, in such conveyances, although the party be not then indebted, the conveyance will be held utterly void, as to subsequent as well as to present creditors, for it is not *bona fide*.

A conveyance, even for a valuable consideration, is not, under the statute of the 13th of Elizabeth, valid in point of law from that circumstance alone. **It must also be** *bona fide;* for if it be made with intent to defraud or defeat creditors, it will be void, although there may, in the strictest sense, be a valuable, nay, an adequate, consideration.

Although voluntary conveyances are, or may be, void as to existing creditors, **they are perfect and effectual as between the parties,** and cannot be set aside by the grantor if he should become dissatisfied with the transaction.

The distinction between existing and subsequent creditors, in reference to voluntary conveyances is that, as to the former, fraud is an inference of law, and as to the latter there must be proof of fraud in fact.

Purchasers, bona fide, for a valuable consideration, without notice of the fraudulent or voluntary grant, are of such high consideration, that they will be protected, as well at law as in equity, in their purchases.

Where the parties are equally meritorious, and equally innocent, the known maxim of courts of equity is, *Qui prior est in tempore, potior est in jure;* he is to be preferred who has acquired the first title.

Another class of constructive frauds of a large extent and over which courts of equity exercise an exclusive and a very salutary control and jurisdiction, consists of those where a man designedly or knowingly produces a false impression upon another, who is thereby drawn into some act or contract, injurious to his own rights or interests.

The wholesome maxim of the law is, that a party who enables another to commit a fraud, is answerable for the consequences; and the maxim, *Fraus est celare fraudem,* is, with proper limitations in its application, a rule of general justice.

In many cases, a man may be innocently silent; for, as has often been observed, *Aliud est tacere, aliud celare.* But in other cases, **a man is bound to speak out**; and his very silence becomes as expressive as if he had openly consented to what is said or done, and had become a party to the transaction.

Thus, if a party having a title to an estate **should stand by and allow an innocent purchaser to expend money** upon the estate, without giving him notice, he would not be permitted in equity to assert that title against such purchaser, at least not without fully indemnifying him for all his expenditures.

Where one of two innocent persons must suffer a loss, and, *a fortiori,* in cases where one has misled the other, he who is the cause or occasion of that confidence by which the loss has been caused or occasioned ought to bear it.

Cases of this sort are viewed with so much disfavor by courts of equity, that **neither infancy nor coverture will constitute any excuse for the party guilty of the concealment** or misrepresentation; for neither infants nor *femes covert* are privileged to practice deception or cheats on other innocent persons.

Another class of constructive frauds consists of those

where a person **purchases with full notice** of the legal or equitable title of other persons to the same property. In such cases he will not be permitted to protect himself against such claims, but his own title will be postponed, and made subservient to theirs.

What shall constitute notice, in cases of *subsequent purchasers,* is a point of some nicety, and resolves itself sometimes into a matter of fact, and sometimes into a matter of law.

Notice may be either actual and positive, or it may be implied and constructive.

Constructive notice is knowledge imputed by the court, on presumption too strong to be rebutted, that the knowledge must have been communicated.

To constitute constructive notice, it is not indispensable that it should be brought home to the party himself. It is sufficient if it is brought home to the agent, attorney, or counsel of the party; for, in such cases, the law presumes notice to the principal, since it would be a breach of trust in the former not to communicate the knowledge to the latter.

Another branch of constructive frauds is that of **voluntary conveyances of real estate**, in regard to subsequent purchasers. This is founded in a great measure upon the provisions of the statute 27th Elizabeth, ch. 4. The object of the statute was to give full protection to subsequent purchasers from the grantor, against mere volunteers, under prior conveyances.

The true construction of the statute is that conveyances are not avoided merely because they are voluntary, but because they are fraudulent.

A voluntary gift of real estate is valid against subsequent purchasers and all other persons, unless it was fraudulent at the time of its execution; and a subsequent conveyance for a valuable consideration is evidence, but by no means conclusive evidence, of fraud in the first voluntary conveyance.

Courts of equity will not interpose, where the property has been conveyed by the voluntary and covenous grantee to a *bona fide* purchaser, for a valuable consideration, without notice. Such a person is always a favorite in equity, and is always protected. His equity is equal to that of any other person, whether he be a creditor or a purchaser of the grantor; and where the equities are equal, the rule applies, *potior est conditio possidentis.*

Where there is a *bona fide* purchaser from the voluntary or fraudulent grantor, and another from the voluntary or fraudulent grantee, the grantees **will have preference according to the priority of their respective titles.**

The beautiful character and pervading excellence of equity jurisprudence is that it varies its adjustments and proportions, so as to meet the very form and pressure of each particular case. Thus, to present **a summary of what has been already stated**: if conveyances or other instruments are fraudulently or improperly obtained, they are decreed to be given up and cancelled. If they are money securities, on which the money has been paid, the money is decreed to be paid back. **If they are deeds, or other muniments of title, detained from the rightful party, they are decreed to be delivered up.** If they are deeds depressed or spoliated, the party is decreed to hold the same rights as if they were in his possession and power. If there has been any undue concealment, or misrepresentation, or specific promise collusively broken, the injured party is placed in the same situation, and the other party is compelled to do the same acts, as if all had been transacted with the utmost good faith.

It may be also stated, by way of summary, that if the party says nothing, but by his expressive silence misleads another to his injury, he is compellable to make good the loss; and his own title, if the case requires it, is made subservient to that of the confiding purchaser. If a party, by fraud or misrepresentation, induces another to do an act injurious to a third person, he is made responsible for it. **If by fraud or misrepresentation he prevents acts from being done, equity treats the case, as to him, as if it were done; and makes him a trustee for the other.** So, if a will is revoked by a fraudulent deed, the revocation is treated as a nullity. And if a devisee obtains a devise by fraud, he is treated as a trustee of the injured party.

ACCOUNT.

One of the most ancient forms of action at the Common Law is the **action of account.**

But the modes of proceeding in that action were found so very dilatory that, as soon as courts of equity began to assume jurisdiction in matters of account, as they did at a very early period, the remedy at law began to decline.

As courts of equity entertain concurrent jurisdiction to the fullest extent with courts of law, in matters of account, the decision as to the proper tribunal must be governed by considerations of convenience.

Courts of equity in suits of this nature proceed, in many respects, in analogy to what is done at law. The cause is referred to a Master (acting as auditor), before whom the account is taken, and he is armed with the fullest powers, not only to examine the parties on oath, but to make all the enquiries by testimony under oath, and by documents and books which are necessary to the due administration of justice.

The whole machinery of courts of equity is better adapted to the purpose of an account, in general, for in a complicated account a court of law would be incompetent to examine it at *Nisi Prius*, with all the necessary accuracy. This is the principle on which courts of equity constantly act, by taking cognizance of matters, which, though cognizable at law, are yet so involved with a complex account, that it cannot be properly taken at law.

The general ground asserted for the jurisdiction is not that there is no remedy at law, but that the remedy is more complete and adequate in equity.

Equity will also entertain jurisdiction in matters of account, not only when there are mutual accounts, but also when the accounts to be examined are on one side only, and *a discovery* is wanted in aid of the account and is obtained.

APPROPRIATION.—In matters of account, where several debts are due by the debtor to the creditor, it often becomes material to ascertain to what debt a particular payment made by the debtor is to be applied. **This is called the appropriation of payments.**

In the case of running accounts between parties where there are various items of debt on one side, and various items of credit on the other side, occurring at different times, and no special appropriation of the payments is made by either party, the successive payments or credits are to be applied to the discharge of the items of debit, antecedently due, in the order of time in which they stand in the account.

Where there are no running accounts between the parties, and the debtor himself makes no special appropriation of any payment, there the creditor is generally at liberty to apply that payment to any one or more of the debts which the debtor owes him, whether it be upon an account or otherwise.

A creditor has no right to apply a general payment to any item of account which is itself illegal, and contrary to law, as a claim for usurious interest.

But if the debtor so apply the payment, he cannot afterwards revoke it.

If neither party has made any appropriation, then the law will make the appropriation according to its notion of the equity and justice of the case, and so that it may be most beneficial to both parties.

APPORTIONMENT.—CONTRIBUTION AND GENERAL AVERAGE are usually treated of under this head, as they are in some measure blended together, and require and terminate in accounts.

In most of these cases a discovery is indispensable for the purposes of justice; and where this does not occur, there are other distinct grounds for the exercise of equity jurisdiction in order **to avoid circuity and multiplicity of actions.**

Apportionment is sometimes used to denote the contribution which is to be made by different persons, having distinct rights, towards the discharge of a common burden or charge to be borne by all of them.

In respect to apportionment, in its application to contracts in general, it is the known and familiar principle of the Common Law, that an entire contract is not apportionable. The reason given is that as the contract is founded upon **a consideration dependent upon the entire performance of the act,** and if from any cause it is not wholly performed, the *casus fœderis* does not arise, and the law will not make provisions for exigencies which the parties have neglected to provide for themselves.

At the common law, the cases are few in which an apportionment under contracts is allowed, the general doctrine being against it, unless specially stipulated by the parties.

Thus, for instance, where a person was appointed a collector of rents for another, and was to receive $100 per annum for his services, and he died at the end of three quarters of the year, while in the service, it was held that his executor could not recover $75 for the three quarters service, **upon the ground** that the contract was entire and there could be no apportionment.

Courts of equity, to a considerable extent, act upon this maxim of the Common Law in regard to contracts. But where equitable circumstances intervene, they will grant redress.

A very important and beneficial exercise of equity jurisdiction, in cases of apportionment and contribution, is when encumbrances, fines, and other charges on real estate are required to be paid off, or are actually paid off by some of the parties in interest.

GENERAL AVERAGE, a subject of daily occurrence in maritime and commercial operations, furnishes another class of cases over which equity exercises jurisdiction.

General average, in the sense of the maritime law, means a general contribution that is to be made by all parties in interest towards a loss or expense which is voluntarily sustained or incurred for the benefit of all.

The principle upon which this contribution is founded is not the result of contract, but has its origin in the plain dictates of natural law.

A court of equity, having authority to bring all the parties before it, and to refer the whole matter to a Master, *to take an account*, and to adjust the whole apportionment at once, affords a safe, convenient and expedient remedy.

CONTRIBUTION BETWEEN SURETIES.—Where, between sureties, who are bound for the same principal, and upon his default, one of them is compelled to pay the money, or to perform any other obligation, for which they all became bound, the surety who has paid the whole is entitled to receive contribution from all the others for what he has done in relieving them from a common burden.

As all are equally bound and are equally relieved, it seems but just that in such a case all should contribute in proportion towards a benefit obtained by all, upon the maxim *Qui sentit commodum, sentire debet et onus.*

The ground of relief does not stand upon any notion of mutual contract, express or implied, between the sureties to indemnify each other in proportion, but arises from principles of equity, independent of contract.

There are many cases in which the relief is more complete and effectual in equity than it can be at law, as, for instance, where an account and discovery are wanted; or where there are numerous parties in interest, which would occasion a multiplicity of suits.

In some cases the remedy at law is inadequate. Thus, if there are four sureties, and one is insolvent, a solvent surety, who pays the whole debt, can recover only one-fourth part thereof, (and not a third part) against the other two solvent sureties. But in a court of equity he will be entitled to recover one-third part of the debt against each of them; for, in **equity, the insolvent's share is apportioned among all the other solvent sureties.**

In some States **courts of law** follow the rule adopted in courts of equity in apportioning the share of an insolvent surety upon those who remain solvent.

Upon like grounds, if one of the sureties dies, the remedy at law lies only against the surviving parties; whereas **in equity it may be enforced against the representative of the deceased party,** and he may be compelled to contribute his share to the surviving surety who shall pay the whole debt.

At law, the release or discharge of one surety by the creditor will operate as a discharge of all the other sureties, even though it may be founded on a mere mistake of law. But this rule does not universally prevail in equity.

Sureties are not only entitled to contribution from each other for moneys paid in discharge of their joint liabilities for the principal, but they are also entitled to the benefit of all securities which have been taken by any one of them to indemnify himself against such liabilities.

And in equity the sureties are entitled, upon payment of the debt due by their principal to the creditor, to have the full benefit of all the collateral securities, both of a legal and equitable nature, which the creditor has taken as an additional pledge for his debt.

It is a rule in equity that a creditor shall not, by his own election of the fund, out of which he will receive payment, prejudice the rights which other persons are entitled to; but they shall either be substituted to his rights, or they may compel him to seek satisfaction out of the fund, to which they cannot resort.

Thus, where a party, having two funds to resort to for payment of his debt, elects to proceed against one, and thereby disappoints another party, who can resort to that fund only,

In such a case, the disappointed party is substituted in the place of the electing creditor, or the latter is compelled to resort, in the first instance, to that fund which will not interfere with the rights of the other.

The surety, upon payment of the debt, is entitled to be subrogated to all the rights of the creditor.

If the surety has a counter-bond or security from the principal, the creditor will be entitled to the benefit of it, and may in equity reach such security to satisfy the debt.

And the surety, by making a new and independent arrangement with the creditor, in regard to the security of the debt, **puts himself in the place of a principal**, and cannot thereafter complain of the creditor for any want of diligence in pursuing the principal.

Contribution lies between partners for any excess which has been paid by one partner beyond his share, against the other partners, if upon a winding up of the partnership affairs, such a balance appears in his favor; or, if, upon a dissolution, he has been compelled to pay any sum for which he ought to be indemnified.

Contribution also lies between joint-tenants, tenants in common and part owners, of ships and other chattels, for all charges and expenditures incurred for the common benefit.

The remedial justice of courts of equity, in all cases of apportionment and contribution, is so complete, and so flexible in its adaptation to all the particular circumstances and equities, that it has, in a great measure, superseded all efforts to obtain redress in any other tribunals.

There are some matters of defence peculiarly belonging to matters of account. Thus, it is ordinarily a good bar to a suit for an account that the parties have already in writing stated and adjusted the items of the account, and struck the balance. In such a case equity will not interfere; for there is a remedy at law, and no ground for resorting to equity.

If there has been any mistake, or omission, or accident, or fraud, or undue advantage, by which the account stated is in truth vitiated, and the balance is incorrectly fixed, a court of equity will not suffer it to be conclusive upon the parties, but will allow it to be opened and re-examined.

What shall constitute, in the sense of a court of equity, a stated account, is in some measure dependent upon the particular circumstances of the case. It is sufficient if it has been examined and accepted by both parties. And this acceptance need not be express, but may be implied from circumstances.

Between merchants at home, an account which has been presented, and no objection made thereto after the lapse of several posts, is treated, under ordinary circumstances, as being, by acquiescence, a stated account.

In regard to acquiescence in stated accounts, although it amounts to an admission or presumption of their correctness, it by no means establishes the fact of their having been settled, even though the acquiescence has been for a considerable time.

A settled account will be deemed conclusive between the parties, unless some fraud, mistake, or omission is shown. For it would be most mischievous to allow settled accounts between the parties, especially where vouchers have been delivered up or destroyed, to be unsettled, unless for urgent reasons.

In matters of account, although not barred by the statute of limitations, courts of **equity refuse to interfere after a considerable lapse of time**, and the original transactions have become obscure or the evidence lost; they act upon the maxim, *Vigilantibus, non dormientibus, jura subveniunt.*

It is said that where there is no legal remedy, it does not therefore follow that there must be an equitable remedy, unless there is also an equitable right. Where there is a legal right, there must be a legal remedy; and if there is no legal right, in many cases there can be no equitable one.

Courts of equity also exercise a concurrent jurisdiction in the *Administration* of the assets of deceased persons, and a similar jurisdiction in regard to *Legacies, Confusion* of *Boundaries, Dower, Marshalling* of *Securities* and *Partition;* all of which the student can only comprehend by a careful perusal of the details as given in the text-books.

PARTNERSHIP.

In cases of **PARTNERSHIP**, where a remedy at law actually exists, it is often found to be very imperfect, inconvenient and circuitous. But in a very great variety of cases, there is, in fact, no remedy at all at law to meet the exigency of the case.

The powers of a court of equity will be found most effective, **by means of a bill of discovery**, to bring out all the facts, as well in controversies between the partners themselves, **as between them and third persons.**

The most extensive, and generally, **the most operative, remedy at law, between partners, is an action of account.** This is the appropriate, and, except under very peculiar circumstances, is the only remedy, at the Common Law, for the final adjustment and settlement of partnership transactions.

But the remedial justice administered by courts of equity **is far more complete, extensive and various,** adapting itself to the peculiar nature of the grievance, and granting relief in the most beneficial and effective manner, where no redress could be obtained at law.

After the commencement, and during the continuance of a partnership, courts of equity will, in many cases, interpose to decree a specific performance of agreements in the articles of partnership.

In case of a partnership existing during the pleasure of the parties, if a sudden dissolution is about to be made, in ill faith, and will **work irreparable injury,** courts of equity will, upon their ordinary jurisdiction to prevent irreparable mischief, grant an injunction against such a dissolution.

Equity will also interfere, by injunction, **to prevent a partner, during the continuation of the partnership, from doing any acts injurious thereto,** as by signing or endorsing notes to the injury of the partnership, or by driving away customers, or by violating the rights of the other parties, or his duty to them, even when a dissolution is not necessarily contemplated.

But equity will not, in all cases, interfere to enforce a specific performance of the articles of partnership. **Where a remedy at law is entirely adequate, no relief will be granted in equity.**

Courts of equity may not only provide for a more effectual settlement of all the accounts of the partnership after a dissolution, but they may take steps for this purpose which courts of law are inadequate to afford.

It is the duty of courts of equity to adapt their practice and course of proceeding to the existing state of society, and not by too strict an adherence to forms and rules, established under different circumstances, to decline to administer justice, and to enforce rights for which there is no other remedy. A general rule, established for the convenient administration of justice, must not be adhered to in cases in which, consistently with practical convenience, it is incapable of application; **it is better to go as far as possible towards justice, than to deny it altogether.**

Where a dissolution has taken place, an account will not only be decreed, but, if necessary, a manager or **receiver will be appointed to close the partnership business,** and make sale of the partnership property: so that a final distribution may be made of the partnership effects. This a court of law is incompetent to do.

The accounts are usually taken before a Master, who examines the parties, if necessary, and requires the production of all the books, papers and vouchers of the partnership, and he is armed from time to time, by the court, with all the powers necessary to effectuate the objects of the reference to him.

A receiver or manager will not be appointed, at the instance of one of the partners, in a suit which does not seek to dissolve the partnership.

The power to dissolve a partnership during the term for which it is stipulated is also exercised by courts of equity. And this is a peculiar remedy which courts of law are incapable of administering.

Such a dissolution may be granted on account of the impracticability of carrying on the undertaking, either at all or according to the stipulations of the articles. **It may be granted on account of the insanity, or permanent incapacity** of one of the partners. **Also on account of the gross misconduct of one or more of the partners.** But trifling faults and misbehavior, which do not go to the substance of the contract, do not constitute sufficient ground to justify a decree for dissolution.

Where the circumstances have so changed, and the conduct of the parties is such as to render it impossible to continue the relation without injury to all the partners, **the court will decree a dissolution.**

The real estate is treated, to all intents and purposes, as **a part of the partnership funds,** whatever may be the form of the conveyance. For equity considers the real estate, to all intents and purposes, as personal estate; and subjects it to all the equitable rights and liens of the partners, which would apply to it if it were personal estate. 21

The creditors of the partnership have the preference to have their debts paid out of the partnership funds, before the private creditors of either of the partners.

And it seems that the separate creditors of each partner are entitled to be first paid out of the separate effects of their debtor, before the partnership creditors can claim anything.

Or, as it is said, where there are partnership property and partnership creditors, and separate property and separate creditors, **each class of creditors must look to their separate estates**, without jostling each other for payment in the first instance.

Each has a priority on its respective estate; **after it is satisfied, the other may come upon the residue,** according to its several legal and equitable rights.

This rule can only become material in cases of insolvency or bankruptcy, where the necessity may arise for marshalling assets. Prior to and independent of this, the rights of creditors remain, to enforce the payment of debts due them at law.

In cases of partnership debts, if one of the partners dies and the survivor becomes insolvent or bankrupt, the **joint creditors have a right to be paid out of the estate of the deceased** partner, through the medium of the equities subsisting between the partners.

The ground of the doctrine is that every partnership debt is joint and several; and, in all such cases, resort may primarily be had for the debt to the surviving partners, or to the assets of the deceased partner.

At law, an execution for the separate debt of one of the partners may be levied upon the joint property of the partnership. In such case, however, the judgment creditor **can levy on the interest only of the judgment debtor,** if any, in the property, after payment of all debts and other charges thereon.

The creditor can take only the same interest in the property which the judgment debtor himself would have upon the final settlement of all the accounts of the partnership. And after the sale of the interest of the partner, the vendee has a right in equity to call for an account, and thus to entitle himself to the interest of the partner in the property, which shall be ascertained to exist.

The remedy for the other partners, if nothing is due to the judgment debtor out of the partnership funds, is to file a bill in equity against the vendee of the sheriff, to have the proper accounts taken.

In the case of two firms dealing with each other where some or all the partners in one firm are partners with other persons in the other firm, **no suit can be maintained at law** in regard to any transactions or debts between the two firms; for in such suit all the partners must join, and be joined; and **no person can maintain a suit against himself,** or against himself and others.

But in equity it is otherwise; for there it is sufficient that all the parties in interest are before the court as plaintiffs or as defendants; and they need not, as at law in such cases, be on the opposite sides of the record.

Equity in all such cases **looks behind the form of the transactions to their substance**; and treats the different firms, for the purposes of substantial justice, exactly as if they were composed of strangers, or were in, fact, corporate companies.

If one partner, in fraud of the partnership rights or credits, should release an action, that release would, *at law*, be obligatory upon all the partners. But equity would not hesitate to relieve the partnership.

Where a discovery, an account, a contribution, an injunction, or a dissolution is sought, in cases of partnership, or where a due enforcement of partnership rights and duties and credits is required, it is plain to perceive that, generally, a resort to courts of law would be little more than a solemn mockery of justice.

It is said that **where there is a right there ought to be a remedy,** and if the *law* gives none, it ought to be administered in equity. This principle is of frequent application in equity, but it is not to be understood as of universal application.

DISCOVERY.

CANCELLATION AND DELIVERY OF INSTRUMENTS.—Every **original bill** in equity may, in truth, be properly deemed **a bill of discovery,** for it seeks a disclosure of circumstances relative to the plaintiff's case.

But that which is usually distinguished by this appellation is **a bill for the discovery of facts, resting in the knowledge of the defendant**, or of deeds, or writings, or other things, in his custody, possession, or power, but seeking no relief in consequence of this discovery, although it may pray for a stay of proceedings at law, until the discovery shall be made.

Courts of law are incompetent to compel such a discovery; and, therefore, it properly falls under the head of the *exclusive* jurisdiction of courts of equity.

The court, having acquired cognizance of the suit for the purpose of *discovery*, will entertain it for the purpose of *relief* in most cases of fraud, account, accident and mistake.

Equity also exercises jurisdiction over cases where the *Rescission, Cancellation or Delivery Up* of agreements, securities, or deeds is sought, or a *Specific Performance* is required of the terms of such agreements, securities, or deeds, as indispensable to reciprocal justice.

Courts of law are utterly incompetent to make a specific decree for any relief of this sort.

Application to a court of equity in all cases of this sort is not, strictly speaking, a matter of absolute right upon which the court is bound to pass a final decree. But it is **a matter of sound discretion** to be exercised by the court, either in granting or in refusing relief.

The principle upon which courts of equity direct the *Delivery Up, Cancellation or Rescission* of agreements, securities, deeds or other instruments, is technically called *quia timet;* that is, for fear that such agreements or other instruments may be vexatiously or injuriously used against him, when the evidence to impeach them may be lost; or that they may now throw a cloud or suspicion over his title or interest.

Equity will generally set aside, cancel and direct to be delivered up agreements and other instruments, however solemn in their form or operation, where they are *voidable*, and not merely void, under the following circumstances: *First*, where there is *actual fraud* in the party defendant, in which the plaintiff has not participated. *Secondly*, where there is *a constructive fraud* against public policy, and the plaintiff has not participated therein. *Thirdly*, where there is *a fraud against public policy*, and the party plaintiff has participated therein, but public policy would be defeated by allowing it to stand. *Lastly*, where there is a construtive fraud by both parties, but they are not *in pari delicto*.

A party ought not to be permitted to avail himself of any agreement, deed or other instrument procured by his own actual or constructive fraud, or by his own violation of legal duty or public policy, to the prejudice of an innocent party.

The third class of cases may be illustrated by the common case of gaming security, which will be decreed to be given up, notwithstanding both parties have participated in the violation of the law.

The fourth class may also be illustrated by cases where although both parties have participated in the guilty transaction, yet the party who seeks relief has acted under circumstances of oppression, imposition, hardship, undue influence or great inequality of age or condition.

Where a delivery up or cancellation of deeds or other instruments is sought, either upon the ground of their original invalidity, or of their subsequent satisfaction, or because the party has a just title thereto, or derives an interest under them, **courts of equity act upon an enlarged and comprehensive policy**; and in granting relief will impose such terms and qualifications as shall meet the just equities of the opposing party.

In case of chattels courts of **equity will not**, ordinarily, interfere to **decree a specific delivery**, because by a suit at law a full compensation may be obtained in damages, although the thing itself cannot be specifically obtained; and when such **a remedy at law is perfectly adequate and effectual**, there is no reason why equity should afford any aid to the party.

But there are cases of personal goods and chattels in which the remedy at law by damages would be utterly inadequate, and leave the injured party in a state of irremediable loss.

In such cases equity will grant relief by requiring the **specific delivery of the thing which is wrongfully withheld.**

This will be done in cases where the principal value of the chattel consists in its high antiquity, or in its being a family relic, ornament, or heirloom; such as ancient gems, medals, coins, paintings of old and distinguished masters, ancient statues and busts.

Relief will also be granted in equity where the party in possession of the chattel has acquired such possession through an alleged abuse of power on the part of one **standing in a fiduciary relation to the plaintiff.**

SPECIFIC PERFORMANCE.

Equity, in obedience to the cardinal rule of natural justice, that **a person should perform his agreement**, enforces, pursuant to a regulated and judicial discretion, the actual accomplishment of a thing stipulated for, on the ground that **what is lawfully agreed to be done ought to be done.**

This branch of equity jurisdiction is of a very ancient date. It may be distinctly traced back to the reign of Edward IV; for in the Year Books of that reign it was expressly recognized by the chancellor as a clear jurisdiction.

The ground of the jurisdiction is that a court of law is inadequate to decree a specific performance, and can relieve the injured party **only by a compensation in damages**, which, in many cases, would fall far short of the redress which his situation might require.

Whenever a party wants the thing *in specie*, and he cannot otherwise **be fully compensated**, courts of equity will grant him **a specific performance.**

With reference to the present subject, *agreements* may be divided into three classes: (1) those which respect **personal property**; (2) those which respect **personal acts**; and (3), those which respect **real property.**

Although the general rule is not to entertain jurisdiction in equity for a specific performance of agreements respecting goods, chattels, stock, choses in action and other things of a merely personal nature; yet the rule is, as we have seen, a qualified one, and subject to exceptions; or rather the rule is limited to cases **where a compensation in damages furnishes a complete and satisfactory remedy.**

Cases of agreements to form a partnership, and to execute articles accordingly, **may be specifically decreed**, although they relate exclusively to chattel interests, and so of a covenant for a lease, or to renew a lease; so of a contract for the sale of the good-will of a trade, and of a valuable secret connected with it; **for no adequate compensation can, in such cases, be made at law.**

And if a party covenants that he will not carry on his trade within a certain distance, or in a certain place within which the other party carries on the same trade, a court of equity will restrain the party from breaking the agreement so made. In such cases the decree operates, *pro tanto,* as a specific performance.

The jurisdiction of courts of equity, to decree a specific performance of contracts, is not dependent upon, or affected by, **the form or character of the instrument.**

It is maintained that courts of equity ought not to decline the jurisdiction for a specific performance of contracts, whenever the remedy at law is doubtful in its nature, extent, operation or adequacy.

It is not necessary to the specific performance of a written agreement **that it should be signed by the party seeking to enforce it**; if the agreement is certain, fair and just in all its parts, and signed by the party sought to be charged, that is sufficient; the **want of mutuality in the signature merely** is no objection to its enforcement.

In cases of specific performance, courts of equity sometimes follow the law, and sometimes go far beyond the law ; and their doctrines, if not wholly independent of the point whether damages would be given at law, are not in general dependent upon it.

Sometimes damages may be recoverable at law, when courts of equity would yet not decree a specific performance ; and, on the other hand, damages may not be recoverable at law, and yet relief would be granted in equity.

The most numerous class of cases in which courts of equity are called upon to decree a specific performance of contracts is that class *respecting land.*

A bill for a specific performance of a contract respecting land may be entertained by courts of equity, although the land is situate in a foreign country, if the parties are resident within the territorial jurisdiction of the court. **The ground of this jurisdiction** is that courts of equity have authority to act upon the person; *Æquitas agit in personam ;* for in all suits in equity the primary decree is *in personam* and not *in rem.*

But a court of equity has no jurisdiction in cases touching lands in foreign countries, unless the relief sought is of such a nature as the court is capable of administering in the given case.

The jurisdiction of courts of equity to decree specific performance, is, in cases of contracts respecting land, universally maintained; whereas, in cases respecting chattels, it is limited to special circumstances.

If a man contracts for a hundred bales of cotton, or boxes of sugar, of a particular description or quality, if the contract is not specifically performed, he may, generally, with a sum equal to the market price, purchase other goods of the same kind and quality; **and thus completely obtain his object and indemnify himself against loss.**

But in contracts respecting a specific messuage or parcel of land it is different; the locality, character, vicinage, soil, easements or accommodations of the land generally, may give it a peculiar and special value in the eyes of the purchaser; so that it cannot be replaced by other land of the same precise value, and, therfore, **a compensation in damages would not be adequate relief.**

Courts of equity will not permit **the forms of law to be made the instruments of injustice**; and they will, therefore, interpose against parties, attempting to avail themselves of the rigid rules of law for unconscientious purposes.

They dispense with that which would make a compliance with what the law requires oppressive; and in various cases of such contracts, they are in the constant habit of relieving a party who has acted fairly, although negligently.

It seems that where the party against whom the decree is sought shows to the satisfaction of the court that he entered into the contract under a *bona fide* **misapprehension in a material point**, the contract will not be carried into effect. Thus, where A by letter offered to sell some property to B for £1,250, and B by letter accepted the offer, and A by mistake inserted £1,250 in his letter, instead of £2,250, and so informed B immediately, equity would not enforce the contract.

He who seeks a specific performance must show an execution, or an offer to execute, on his part.

Equity will not decree a specific performance where the contract **is founded in fraud, imposition, mistake, undue advantage, or gross misrepresentation**; or where from a **change of circumstances**, or otherwise, it would be unconscientious to enforce it.

Specific performance will be decreed where the contract is in writing, and is certain, and is fair in all its parts, and is for an adequate consideration, and is capable of being performed.

In some cases courts of equity will decree the specific performance of contracts respecting lands, **where they are within the provisions of the statute of frauds and perjuries.** That statute has been generally re-enacted or adopted in this country. 29 Car. II, ch. 3.

It enacts "That all interest in lands, tenements, and hereditaments, except leases for three years, **not put in writing and signed by the parties** or their agents authorized by writing, shall not have, nor be deemed in law or equity to have, any **greater force or effect than leases on estates at will.**" It further enacts, "That no action shall be brought, whereby to charge any person upon any agreement made upon consideration of marriage, or upon any contract or sale of lands, tenements, or hereditaments, or any interest in or concerning the same, or **upon any agreement that is not to be performed within the space of one year from the making thereof,** unless the agreement upon which such action shall be brought, or some memorandum or note thereof, **shall be in writing and signed by the party or his lawful agent.**"

The objects of this statute are such as the very title indicates, to prevent the fraudulent setting up of pretended agreements, and then supporting them by perjury.

Besides, there is a manifest policy in requiring all contracts of an important nature to be *reduced to writing*, since otherwise, from the imperfection of memory, and the honest mistakes of witnesses, it must often happen, either that the specific contract is **incapable of exact proof,** or that it is unintentionally **varied from its precise original terms.**

Equity will enforce a specific performance of a contract within the statute, *not in writing*, where it is fully set forth in the bill, and is confessed by the answer of the defendant. But even where the answer confesses the parol agreement, if it insists, by way of defence, upon the protection of the statute, the defence must prevail as a bar.

So will equity enforce a specific performance of a contract within the statute, **where the parol agreement has been partly carried into execution.**

Otherwise one party would be able to practice a fraud upon the other; and it could never be the intention of the statute to enable any party to commit such a fraud with impunity.

Where one party has executed his part of the agreement, in the confidence that the other party would do the same, it is obvious that if the latter should refuse, it would be a fraud upon the former to suffer this refusal to work to his prejudice.

It was formerly thought that a deposit, or security, or payment of the purchase-money, or of a part of it, was such **a part performance** as took the case out of the statute. But this doctrine is overthrown.

One ground why part payment is not deemed a part performance, sufficient to lift a case out of the statute, is that **the money can be recovered back again at law**, and therefore the case admits of full and direct compensation.

Another ground is that the statute has said in another clause (that which respects contracts for goods) that part payment, by way of earnest, shall operate as a part performance. And hence the **courts have considered this clause as excluding, by implication, agreements for lands.**

But the general rule in cases of this sort is that **nothing is to be considered as a part performance** which does not put the party into a situation which is **a fraud upon him**, unless the agreement is fully performed.

Thus, where a vendee, upon a parol argreement for a sale of land, should proceed to build a house on the land, in the confidence of a due completion of the contract,—in such a case, it **would be a manifest fraud upon the party to permit the vendor to escape** from a strict fulfillment of such agreement.

To take a case out of the statute because of part performance of a parol contract, it is indispensable that **the acts done should be clear and definite**, and referable exclusively to the contract; and **the contract should also be established by competent proofs** to be clear, definite and unequivocal in all its terms.

A contract cannot rest partly in writing and partly in parol. The writing is the highest evidence, and does away with the necessity and effect of the parol evidence, if it is contradictory to it.

When the court simply *refuses* to enforce the specific performance of a contract, **it leaves the party to his remedy at law.**

Equity will allow the defendant to show that by fraud, accident, or mistake, the thing bought is different from what he intended; or that material **terms have been omitted in the**

written agreement; or that there has been a variation of it by parol; or that there has been **a parol discharge of a written contract.**

The ground of this doctrine is that courts of equity ought not to be active in enforcing claims which are not, under the actual circumstances, just, as between the parties.

In general, it may be stated that **to entitle a party to a specific performance,** he must show that he has been in no default in not having performed the agreement, and that he has taken all proper steps towards performance on his own part.

If the plaintiff has been guilty of gross laches, or if he applies for relief after a long lapse of time, unexplained by equitable circumstances, his bill will be dismissed; for courts of equity do not, any more than courts of law, administer relief to the gross negligence of suitors.

In some cases courts of equity will decree a specific execution, **not according to the letter of the contract, if that will be unconscientious;** but they will modify it according to the change of circumstances.

A court of equity will also decree specific performance, in some cases, **where the action at law has been lost by the default of the party seeking the specific performance,** if it be, notwithstanding, *conscientious* that the agreement should be performed.

Time is not generally deemed in equity to be of the essence of the contract, unless the parties have expressly so stated it, or it necessarily follows from the nature and circumstances of the contract.

But courts of equity have regard to time, so far as it respects the good faith and diligence of the parties. If, however, circumstances of a reasonable nature have *disabled the party* from a strict compliance, or if he comes, *recenti facto*, to ask for a specific performance, the suit will be treated with indulgence, and, generally, with favor by the court.

Equity will also relieve the party vendor, by decreeing a specific performance where he has been unable to comply with his contract according to the terms of it, **from the state of his title at the time,** if he comes within a reasonable time, and the defect is cured.

So, if he is unable to make a good title **at the time when the bill is brought,** if he is in a condition to make such a title at or before the time of the decree.

Where there is a substantial defect in the estate sold either in the title itself, or in the representation or description, or the nature, character, situation, extent, or quality of it **which is unknown to the vendee,** and in regard to which he is not put upon enquiry, there a specific performance will not be decreed against him.

The general rule is that the *purchaser,* if he chooses, **is entitled to have the contract specifically performed,** as far as the vendor can perform it, and to have abatement out of the purchase-money or compensation for any deficiency in the title, quantity, quality, description, or other matters touching the estate.

But if the purchaser should insist upon such a performance, the court will grant relief only upon his **compliance with equitable terms.**

If a man in confidence of the parol promise of another to perform the intended act, should omit to make certain provisions, gifts, or arrangements for other persons, *by will or otherwise,* **such a promise would be specifically enforced in equity** against such promisee; although founded on a *parol declaration,* creating a trust contrary to the statute of frauds; **for it would be a fraud upon all the other parties** to permit him to derive a benefit from his own breach of duty and obligation.

Thus, where a testator was about altering his will, for fear that there would not be assets enough to pay all the legacies, and his heir-at-law persuaded him not to alter it, promising to pay all the legacies, he was decreed specifically to perform his promise.

Privity of contract between the parties is, in general, **indispensable to a suit at law**; but courts of equity act in favor of all persons claiming by assignment under the parties, independent of any such privity.

If a person has, in writing, contracted to sell land, and afterwards refuses to perform his contract, and then sells the land to a purchaser with notice of the contract, **the latter will be compelled to perform the contract of his vendor,** for he stands upon the same equity; and although he is not personally liable on the contract, yet he will be decreed to convey the land, for **he is treated as a trustee of the first vendee.**

In general, where the specific execution of a contract respecting lands **will be decreed between the parties, it will be decreed between all persons claiming under them in privity of estate,** or representation, or of title, unless other controlling equities are interposed.

The general principle upon which this doctrine proceeds is that from the time of the contract for the sale of the land, the vendor, as to the land, **becomes a trustee for the vendee**, and the vendee, as to the purchase-money, a **trustee to the vendor**, who has a lien upon the land therefor. And every subsequent purchaser from either, with notice **becomes subject to the same equities** as the party would be from whom he purchased.

Where a man has entered into a valid contract for the purchase of land, **he is treated in equity as the equitable owner of the land, and the vendor is treated as the owner of the money.** The purchaser may devise it as land, even before the conveyance is made, and it passes by descent to his heir as land. The vendor is deemed in equity to stand seized of it for the benefit of the purchaser.

The vendor may come into equity for a specific performance of the contract on the other side, and to have the money paid; for **the remedy in cases of specific performance is mutual**, and the purchase-money is treated as the personal estate of the vendor, and goes as such to his personal representatives.

In respect to voluntary contracts, or such as are not founded in a valuable consideration, **courts of equity do not enforce them,** either as against the party himself or as against other volunteers claiming under him.

Where there is any matter affecting the contract, about which the party might *bona fide* make a mistake, **and he swears positively that he did make such mistake,** a court of equity will not decree specific performance against him.

Where the party agrees to convey the land with full covenants of warranty and release of dower and he is unable to procure the release of dower, a decree of specific performance will be made with compensation for the right of dower and an exception to that extent in the covenants.

Courts of equity exercise a discretion in decreeing specific performance, and **where the title to any portion of the estate fails,** or is not of a marketable character, it will not be forced upon the purchaser.

COMPENSATION AND DAMAGES.

It may be stated as a general proposition, that, for breaches of contract and other wrongs and injuries cognizable at law, **courts of equity do not entertain jurisdiction to give redress by way of compensation or damages where these constitute the sole objects of the bill.**

Wherever the matter of the bill is **merely for damages**, and there is a perfect remedy therefor at law, **it is far better that they should be ascertained by a jury** than by the conscience of an equity judge.

Compensation or damages will, ordinarily, be decreed in equity only as **incidental to other relief** sought by the bill and granted by the court, **or where there is no adequate remedy at law.**

The mode in which such damages are ascertained is either by a reference to a Master, or by directing an issue, *quantum damnificatus,* which is trial by a jury.

INTERPLEADER.

The jurisdiction of a court of equity to compel an interpleader follows, to some extent, the analogies of the law.

Interpleader is applied to cases **where two or more persons claim the same debt, duty, or thing from another, by different or separate interests**, and he, not insisting upon any right in the matter, and not knowing to which of the claimants he ought rightly to render such debt, duty, or thing, but fearing that he may suffer injury from their conflicting claims, can file a bill of interpleader, which is in its nature an original bill for relief.

Generally the bill should be filed before any judgment at law settling the right of the respective parties to the property in question: **the object of the bill** being to protect the complainant from the vexation attendant upon defending all the suits that may be instituted against him for the same property.

If an interpleader at law will lie in the case, and it would be effectual for the protection of the party, then the jurisdiction in equity fails.

EQUITY.

The true ground upon which the plaintiff comes into equity is that claiming no right in the subject-matter himself, he is, or may be, vexed by having two legal or other processes, in the names of different persons, going on against him at the same time.

Courts of equity dispose of questions, arising upon bills of interpleader, in various modes, according to the nature of the question, and the manner in which it is brought before the court.

BILLS QUIA TIMET.

Bills in equity, *quia timet*, are in the nature of bills of prevention, to accomplish the ends of precautionary justice. They are ordinarily applied **to prevent wrongs or anticipated mischiefs**, and not merely to redress them when done.

The party seeks the aid of a court of equity, **because he fears**, *quia timet,* **some future probable injury to his rights** or interests, and not because an injury has already occurred, which requires any compensation or other relief.

The manner in which this aid is given by courts of equity is dependent upon circumstances. They interfere sometimes by the appointment of a receiver to receive rents or other income, sometimes by an order to pay a pecuniary fund into court, sometimes by directing security to be given, or money to be paid over, and sometimes by the mere issuing of an injunction or other remedial process.

The appointment of a receiver, when directed, is made for the **benefit and on behalf of all the parties** in interest, and not for the benefit of the plaintiff, or of one defendant only.

The appointment of a receiver is **a matter resting in the sound discretion of the court;** and the receiver, when appointed, is treated as virtually **an officer and representative of the court**, and subject to its orders.

A receiver, when in possession, **has very little discretion allowed him; but he must apply, from time to time, to the court for authority** to do such acts as may be beneficial to the estate. Thus, he is not at liberty to bring or to defend actions, or to let the estate, or lay out money, unless by the special leave of the court.

Where a receiver is appointed, and **the property is in possession of a third person, who claims he has a right to**

retain it, the receiver must either proceed by a suit in the ordinary way, to try his right to it, or the plaintiff in equity should make such third person a party to the suit, and apply to the court to have the receivership extended to the property in his hands.

It is not infrequent for a bill *quia timet* to ask for the appointment of a receiver, **against a party who is rightfully in possession,** or who is entitled to possession of the fund, or who has an interest in its due administration.

But equity will not withdraw the fund from him by the appointment of a receiver, unless the facts averred and established in proof show that **there has been an abuse, or is danger of abuse, on his own part.**

Thus, whenever the appointment of a receiver is sought against an executor or administrator, it is necessary to establish, by suitable proofs, that there is some positive loss, or danger of loss, of the funds; as, for instance, some waste or misapplication of the funds, or some apprehended danger from the bankruptcy, insolvency, or personal fraud, misconduct, or negligence of the executor or administrator.

So, where the tenants of particular estates for life, or in tail, neglect to keep down the interest due upon encumbrances upon the estates, courts of equity will appoint a receiver **to receive the rents and profits,** in order to keep down the interest.

It is a rule in equity to follow trust-money whenever it may be found in the hands of any person who has not *prima facie* a right to hold it, and order him to bring it into court.

Where there is a future right of enjoyment of personal property, equity will interfere and grant relief upon a bill *quia timet,* where there is any danger of loss, or deterioration, or injury to it in the hands of the party who is entitled to the present possession.

There are other cases where a remedial justice is applied in the nature of bills *quia timet,* as where courts of equity interfere to prevent the waste or destruction of property, *pendente lite,* or to prevent irreparable mischief. But these cases will more properly come under the head of injunctions.

BILLS OF PEACE.

By a Bill of Peace we are to understand a bill brought by a person to establish and perpetuate a right, which he claims, and which, from its nature, may be controverted by different persons, at different times and by different actions.

Bills of peace sometimes **bear a resemblance** to bills *quia timet*. But the latter, however, are quite distinguishable from the former in several respects, and are always **used as a preventive process before a suit is actually instituted**; whereas bills of peace, although sometimes brought before any suit is instituted to try a right, **are most generally brought after the right has been tried at law.**

The obvious design of such a bill is to procure repose from perpetual litigation, and, therefore, it is justly called a bill of peace.

It may be resorted to, where **one person claims or defends a right against many**, or where **many claim or defend a right against one**. In such cases equity interposes in order to prevent a multiplicity of suits.

To entitle a party to maintain a bill of peace, it must be clear that there is **a right claimed which affects many persons**, and that a suitable number of parties in interest are brought before the court.

Bills of peace are also applied to cases where the plaintiff has, **after repeated and satisfactory trials, established his right at law**; and yet is in **danger of further litigation** and obstruction to his right from new attempts to controvert it.

In such cases equity will interfere by perpetual injunction to quiet the possession of the plaintiff, and to suppress future litigation of the right.

INJUNCTIONS.

A writ of injunction may be described to be a judicial process, whereby a party is required to do a particular thing, or to refrain from doing a particular thing, according to the exigency of the writ.

The most common form of injunction is that which operates as a *restraint* upon the party in the exercise of his real and supposed rights; and is sometimes **called the remedial writ of injunction.**

The other form, **commanding an act to be done**, is sometimes called the *judicial writ*, because it issues after a decree, and **is in the nature of an execution to enforce the same.**

The object of this process is generally preventive and protective, rather than restorative; although it is by no means confined to the former. **It seeks to prevent a meditated wrong more often than to redress an injury already done.**

The granting or refusal of injunctions is a matter resting in the sound discretion of the court; but injunctions are now more **liberally granted** than in former times.

The writ of injunction is peculiar to courts of equity, although there are some cases where courts of law may exercise *analogous powers;* such as by the writ of prohibition and estrepement in cases of waste.

Injunctions, when granted on bills, are either temporary, as until the coming in of the defendant's answer, or until the further order of the court, or until the hearing of the cause, or until the coming in of the report of the Master; **or they are perpetual,** as when they form a part of the decree after the hearing upon the merits, and the defendant is perpetually enjoined from any assertion of a particular right, or perpetually restrained from the doing of a particular act.

Injunctions to stay proceedings at law are sometimes granted to stay trial; or, after verdict, to stay judgment; or, after judgment, to stay execution; or, if the execution has been effected, to stay the money in the hands of the sheriff.

A writ of injunction, for these purposes, is in no just sense a prohibition to the courts of Common Law in the exercise of their jurisdiction. It is not addressed to those courts. **It does not even affect to interfere with them.** The process, when its object is to restrain proceedings at law, **is directed only to the parties.** It neither assumes any superiority over the court in which the proceedings are had, nor denies its jurisdiction.

Without a jurisdiction of this sort to control the proceedings, or to enjoin the judgments of parties at law, it is most obvious that **equity jurisprudence, as a system of remedial justice, would be grossly inadequate** to the ends of its institution.

The great mass of cases in which an injunction is ordinarily applied for, **to stay proceedings at law,** is where the rights of the party are *wholly equitable* in their own nature or are incapable, under the circumstances, of being *asserted* in a court of law.

The occasions on which an injunction may be used to stay proceedings at law are almost *infinite* in their nature and circumstances. Generally, in all cases where, by accident, or mistake, or fraud, or otherwise, a party has an **unfair advantage in proceedings in a court of law,** which must necessarily make that court an instrument of injustice, and it is, therefore, against conscience that he should use that advantage, a court of equity will interfere by injunction.

The injunction is not confined to any one point of the proceedings at law; but it may, upon a proper case being presented to the court, be **granted at any stage of the suit.**

Injunctions to restrain suits at law are usually spoken of as *common* or *special*. **The common injunction** is the writ of injunction issued upon and for the default of the defendant, in not appearing to answer the bill. It is also granted where the defendant obtains an order for further time to answer, or for a commission to take his answer.

All other injunctions granted upon other occasions, or involving other directions, are called *special* injunctions.

It is asserted, as a general rule, that *a defence* cannot be set up **as the ground of a bill in equity for injunction which has been fully and fairly tried at law,** although it may be the opinion of a court of equity that the defence ought to have been sustained at law.

But relief will be granted where the defence could not at the time, or under the circumstances, be made available at law, without any laches of the party.

Thus, if a party should recover a judgment at law for a debt, and the defendant should afterwards find a receipt under the plaintiff's own hand for the very money in question, the defendant would be relieved by a perpetual injunction.

Relief will not be granted by staying proceedings at law, after a verdict, **if the party applying has been guilty of laches as to the matter of defence,** or might, by reasonable diligence, have procured the requisite proofs before the trial.

If a matter has been already investigated in a court of

justice, according to the common and ordinary rules of investigation, a court of equity cannot take on itself to enter into it again. It is more important that **an end should be put to litigation** than that justice should be done in every case.

When both parties to a suit in a foreign country are residents within the territorial limits of another country, the courts of equity in the latter may act *in personam* upon those parties, and direct them, by injunction, to proceed no further in such suit.

But as an exception to this rule, it is held that the state courts cannot enjoin proceedings in the courts of the United States; nor the latter in the former courts. And the like doctrine has been applied by the state courts to suits and judgments in other American state courts, where the latter are competent to administer the proper relief.

Courts of equity will grant injunctions in cases where the aggrieved party has equitable rights only; and, indeed, it is said that these courts will grant them more strongly where there is a trust estate.

Injunctions are frequently used in cases of waste, when the remedy at law is imperfect, or is wholly denied; when the nature of the injury is such that a preventive remedy is indispensable, and it should be permanent; where matters of discovery and account are incidental to proper relief.

Injunctions are also used in cases of nuisances. And nuisances may be of two sorts: first, such as are **injurious to the public at large,** or to public rights; secondly, such as are **injurious to the rights and interests of private persons.**

In cases of public nuisances, properly so called, **an indictment lies to abate them,** and to punish the offenders.

But **an information also lies in equity** to redress the grievance by way of injunction.

But **the question of nuisance or not, must, in cases of doubt, be tried by a jury;** and the injunction will be granted or not, as that fact is decided. And the court, in the exercise of its jurisdiction, **will direct the matter to be tried upon an indictment,** and reserve its decree accordingly.

The ground of this jurisdiction of courts of equity in cases of public nuisances is their ability to give **a more complete and perfect remedy** than is attainable at law. They can interpose, where the courts of law cannot, to restrain and prevent such nuisances, **which are threatened**, or are in progress, as well as **to abate those already existing.**

Also, by a perpetual injunction, the remedy is made complete through all future time; whereas an information or indictment at the Common Law can only dispose of the present nuisance and for future acts new prosecutions must be brought; and then **the remedial justice in equity may be prompt and immediate,** before irreparable mischief is done; whereas, at law, nothing can be done, except after a trial, and upon the award of judgment.

But courts of equity will grant an injunction to restrain a public nuisance, **only in cases where the fact is clearly made out upon satisfactory evidence.** For if the evidence be conflicting, and the injury to the public doubtful, that alone will constitute a ground for withholding this extraordinary interposition.

In regard to private nuisances, the interference of courts of equity by way of injunction is founded upon the ground of restraining irreparable mischief, or of suppressing oppressive and interminable litigation, or of preventing multiplicity of suits.

A court of equity will restrain acts in violation of an agreement, where the injury to the plaintiffs would be irreparable, and the recovery of damages at law no adequate redress.

Where the injury is irreparable, as where loss of health, loss of trade, destruction of the means of subsistence, or permanent ruin of property, may or will ensue from the wrongful act or erection; in every such case courts of equity will interfere by injunction.

Cases of a nature calling for the like remedial interposition of equity are the obstruction or pollution of watercourses, the diversion of streams from mills, the backflowage on mills and the pulling down of the banks of rivers, and thereby exposing adjacent lands to inundation.

Courts of equity will also interfere by injunction to **restrain adjoining land-owners** from so digging in the soil of their own land as to endanger their neighbors' buildings.

These courts also interfere in cases of trespasses, that is to say, to prevent irreparable mischiefs, or to suppress multiplicity of suits and oppressive litigation; and upon the same grounds **they interfere in cases of patents for in-**

ventions, and in **cases of copyrights**, to secure the rights of the inventor, or author.

Injunctions are also granted **to prevent the use of names, marks, letters** or other *indicia* of a tradesman, by which to pass off goods to purchasers as the manufacture of that tradesman, when they are not so.

The true ground of enjoining the use of a trade-mark is that its similarity to plaintiffs was intended by defendants to give purchasers to understand the goods were the same, and that it would be likely to produce that effect with the majority of purchasers.

There are many cases in which courts of equity will interfere by injunction to prevent the sale of real estate; as to restrain the vendor from selling to the prejudice of the vendee, pending a bill for the specific performance of a contract respecting an estate.

In like manner, **sales may be restrained** in all cases **where they are inequitable, or may operate as a fraud** upon the rights or interests of third persons; as in cases of trusts, and special authorities, where the party is abusing his trust or authority.

Where land is sold with covenant from the grantee, or upon condition that the erections upon it shall be of a prescribed character, the performance of **such stipulations will be enforced in equity by restraining any departure from them.**

A preliminary injunction is commonly granted upon such conditions as the court deem reasonable and prudent.

No injunction will be granted whenever it will operate oppressively, or inequitably, or contrary to the real justice of the case, or where it is not the fit and appropriate mode of redress under all the circumstances of the case; or, where it will or may work an immediate mischief, or fatal injury.

It may be said, **in relation to special injunctions**, that **courts of equity constantly decline to lay down any rule which shall limit their power and discretion** as to the particular cases in which such injunctions shall be granted or withheld; for it is impossible to foresee all the exigences of society which may require their aid and assistance to protect rights, or redress wrongs.

EQUITY. 343

There is no power, the exercise of which is more delicate, which requires greater caution, deliberation and sound discretion, or is more dangerous, in a doubtful case, **than the issuing of an injunction.** It is the strong arm of equity, that never ought to be extended, unless to cases of great injury where courts of law cannot afford an adequate or commensurate remedy in damages. **The right must be clear, the injury impending or threatened,** so as to be averted only by the protecting preventive process of injunction. **If it issues erroneously,** an irreparable injury is inflicted, **for which there can be no redress,** it being the act of a court, not of the party who prays for it.

TRUSTS.

A trust, in its enlarged sense, may be defined to be an equitable right, title or interest in property, real or personal, distinct from the legal ownership thereof.

The legal owner holds the direct and absolute dominion over the property in the view of the law, but the income, profits, or benefits thereof in his hands, belong wholly, or in part, to others.

Three things are said to be indispensable to constitute a valid trust; *first,* sufficient words to raise it; *secondly,* a definite subject; *thirdly,* a certain or ascertained object.

For the most part, **matters of trust and confidence are exclusively cognizable in courts of equity;** there being few cases, **except bailments, and rights founded in contract,** and remedial by an action of *assumpsit,* and especially by an action for money had and received, in which a remedy can be administered in the courts of law.

It is also said that **a trust is where there is such a confidence between parties** that no action at law will lie, but is merely a case for the consideration of a court of equity.

Trusts constitute a very important and comprehensive branch of equity jurisprudence; and when the remedy in regard to them ends at law, then the exclusive jurisdiction in equity, for the most part, begins.

It is quite probable that those trusts, which are exclusively cognizable in courts of equity, were, in their origin, derived from the Roman law.

The Statute of Frauds, 29 Charles II, ch. 3, sec. 7, which has been generally adopted in this country, **requires all declarations or creations of trusts or confidences of any lands,** tenements and hereditaments to be manifested and **proved by some writing, signed by the party** entitled to declare such trusts, or by his last will in writing.

From the terms of the statute, it is apparent that **it does not extend to declarations of trusts of personalty.** Neither does it prescribe any particular form or solemnity in writing; nor that the writing should be under seal.

Any writing sufficiently evincive of a trust, as a letter, or other writing of a trustee, stating the trust, or any language in writing, clearly expressive of a trust, intended by the party, **although in the form of a desire or a request, or a recommendation, will create a trust by implication.**

Uses or trusts, to be raised by any covenant or agreement of a party in equity, must be founded upon some valuable consideration; for courts of equity will not enforce a mere gratuitous gift, or a mere moral obligation.

Trusts in real property, which are exclusively cognizable in equity, are in many respects **governed by the same rules as the like estates at law** and afford a striking illustration of the maxim *æquitas sequitur legem.*

Where a trust is created for the benefit of a party, it is not only alienable by him by his own proper act and conveyance, but it is also liable to be disposed of by operation of law *in invitum*, like any other property.

In general a trustee is only suable in equity in regard to any matters touching the trust.

It is a general rule in equity, that whenever a trust exists, either by the declaration of the party, or by intendment or implication of law, and **the party creating the trust has not appointed any trustee to execute it,** equity will follow the legal estate, and decree the person in whom it is vested (not being a *bona fide* purchaser for a valuable consideration without notice,) to execute the trust. For it is a rule in equity which admits of no exception, that **a court of equity never wants a trustee.**

The power of a trustee over the legal estate or property vested in him, properly speaking, exists only for the benefit of the *cestui qui trust.*

What powers may be properly exercised over trust property, by a trustee, **depends upon the nature of the trust**, and sometimes upon the situation of the *cestui que trust*. Where the *cestui que trust* is of age, or *sui juris*, the **trustee has no right** (unless power is given) **to change the nature of the estate**, as by converting land into money, or money into land, so as to bind the *cestui que trust*.

Trusts are usually divided into *Express Trusts* and *Implied Trusts*, the latter comprehending all those trusts which are called *constructive* and *resulting* trusts.

Express trusts are those which are created by the direct and positive acts of the parties by some writing, or deed, or will.

Implied trusts are those which are deducible from the nature of the transaction, as a matter of clear intention, **although not found in the words of the parties**; or which are superinduced upon the transaction by operation of law, as matter of equity, independent of the particular intention of the parties.

A resulting trust is created by one man furnishing the money to pay the price of land purchased by another, and by agreement of the parties conveyed to the latter for the benefit of the former.

MORTGAGES.

As to what constitutes a mortgage there is no difficulty whatever in courts of equity, although there may be technical embarrassments in courts.

The particular form or words of the conveyance are unimportant.

It is a general rule, subject to few exceptions, that wherever a conveyance, assignment or other instrument, transferring an estate, **is originally intended between the parties as a security for money**, or for any other encumbrance, whether this intention appear from the same instrument or from any other, it **is always considered in equity as a mortgage**, and consequently is redeemable upon the performance of the conditions or stipulations thereof.

Parol evidence is admissible in some cases, as in cases of fraud, accident and mistake, **to show that a conveyance, absolute on its face**, was intended between the parties to be **a mere mortgage** or security for money.

The estate of the mortgagee, being treated in equity as a mere security for the debt, it follows the nature of the debt. And although where the mortgage is in fee, the legal estate descends to the heir, yet, in equity, it is deemed a chattel interest and personal estate, and belongs to the personal representatives, as assets.

A mortgage may be created by a conditional deed, as well as by a conveyance and mortgaging back. And the assignee of a mortgage takes it subject to all the equities which existed as against the mortgagee.

Mortgages may not only be created by the express deeds and contracts of the parties, but they may also be *implied* in equity, from the nature of the transactions between the parties; and then **they are termed equitable mortgages.**

In equity, whatever property, personal or real, is capable of absolute sale, may be the subject of a mortgage.

Mortgages are often given **to secure future advances,** and in such cases, where the mortgagee **has notice of a subsequent mortgage,** he cannot hold his security for advances made after such notice.

A mortgage of personal property differs from a pledge. The former is a conditional transfer or conveyance of the property itself; and, if the condition is not fully performed, **the whole title vests absolutely at law in the mortgagee,** exactly as it does in the case of a mortgage of lands. **The latter only passes the possession,** or, at most, a special property only to the pledgee, with a right of retainer until the debt is paid.

In mortgages of personal property there exists, as in mortgages of land, **an equity of redemption,** which may be asserted by the mortgagor. But there is a difference between mortgages of land and mortgages of personal property, in regard to the rights of the mortgagee, after a breach of the condition. In the latter case the mortgagee, upon due notice, may sell the personal property mortgaged, without a bill of foreclosure.

It is said that goods pledged or leased by the defendant in execution may be levied upon, subject to the rights of the pawnee or lessee.

The satisfaction of the principal debt, by payment, or otherwise, will be deemed in equity an **extinguishment of the**

EQUITY.

mortgage, unless there is an express or implied contract for keeping alive the original security.

An extinguishment of the debt will also ordinarily take place where the mortgagee becomes also the absolute owner of the equity of redemption, for **then the equitable estate becomes merged in the legal.**

When the mortgage debt is once paid off, the security is so effectually extinguished that it cannot be made a continuing security for further advancements.

ASSIGNMENTS.

Courts of equity take notice of assignments of property, and enforce the rights growing out of the same, in many cases where such assignments are not recognized at law as valid or effectual to pass titles.

It is a well known rule of the common law that no possibility, right, title, or *thing in action* can be granted to a third person. For it was thought that a different rule **would be the occasion of multiplying contentions and suits,** as it would in effect be transferring a law suit to a stranger.

Hence, at Common Law, the assignment of a chose in action could not be made so as to vest in the assignee **a right of action in his own name.** And this, with the exception of negotiable instruments, and some few other securities, still continues to be the general rule, unless the debtor assents to the transfer.

But courts of equity totally disregard this nicety. They give effect to assignments of trusts, and possibilities of trusts, and contingent interests, and expectancies, whether they are in real or personal estate, as well as to **assignments of choses in action.**

Every such assignment is considered in equity as amounting to **an agreement to permit the assignee to make use of the name of the assignor,** in order to recover the debt, or reduce the property into possession.

In some of the states, the common law rule has been relaxed, and all choses in action, such as bonds, mortgages, notes, judgments, debts, contracts, agreements, as well relating to personal as real estate, are assignable, and will pass to the assignee **a right of action, in the name of the assignee.**

In order to constitute an assignment of a debt, or other chose in action, in equity, **no particular form is necessary.** And an assignment of a debt may be **by parol, as well as by deed.**

A draft drawn by A on B, in favor of C, for a valuable consideration, amounts to a valid assignment to C of so much of the funds of A in the hands of B.

Indeed, any order, writing, or act, which makes an appropriation of a fund, **amounts to an assignment of that fund.**

As the assignee is generally **entitled to all the remedies** of the assignor, so he is generally **subject to all the equities** between the assignor and his debtor.

In order to perfect his title against the debtor, it is indispensable that the assignee should immediately **give notice of the assignment to the debtor;** for, otherwise, a priority of right may be obtained by a subsequent assignee, or **the debt may be discharged by a payment to the assignor before such notice.**

In cases of assignments of a debt, **where the assignor has collateral security** therefor, the **assignee will be entitled to the full benefit of such securities,** unless it is otherwise agreed between the parties.

It is principally in cases of assignments that courts of equity have occasion to examine into the doctrine of *champerty* and *maintenance.*

Where there is no contract to have a part of the thing in suit, the party so intermeddling is said to be guilty of **maintenance.** But if the party stipulates to have part of the thing in suit, his offence is called **champerty.**

Courts of equity are ever solicitous to enforce all the principles of law respecting champerty and maintenance; and they will not, in any case, uphold an assignment which involves any such offensive ingredients.

WILLS.

The construction of wills often presents embarrassing questions, which call for the interposition of courts of equity to expound.

In equity, executors and administrators are considered as trustees, and the persons to whom bequests are made, as the *cestuis que trust,* and in that character are peculiarly entitled to the protection of courts of equity.

EQUITY.

Incidental to the jurisdiction over trusts is the duty of giving the true **construction of wills, and of compelling their execution** by the executors, or other persons to whom a duty in relation thereto is confided.

The cardinal rule in the construction of wills is that **the intention of the testator is to govern, if consistent with the rules of law;** that is, the testator cannot create a trust which the law prohibits, or suspend the power of alienation, or the absolute ownership of property, beyond the period allowed by law.

The testator is to be presumed to have used words in their natural or primary sense, unless there is something in the situation of the family or in his will to lead to a contrary conclusion.

He is not bound to use any particular form of words, to devise or bequeath a legal interest in property, or to designate the objects of his bounty, provided he uses language sufficient to show his intention.

The intention of the testator is to be ascertained from the whole will taken together, and not from the language of any particular provision or clause, when taken by itself.

For the purpose of construction, **a will and a codicil may be considered together,** and construed as different parts of the same will.

The word "and" may be understood disjunctively for "or," and "or" for "and," when it is clear such was the intention of the testator.

The construction will be most favored which will prevent a total failure of a bequest, if *specific*, and the intent is to be gathered from the words of the will itself.

Where the language employed in a will is obscure or ambiguous, and words are made use of in one connection, with a meaning apparently at variance with the sense of the same words in another clause, **extrinsic circumstances may be resorted to** for the purpose of aiding the court in arriving at the intention of the testator.

In such a case, the situation of the testator's property, the condition of his family and the apparent beneficiaries, may be considered as landmarks to guide the court in the duty of interpretation.

But extrinsic evidence is inadmissible to influence the

construction of a will, **when the language is clear** and capable of construction by well-settled rules.

Effect should be given to every part of a will, and no portion is to be disregarded unless entirely repugnant to another portion.

No two wills are in all respects alike. But where the same precise form of expression occurs in a will that has been the subject of some former adjudication, unaffected by any different intention in some other part of the will, the courts, with a view to certainty and stability of titles, will follow the judicial precedent.

The intention is to be gathered from the entire instrument; but, **rather than sacrifice what is clearly the whole scheme of the testator**, incongruous and insensible words must give way.

Where words taken in their technical signification would defeat the testator's intention, as collected from the whole will, a *liberal* and *popular* meaning may be given to them.

Where the intention depends upon **words which admit of a two-fold construction**, one of which would render it void, and the other uphold it, the court will give the latter construction.

One name may be substituted for another, in the construction of a will, where it is manifest, not only that the name used was not intended, but that a certain other name was necessarily intended.

The strict grammatical sense is not always regarded, but the words of a will may be transposed to make a limitation sensible, or to carry into effect the general intent of the testator.

The court will abide by the settled meaning of the words, until driven out by strong, solid and rational interpretation put upon, and plain inference drawn from, the rest of the will.

If the language admits of two constructions, one reasonable and natural, and the other less so, the court will adopt the former.

It sometimes happens in wills that there are clauses inconsistent with each other, in which both cannot take effect. In analogy to the fact that the last will of a testator is to prevail in preference to an earlier one, the **courts treat the subsequent words in the will as indicating a subsequent**

intention, unless there be other expressions of the will which make it apparent that the *first* should take effect.

Sometimes a will is *ambiguous* in its terms, and the true construction of it cannot be made without the aid of a court of equity. **The question then arises whether the ambiguity can be explained by a resort to parol evidence,** or whether it must be determined solely by a resort to other parts of the will.

Ambiguities are of two sorts. One is called a *latent* and the other a *patent* ambiguity.

The first occurs where the deed or instrument is sufficiently certain and free from ambiguity; but the ambiguity is produced by evidence of something extrinsic, or some collateral matter out of the instrument.

A latent ambiguity, which is raised by extrinsic evidence, may be explained in the same manner. Thus, if a person grant his manor of S to one of his heirs, so far there appears no ambiguity; but if it should be proved that the grantor has the manors both of South S and North S, this ambiguity is matter of fact, and parol evidence may be admitted to show which of the two manors the party intended to convey.

A patent ambiguity is such as appears on the face of the instrument itself.

In cases of patent ambiguities, the apparent uncertainty may be removed by collecting the general intention from other parts of the instrument, so as to make the whole consistent, and **this is a legitimate mode of explaining the ambiguity.**

But when, after comparing the several parts of a written instrument, and collecting all the lights which *the writing itself supplies,* the intention of the parties still appears to be uncertain, **parol evidence of their intention is not admissible.**

If any devise is expressed doubtfully and with uncertainty, the only construction which it is capable of receiving is **by comparing it with other parts of the will; and declarations of the testator are not admissible to remove the apparent ambiguity, or to explain his intention.**

The rule which excludes parol evidence to explain a patent ambiguity in a deed or will should not be carried to the extent of shutting out **evidence of the situation and circumstances of the parties,** for the purpose of assisting them in putting a construction on wills that are not clearly expressed.

A latent ambiguity sometimes relates to **the person of the legatee,** and sometimes to **the subject of the bequest;** but in either case, if the doubt be created by extrinsic evidence, it may be removed in the same way.

The reason of the rule which excludes parol evidence to explain a patent ambiguity is that **the law will not couple and mingle matter of specialty,** which is of the higher account, **with matter of averment,** which is of inferior account in law; for that were to make all deeds hollow and subject to averment, and so, in effect, **to make that pass without deed which the law appoints shall not pass but by deed.**

Ambiguity of language is, however, to be distinguished from unintelligibility and inaccuracy; for **words cannot be said to be ambiguous, unless** their signification seem doubtful and uncertain to persons of competent skill and knowledge to understand them.

The general presumption is that **the testator expects the words of his will to speak from his death.** A different construction will not therefore be admitted unless very obviously intended.

Upon the construction of wills we are not much assisted by a reference to cases, unless the will, or the words used, are very similar. If this is not so, they are more likely to mislead than to assist, in coming to a correct conclusion.

ELECTION.

Election, in the sense here used, is the obligation imposed upon a party **to choose between two inconsistent or alternative rights or claims,** in cases where there is clear intention of the person from whom he derives one, **that he should not enjoy both.**

Every case of election presupposes a plurality of gifts or rights, with an intention, express or implied, of the party who has a right to control one or both, that one should be a substitute for the other. **The party who is to take has a choice, but he cannot enjoy the benefits of both.**

Thus, if a testator should, by his will, give to a legatee an absolute legacy of ten thousand dollars, or an annuity of one thousand dollars per annum during his life, at his election, it would be clear that he ought not to have both, and **should be compelled to make an election.**

Election may be, first, *express and positive;* secondly, *implied or constructive.*

Courts of equity adopt the rational exposition of the will, that **there is an implied condition that he who accepts a benefit under the instrument shall adopt the whole,** conforming to all its provisions and **renouncing every right inconsistent with it.**

The doctrine of election is equally applicable to all interests, whether they are immediate or remote, vested or contingent, of value or of no value, and whether these interests are in real or personal estate.

SATISFACTION.

Satisfaction may be defined in equity to be the donation of a thing, with the intention, express or implied, that it is to be an extinguishment of some existing right or claim of the donee.

What is given by a will ought, from the character of the instrument, ordinarily to be deemed as **given as a mere bounty,** unless a contrary intention is apparent on the face of the instrument.

But equity has proceeded upon an opposite ground; **and the donation is held to be a satisfaction,** unless that conclusion is repelled by the nature of the gift, the terms of the will, or the attendant circumstances.

Questions of satisfaction usually come before courts of equity in three classes of cases: *First,* in cases of portions secured by a marriage settlement; *Secondly,* in cases of portions given by a will, and an advancement to the donee afterwards in the lifetime of the testator; *Thirdly,* in cases of legacies to creditors.

CHARITIES.

Courts of equity take jurisdiction in carrying into effect charitable bequests, however general are the purposes and objects intended, if sufficiently certain to be intelligible; and without regard to the fact of the existence of a trustee capable of holding the legal estate.

In carrying into execution a bequest to an individual, **the mode** in which the legacy is to take effect is deemed to be of the *substance* of the legacy; yet where the legacy is to a charity, the court will consider **charity as the substance;** and in such cases only, if the mode pointed out fail, it will provide another mode by which the charity may take effect.

Another principle is that if the bequest be for charity, **it matters not how uncertain the persons or the objects may be,** or whether the persons, who are to take are in *esse,* or not; or whether the legatee be a corporation capable in law of taking, or not; or whether the bequest can be carried into exact execution, or not; for in all these, and the like cases, **the court will sustain the legacy.**

Where a literal execution becomes inexpedient or impracticable, the court will execute it, as nearly as it can, according to the original purpose, or, as the technical expression is, *cy pres.*

The general rule is that if lands are given to a corporation for any charitable uses, which the donor contemplates to last forever, **the heir never can have the land back again.**

When the increased revenues of a charity extend beyond the original objects, the general rule as to the application of such increased revenues is that **they are not a resulting trust for the heirs at law;** but they are to be applied to similar charitable purposes, and to the augmentation of the benefits of the charity.

Courts of equity will not transfer the administration of a charity to a new trustee, unless there is proof of incapacity, or unfaithfulness, in the trustee named in the gift; or where there has occurred a failure of the objects of the charity.

All these doctrines proceed upon the same ground; that it is the duty of the court to **effectuate the general intention of the testator.** And, accordingly, the application of them ceases whenever such general intention is not to be found.

If the testator means to create a trust, and the trust is not effectually created, or fails, **the next of kin must take.**

The jurisdiction of a court of equity, with respect to charitable bequests, is derived from its **general authority to carry into execution the trusts of a will or other instrument,** according to the intention expressed in that will or instrument.

If the trustees of a charity should grossly abuse their trust, a court of equity may go to the length of taking it away from them, **and commit the administration of the charity to other hands.** But this is no more than the court will do, in proper cases, for any gross abuse of other trusts.

EQUITY.

Courts of equity exercise a benign authority in the administration of trusts, **to prevent the misapplication of property accumulated for one purpose, from being devoted to another and different object.**

The cardinal design is to carry out the intent of the donor, when consistent with the rules of law. If the application of the ordinary doctrines of the court works injustice, or if, by the lapse of time or other causes, the public good would be **promoted by a diversion of the funds to other objects**, in whole or in part, **the remedy is with the legislature, and not with the courts.**

It should be stated that the *cy pres* doctrine of the English courts of chancery **does not exist in all its force, if at all, in the equity courts of some of our states**; and that the courts of equity in those states are not clothed with the power, or charged with the duty of devising a scheme of charity, and decreeing its execution, where no scheme was framed by the testator.

In general, the courts of equity in this country must deal with bequests and trusts, for charitable uses, as they deal with bequests and trusts for other lawful purposes, and decide them upon the same principles.

And if the object to be benefited is so indefinite, and so vaguely described that the bequest or trust cannot be supported in the case of an ordinary trust, **it cannot be established in any court of equity upon the ground that it is a charity.**

IMPLIED TRUSTS.

All trusts are either *express trusts*, which are raised and created **by act of the parties**; or *implied trusts*, which are raised or created **by act or construction of law.**

Express trusts are declared either by word or writing; and these declarations appear either by direct and manifest proof, or violent and necessary presumption.

Implied trusts may be divided into two general classes: *first*, those which stand upon the presumed intention of the parties; *secondly*, those which are independent of any such intention, and are forced upon the conscience of the party by operation of law. As, for example, in cases of meditated fraud, imposition, notice of an adverse equity, and cases of similar nature.

It is a general rule that a trust is never presumed or implied as intended by the parties, unless, taking all the circumstances together, that is the fair and reasonable interpretation of their acts and transactions.

Where a man buys land in the name of another, and pays the consideration money, the land will generally be held by the grantee **in trust for the person who pays the consideration money.**

As the doctrine of resulting uses and trusts is founded upon a mere implication of law, **parol evidence is generally admissible for the purpose of rebutting such resulting use or trust.**

But whether, after the death of the supposed nominal purchaser, parol proof alone is admissible against the express declaration of the deed, is not so clear.

Where real estate is purchased for partnership purposes, and on partnership account, it is immaterial, in the view of a court of equity, in whose name or names the purchase is made, and the conveyance is taken; **it is in equity deemed partnership property, not subject to survivorship;** and the partners are deemed the *cestuis que trust* thereof.

Such real estate, belonging to a partnership, is generally, if not universally, treated as personal property of the partnership.

Generally speaking, **whatever is purchased with partnership property,** to be used for partnership purposes, **is treated as a trust for the partnership,** in whosever name the purchase may be made.

So, in the case of a purchase of land by a trustee in his own name, in pursuance of the trust, the *cestui que trust* is entitled to the estate.

In every case where the trust money can be distinctly traced, a court of **equity will fasten a trust upon the land** in favor of the person beneficially entitled to the money.

Whatever acts are done by trustees in regard to trust property shall be deemed to be done for the benefit of the *cestui que trust*, and not for the benefit of the trustee.

If a trustee should misapply the funds of the *cestui que trust*, the latter would have **an election either to take the security, or other property** in which the funds were wrongfully invested, **or to demand repayment from the trustee of the original funds.**

The same principle will apply to persons standing in other fiduciary relations to each other. Thus, for example, if an agent, who is employed to purchase for another, purchases in his own name, or for his own account, he will be held to be a trustee of the principal at the option of another.

Another class of cases, illustrating the doctrine of implied trusts, is that which embraces what is commonly called **the equitable conversion of property.**

By this is meant an implied or equitable change of property from real to personal, or from personal to real; **so that each is transferable and descendible according to its new character,** as it arises out of the contracts or other acts and intentions of the parties.

This change is a mere consequence of the common doctrine of courts of equity that **where things are agreed to be done, they are to be treated, for many purposes, as if they were actually done.** Thus, where a contract is made for the sale of land, the vendor is in equity deemed a trustee for the vendee of the real estate, and the vendee is decreed a trustee for the vendors of the purchase-money.

Under such circumstances, **the vendee is treated as the owner of the land**, and it is devisable and descendible as his real estate. **And the money is treated as the personal estate of the vendor,** and is subject to the like modes of disposition by him as other personalty, and is distributable in the same manner, on his death.

Land, articled to be sold and turned into money, **is reputed money**; and money, articled or bequeathed to be invested in land, is ordinarily **deemed to be land.**

Another class of implied trusts arises from what are properly called **equitable liens**; by which we are to understand such liens as exist in equity, and of which courts of equity alone take cognizance.

A lien is not, strictly speaking, either a *jus in re*, or a *jus ad rem;* that is, it is not a property in the thing itself, nor does it constitute a right of action for the thing. **It more properly constitutes a charge upon the thing.**

At law, **a lien is usually deemed to be a right to possess and retain a thing,** until some charge upon it is paid or removed.

Liens at law generally arise either by the express agreement of the parties, or by the usage of trade, which amounts to an implied agreement, or by mere operation of law.

But there are liens recognized in equity whose existence is not known or obligation enforced at law; and in regard to these liens, it may be generally stated that **they arise from constructive trusts.**

Such liens, therefore, are wholly **independent of the possession of the thing to which they are attached,** as a charge or encumbrance; and they can be enforced only in courts of equity.

The usual course of enforcing a lien in equity, if not discharged, is by a sale of the property to which it is attached.

In equity, the vendor of land has a lien on the land for the amount of the purchase-money, **not only against the vendee himself, and his heirs,** and other privies in estate, but also against **all subsequent purchasers having notice** that the purchase-money remains unpaid.

Where a conveyance is made prematurely, before money paid, the money is considered as a lien on that estate in the hands of the vendee. So, **where money is paid prematurely,** the money would be considered as a lien on the estate of the vendor for the personal representatives of the purchaser.

The general rule seems to be that the **absolute dominion over property sold is not acquired by the purchaser until he has paid the price,** or has otherwise satisfied it, unless the vendor has agreed to trust to the personal credit of the buyer. For a thing may well be deemed to be unconscientiously obtained, when the consideration is not paid.

Generally speaking, the lien of the vendor exists; and the burden of proof is on the purchaser to establish that, in the particular case, it has been intentionally displaced, or waived by the consent of the parties. If, under the circumstances, it remains in doubt, then the lien attaches.

The taking of a security for the payment of the purchase-money is not, of itself, a positive waiver or extinguishment of the lien.

Where the vendee has sold to a *bona fide* **purchaser without notice,** if the purchase-money has not been paid, the original vendor may proceed against the estate for his lien, or against the purchase-money in the hands of such purchaser for satisfaction; for in such case the latter, **not having paid his money, takes the estate** *cum onere,* at least to the extent of the unpaid purchase-money.

It is also a general rule in equity that where there is a lien upon different parcels of land for the payment of the same debt, and some of those lands still belong to the person who, in equity and justice, owes, or ought to pay, the debt, and other parcels of the land have been transferred by him to third persons, **his part of the land,** as between himself and them, **shall be primarily chargeable with the debt.**

Another species of lien is that which results to one joint owner of any real estate, or other joint property, from **repairs and improvements made upon such property for the joint benefit,** and for disbursements touching the same.

The doctrine of contribution in equity is larger than it is at law; and, in many cases, repairs and improvements will be held to be **not merely a personal charge, but a lien on the estate itself.**

Thus, it is held that if two or more persons make a joint purchase, and afterwards **one of them lays out a considerable sum of money in repairs** or improvements, and dies, this will be a *lien* on the land, and a *trust* for the representatives of him who advanced it.

Courts of equity have not confined the doctrine of compensation, or lien, for repairs and improvements, **to cases of agreement or of joint purchases.** They have extended it to other cases, where the party making the repairs and improvements has acted *bona fide* and innocently, and there has been **a substantial benefit conferred on the owner,** so that, *ex æquo et bono,* he ought to pay for such benefit.

Thus, where a party, lawfully in possession under a defective title, **has made permanent improvements,** if relief is asked in equity by the true owner, **he will be compelled to allow for such improvements.**

So, if the true owner stands by, and suffers improvements to be made on an estate, **without notice of his title,** he will not be permitted in equity to enrich himself by the loss of another; **but the improvements will constitute a lien on the estate.**

In all cases of this sort, however, the doctrine proceeds upon the ground either that there is some *fraud,* or that the aid of a court of equity is required; **for if a party can recover the estate at law,** a court of equity will not, unless there is some *fraud,* relieve a purchaser, or *bona fide* possessor, on account of money laid out in repairs and improvements.

Generally, all encumbrances upon land descended or devised are made **a primary charge upon the lands,** and not entitled to **exoneration out of the personal estate,** unless in the case of a will there shall be some expression of an intention to that effect.

Where a person becomes entitled to an **estate subject to a charge,** and then covenants to pay it, **the charge still remains** primarily on the real estate; **and the covenant is only a collateral security,** because the debt is not the original debt of the covenantor.

Having considered some of the important classes of *implied trusts,* arising from the **presumed intention of the parties,** we may now pass to the consideration of their implied, or their constructive, trusts, which are **independent of any such intention,** and are forced upon the conscience of the party **by the mere operation of law.**

One of the most common cases in which a court of equity acts upon the ground of implied trusts *in invitum* is where a party has received money which he cannot conscientiously withhold from another party.

Courts of law entertain jurisdiction in many cases of this sort where formerly the remedy was solely in equity; as, for example, in an action of *assumpsit* for money had and received, where the money cannot conscientiously be withheld by the party.

Where a party purchases trust property, knowing it to be such, from the trustee, in violation of the objects of the trust, courts of equity force the trust upon the conscience of the guilty party, and **compel him to perform it,** and to hold the property subject to it

It is a general proposition, both at law and in equity, that **if any property, in its original state and form, is covered with a trust** in favor of the principal, **no change of that state and form can divest it of such trust,** or give the agent or trustee converting it, or those who represent him in right, (not being *bona fide* purchasers for a valuable consideration without notice,) any more valid claim in respect to it than they respectively had before such change.

Thus, if A is trusted by B with money to purchase a horse for him, and A purchases a carriage with that money, in violation of the trust, B is entitled to the carriage, and may, if he chooses so to do, sue for it at law.

When a trustee or other person, standing in a fiduciary relation, makes a profit out of any transactions within the scope of his agency or authority, that profit will belong to his *cestui que trust.*

And one who assumes to act in relation to trust property, without just authority, however *bona fide* may be his conduct, shall be held responsible both for the capital and the income, to the same extent as if he had been *de jure* trustee.

The principle of following trust funds in the hands of a defaulting trustee **applies against the assignees of such trustee** as fully as against the trustee himself.

Wherever a trustee is guilty of a breach of trust, by the sale of the trust property to a *bona fide* purchaser, **for a valuable consideration without notice, and the purchase-money has been paid, the trust in the property is extinguished.**

But if afterwards the trustee should repurchase, or otherwise become entitled to the same property, **the trust would revive,** for a party shall not, by his own wrongful act, acquire an absolute title to that which he is in conscience bound to preserve for another. In equity, even more strongly than at law, the maxim prevails that **no man shall take advantage of his own wrong.**

A fraudulent purchaser will be held a mere trustee for the honest, but deluded and cheated, vendor. **And a person who lies by,** and without notice suffers his own estate to be sold and encumbered in favor of an innocent purchaser or lender, **will be held a trustee of the estate for the latter.**

In general, a trustee is bound by his implied obligation **to perform all those acts which are necessary and proper for the due execution of the trust** which he has undertaken.

He would seem, upon the analogous principles applicable to bailments, bound only to **good faith and reasonable diligence;** and, as in the case of a gratuitous bailee, **liable only for gross negligence.**

The rule is that where a trustee acts by other hands, either from necessity, or conformably to the common usage of mankind, **he is not to be made answerable for losses.**

In all cases, however, **where a trustee places money in the hands of a banker, he should take care to keep it separate,** and not mix it with his own in a common account; for, if he should so mix it, he would be deemed to have treated the whole as his own; and he would be held liable to the *cestui que trust* for any loss sustained by the banker's insolvency.

Where a trustee has acted in good faith, in the exercise of a fair discretion, and in the same manner as he would ordinarily do in regard to his own property, he ought not to be held responsible for any losses accruing in the management of the trust property.

Joint trustees are responsible for the acts of each other, in the misapplication of the trust funds, where they have put the funds in the power of one of their number.

The general rule is that **if a trustee has made interest upon the trust funds,** or ought to have invested them so as to yield interest, he shall, in each case, be chargeable with the payment of interest. The rule in equity is that all the gain shall go to the *cestui que trust.*

Co-trustees are not responsible for the **fraud and forgery of one of their number,** to which they in no way contribute, either directly or remotely.

When the trustee makes an improper investment of trust funds he becomes responsible for the same, with interest.

Trustees have all equal power, interest and authority, and cannot act separately, as executors may, but must join, both in conveyances and receipt.

Where there are two executors, each has a several right to receive the debts due the estate, and all other assets which shall come to his hands; and he is consequently solely responsible for the assets which he receives.

If they join in a receipt, it is their own voluntary act, and equivalent to an admission of their willingness to be jointly accountable for the money.

If an executor knows that the moneys received by his co-executor are not applied according to the trusts of the will, and stands by and acquiesces in it, without doing anything on his part to procure the due execution of the trust, he will, in respect to that negligence, be himself charged with the loss.

It is held that if two executors, guardians, or trustees, join in a receipt for trust money, it is *prima facie*, although **not absolutely conclusive, that the money came to the hands of both.** Either of them may show, by satisfactory proof, that his joining in the receipt was necessary, or merely formal, and **that the money was, in fact, all received by his companion.**

If, by any positive act, direction, or agreement of one joint executor, guardian, or trustee, the trust-money is paid over, and comes into the hands of the other, when it might and should have been otherwise controlled or secured by both, then **each of them will be held chargeable for the whole.**

If there has been a clear breach of trust by a trustee, yet, if the *cestui que trust,* or beneficiary, has **for a long time acquiesced in the misconduct of the trustee, with a full knowledge of it,** a court of equity will not relieve him: *Vigilantibus, non dormientibus, æquitas subvenit.*

In general, *concurrence* is required in regard to trusts of a private nature. But in regard to such trusts as are of a public nature, the trustees **may act by the majority.**

All trusts which partake of an official character, such as that of executors and administrators in the settlement of estates, **may be performed severally,** as in the collection of debts.

Where a trust is to be executed, **if the parties have become so hostile to each other that they will not act together,** or there is positive evidence of misconduct, or such acts or omissions as endanger the trust property, or show a want of honesty or proper capacity to execute the duties of the trust, **a court of equity will displace them.**

PENALTIES AND FORFEITURES.

In cases of **Penalties and Forfeitures for breaches of Conditions and Covenants,** there was, originally, no remedy at law; but the only relief which could be obtained was exclusively sought in courts of equity.

Now, by the operation of statutes made for the purpose, **relief may be obtained at law.** The original jurisdiction, however, of courts of equity, still remains, notwithstanding the concurrent remedy at law.

At law, and in general the same is true in equity, **if a man undertake to do a thing,** either by way of *contract* or by way of *condition,* and it is practicable to do the thing, **he is bound** to perform it, or he must suffer the ordinary consequences: that is to say, if it be a matter of contract, he will be liable at law for damages for the non-performance; if it be a condition, then his rights, dependent upon the performance of the condition, will be gone by the non-performance.

The difficulty which arises is to ascertain what shall be the effect in cases **where the contract or condition is impossible to be performed**, or where it is against law, or repugnant in itself, or to the policy of the law.

Conditions may be divided into four classes: *first*, those which are possible at the time of their creation, but afterwards become impossible, either by the act of God, or by the act of the party; *secondly*, those which are impossible at the time of their creation; *thirdly*, those which are against law, or public policy, or are *mala in se* or *mala prohibita* ; *fourthly*, those which are repugnant to the grant or gift by which they are created, or to which they are annexed.

The general rule of the common law in regard to conditions is that if they are impossible at the time of their creation, or afterwards become impossible by the act of God, or of the law, or of the party who is entitled to the benefit of them, or if they are contrary to law, or if they are repugnant to the nature of the estate or grant, **they are void.**

But if they are possible at the time, and become subsequently impossible **by the act of the party** who is to perform them, then he is treated as *in delicto*, and the condition is valid and obligatory upon him.

At the Common Law, a condition is considered as impossible **only when it cannot, by any human means, take effect.**

Conditions will have a very different operation where they are **conditions precedent** from what they will have where they are **conditions subsequent.**

Thus, if an estate is granted upon a condition subsequent, that is to say, to be performed after the estate is vested, and the condition is void for any of the causes just stated, there the estate becomes absolute.

But if the condition is precedent, or to be performed before the estate vests, there, the condition being void, the estate which depends thereon is void also, and the grantee shall take nothing by the grant; **for he hath no estate until the condition is performed.**

It is obvious that **if a condition or covenant was possible to be performed**, there was an obligation on the party, at the Common Law, to perform it punctiliously. If he failed so to do, it was wholly immaterial whether the failure was by accident, or mistake, or fraud, or negligence; his responsibility dependent upon it became absolute.

Courts of equity, however, do not hold themselves to such rigid rules; but they are accustomed to administer, as well as to refuse, relief in many cases of this sort, upon principles peculiar to themselves.

In the first place, as to **relief in cases of penalties annexed to bonds and other instruments**, the design of which is to secure the due fulfillment of the principal obligation, **the general principle adopted is** that wherever a penalty is inserted merely to secure the performance or enjoyment of a collateral object, the latter is considered as the principal intent of the instrument, and **the penalty is deemed only as accessory**, and, therefore, as intended only to secure the due performance thereof, or the **damages really incurred** by the non-performance.

If the penalty is to secure **the mere payment of money**, courts of equity will relieve the party, upon paying the principal and interest.

The foundation of this relief in equity is that as the penalty is designed as a mere security, if the party obtains his money, or his damages, **he gets all that he expected**, and all that, in justice, he is entitled to.

The whole system of equity jurisprudence proceeds upon the ground that **a party having a legal right shall not be permitted to avail himself of it for the purposes of injustice**, or fraud, or oppression, or harsh and vindictive injury.

But we must carefully **distinguish between cases of penalties**, strictly so called, and **cases of liquidated damages**.

Cases of liquidated damages occur when the parties have agreed that, in case one party shall do a stipulated act, or omit to do it, the other party shall receive a certain sum as the just, appropriate and conventional amount of the damages sustained by such act or omission.

In cases of this sort courts of equity will not interfere to grant relief; but will deem the parties entitled to fix their own measure of damages; **provided the damages do**

not assume the character of **gross extravagance**, or of wanton and unreasonable disproportion to the nature and extent of the injury.

It is a universal rule in equity never to enforce either a penalty or a forfeiture. Therefore courts of equity will never aid in the divesting of an estate, for a breach of a covenant, or a condition subsequent; although they will often interfere to prevent the divesting of an estate for a breach of covenant or condition.

Where a party, or his agent, who is entitled to the benefit of the forfeiture, **has waived such benefit, and treated the contract as still subsisting for some purpose,** he will not be allowed to insist upon the forfeiture for any purpose.

And where any penalty or forfeiture is imposed by statute upon the doing or omission of a certain act, courts of **equity will not interfere to mitigate the penalty or forfeiture,** if incurred, for it would be in contravention of the direct expression of the legislative will to grant relief in such cases.

INFANTS.

Whatever may be the true origin of the jurisdiction of courts of equity **over the persons and property of infants,** it is now conceded, on all sides, to be **firmly established, and beyond the reach of controversy.**

Courts of equity will appoint a suitable guardian to an infant, when there is none other, or none other who will or can act, at least where the infant has property; for **if the infant has no property,** the court will perhaps not interfere.

Guardians appointed by the court are treated as officers of the court, and are held responsible accordingly to it.

Courts of chancery will not only remove guardians appointed by their own authority, but **will also remove guardians at the common law, and even testamentary or statute guardians,** whenever sufficient cause can be shown for that purpose.

The court will, upon special application, **interfere, and regulate, and direct the conduct of the guardian in regard to the custody,** and education, and maintenance of the infant, and, if necessary, will inhibit him from carrying the infant out of the country, and will even appoint the school where he shall be educated.

The jurisdiction extends to the care of the person of the infant, so far as necessary for his protection and education; and as **to the care of the property of the infant**, for its due management and preservation, and proper application for his maintenance.

It is only in cases of gross misconduct that paternal rights are interfered with. And as between husband and wife, **the custody of the children generally belongs to the husband.**

If the infant be a daughter, and of very tender years, and the mother, under all the circumstances, be the most suitable to take care of her person and education, a court of **chancery will confer the custody on the mother;** when, if the infant were of riper years, and more discretion, and especially if a son, he would be intrusted for his education and superintendence to the custody and care of his father, **if no real objection to his character and conduct existed.**

The jurisdiction to remove infant children from the custody of their parents, and to superintend their education and maintenance, **is admitted to be of extreme delicacy;** but it is a jurisdiction which seems indispensable to the sound morals, the good order and the just protection of civilized society.

Equity will only apply the income of the estate of the infant towards his support and education when the father is not of sufficient ability, or in some other exceptional cases, as where it is desirable to educate the infant with a view to establishment in life beyond that which the law requires of the father.

A court of equity acts throughout with all the anxious care and vigilance of a parent; and it allows neither the guardian, nor any other person, to do any act injurious to the rights or interests of the infant.

In allowing maintenance, the court usually confines itself **within the limits of the income of the property.** But where the property is small, and more means are necessary for the due maintenance of the infant, **the court will sometimes allow the capital to be broken in upon.**

If a man intrudes upon the estate of an infant and takes the profits thereof, **he will be treated as a guardian,** and held responsible therefor, to the infant, in a suit in equity.

,Guardians will not ordinarily be permitted to change the personal property of the infant into real property, or the real property into personalty; since it may not only affect the rights of the infant himself, but also of **his representatives, if he should die under age.**

When a court directs any such change of property, **it directs the new investment to be in trust** for the benefit of those who would be entitled to it if it had remained in its original state.

MARRIED WOMEN.

At common law, husband and wife are treated, for most purposes, **as one person**; that is to say, the very being or legal existence of the woman, as a distinct person, is suspended during the marriage, or, at least, is incorporated and consolidated with that of her husband.

For this reason, if the wife be injured in her person or property during the marriage, **she can bring no action for redress without the concurrence of her husband,** neither can she be sued without making her husband also a party in the cause.

Courts of equity, however, for many purposes, **treat the husband and wife** as the *civil law* treats them, **as distinct persons,** capable, in a limited sense, of **contracting with each other, of suing each other,** and of having separate estates, debts and interests.

By the general rules of *law*, the contracts made between husband and wife, before marriage, **become, by the matrimonial union, utterly extinguished.**

But courts of equity, although they generally follow the same doctrine, **will, in special cases,** in furtherance of the manifest intentions and objects of the parties, **carry into effect such a contract,** made before marriage, between the husband and wife, although it would be avoided at law. For equity will not suffer the intention of the parties to be defeated by the very act which is designed to give effect to such a contract.

As to contracts made between husband and wife, **after marriage,** the principles of the Common Law apply to pronounce them **a mere nullity**; for there is deemed to be **a positive incapacity** in each to contract with the other.

But here again, although courts of equity *follow the law*, **they**

EQUITY.

will, under particular circumstances, give **full effect and validity to post-nuptial contracts.**

So, in equity, **a wife may become a creditor of her husband,** by acts and contracts during marriage; and her rights as such will be enforced against him and his representatives.

In respect to gifts or grants of property by a husband to his wife **after marriage,** they are ordinarily, but not universally, void at law. But courts of **equity will uphold them in many cases** where they would be held void at law; although in other cases, the rule of law will be recognized and enforced.

In some of the states, the equitable rights of married women, which have been, for over a century, enforced only in courts of equity, are now, as the direct result of remedial legislation, **changed into legal rights,** and the Common Law courts, by virtue of the statute law, afford as complete protection to married women as they have ever enjoyed in the equity courts.

Indeed, in some of the states, the rights of married women over their separate estates have been carried far beyond the established principles of these courts, and a *feme covert* is now permitted *at law* to **dispose of her own property at pleasure, without the assent of her husband,** and may enter into contracts, and **sue and be sued in her own name,** as fully as if she were single.

Thus, in respect to the separate estate of the wife, **most all of the old common law disabilities of coverture, originating in the feudal system, have been swept away,** just as the most oppressive of the feudal tenures were extirpated and demolished by the memorable statute 12 Charles II. **All of the states,** however, **have not advanced as far as this** in overturning the Common Law rules governing the marital relation, and it is safe to say that no two states have legislated exactly alike upon the subject.

BILLS OF DISCOVERY.

Every bill in equity may properly be deemed a bill of discovery, since it seeks a disclosure from the defendant, on his oath, of the truth of the circumstances constituting the plaintiff's case as propounded in his bill.

But that which is usually called a bill of discovery **is a bill which asks no relief, but which simply seeks the dis-**

covery of the facts resting in the knowledge of the defendant, or the discovery of deeds, or writings, or other things in the possession or power of the defendant, in order to maintain the right or title of the party asking it in some suit or proceeding in another court.

The sole object of such a bill, then, being a particular discovery, when that discovery is obtained by the answer, there can be no further proceedings thereon.

To maintain a bill of discovery it is not necessary that the party should otherwise be without any proof of his case; for he may maintain such a bill either because he has no proof, or because he wants it in aid of other proof.

In general it seems necessary, in order to maintain a bill of discovery, that an action should be already commenced in another court, to which it should be auxiliary; still it is not always essential.

It must clearly appear upon the face of the bill that the plaintiff has a title to the discovery which he seeks; or that he has an interest in the subject-matter to which the discovery is attached, capable and proper to be vindicated in some judicial tribunal.

He must also state a case which will, if he is the plaintiff at law, constitute a good ground of action, or, if he is the defendant at law, show a good ground of defence, in aid of which the discovery is sought.

The substantial requisites of a bill for discovery, which must be alleged therein, are that the plaintiff has a good cause of action or defence, as the case may be; that he is without proof except from the testimony of the defendants in the bill, whose testimony he cannot obtain except in this mode, and that he expects by such testimony to establish his case.

Courts of equity will not entertain a bill for a discovery, to aid the promotion or defence of any suit which is not purely of a civil nature. Thus, for example, they will not compel a discovery in aid of a criminal prosecution; or of a penal action; or of a suit in its nature partaking of such a character.

And equity will not entertain a bill for a discovery to assist a suit in another court, if the latter is of itself competent to grant the same relief; for in such a case the proper exercise of the jurisdiction should be left to the functionaries of the court where the suit is pending.

A defendant may object to a bill of discovery that he is a *bona fide* purchaser of the property for a valuable consideration, without notice of the plaintiff's claim.

But to entitle himself to protection, the purchaser must not only be a *bona fide* purchaser without notice, and for a valuable consideration, **but he must have also paid the purchase-money.**

Even the purchaser of an equity is bound to take notice of, and is **bound by, a prior equity**; and between equities the established rule is that **he who has the prior equity in point of time** is entitled to the like priority in point of right.

The rule in equity is that **if a defendant has in conscience a right equal to that claimed by the person filing a bill against him**, although he is not clothed with a perfect legal title, this circumstance, in his situation as defendant, renders it improper for a court of equity to compel him to make a discovery which may hazard his title.

BILLS TO PERPETUATE TESTIMONY are also entertained by courts of equity. **The object of such bills is to preserve and perpetuate testimony, when it is in danger of being lost**, before the matter to which it relates can be made the subject of judicial investigation.

Bills of this sort are indispensable for the purposes of public justice, as it may be utterly impossible for a party to bring his rights presently to a judicial decision; and unless in the intermediate time he may perpetuate **the proofs of those rights, they may be lost without any default on his side.**

The equity courts **do not generally entertain bills** to perpetuate testimony, for the purpose of being used upon a future occasion, **unless where it is absolutely necessary to prevent a failure of justice.**

If, therefore, it be possible that the matter in controversy can be made **the subject of immediate judicial investigation** by the party who seeks to perpetuate testimony, courts of equity will not entertain any bill for the purpose.

As to the right to maintain a bill to perpetuate testimony, **there is no distinction whether it respects a title or claim to real estate, or to personal estate, or to mere personal demands**; or whether it is to be used as a matter of proof in support of the plaintiff's action, or as a matter of defence to repel it.

If the bill is sustained, and the testimony is taken, **the suit terminates with the examination**; and, of course, is not brought to a hearing.

The decretal order of the court granting the commission directs that the depositions when taken **shall remain to perpetuate the memory thereof**, and to be used, in case of the death of the witnesses or their inability to travel, as there shall be occasion.

PECULIAR DEFENCES AND PROOFS.

There are some defences which are peculiar to courts of equity, and are unknown to courts of Common Law. So, also, there are some **peculiarities in relation to evidence**, unknown to the practice of the latter courts, which yet lie at the very foundation of the practice of the former.

The statutes of limitations, where they are addressed to courts of equity, as well as to courts of law, as they seem to be in all cases of concurrent jurisdiction at law and in equity, **are equally obligatory on each court**.

Thus, for example, if a legal title would, in ejectment, be barred by twenty years adverse possession, courts of **equity will act upon the like limitation**, and apply it to all cases of relief sought upon equitable titles or claims touching real estate.

So, **if the judgment creditor has lain by** for twenty years without any effort to enforce his judgment, and it has not been acknowledged by the debtor within that time, **it will be presumed to be satisfied**.

And in all these cases, courts of equity will act upon these facts **as a positive bar to relief in equity**; for these courts have always refused their aid to stale demands, **where the party has slept upon his rights**, and acquiesced for a great length of time. Nothing can call these courts into activity but **conscience, good faith and reasonable diligence**.

A court of equity will not allow a dormant claim to be set up **when the means of resisting it**, if unfounded, **have perished**.

The personal representative is affected by the delay or acquiescence of the decedent, to the same extent as if it were his own. **But acquiescence without full knowledge of the facts cannot affect the rights of anyone.**

EQUITY.

Courts of equity not only act in obedience and in analogy to the Statutes of Limitations, in proper cases, but **they also interfere in many cases to prevent the bar of the statutes,** when it would be inequitable or unjust.

Thus, for example, **if a party has perpetrated a fraud, which has not been discovered until the statutable bar may apply to it at law,** equity will interpose and remove the bar out of the way of the other injured party.

In general, it may be said that the rule of courts of equity is that **the cause of action or suit arises** when and as soon as the party has **a right to apply to a court of equity for relief.**

In cases of fraud or mistake, the bar of the Statute of Limitations **begins to run from the time of the discovery of such fraud or mistake, and not before.**

An acknowledgment of a debt or judgment, to take the case out of the Statute of Limitations, or bar by lapse of time, **must be made, not to a mere stranger, but to the creditor, or some one acting for him,** and upon which the creditor is to act or confide.

It is a rule, both at law and in equity, **that an endorsement upon a promissory note, or other written** evidence of debt, in order to take the case out of the Statute of Limitations, **if made by the creditor** or holder, must be shown to have been made **before the statutory bar took effect.**

Where one indebted on three promissory notes was applied to for payment on account of interest, and paid £5, and at this time two of the notes were barred by the Statute of Limitations, it was held that **the payment must be considered as made exclusively upon the note not barred,** and its effect was to prevent the operation of the statute as to that note.

A devise in trust to pay the debts of the devisor will remove the bar of the Statute of Limitations.

It is on the ground of part-performance, and to prevent fraud, that the courts of equity are enabled to **treat an absolute deed,** given to secure a debt, **as a mortgage, where the condition of defeasance rests in parol merely.**

A former decree in a suit in equity between the same parties, and for the same subject-matter, **is also a good defence in equity,** even although it be a decree merely dismissing the bill, if the dismissal is not expressed to be without prejudice.

The **want of proper parties to a bill** is also a good defence in equity, at least until the new parties are made, or a good reason shown why they are not made.

It is the **great object of courts of equity to put an end to litigation**; and to settle, if possible, **in a single suit**, the rights of all parties interested or affected by the subject-matter in controversy.

Hence, the **general rule in equity is that all persons are to be made parties** who are either **legally or equitably** interested in the subject-matter and result of the suit, **however numerous they may be**, if they are within the jurisdiction, and it is, in a general sense, practicable to do so.

In general, it may be stated that **the rules of evidence are the same in equity as they are at law**, and that questions of the competency or incompetency of witnesses, and of other proofs, are also the same in both courts.

Almost all testimony is positively required by courts of equity to be by written deposition; the admission of *viva voce* evidence at the hearing, being limited to a very few cases, such as proving a deed or a voucher referred to in the case.

The same general rule prevails in equity, as at law, that **parol evidence is not admissible to contradict**, qualify, extend, **or vary written instruments**; and the interpretation of them must depend upon their own terms. But in cases of **accident, mistake, or fraud**, courts of equity are constantly **in the habit of admitting parol evidence to qualify** and correct, and even **defeat**, the terms of written instruments.

ESTOPPEL IN EQUITY.

The subject of equitable estoppels, or **estoppels in fact**, applies to all cases **where rights once valid are lost by delay, and the implied acquiescence resulting from such delay.**

Lapse of time and acquieseence on the part of the party whose interests are alleged to have been injuriously affected by irregular proceedings **will be a complete bar**, unless the transaction is **tainted with fraud**, meaning thereby an act involving grave moral guilt.

In cases of actual fraud, courts of equity feel great reluctance to interfere where the party complaining does not apply for redress at the earliest convenient moment after the fraudulent character of the transaction comes to his knowledge.

Upon similar grounds, courts **refuse to disturb settlements long acquiesced in,** although between parties holding confidential relations to each other, and of such a nature as to give one great advantage over the other in making such settlements; as, for instance, between trustee and *cestui que trust.*

The equitable rule as to the effect of a person **lying by, and allowing another to expend money on his property,** does not apply where the money is expended **with knowledge of the real state of the title.**

Where a party, by misrepresentation, draws another into a contract, he may be compelled to make good the representation, if that be possible; but if not, the other party may avoid the contract.

And the same principle applies, although the party making the representation **believed it to be true,** if, in the due discharge of his duty, **he ought to have known the fact.**

Third parties who by false representations, induce others to enter into contracts are estopped from afterwards falsifying their statements, and, if necessary, **may be compelled to make them good.** But where a contract is entered into upon the false statement of one not a party, **it is no ground of avoiding the contract.**

Misrepresentation may be either by the suppression of truth or the suggestion of falsehood; but to be the ground for avoiding the contract, it must be such that it is reasonable to infer that **in its absence the party deceived would not have entered into the contract.**

The doctrine of estoppel *in pais,* or equitable estoppels, **is based upon a fraudulent purpose and a fraudulent result.** If, therefore, the element of fraud is wanting, there is no estoppel.

As if both parties were equally conusant of the facts, and the declaration or silence of one party produced no change in the conduct of the other, **he acting solely upon his own judgment.**

It is a universal law that if a man, either by words or by conduct, has intimated that he consents to an act which has been done, and that he will offer no opposition to it, although it could not have been lawfully done without his consent, **and he thereby induces others to do that from which they otherwise might have abstained,** he cannot question the legality of the act he had so sanctioned to the prejudice of those who have so given faith to his words, **or to the fair inference to be drawn from his conduct.**

It is equally true that if a party has an interest to prevent an act being done, and acquiesces in it, so as to induce a reasonable belief that he consents to it, and **the position of others is altered by their giving credit to his sincerity,** he has no more right to challenge the act to their prejudice than he would have, had it been done **by his previous license.**

And here we must bring this abridgment of equity jurisprudence to a close. But, to use the language of Mr. Justice Story, let not the ingenuous youth imagine that he also may here close his own preparatory studies of equity jurisprudence, or content himself, for the ordinary purposes of practice, with the general survey which has thus been presented to his view. What has been here offered to his attention is designed only to open the paths for his future enquiries; to stimulate his diligence to wider and deeper and more comprehensive examinations; to awaken his ambition to the pursuit of the loftiest objects of his profession, and to impress him with a profound sense of the ample instruction and glorious rewards which await his future enterprise and patient devotion in the study of the *first of human sciences*, THE LAW.

SUGGESTIONS TO STUDENTS.

THE START.

Melancholy and untrue is the picture which they draw of the legal study who represent its prominent features to be those of subtlety and impudence, and of a labor dry and barren. Rather would I compare it to a mountain, steep and toilsome, in its first approaches, but easy and delightful in its superior ascent, and whose top is crowned with a rich and lasting verdure. Be a student, then, according to your own acceptation of the idea; and remember this as a maxim which arises from the very character of the study, that *he who is a great lawyer must be a great and a good man.* Be not impatient of your progress if you find it at first difficult and tardy; this will be but a natural consequence; you may, however, find it less so than you now imagine. Should this prove the case, do not babble to every one you meet the great plans which you have formed, or the achievements you have executed; this will expose you to ridicule or envy, and will be unworthy of you. I know not a more accurate criterion of a noble mind than that silent confidence in its own powers which incites to great endeavors and leaves the event to time. The labors of such a mind will be secret but ardent; and its success will be known to the world only by the superiority of the actions it incites. In the outset, let me say, that he who has not a mind susceptible of the habits of labor, or willing to acquire them, *will never succeed at the bar:* if such a man should entertain a design of studying the law, I would advise him to lay it aside.—*Raithby, Study and Practice of the Law.*

WHEN TO ENTER AN ATTORNEY'S OFFICE.

Many young men on leaving college at once place themselves in a law-office; and are frequently made mere drudges to copy long declarations, pleas, bills in chancery, deeds, letters, etc., which the proprietor of the office was either too much engaged or too indolent to copy himself; and which neither improve the students hand-writing, nor add one mite to his legal stores. Others are suffered to grope through the intricacies of the law without torch or clue, and destitute of all method. Left to self-direction, they essay the perusal of some black-lettered folio, as the herculean task alone necessary to be surmounted; the difficulties of this widely diffused science are then to vanish, and this musty and ponderous folio is to be the avenue through which they are to pass, as by enchantment, into smooth and uninterrupted paths. Disappointment, however, is the certain reward of such students. Their minds are not prepared for so vast an undertaking. The first beams of legal knowledge have not been felt, when they ignorantly and rashly fly, like Icarus, into the very face of the sun, and meet with the same inevitable and ruinous fate. Some, again, are contented with the *scraps* and *bits* of knowledge gleaned from writing deeds and declarations, from listening to the protracted narratives of clients to their counsel, and the hasty advice which the former receive from the latter; or from an occasional attendance on courts of justice; whilst the remainder of their *office hours* are dedicated to politics and pamphlets, or the ephemeral and amusing productions of the day. In this round of *time-slaughtering*, the three or four years originally appropriated as the period of legal study have elapsed; and the student must now embark in the practice of a profession, the very rudiments and general contour of which have never been fully presented to his mind. This is by no means a picture of too high coloring, but a faithful sketch of the history of many students of law. We, therefore, earnestly entreat the student to devote three-fourths of the period allotted for his legal apprenticeship to private study, and by no means to enter an office until the year previous to his entering into the practice of his profession. If the public records be accessible to him, he should read occasionally the entire record of a case carried from an inferior tribunal to the supreme court: the perusal of a few records of this kind would impress on his mind a distinct view of the whole routine of an action, through perhaps a hundred different forms or entries, to the return of the executory process.—*Hoffman's Course of Legal Study.*

QUICK PERCEPTION AND ANALYSIS.

There are certain qualities of the mind, of a very noble nature, the want of which cannot be dispensed with in that man who is determined to be eminent at the bar. A clear intellect, by which I mean the *faculty of darting in a moment upon the truth*, is indeed a choice gift of nature; it may be improved, but it never can be acquired; it is that wonderful power before which ambiguity and confusion fly away; it is that mighty influence which irradiates whatever system it pervades; which separates in an instant the most entangled and perplexed ideas; this it is which descends to the minutest circumstances in the affairs of men, and, dissipating the mists with which they may be enveloped by craft or by ignorance, draws forth to the light the little secret motive which gives them their real character, and which is so often sought in vain.—*Raithby, Study and Practice of the Law.*

LAW AND PRACTICE.

The *study* of the law, though it require vigorous comprehension, and habits of patient thinking, demands, however, no very peculiar modification of talent. Whoever can be made to understand with facility may soon comprehend its system; whoever can think minutely may soon be master of its niceties: As to its *practice*, it is otherwise. Men who in solitude think correctly, and reason clearly, are, in public, masters neither of their own thoughts nor their words. The happy exposition of a subject, the ingenious elucidation of difficulties, the fluency of utterance, the rapidity and skill of forensic evolutions, are impracticable to themselves, and irresistible in others. When an intricate controversy must be unfolded in a perspicuous manner to the mind of the judge, or a tangled tissue of blended facts and law must be familiarly unravelled to a jury,—that is, at the very crisis, when the contest is to be decided by the authority of the land, learning and judgment are of no avail to the client or his counsel without the assistance of an *eloquent voice* to make them known. Then it is that all the arts of the orator are called into action, and that every part of a rhetorical discourse finds its place for the success of the cause. The diamond in the mine is no brighter than the pebble upon the beach. From the hand of the lapidary must it learn to sparkle in the solar beam, and glitter in the imperial crown. The crowd of clients, the profits of practice and the honors of reputation will all inevitably fly to him who is known to possess, not only the precious treasures of legal learning, but the *keys*, which alone can open them to the public eye.—*Adams' Harvard Law Lectures.*

WHAT YOU MUST POSSESS.

The studies by which a man may gain the summit of legal excellence are infinitely varied: he must possess the most opposite qualities, and be capable of exercising them; he must have a quick discernment, and yet a steady understanding; he must not be destitute of imagination, yet must he possess a sound judgment; he must know books, yet be *well learned in mankind;* the subtle technicality of law, and the enlarged beauties of classical learning; the solitary habits of study and the easy refinement of active life must equally distinguish him. In fine, he must unite in himself all those noble qualities by which he may at once command the attention of the acute and the learned, and render himself intelligible to the most ordinary capacity. Let him remember that every eye is busy in the discovery of his weaknesses, and that every ear is open to the detection of his errors. I know of no scenes in life where men stand or fall more completely by the strength or the weakness of their talents than in our courts of law. The utmost tenderness is shown to the embarrassment of inexperience, but ignorance finds no mercy. It is true, it is not hissed off the stage, but it sinks beneath the awful, chilling influence of surrounding wisdom.—*Raithby.*

UNWRITTEN LAW OF THE FORUM.

The talented author of Reed's Practical Suggestions, in speaking of the art of conducting a law suit, says: The law, as written in the text books, and revealed by the reports, is not the same as that administered by judges and juries. The reports over which we pore day and night have no presentations of the faces, character, voices, dress, deportment and evident bias, one way or the other, of the parties and witnesses. The glance of intelligence of a juror not knowing he is watched, the

SUGGESTIONS TO STUDENTS.

frown of another, and the smile of still another—all these are missed. But they are signs by which the lawyer has been guided, almost unconsciously to himself. There is no place in the world where the feelings have more unconstrained play than in a crowded court room during an important and exciting trial. The great crowd goes along with everything, as well as the audience follows the play in the theatre, and though the sheriffs and bailiffs keep the best of order, that whole throng of listeners perceptibly manifest their approval or disapproval of everything that is said or done. The bar feel this influence—they have brothers and fathers in that company. The judge feels it, too, and he has an almost fraternal feeling for those people out there; and the jury,—why, they came from that multitude; and all of them, judge, counsel, witnesses, parties, jury and audience are men and women, and, like other men and women, have their weaknesses and infirmities, their loves and hatreds, their vices and their many virtues too. All of them *live in their feelings*, and these impulsive heady feelings are ever *running away with their reasons* in unguarded moments. And thus is there a *different law* administered at *nisi prius* from that which is found in Blackstone and Story. And this law must be learned by him who would be a successful lawyer.

FLUENCY AND READINESS AT THE BAR.

In the exercises of the forum, everything depends upon ease and fluency of speech. The talent is rendered a peculiar one: two circumstances have made it so; the *variety* and *instantaneousness* of the occasions. Hence not only terseness and elegance are required from the advocate upon important and elaborate matters, but a quickness of expression also, calculated for short and shrewd debate; for you must have observed that there are numberless occasions, in the course of practice, in which a readiness of observation and reply have stood him in better stead than all the most solid powers of the judgment combined together at that moment could perform. Men are apt to be caught by the activity of speech, which, as it is often the talent of an inferior mind, is not to be regarded as the standard of great powers, but which will ever be advantageous in this sort of commerce with the world. A superficial man, even in cases of importance, if he possesses a liveliness and rapidity of speech, will be often more welcome than the hesitating, tedious man of judgment.

How often do people say, when describing a speaker, "Why, to be sure, there is not much depth in him, but then he is never at a loss; he speaks charmingly; his words seem always ready!" On the other hand, "I cannot bear to hear that man; I dare say he is a very wise man, but he keeps me in constant pain; he seems always so much in want of words, that absolutely one expects he will every moment stop in the middle of his speech. I would rather give up my law suit than be bound to hear that man speak frequently." Now this is a very common sentiment, expressed by the vulgar, indeed, but by which the wise man is not wholly unaffected; and I may here add, that it is not by the suffrage of the *wise alone* that the advocate rises in his profession. Fluency of speech I conceive to be an art, and, like any other art, it is to be acquired by observation and diligence.—*Raithby.*

THE JUDGE.

The perfect judicial character has been sketched more than once by the hand of a master. Lord Bacon says: "If any one sues to be made a judge, for my own part, I should suspect him. Let not a judge meet a cause halfway, nor give occasion to the party to say his counsel or proofs were not heard." Judge Hutton is advised to be "a light to jurors to open their eyes, but not a guide to lead them by the nose; that he should not affect pregnancy and expedition, by an impatient and catching hearing of the counsellors at the bar." So in another place he says, "Patience and gravity of hearing is an essential part of justice, and an overspeaking judge is no well-tuned cymbal; it is no grace to a judge first to find that which he might have heard in due time from the bar; or to show quickness of conceit in cutting off evidence or counsel too short, or to prevent information by questions, although pertinent. Judges ought to be more learned than witty, more reverend than plausible, more advised than confident. Above all things, *integrity* is their portion and proper virtue." Another writer says, "The judge should know nothing of the parties, but their *names* on his docket; nothing of the cause, but from the evidence; nothing of the result and its consequences, but the judgment which the LAW pronounces." Sir John Fortescue in speaking of the courts in his time (1470) says, "The judges of England do not sit in the King's Courts above three hours in the day; that is, from eight in the morning till eleven. The courts are not open in the afternoon. The judges, when they have taken their refreshments, spend the rest of the day in the STUDY OF THE LAWS AND READING OF THE HOLY SCRIPTURES.

WHAT IS NEEDED IN COURT.

Those who have frequented the criminal courts cannot but sometimes have witnessed the unpleasing triumph of a loquacious wrangler over deep discriminations and profundity of thought. These, indeed, are busy scenes, in which if you mix and hope to succeed, you must unite these jarring capacities. The crowd are gaping for a smart speech, and some of the attorneys that conduct business in these courts have been long accustomed to all the lively keennesses of practice; they therefore expect to see a congenial capacity in those they employ as counsel; and, in short, will never think of giving a case to that man who *has it not*, however extended or refined his knowledge may be. To be able to meet every opponent upon his own ground is an art which the lawyer must condescend to learn, seeing there are occasions that may demand the exercise of it; and it is not an art which has been acquired and exercised heretofore by many great men. You must be able at once to influence the passions of a jury, and to convince the understanding of the judge; you must appear in all the varied characters of the abstract reasoner, and the lively wit; the accurate definer, and the polished rhetorician. The dignity of wisdom and the facility of business, the nervousness of eloquence and the easy familiarity of colloquy, must take their turns in the varieties of your practice. In short, *all that is excellent* in general knowledge and refined in legal intelligence must be called in to complete the character of *a leader in the courts*. In the court of chancery, for instance, the scene is entirely altered; the wrangling of the forum is exchanged for the reasoning of the schools. The decisions of the court are not at the disposal of twelve men; they lie in the breast of one man, who is himself governed, not only by the decisions of his predecessors, but by a peculiar kind of equity which professes to aid the sterility or to correct the severity of the Common Law, without opposing its dictates or violating its principles. In this court, therefore, there is no jury, whose imaginations the orator can hope to influence, or whose passions to mislead; all here is *cool reasoning and nice disquisition.* Here, too, is agitated some of the most abstruse and difficult learning of the law.—*Raithby.*

READING AT THE BAR.

Nothing is more wearisome to the auditors of the advocate than the long citations he is under the necessity of making from legal authorities, except it be the drawling and careless manner in which they are read. The reading of an authority, if not the signal for inattention, especially to juries, is at least a forewarning of fatigue. Policy, therefore, might dictate more attention to this matter. Lord Mansfield, it is said, possessed the art, by the agreeableness of his reading, to render even a *statute* interesting.—*Hoffman.*

HISTORY AND LAW.

To assert that he whose professional life depends upon his powers of reasoning and argument, and whose argument rests upon his knowlege of the laws, may be ignorant of the circumstances that have contributed to the formation of their original nature, and succeed, is an outrage upon common sense. As well may you say a statesman can govern without a knowledge of the genius of the people whose affairs he is to direct, or a physician judge of a disease without an acquaintance with the previous and accompanying symptoms, as that the lawyer should understand the laws of a country while the events that gave them birth and the systems by which they have been formed, are unknown to him. A good lawyer MUST BE FAMILIAR WITH HISTORY. How often would it have proved a most tedious and almost insupportable task to those whose high office it is to hear and determine upon the arguments of counsel had they who have filled the character of an advocate at the bar been generally unversed in the events recorded in history! How confined would, to this moment, have been the legal notions of our courts! How spiritless and perhaps unjust their interpretations of the law, had they who preside in those august tribunals derived their principles of truth, in the administration of civil and criminal justice, from the letter of the law alone! On the other hand, what grand and striking displays of the reasoning powers, what extensiveness of remark, what acumen of comparison, what a various energy of combination mark the argument of that advocate whose mind has been illuminated by a contemplation of the hidden causes from which, as we have already remarked, laws in particular, among all other human subjects, derive their true character and complete force! Persevere, then, in this study, and you shall pluck, at length, a fruit, which, if long in ripening, will nevertheless be truly valuable. You may not, perhaps, at first sight, perceive the advantages which the perusal of history will present to you as a lawyer; but regard not this; *read on with diligence, persevere*, and, unless I am deceived, you will in the end find no reason for regret.—*Raithby*.

TWO EXAMPLES.

This is what is said of Lord Eldon, one of England's great counsellors: "He rose in the morning at four, took little exercise, made short and abstemious meals, and sat up studying late at night, with a wet towel round his head to drive away drousiness." And this was the son of a Newcastle coal dealer, who worked his way up from his father's office to the woolsack, where his decisions in chancery, for a quarter of a century, have enriched the equity jurisprudence of his country and placed his name high on the roll of her distinguished chancellors. His contemporary, the celebrated English advocate, Lord Erskine, whose remarkable speeches at the bar have never ceased to be the wonder and admiration of the profession, was also a man whose great energy and determination to excel raised him from scenes of want and obscurity to the highest round in the profession, where he stands, as Lord Campbell says, without an equal, as an advocate, in ancient or modern times.

And need I tell you that it was by work, hard work, day by day, year in and year out that these men ascended from the humble walks of life to the MARBLE CHAIR and the peerage. Whether before, or on, the bench; whether as advocates, or keepers of the great seal, they enjoyed not only the esteem and confidence of their sovereign and fellow-countrymen, but that which a lawyer would prize more than all else, the *admiration* and *applause* of that venerable temple of justice, WESTMINSTER HALL. Take courage, then, young man, take courage. The great lights of the profession everywhere were once hard-struggling, brave young men, with chances no better, perhaps, than yours. Take courage; only the hard-fought battles live in history; success lies only at the end of effort. On, on with you, then, through hail and storm, through fire and flood; sweep forward with a high resolve, to stand abreast with the mighty victors of the past who have gained the summit of glory and renown!

PATIENCE AND GRIT.

When a man sets out in the pursuit of a science like that of the law, he will naturally be struck with the variety and intricacy of its different branches, and, by an almost unavoidable transition, he will take a view of the extent of the talents that are necessary to their development and investigation. Now if this view be taken at the first, under the impression of self-mistrust or despondency, everything will appear in its inverted proportions. The task you have undertaken will seem to be obstructed by almost insuperable difficulties, whilst your powers dwindle away to nothing in your distempered apprehension. If, then, in the beginning of your career you find this unhappy influence coming over you, do not tamely yield to it; be not affrighted by the horrible pictures it would draw of the profundity and intricacy of the legal science: the treasures of that science are ever open to a *good understanding* and *diligent application*. At first you will no doubt feel yourself somewhat disgusted at the apparent dryness and repetition of the subjects of your labor; you will be apt to conceive that, however wonderfully the ends of justice may be answered by such tedious forms, those of reason are violated and overthrown. Have patience; in the course of a little time you will be induced to alter your opinion; a ground which at first you did not perceive, a reason which did not discover itself, an order, a connection which were hidden from your view will arise gradually to your observation, and when once this important discovery is made, the confusion and irrationality that appeared to hang around your labors will disperse, the clouds of obscurity that heretofore have seemed to enwrap the legal science will depart, and STRENGTH AND ORDER WILL APPEAR.—*Adam's Lectures.*

THE SACRED SCRIPTURES.

The Bible forms a very natural introduction to the student's course, as recording a form of government and law originating in the great Legislator of the universe, whose pleasure it was to enjoin, by a direct communication of his will, those duties and declare those obligations which, when by reasoning on the nature and relations of man we have concluded to be such, we consider as the dictates of the law of nature. The purity and sublimity of the morals of the Bible have at no time and in no country been questioned; IT IS THE FOUNDATION OF THE COMMON LAW OF EVERY CHRISTIAN NATION. The Christian religion is a part of the law of the land, and as such should certainly receive no inconsiderable portion of the lawyer's attention. Sir William Jones says: "I have carefully and regularly perused these Holy Scriptures, and am of opinion that the volume, independently of its divine origin, contains more *sublimity,* purer *morality,* more important *history,* and finer strains of *eloquence* than can be collected from any other book, *in whatever language it may have been written.*" An American, recently writing from London, says: "A young man cannot graduate at Oxford without passing a thorough examination in the Old Testament history, the Gospels and the Acts in their original Greek, and repeat the thirty-nine articles almost word for word. It is curious to note how familiar this makes the educated classes with the Bible. An allusion to a Scripture incident is made and understood as readily in Parliament as it would be with us in a Presbyterian Synod, and I have heard a Queen's counsel catch up such an allusion and dwell upon it in a way that showed a minute acquaintance with the very text of the Bible itself." A thorough knowledge of it will be of incalculable service to you in your practice at the bar, where most all great lawyers have felt and recognized its power; beyond and above this, it may, under the benign influence of the GREAT AUTHOR of your being, become the happy means of securing success and prosperity for you in this world and a triumphal entry into the next. Remember that the *last case* you are to try will be your own; not at NISI PRIUS, not at the QUARTER SESSIONS, where you may have practiced so long, but before the awful presence of the GREAT MAGISTRATE of the universe. I beseech you, then, look well to the preparation of *this* case, and see to it that *not one* of all the cases arising in your whole life's practice here can be possibly used to overwhelm and convict you there. Since your lot was so happily cast in a land of liberty, civil and religious, where the revealed law has been most thoroughly and liberally expounded, I fear you will find no recognized equity in appeals for mercy grounded on the slightest ignorance of those pure and simple laws which have been daily before your eyes, like the sunlight of the universe.

INDOLENCE.

A habit of *indolence* is a most powerful enemy to those whose profession in life demands the utmost exertion. I mean not here to allude to that shocking intemperance of idleness which utterly precludes every hope; no man of sense is likely on a sudden, or perhaps ever, to fall into so disgraceful an inactivity. I mean that indolence which steals upon us by degrees, even while we flatter ourselves all is activity and diligence; which does not boldly rob us of our time and powers at once, but which persuades us that we are already sufficiently industrious; which is eternally whispering into our willing ears: "Now is the time for repose; you have done enough; you pursue your studies with an unnecessary attention; recreate yourself; you have a right to recreation; you have done more than is commonly done." This is the language, this is the sentiment, that beguiles us of apparently small, but really valuable, portions of time, and that defrauds us of excellence. You have taken up the profession of the law; that is the science to which your principal attention henceforth is to be directed, and excellence in it is the point towards which all the best and most vigorous faculties of your mind are to be exerted. Refuse not to labor at a settled point, and in the end you will reap the fruits of your labor. We are men, and we must bend to the conditions of mortality. The most prominent of these conditions is that we should get our bread by the sweat of our brow, and from this lot, in some degree or other, no man is exempt. But does it necessarily follow that we are therefore to lose every degree of spirit? Must we as a consequence give up every hope? Far from it. He whose labors are regularly directed to some certain study that may make him respectable in his own eyes and useful to the community, however he may for a moment be the derision of the wit and the contempt of the universal genius, will not only be a more happy, but a more estimable, character.

> "His be the praise, who, looking down in scorn
> On the false judgment of the partial herd,
> Consults his own clear heart, and nobly dares
> To *be*, not to be *thought*, an honest man."
>
> —*Raithby*.

ONE THING AT A TIME.

The student who abandons a subject without understanding it is like a commander who leaves an enemy in his rear; he advances without the cheering certainty of being fully master of the road over which he has travelled, and most generally finds the difficulty, which he has left without overcoming, start up in the course of his progress in a hundred different shapes and a hundred different subjects, to harass and perplex him.—*Hoffman*.

EXAMINATION OF WITNESSES.

An interested witness in the hands of a ready examiner, even though he be not a man of great parts, will frequently be surprised out of the truth which he has determined to hide. The multitude and variety of questions, not asked, perhaps, with the exactest judgment, but running one upon the heels of another, with a wonderful rapidity, amaze and frighten him; he conceives there are multitudes yet behind; he concludes that all his secrets are discovered; he confesses everything in mere despair. Not such is the influence of that advocate, who, with greater mental powers, is deficient in this useful and necessary faculty; his judgment points out, with little difficulty, the questions that are proper to be asked, but by some unhappy influence he has no adequate expression at command. This very want of words produces not only hesitation, but, in the end, questions full of words, and arriving with difficulty at the proposed point.

While all this is preparing, what is the witness about? Does he suffer these immense spaces of leisure to pass unemployed? Oh, no; he is framing answers by which he may hope at once to elude confession and perplex his loitering examiner.—*Raithby*.

COKE UPON LITTLETON.

It is related by Lord Campbell, that when he commenced his legal curriculum, he was told this anecdote : "A young student asked Sir Vicary Gibbs how he should learn his profession. *Sir Vicary:* 'Read Coke upon Littleton.' *Student:* 'I have read Coke upon Littleton.' *Sir Vicary:* 'Read Coke upon Littleton over again.' *Student:* 'I have read it twice over.' *Sir Vicary:* 'Thrice?' *Student:* 'Yes, three times over very carefully.' *Sir Vicary:* 'You may now sit down and make an abstract of it.'" And Campbell adds : "If my opinion is of any value I would heartily join in the same advice. The book contains much that is obsolete, and much that is altered by statutable enactment; but no man thoroughly understands the law as it is without knowing the changes it has undergone, and no man can be acquainted with its history without being familiar with the writings of Lord Coke."

MODESTY.

It is by no means a necessary consequence, because it falls to a man's lot to address a number of persons, that he is therefore the *wisest* man of that number. The gift of eloquence is a very noble gift, and wherever it is allied to a sound judgment, it will at one time or another elevate the man who possesses it above his contemporaries; but it will only elevate him as it is manifested, and as it makes an impression upon men's minds; and nothing so effectually convinces men of the good understanding of a public speaker as the appearance of *modesty*. By this he acknowledges the inferiority of his own single opinion to the aggregate wisdom of the body he is addressing, yet because the aggregate wisdom of every society of men is a composition of separate efforts of individual understandings, he does not relinquish his own opinion, but continues to enforce it, until by some solemn act of the auditory the public opinion is clearly demonstrated.

We see that the wisest men do not advance their observations or their arguments in a tone of confidence, or with an unblushing boldness. Experience and knowledge have taught them that, like other men, they may err; still, conscious of their superiority, they take upon them to inform and instruct mankind, but their lessons are delivered in the *chastened style of modesty;* they remember that they themselves have *something yet to learn.* The man who never speaks before the tribunals of justice but in the tones of confidence and audacity, may excite a temporary amazement; he may delude for the moment, but when the reason of men returns, he will be taught to feel that there is a dreadful distance between himself and that character which is formed to EXPOUND THE SCIENCE AND TO ELEVATE THE PROFESSION OF THE LAW. In argument, whether addressed to the judge upon the bench or to the jury, or in the examination of witnesses, bear continually in your recollection that you are in the presence of those to whom all respect is due, who are able to distinguish, with a piercing eye, what is necessary to the completion of your character, and against whom effrontery must be no inferior offence; while they contemplate the modesty of the ingenuous advocate with sensations of benignity and pleasure.—*Raithby.*

LAW AND LAWYER.

The student will ever bear in mind that notwithstanding the word *law* is of comprehensive signification, LAWYER is still more so; embracing the richness and solidity of learning, the profundity of wisdom, the purity of morals, the soundness of integrity, the ornaments of literature, the amiableness of urbanity, the graces of modesty, and, generally, the decorations and amenities of life. The instructor of a law student should never cease to press upon his pupil, that all the learning of the schools will not make *a great lawyer,* without a sound system of morals and a nice sense of right and wrong.—*Hoffman.*

INTEGRITY.

In the course of your practice you may meet with some occasions in which, by taking advantage of the negligence or ignorance of your opponent in some particular form, you might recommend yourself to a sharp or selfish client. Here integrity will be very useful; it will not let you make of such accidents any undue or dishonest advantage; it will not suffer you to be so far smitten with the character of a *keen man,* that you will obtain it at any rate. What, alas, will a little temporary profit avail in the estimation of the man who has been tempted by the hope of it to do that upon which he can reflect with no honest pride? for I again remark that even in point of profit, this sharp, this catching spirit does not always, in the end, bear away the palm. Like the bubbling of a disturbed rivulet, it may excite a momentary attention, while the noble, silent swell of the river passes unnoticed; but like the rivulet, its shallowness will presently be discovered; we shall turn from it with contempt, content only with that perennial stream of talent and integrity that is rolling on with a majestic and unruffled course towards the great ocean of immortality. The advocate who is influenced by *integrity* will never forget that the cause of his client is his own : this is a happy consequence of that animating principle. What a glow, what a fervor does it impart to every look and every action! And is it not as much to his interest as his honor? Men are charmed when they find their business thus warmly undertaken. When they perceive that everything they themselves could think is said for them, they are led insensibly into the idea that the lawyer perceives and is affected by the justice of their cause. If this be a delusion, it is a delusion that is most readily supported by their self-complacency; and the name of that lawyer is presently spread in the world, who appears to argue rather from the affection he has towards the cause of his client than from LOVE OF THE GOLDEN FEE.—*Raithby.*

FOUR WAYS.

We are told by Lord Campbell that "it used to be said that there were four, and only four, ways in which a young man could get on at the bar: 1. By *huggery.* 2. By writing a law book. 3. By Quarter Sessions. 4. By a miracle. The first was successfully practiced by that great *nisi prius* leader, Tom Tewkesbury, who not only gave dinners at his chambers to the attorneys, but suppers to their clerks." "The miracle," says Campbell, "consists in the conjunction of an opportunity to make a great speech in some very popular cause, with full ability to improve the advantage." Perhaps the most remarkable instance in the miracle way is that furnished us by the great Erskine. "Living in small lodgings, dressed shabbily, and subsisting on 'cow-heel and tripe,' he was suddenly to be the idol of all ranks of the community, and to wallow in riches. Such a quick transition from misery to splendor is only equalled in the Arabian Nights, when the genii of the wonderful lamp appeared, to do the bidding of Aladdin. A sunrise within the tropics displays some fleeting crepuscular tints between utter darkness and the full solar blaze, and therefore cannot be used to give a just notion of Erskine's first appearance to the dazzled eyes of the British public." His reputation was made in his first case—*The King v. Baillie.* "The impression made upon the audience by his address is said to have been unprecedented, and I must own that, all the circumstances considered, it is the most wonderful forensic effort of which we have any account in our annals. It was the *debut* of a barrister just called and wholly unpracticed in public speaking, before a court crowded with men of the highest distinction. He came after four eminent counsel, who might be supposed to have exhausted the subject. He was called to order by a venerable judge, Lord Mansfield, whose word had been law in that hall above a quarter of a century. A commonplace declaimer would have thought it necessary to conclude with some noisy, mouthing sentences. How much more effective must have been the lowered tones of the man who knew instinctively how much to touch the feelings, speaking in an assembly where every look was fixed upon him, where every syllable he uttered was eagerly caught up, where breathing was almost suspended, and as often as he paused a flake of snow would have been heard to fall.

"Briefs and fees, large and small, now flowed in a continual stream into the chambers of the counsellor who had so astonished the world. He was at once in full business; and it should be recorded, for the honor of the 'long robe,' that although he passed over the heads of many who had fully established themselves in Westminster Hall, there was no caballing against him; he had not even to encounter envy or ill-will; he was hailed by his competitors *as conferring new honors upon them*, and bearing his faculties most meekly, he became and ever continued a favorite with all ranks of the profession."

DO NOT BE IN HASTE.

I would here warn you against a very prevalent delusion. Is it not common for young men to say, "What is the use of studying so much beforehand? Cannot I acquire the learning as I want it? Does not every case carry its own law?" Depend upon it, such reliance upon future opportunities will deceive you. Should your mind be unversed in general doctrines, you will find unexpected difficulties in the search for particular examples, as well as in the application of them. We daily see men at the bar with a respectable share of book learning, nay, with no small degree of a certain sort of talent for eloquence, and yet we venture to pronounce secretly of these men that they will never soar above mediocrity. This is a sort of feeling which rests satisfied with its own prophetic certainty, and therefore the reasons that produce it are seldom analyzed; but should the question be asked, the answer would in a moment doubtless be: "He has been in TOO GREAT HASTE; he knows nothing of the world or himself."—*Raithby.*

SELECTION OF BOOKS.

If a man should calculate on living to the age of sixty years, and should appropriate with great industry forty of these years to the study of books, the most that could be accomplished in this time would be the perusal of about *sixteen hundred* octavo volumes of *five hundred* pages each. What is this number compared with the millions of volumes out of which he has to select! How important is it, therefore, that the choice should be judicious, and that after it is made the whole should be studied with method; and how much more necessary it is to those who, instead of forty years devotion to books, appropriate not more than a fourth-part of that period. Lord Bacon has quaintly observed: "Some books are to be tasted, others to be swallowed, and some few to be chewed and digested; that is, some books are to be read only in part, others to be read, but not curiously, and some few to be read wholly, and with diligence and attention."—*Hoffman.*

DEPORTMENT.

Manner is that invisible quality which insensibly pervades, with the happiest effect, the works of pure genius. It animates the pencil of the artist, the pen of the poet, and the sentiments of the orator; it spreads an inexpressible glow of charms over every effort of art; it communicates a peculiar sweetness to the keenest truths; an air of majesty to the simplest figures. It allures while it awes the mind; it speaks a language that no power but itself can express, and it is that Attic fire that enlivens every object to which it communicates its influence.

In the advocate it is more immediately discerned than in any other character; consequently in him the want of it will more easily be detected. How shall we express what this manner is! It appears to be a quality arising from some internal influence, and cannot therefore, perhaps, be absolutely acquired; but that it may be improved appears by the same reason that governs the improvement of all similar qualities, and by the same means. It communicates itself by a thousand mediums to the action of the speaker, even in the most minute particulars; it may be seen in the countenance, in the movement of a finger, yet it cannot be well designated by any single action. It is felt in the tones of the voice; yet any particular sort of expression will not be adequate to the description of it. It is an indescribable combination of ease and dignity; it mixes with and elevates the character, without seeming to form any denominate part of it. It is of a dignified nature, and is the result only of a penetrating judgment, a refined and enlarged sentiment, a superior virtue and an extensive commerce with mankind. Thus is the rarity of its appearance in the world accounted for. Has nature favored you with the materials? Improve them by studying the exalted principles of truth.—*Raithby.*

A CHIEF JUSTICE.

It will be no loss of time for the student to pause for a moment to read the following sketch of the illustrious John Jay, first Chief Justice of the United States. Doubtless it will convince you that to be a great lawyer, statesman or judge, manifestly means something more than to be greatly learned. According to the English system of conferring titles of nobility, it is possible that our plain, republican John Jay would have lost his family name when he became Chief Justice, and we should probably read of him now as the noble Lord Bedford. But no title of nobility could add any lustre to his name. No royal patent could make him nobler than he was. His deportment was tranquil and unassuming, and one who had met him, not knowing who he was, would not have been led to suppose that he was in the presence of one eminently gifted by nature with intellectual power, and who had sustained so many offices of high trust and honor. Mr. Jay's character is disclosed in the record of his life. His moral and intellectual qualities were in harmony. His public principle commanded the respect of the *world. His private virtues attracted the affection and homage of his friends. He was modest, claimed no merit, assumed no importance, and seldom alluded to the great events of his life. He was charitable, not impulsively bestowing his means without discrimination, 'like Goldsmith's village preacher, whose "pity gave ere charity began," but with a judicious selection, and from a sense of duty. His economy was exact, but liberal. "A wise man," he said, "has money in his head, but not in his heart." The recipients of his bounty were numerous. 'He had an elevated sense of justice and of the claims of humanity. His religion was a part of his being, and displayed itself in the uniform tenor of his life. He acted under the habitual conviction of accountability. "All his serious thoughts had rest in heaven." His feelings were always under the control of his will, and hence he was never guilty of those extravagances of conduct which too often mar the career of genius. He was tenacious in his friendships, and equally so, we suspect, in his enmities. Having once had good cause to doubt a man's sincerity or integrity, he never after trusted him. His disposition was cheerful, his conversation equally instructive and interesting.

His intellectual endowments are easily described. His mind was vigorous, exact and logical. To genius he could make no pretensions. Judgment—discriminative, penetrating—was the characteristic of his understanding. If over his other faculties imagination had presided, the compass of his thought would have been enlarged, and grace and flexibility been imparted to his mind. Jay was not a variously-learned man. Modern genius did not delight him. Of the ancients, Cicero was his favorite. The Bible was his constant study. Observing throughout his life the great principles of justice and rectitude, he "ascended to the temple of honor through the temple of virtue."—*Flanders' Lives of the Chief Justices.*

URBANITY.

Those who have written upon the decorations of life have agreed to mark *urbanity* as the chief amongst them. Its good effects are conspicuous in every movement, in every word, in every action; it possesses an engaging condescension that adds fresh lustre to the dignity of our manners; it softens the tone of the voice and relaxes the awful countenance of wisdom. In addressing the judge or jury it will give at once an elegant and respectful air to every sentiment; in arguing with a learned friend it will produce a tone of yielding diffidence, without impairing the firmness or blunting the point of our conclusion; in examining a witness it will guard us against *insulting the humble* or *deriding the modest;* it will clothe the countenance with a pleasing seriousness when undesigning ignorance only presents itself; to the crafty and audacious it will exhibit an aspect adverse and terrific in the highest degree. Thus will urbanity raise up a character that will prove obnoxious to those only to whom virtue and elegance are obnoxious. It may appear ludicrous to class urbanity among the serious studies of the lawyer; but if it be a trifling thing, it may be recollected that upon things thus lightly esteemed the most important occurrences of life have depended, important both in their own intrinsic nature and in the consequences they have produced.—*Raithby.*

POINTS TO BE OBSERVED IN PRACTICE.

The freedom of speech allowed to counsel, in conducting the cases of their clients, is manifestly indispensable for the administration of justice. It is, however, a weapon which ought never to be wielded but by a GENTLEMAN, who will cautiously keep in view the true reason of the existence of the right, and be governed, in exercising it, by uniform delicacy and considerateness. It is, however, a matter entirely within his own discretion. If *real* vice, fraud, falsehood, cruelty, meanness, or oppression, are to be denounced, let it be done fearlessly, and with all the power and eloquence which the advocate may be able to command; but still, let him remember the character which he has individually to sustain, and the dignity of that profession of which he has become a member. To indulge in unbridled license of speech, simply because one has the *power* of doing so—under the shelter then, surely, of a most ignominious impunity—is inexpressibly brutal, mean and cowardly, and proves him who is guilty of it to have no pretentions whatever to the title of gentleman. One should bear in mind the agony which one may be inflicting, in every word that is uttered, upon a person possibly of spotless integrity, of the highest delicacy of feeling—whose conduct one may have totally misunderstood, of whose real motives one is altogether ignorant, yet is recklessly endeavoring to expose such a person to the ridicule, scorn, and hatred of his friends, and the public,—to inflict upon his character injury irreparable. Let not, however, the insolent speaker imagine that he always *succeeds* in doing this: he is far more likely to render the victim of his vituperation an object of sympathy, and earn for himself the character of a hard-mouthed bully; one who is despised by the *gentlemen* who belong to the profession which he is dishonoring, and by those who sit upon the bench. You should also be uniformly respectful, but never servile, to the court. Be *firm*, if you please, but approach not the confines of flippancy, familiarity, or presumption. A rebuke under such circumstances will be justly galling and humiliating. The ear of the court is gained by modesty, and by speaking briefly and to the point. It is closed against assurance, volubility, prolixity, repetition. How disgusting and intolerable is it to hear a man going doggedly over ground already gone over, as if the judges had not heard or understood your senior, as if there were no other case to be heard but your own, as if you were not the subject of the "curses, not loud but deep," of those whom you keep waiting to be heard in their own cases, possibly of far greater importance than that with which you are pestering the court *ad nauseam!* Observe how differently the court listens to a sinner of this sort, and to a man who has earned the character of being brief and lucid! Do not give up too easily; but the accursed pertinacity which you may occasionally see exhibited—look at the faces of the judges while suffering under the infliction! Be courteous to your opponents. When you find you are *being beaten*, then is the moment to guard against the least manifestation of a ruffled temper, of irritability, or snappishness, or downright ill-humor. It will provoke only laughter, or dislike. 'Tis at this pinching point that you may infallibly distinguish between the temper and breeding of different men, between the man well-bred, and him under-bred, or ill-bred. A gentleman is a gentleman to the end of the chapter. Never take offence at what is said or done by your opponent, unless you deliberately believe that *offence was intended.* If that be the case, you must act as your own sense of self-respect may prompt, with spirit, but prudence. Never permit yourself to speak in a disparaging tone of any of your brethren in the presence of clients. If you cannot praise, be silent. Do not expose a slip or error; but, if possible, and consistent with your duty to your own client, conceal that slip or error as you would wish your own to be concealed.—*Warren's Law Studies.*

SHORT AND SHARP.

The minds of very few men are patient of a long or thorough investigation, even where the thing in contemplation requires it; much less will it be borne where the determinate quality of the subject is lightness or velocity. For this reason, I have seen much impatience in a court, where a man of superior understanding, but of a deliberative turn, and slow of speech, has been many minutes gravely combating the trivial position of some artful adversary, who, though his inferior in every other respect, knew he could conquer him in this. In such a case, to what end served his profundity? However valuable it might be on other occasions, at this moment no man attended to it but with pain and reluctance; when ten words of a gay and lively import would have abashed his adversary, and procured him a triumph, five hundred have been uttered with prodigious labor only to produce him vexation and defeat.—*Raithby.*

THE END.

And now, as a parting word of advice, let me ask the student to bear in mind what Hamlet says in the following expressive lines. Remember that after your professional career is ended, and your final exit made, however eminent you may have been while living, it is possible that some unfeeling grave-digger may bang your skull without *battery* and jestingly proclaim you an *outlaw.*

"Why may not that be the skull of a lawyer? Where be his

quiddits now, his quillets, his cases, his tenures, and his tricks? why does he suffer this rude knave now to knock him about the sconce with a dirty shovel, and will not tell him of his action of battery? Humph! This fellow might be in's time a great buyer of land, with his statutes, his recognizances, his fines, his double vouchers, his recoveries. Is this the fine of his fines and the recovery of his recoveries, to have his fine pate full of fine dirt? Will his vouchers vouch him no more of his purchases, and double ones too, than the length and breadth of a pair of indentures? The very conveyances of his lands will hardly lie in this box; and must the inheritor himself have no more? ha!"

GLOSSARY.

LAW TERMS AND MAXIMS.

A.

A fortiori. By so much the stronger; by a more powerful reason.
A mensa et thoro. "From bed and board." A divorce between husband and wife, which does not make the marriage void *ab initio,* or from the beginning.
A prendre. to take; to seize.
A priori. From the former.
A verbis legis non est recedendum. From the words of the law there should be no departure.
A vinculo matrimonii. From the bond of marriage.
Ab initio. From the beginning.
Ab origine. From the beginning.
Absoluta sententia expositore non indiget. An absolute, unqualified sentence, or proposition, needs no expositor.
Actio accrevit. An action has accrued.
Actio personalis moritur cum persona. A personal action dies with the person.
Actor sequitur forum rei. The plaintiff must follow the forum of the thing in dispute.
Actus curiæ neminem gravabit. An act of the court shall prejudice no man.
Actus Dei neminem facit injuriam. The act of God does wrong to no one; i. e., no one is responsible in damages for inevitable accidents.
Ad finem litis. To the conclusion of the suit.
Ad idem. "To the same." To the like intent.
Ad infinitum. "To eternity." To the utmost.
Ad inquirendum. To make inquiry.
Ad libitum. At pleasure; at will.
Ad litem. To (or in) the suit (or controversy).
Ad sectam. At the suit of.

GLOSSARY.

Administrator de son tort. Administrator in his own wrong.
Æquitas agit in personam. Equity acts upon the person.
Æquitas sequitur legem. Equity follows the law.
Affectio tua nomen imponit operi tuo. Your motive gives a name to your act.
Affirmantis est probatio. He who affirms must prove.
Alias ca. sa. Another writ to take (the person), to make satisfaction.
Alias scire facias. "That you again cause to be informed." A second writ of *scire facias.*
Alibi. "In another place."
Alibi natus. Born in another place.
Aliud est celare, aliud tacere. To conceal is one thing, to be silent another.
Allegari non debuit quod probatum non relevat. That ought not to be alleged which, if proved, would not be relevant.
Ancient demesne. An ancient inheritance.
Animo furandi. With intent to steal.
Animo lucrandi. With intention to gain a profit.
Animalia feræ naturæ. Animals of a wild nature.
Animus hominis est anima scripti. The intention of the party is the soul of the instrument.
Apices juris non sunt jura. Legal niceties are not laws.
Assumpsit. He undertook (or promised).
Assumpsit pro rata. He undertook agreeably to the proportion.
Autre droit. Another's right.

B.

Banco. "In bench." As "*dies in banco,*" or days in which the court sits.
Bancus ruptus. "A broken bank." From which the word "bankrupt."
Baron et feme. The husband and wife.
Benignius leges interpretandæ sunt quo voluntas carum conservetur. Laws are to be more favorably interpreted, that their intent may be preserved.
Billa vera. A true bill.
Bona fide. In good faith.
Bona fides exigit ut quod convenit fiat. Good faith demands that what is agreed upon shall be done.
Bonus. A consideration given for what is received; a premium paid to a grantor or vendor.

C.

Capias "You may take." A writ authorizing the defendant's arrest.

Capias ad computandum. That you take (defendant) to make account.

Capias ad respondendum. That you take (defendant) to make answer.

Capias ad satisfaciendum. That you take (defendant) to make satisfaction.

Capias ad valentiam. That you take to the value.

Capias in withernam. That you take a reprisal.

Capias pro fine. That you take for a fine.

Causa causans. The moving cause.

Causa impotentiæ. On account of impotence.

Causa causæ est causa causati. The cause of a cause is the cause of the effect.

Causa mortis. On account of death; in prospect of death.

Casus fœderis. A cause which comes within the terms of a compact.

Caveat. That he beware; a warning.

Caveat emptor. Let the purchaser beware.

Caveat venditor. Let the seller beware.

Cepi corpus. I have taken the body.

Certiorari. "To be certified of; to be informed of." A writ directing the proceedings or record of a cause to be brought before a superior court.

Cessante causa, cessat effectus. The cause ceasing, the effect must cease.

Cestui que trusts. Persons for whose use another is seized of lands, etc.

Cestui que use. A person for whose use land, etc., is given or granted.

Cestui que vies. Persons for whose lives a gift or grant is made.

Chose in action. A thing in action.

Clausum fregit. He broke the close or field.

Commodum ex injuria sua non habere debet. No man ought to derive any benefit of his own wrong.

Compensatio criminis. A compensation for crime.

Compos mentis. "Of sound mind." A man in such a state of mind as to be qualified legally to sign a will or deed, etc.

Contra bonos mores. Against good morals.

Contractus legem ex conventione accipiunt. The agreement of the parties makes the law of the contract.

Conventio vincit legem. The agreement of the parties overcomes or prevails against the law.

Corpora cepi. I have taken the bodies.

Covert. Married.

Crim. con. Illicit connection (adultery).

Cuilibet in arte sua perito est credendum. Credence should be given to one skilled in his peculiar art.

Cujus est solum ejus est usque ad cœlum. He who owns the soil owns it up to the sky.

Culpa lata dolo æquiparatur. Gross neglect is equivalent to fraud.

Currit tempus contra desides et sui juris contemptores. Time runs against the slothful and those who neglect their rights.

Cy pres. By approximation.

D.

Damage feasant. Doing damage.

Data. "Things granted." We must proceed on certain "*data;*" that is, on matters previously admitted to be correct.

Datum. A thing granted; a point fixed upon; a first principle.

De bene esse. Conditionally.

De bonis non. Of goods not (administered).

De bonis non administrandis. Of goods unadministered.

De die in diem. From day to day.

De facto. Of the deed; in fact.

De gratia. As a matter of grace or favor.

De jura judices, de facto juratores, respondent. The judges answer concerning the law, the jury concerning the facts.

De jure—de facto. "From the law; from the fact." Sometimes an offender is guilty the moment the wrong is committed; then he may be said to be guilty "*de facto.*" In other cases he is not guilty until he be convicted *by law;* then he is guilty "*de jure.*"

De minimis non curat lex. The law does not notice trifling matters.

De novo. Anew; afresh.

De præsenti. Of the present time.

De son don. Of his gift.

De son tort. "Of his own wrong." This was part of a plea very similar to *son assault demesne.*
Debet et detinet. He owes and detains.
Debet quis juri subjacere ubi delinquit. Everyone ought to be subject to the law of the place where he offends.
Debile fundamentum, fallit opus. Where there is a weak foundation the work falls.
Defeasance. A conditional undertaking to annul the effect of a bond, etc.
Delegata potestas non potest delegari. A delegated authority cannot be again delegated.
Delictum. A fault, offence, or crime.
Detinet. He keeps. He detains.
Detinuit. He has detained.
Deus solus hæredem facere potest, non homo. God alone, and not man, can make an heir.
Devastavit. He wasted.
Devastavit nolens volens. He wantonly (or wickedly) committed waste.
Dicta. Sayings; remarks; observations.
Dies dominicus non est juridicus. Sunday is not a day in law.
Discretio est discernere per legem quid sit justum. Discretion is to discern through law what is right.
Distringas. That you distrain.
Divinatio non interpretatio est, quæ omnino recedit a litera. It is a guess, not interpretation, which altogether departs from the letter.
Dolus circuitu non purgatur. Fraud is not purged by circuity.
Domesday—or *Domesday Book.* A book showing the tenures, etc., of most of the lands in England, in the time of William the Conqueror.
Dominium non potest esse in pendenti. The right of property cannot be in abeyance.
Donatio. A gift; a donation.
Dormiunt aliquando leges, nunquam moriunter. The laws sometimes sleep, but never die.
Droit des gens. The law of nations.
Duces tecum. "That you bring with you." A subpœna, so called, when the person is commanded to produce books, papers, etc., to the court and jury.

E.

E converso. On the other hand; on the contrary.
Eat sine die. Let him go without day (or be discharged).
Elegit. "He has chosen." A judicial writ directed to the sheriff, empowering him to seize one moiety of the defendant's lands for damages recovered.
En ventre sa mere. In the womb.
Enciente. Pregnant.
Enumeratio unius est exclusio alterius. Specification of one thing is an exclusion of the rest.
Error coram nobis. Error (lying) before us.
Error coram vobis. Error before you.
Error nominis nunquam nocet, si de identitate rei constat. Mistake in the name never injures, if there is no doubt as to the identity of the thing.
Error scribentis nocere non debet. An error made by a clerk ought not to injure; a clerical error may be corrected.
Eruditus in lege. "Learned in the law;" a counsel.
Escrow. A deed or writing left with another, to be delivered on the performance of something specified.
Estoppel. "A stop;" a preventive plea.
Estovers. Wood cut from a farm by the tenant, which by the common law he has a right to use on the estate for necessary purposes.
Et ad huc detinet. And he still detains.
Et non alibi. And in no other place.
Ex æquo et bono. In equity and good conscience.
Ex contractu. By way of agreement.
Ex curia. Out of court.
Ex delicto. By (or from) a fault or offence.
Ex dolo malo non oritur actio. A right of action cannot arise out of fraud.
Ex facto. From (or by) the deed.
Ex justa causa. For a good reason (or cause).
Ex lege. An outlaw.
Ex nudo pacto non oritur actio. No action arises on a contract without a consideration.
Ex officio. Officially; by virtue of the office.
Ex parte materna. On the part of the mother.
Ex parte paterna. On the part of the father.
Ex parte quærentis. On the part of the plaintiff.

Ex post facto. From (or by) an after act.
Ex relatione. "By (or from) relation." Sometimes the words mean "*by the information.*"
Ex tempore. Off hand (without delay or premeditation).
Ex tota materia emergat resolutio. The construction or explanation should arise out of the whole subject-matter.
Ex visitatione Dei. From the visitation of God.
Exceptio probat regulam de rebus non exceptis. An exception proves the rule concerning things not excepted.
Executor de son tort. "An exector of his own wrong;" one who acts illegally in the office.
Exoneretur nunc pro tunc. Let him (or it) be now discharged, instead of at some past time.
Expressa nocent, non expressa non nocent. Things expressed may be prejudicial; things not expressed, are not.

F.

Fac simile. Do the like; a close imitation.
Facias. That you do (or cause to be done).
Factum negantis nulla probatio. No proof is incumbent on him who denies a fact.
Factum unius alteri nocere non debet. The deed of one should not hurt another.
Falsa demonstratio non nocet. A false description does not vitiate.
Falsare curiam. To deceive the court.
Falsus in uno, falsus in omnibus. False in one thing, false in everything.
Felo de se. A suicide; a self-murderer.
Feme covert. A married woman.
Feme sole. An unmarried woman.
Feme sole sub modo. A single woman to a certain extent.
Feoffare. To enfeoff, or grant in fee.
Feudum. A fee; land held in fee simple.
Fiat. Let it be done.
Fiat justitia ruat cœlum. Let justice be done, though the heavens should fall.
Fictio legis neminem lædit. A fiction of law injures no one.
Fief. "A fee." What we call a fee is, in other countries, the contrary to *chattels.* In Germany, certain districts or territories are called "*Fiefs,*" where there are *Fiefs* of the Empire.
Fieri. To be made or done.

Fieri facias. That you cause to be made or done, or levied. A writ of execution so called.
Flotsam. Goods floating on the sea.
Forma legalis. A legal form.
Forum. A court or place of justice.
Frank-almoign. A free gift.
Fraus est celare fraudem. It is fraud to conceal fraud.
Fraus est odiosa et non præsumenda. Fraud is odious and not to be presumed.
Furiosi nulla voluntas est. A madman has no will.
Furiosus solo furore punitur. A madman is punished by his madness alone.

G.

Gavelkind. A peculiar tenure of land.
Generale nihil certum implicat. A general expression implies nothing certain.
Guardian ad litem. A guardian in the suit.

H.

Habeas corpora. That you have the bodies.
Habeas corpus. "That you have the body." The great writ of the people's liberty.
Habeas corpus ad respondendum. That you have the body to answer.
Habeas corpus ad satisfaciendum. That you have the body to make satisfaction.
Habeas corpus ad testificandum. That you have the body to give evidence.
Habeas corpus cum causa. That you have the body with the cause (why he is arrested).
Habendum et tenendum. To have and to hold.
Habere facias possessionem. That you cause to take possession.
Habere facias seisinam. That you cause to have the possession.
Hæredum appellatione veniunt hæredes hæredum in infinitum. By the title of heirs come the heirs of heirs to infinity.
Hæres hæredis mei est meus hæres. The heir of my heir is my heir.
Hominum causa jus constitutum est. Law is established for the benefit of man.

I.

Id certum est quod certum reddi potest. That is certain which may be rendered certain.

Idem dies. The same day; a like day.

Idem est facere, et nolle prohibere cum possis. It is the same thing to do a thing as not to prohibit it when in your power.

Ignoramus. "We are ignorant." A word written on a bill of indictment when the evidence is insufficient to put the accused on his trial.

Ignorantia facti excusat, ignorantia juris non excusat. Ignorance of facts excuses; ignorance of law does not excuse.

Ignorantia legis neminem excusat. Ignorance of law excuses no one.

Imparlance. A time granted by the court for the defendant to plead.

Impossibilium nulla obligatio est. There is no obligation to perform impossible things.

Impotentia excusat legem. Impossibility is an excuse in the law.

In articulo mortis. At the point of death.

In autre droit. In right of another.

In banco regis. In the King's Bench.

In capite. In chief. Lands held "*in capite*" are those held of the chief lord of the fee.

In colloquio. In a discourse.

In criminalibus, probationes debent esse luce clariores. In criminal cases the proofs ought to be clearer than the light.

In delicto. In an offence, or in default.

In dominio suo. In his demesne or lordship.

In dorso. On the back.

In dubiis. In doubtful cases.

In esse. In being.

In extenso. At large; to the extent.

In extremis. In the last moments; near death.

In infinitum. To infinity; time without end.

In invitum. Against an unwilling party, by operation of law.

In jure non remota causa, sed proxima spectatur. In law, the proximate and not the remote cause is to be looked to.

In loco parentum. In the place of the parents.

In maleficiis voluntas spectatur non exitus. In offences, the intention is regarded, not the event.

In mortua manu. In mortmain; in a dead hand or possession.

In omnibus obligationibus, in quibus dies non ponitur, præsenti die debetur. In all obligations, when no time is fixed for the payment, the thing is due immediately.

In pais. In the country.

In pari delicto. In a like offence (or crime).
In pari delicto melior est conditio possidentis. When the parties are equally in the wrong, the condition of the possessor is better.
In presenti. At the present time.
In proprio jure. In (his) proper (or peculiar) right.
In propria persona. In his own person; in personal attendance.
In re. In the matter of.
In re dubia magis inficiatio quam affirmatio intelligenda. In a doubtful matter the negative is to be understood rather than the affirmative.
In rem. To or against the property; to the point.
In rerum natura. In the nature (or order) of things.
In stirpes. To the stock or lineage.
In suo jure. In his own right.
In terrorem. By way of terror (or warning).
In toto. In the whole; altogether; entirely.
In transitu. "In the passage." Merchandise is said to be "*in transitu*" while on its way to the consignee.
In vadio. In pledge.
In ventre sa mere. In its mother's womb.
Incipitur. It is begun.
Infeudare. To enfeoff; grant in fee.
Injuria non excusat injuriam. A wrong does not excuse a wrong.
Injuria propria non cadet in beneficium facientis. No one shall profit by his own wrong.
Inscriptum. An endorsement.
Intentio mea imponit nomen operi meo. My intent gives a name to my act.
Inter mœnia. Within the walls; within the domicile.
Inter nos. Between ourselves; that is, (*inter nos*,) to keep a secret.
Interpretatio fienda est ut res magis valeat quam pereat. Such a construction is to be made that the subject may have an effect rather than none.
Interregnum. A space between two reigns.
Interregnum quare clausum fregit? In the mean time, why did he break the close?
Ipso facto. By the fact itself; positively.
Ipso jure. By the law itself, or by that right.
Ira furor brevis est. Anger is a short insanity.
Ita lex scripta. So the law is written.

J.

Jetsam. Goods thrown into the sea.
Judex æquitatem semper spectare debet. A judge ought always to regard equity.
Judici officium suum excedenti non paretur. To a judge who exceeds his office or jurisdiction no obedience is due.
Judicis est jus dicere non dare. It is the duty of a judge to declare the law, not enact it.
Judicia posteriora sunt in lege fortiora. The latter decisions are stronger in law.
Jura in re. Rights in the matter or thing.
Jura personarum. The rights of persons.
Jura publica ante ferenda privatis. Public rights are to be preferred to private.
Jura rerum. The rights of things.
Juratores sunt judices facti. Jurors are the judges of the facts.
Jure divino. By right divine.
Jure gentium. By the law of nations.
Jure humano. By human law (or right).
Jure mariti. In right of the husband.
Jure naturæ. By the law of nature.
Jure uxoris. In right of the wife.
Jus ad rem. A right to the property.
Jus civile. The civil (or municipal) law.
Jus ex injuria non oritur. A right cannot arise from a wrong.
Jus in re. The right in the property.
Jus suum. His own right.
Justitia non est neganda, non differenda. Justice is not to be denied nor delayed.

L.

Laches. Neglect; supineness.
Lata culpa dolo æquiparatur. Gross negligence is equal to fraud.
Leges posteriores priores contrarias abrogant. Subsequent laws repeal prior conflicting ones.
Levari facias. That you cause to be levied.
Levari facias de bonis. That you cause to be levied of the goods.
Lex dilationes semper exhorret. The law always abhors delay.
Lex est dictamen rationis. Law is the dictate of reason.
Lex est norma recti. Law is a rule of right.
Lex fori. The law of the court.

Lex neminem cogit ad vana seu inutilia peragenda. The law forces no one to do vain or useless things.

Lex nemini facit injurianom. The law does wrong to no one.

Lex non scripta. The unwritten or common law; that which has been received from time immemorial by tradition.

Lex scripta. The written or statute law.

Lex semper dabit remedium. The law will always give a remedy.

Lex semper intendit quod convenit rationi. The law always intends what is agreeable to reason.

Lex talionis. The law of requital in kind: "An eye for an eye," etc., as in the Mosaic law.

Lex uno ore omnes alloquitur. The law speaks to all with one mouth.

Libelli famosi. Libels; infamous writings.

Libellus sine scriptis. An unwritten libel.

Liber homo. A free man.

Liberari facias. That you cause to be delivered.

Loco parentis. In the place of the parent.

Locus contractus regit actum. The place of the contract governs the act.

Locus penitentiæ. A place of repentance; a power of drawing back from a contract or bargain before any act is done to confirm it in law.

L. S.—Locus sigilli. The place of the seal.

Longa patientia trahitur ad consensum. Long sufferance is construed as consent.

Longa possessio est pacis jus. Long possession is the law of peace.

M.

Magna Charta. The Great Charter. The bulwark of English liberty.

Magna culpa dolus est. Great neglect is equivalent to fraud.

Mahemium est homicidium inchoatum. Mayhem is incipient homicide.

Majori summæ minor inest. The lesser is included in the greater.

Mala fide. In bad faith; with intent to deceive.

Mala prohibita. Wrongs forbidden (by common law).

Malfeasance. Doing wrong; a bad act.

Malo animo. With bad intentions.

Malum in se. Bad in itself; wrong in its own nature.

Malum prohibitum. A prohibited offence.

Mandamus. "We command." A peremptory writ, issued for many purposes.
Manu forti. With a strong hand; by violence.
Matrimonium subsequens tollit peccatum præcedens. A subsequent marriage cures preceding criminality.
Melior est causa possedentis. The cause of the possessor is preferable.
Melior est conditio defendentis. The cause of the defendant is the better.
Mesne. "Middle; intervening." The middle between two extremes, and that either in time or dignity.
Misfeasance. A misdeed.
Modo et forma. In manner and form.
Modica circumstantia facti jus mutat. A small circumstance attending an act may change the law.
Mortmain—Manus mortua. A dead hand, or an unchangeable possession.
Mutatis mutandis. The necessary changes.

N.

Narratio, often abbreviated *Narr'.* A declaration; a count.
Naufrage. Shipwreck.
Nemo contra factum suum venire potest. No man can contradict his own deed.
Nemo debet rem suam sine facto aut defectu suo amittere. No one should lose his property without his act or negligence.
Nemo est hæres viventis. No one is an heir to the living.
Nemo ex proprio dolo consequitur actionem. No one acquires a right of action from his own wrong.
Nemo plus juris ad alienum transferre potest, quam ipse habet. One cannot transfer to another a larger right than he himself has.
Nemo potest facere per obliquum quod non potest facere per directum. No one can do that indirectly which cannot be done directly.
Nemo tenetur se ipsum accusare. No one is bound to accuse himself.
Nihil debet. He is not indebted.
Nihil dicit. He says nothing.
Nihil habit forum ex scena. The court has nothing to do with what is not before it.
Nihil quod est contra rationem est licitum. Nothing against reason is lawful.

Nil debet. "He owes nothing." The usual plea in an action of debt.

Nil debit in assumpsit. He is not indebted in (the action of) assumpsit.

Nil dicit. He says nothing.

Nolle prosequi. "To be unwilling to proceed." Generally used in criminal cases, when further proceedings are discontinued.

Non cepit. He did not take.

Non compos mentis. Not of sound mind; in a delirium of lunacy.

Non damnificatus. Not damnified; not injured.

Non deberet alii nocere, quod inter alios actum esset. No one ought to be injured by that which has taken place between other parties.

Non debet. He does not owe.

Non decepitur qui scit se decipi. He is not deceived who knows himself to be deceived.

Non differunt quæ concordant re, tametsi non in verbis iisdem. Those things which agree in substance, though not in the same words, do not differ.

Non est inventus. "He is not found." The return made by a sheriff when the defendant is not found in his county.

Non est regula quin fallat. There is no rule but what may fail.

Non omne damnum inducit injuriam. Not every loss produces an injury.

Non pros'. He will not prosecute.

Non prosequitur. He does not proceed; he is nonsuited.

Non refert an quis assensum suum præfert verbis, an rebus ipsis et factis. It is immaterial whether a man gives his assent by words or by acts and deeds.

Non refert quid notum sit judici, si notum non sit in forma judicii. It matters not what is known to the judge, if it is not known to him judicially.

Non refert verbis an factis fit revocatio. It matters not whether a revocation be by words or by acts.

Non sum informatus. I am not informed; I am ignorant.

Non tenuit. He did not occupy (or hold).

Nonfeasance. Non-performance.

Nuda pactio obligationem non parit. A naked promise does not create an obligation.

Nudum pactum. A bare (or naked) contract; one not binding in law.

Nul assets ultra. No further effects.
Nul tiel corporation. No such corporation.
Nul tiel record. "No such record." This is part of the plaintiff's rejoinder that there is no such record, where the defendant alleges matter of record in bar of the plaintiff's action.
Nul tort. "No wrong." A plea in a real action that *no wrong* was done, and is a species of the general issue.
Nulla bona. No effects.
Nullus videtur dolo facere qui suo jure utitur. No man is to be esteemed a wrongdoer who avails himself of his legal right.
Nunc pro tunc. "Now for that time." These words are frequently used in legal or equitable proceedings, where something is permitted to be done "*eo instanti*" which should have been performed some time before.
Nunquam res humanæ prospere succedunt ubi negliguntur divinæ. Human things never prosper when divine things are neglected.

O.

Omne actum ab intentione agentis est judicandum. Every act is to be estimated by the intention of the doer.
Omne sacramentum debet esse de certa scientia. Every oath ought to be founded on certain knowledge.
Omnes licentiam habere his quæ pro se indulta sunt, renunciare. All shall have liberty to renounce those things which have been established in their favor.
Omnia præsumunter rite et solemniter esse acta. All things are presumed to have been rightly and regularly done.
Omnis exceptio est ipsa quoque regula. An exception is in itself also a rule.
Omnis ratihabitio retro trahitur et mandato æquiparatur. Every subsequent ratification has a retrospective effect, and is equivalent to a prior command.
Opinio quæ favet testamento est tenenda. That opinion is followed which favors the will.
Optima enim est legis interpres consuetudo. Usage is the best interpreter of law.
Origo rei inspici debet. The origin of a thing ought to be inquired into.
Ouster. A dispossession.
Overt. Open; public.

Owelty. The difference which is paid or received by one coparcener to another, for the purpose of equalizing a partition.

Oyer et terminer. To hear and determine.

P.

Parole. Verbally.

Parum proficit scire quid fieri debet, si non cognoscas quomodo sit facturum. It avails little to know what ought to be done, if you do not know how it is to be done.

Pendente lite. Whilst the contest (or suit) is depending.

Per annum—per diem. By the year; by the day.

Per autre vie. For the life of another.

Per capita. "By the heads or polls;" a division, share and share alike.

Per duellum. By single combat.

Per se. By himself, herself, or itself.

Per stirpes. By stock; by lineage.

Per totam curiam. By the whole court.

Per verba de futuro. By words of future acceptation.

Per verba præsenti. By words of the present time.

Per viam eleemosynæ. By way of charity, or alms.

Pendente lite nihil innovetur. During litigation nothing should be changed.

Periculum rei venditæ, nondum traditæ, est emptoris. The purchaser runs the risk of the loss of a thing sold, though not delivered.

Plena fides. Full credit.

Pluries. "Very often." Also the name of a third writ, after two have issued against a defendant.

Plus peccat auctor quam actor. The instigator of a crime is worse than he who perpetrates it.

Pone. "Put." The name of a writ or process in replevin.

Ponderantur testes non numerantur. Witnesses are weighed, not counted.

Posse comitatus. "The power of the county." Which the sheriff is authorized to call out whenever an opposition is made to his writ or to the execution of justice.

Post diem. After the day.

Post mortem. After the death.

Post nati. After-born.

Post obit. After the death.

Post terminum. After the term.

Postea. "Afterwards." The name given to the endorsement of the verdict made on the record.
Potentia non est nisi ad bonum. Power is not conferred but for the public good.
Potest quis renunciare pro se, et suis, jus quod pro se introductum est. A man may relinquish, for himself and those claiming under him, a right which was introduced for his own benefit.
Præcipe. Command.
Præcipe in capite. A writ of right, so called.
Præsumptio violenta, plena probatio. Violent presumption is full proof.
Prima facie. On the first view or appearance of the business.
Prochein ami. The nearest friend.
Pro rata. According to the rate, proportion, or allowance.
Pro tanto. For so much.
Prohibetur ne quis faciat in suo quod nocere possit alieno. It is prohibited to do on one's own property that which may injure another's.
Pueri sunt de sanguine parentum, sed pater et mater non sunt de sanguine puerorum. Children are of the blood of their parents, but the father and mother are not of the blood of their children.
Pur autre vie. For the life of another.

Q.

Quæ in curia acta sunt rite agi præsumuntur. Whatever is done in court is presumed to be rightly done.
Quæcunque intra rationem legis inveniuntur, intra legem ipsam esse judicantur. Whatever appears within the reason of the law, is considered within the law itself.
Quando aliquid mandatur, mandatur et omne per quod pervenitur ad illud. When any thing is commanded, every thing by which it can be accomplished is also commanded.
Quando lex aliquid alicui concedit, concedere videtur id sine quo res ipsa esse non potest. When the law gives anything, it gives the means of obtaining it.
Quando verba et mens congruunt, non est interpretationi locus. When the words and the mind agree, there is no place for interpretation.
Quantum damnificatus. Amount of damage.
Quantum valebat. As much as it was worth.
Quare clausum fregit? Wherefore (or why) did he break the close?

Quasi ex contractu. In nature of a contract.
Quasi ex delicto. As of an offence (or crime).
Qui facit per alium facit per se. He who acts by or through another, acts himself.
Qui hæret in litera, hæret in cortice. He who adheres to the letter adheres to the bark.
Qui jure suo utitur, nemini facit injuriam. He who uses his legal rights harms no one.
Quid pro quo. A mutual consideration.
Quo animo. With what intent.
Quo warranto. "By what authority." The name of a writ against a person who has usurped a franchise or office.
Quoad hoc. With respect to this.
Quod ab initio non valet, in tractu temporis non convalescet. What is not good in the beginning cannot be rendered good by time.
Quod alias non fuit licitum necessitas licitum facit. Necessity makes that lawful which otherwise were unlawful.
Quod detinuit. Which he (or she) detains.
Quod initio vitiosum est non potest tractu temporis convalescere. Time cannot render valid an act void in its origin.
Quod quis ex culpa sua damnum sentit, non intelligitur damnum sentire. He who suffers damage by his own fault is not held to suffer damage.
Quod quis sciens indebitum dedit hac mente, ut postea repeteret, repetere non potest. What one has paid knowing it not to be due, with the intention of recovering it back, he cannot recover back.
Quousque debitum satisfactum fuerit. Until the debt be satisfied.

R.

Ratio legis est anima legis. The reason of the law is the soul of the law.
Rectus in curia. "Untainted in court;" with clean hands.
Reddendum. To pay; to yield; to render. The reservation of rent, etc., in a deed.
Registrum. A registry; a place for depositing wills, deeds, etc.
Remittitur. To restore (or send back).
Replegiari facias. That you cause to be replevied.
Res inter alios judicatæ nullum aliis præjudicium faciant. Matters adjudged in a cause do not prejudice those who were not parties to it.

GLOSSARY.

Res integra. An entire (new or untouched) matter.
Res judicata pro veritate accipitur. A thing adjudged must be taken for truth.
Rescous. A rescue.
Residuum. "The remainder." Frequently applied to that part of the testator's estate not especially disposed of.
Respondere non debet. He ought not to answer.
Retorna brevium. The return of writs.
Retorno habendo. That a return be had.
Reversetur. Let it be reversed.
Rex non potest peccare. The king can do no wrong.
Rex nunquam moritur. The king never dies.

S.

Sans issue. Without children.
Scienter. Knowingly; willfully.
Scientia utriusque par pares contrahentes facit. Equal knowledge on both sides makes the contracting parties equal.
Scintilla. A tittle; a spark.
Scire facias. That you make known. This is the name of a writ for many purposes, commanding the defendant to show cause why a certain specific thing thould not issue on an old judgment, etc.
Scire fieri. To be informed.
Scribere est agere. To write is to act.
Secta. A suit; litigation. Also, the pledges produced that the plaintiff should prosecute his claim.
Sed per curiam. But by the court.
Semble. It seems.
Semper qui non prohibit pro se intervenire, mandare creditur. He who does not prohibit the intervention of another in his behalf is supposed to authorize it.
Sequestrari facias. That you cause to be sequestered.
Si judicas, cognosce. If you judge, understand.
Sine die. "Without day." As, the court adjourned "*sine die*"— no day being mentioned for sitting again.
Sine qua non. An indispensable condition.
Son assault. His own assault.
Sponsalia. Marriage contracts.
Sponsio judicialis. A judicial agreement.
ss. (Scilicet). To wit; namely.

Stabit præsumptio donec probetur in contrarium. A presumption will stand good until the contrary is proved.

Stare decisis. To abide by or adhere to decided cases.

Statutum generaliter est intelligendum quando verba statuti sunt specialia, ratio autem generalis. When the words of a statute are special, but the reason of it general, it is to be understood generally.

Stirpes. The stock; lineage; race.

Stricti juris. Of strict right (or law).

Sub finem. Under a penalty.

Sub modo. Under a condition; within bounds.

Sub potestate viri. Under the control of the husband.

Subpœna. "Under a penalty." A writ, so called, to procure the attendance of witnesses.

Subpœna ad testificandum. A subpœna to give evidence.

Subpœna duces tecum. "Bring with you, under a penalty." The name of a writ by which a witness is commanded to produce something in his possession, to be given in evidence.

Subsidium justitiæ. An aid to justice.

Suggestio falsi. A suggestion (or incitement) to falsehood or wrong.

Sui generis. "Of his own kind;" not to be classed under any ordinary description.

Sui juris. Of his own right.

Supersedeas. "You may remove or set aside." A writ so called, to stay proceedings.

Supra protest. An acceptance of a bill *after protest*.

Suppressio veri, expressio falsi. Suppression of the truth is (eqivalent to) the expression of what is false.

Sur trover et conversion. Upon trover and conversion.

T.

Tenendum. "To hold." That clause in a deed wherein the tenure of the land is created and limited.

Terminus. The end, limit, or boundary. Sometimes it means the stock or root to which, by reference, the future succession is to be regulated.

Terra transit cum onere. Land passes with the incumbrances.

Terre tenant. The tenant who occupies the land; he who has the actual possession.

Testari. To be witnessed.

GLOSSARY.

Testatum. It is testified.

Testatum capias. That you take the person testified (or to have been proceeded against elsewhere).

Testatum fieri facias. That you cause the testified writ to be executed.

Testatum pluries. A testified process issued more than twice.

Teste. The date; the supposed issuing of process.

Testis de visu præponderat aliis. An eye-witness outweighs others.

Tort. A wrong; an injury.

Tort-feasor. A wrong-doer; a trespasser.

Traditio loqui facit chartam Delivery makes the deed speak.

Trespass, quare clausum fregit. Trespass, wherefore he broke the close.

Trespass vi et armis, de uxore rupta et abducta. Trespass with force and arms, concerning a wife taken and carried away.

Triatio ibi semper debet fieri, ubi juratores meliorem possunt habere notitiam. Trial ought always to be had where the jury can have the best knowledge.

Tutius erratur ex parte mitiori. It is safer to err on the side of mercy.

U.

Ubi jus, ibi remedium. Where there is a right there is a remedy.

Ubi jus incertum, ibi jus nullum. Where the law is uncertain there is no law.

Ubi pugnantia inter se in testamento juberentur, neutrum ratum est. When two directions conflicting with each other are given in a will, neither is held valid.

Ubi quis delinquit ibi punietur. Let a man be punished where he commits the offence.

Ubi verba conjuncta non sunt, sufficit alterutrum esse factum. Where words are used disjunctively, it is sufficient that either one of the things enumerated be performed.

Ultra mare. Beyond sea.

Usance. Usury; interest.

V.

Vacatur. It is set aside; vacated.

Vani timoris justa excusatio non est. A frivolous fear is not a legal excuse.

Venditioni exponas. That you expose to sale

Venire. To come.
Venire ad respondendum. To come to make answer.
Venire dō nove. To come anew.
Venue. The place from which the jury come.
Verba intentioni, non e contra, debent inservire. Words ought to be made subservient to the intent, not contrary to it.
Vi et armis. By force and arms; by unlawful means.
Via antiqua via est tuta. The old way is the safe way.
Vicarius non habet vicarium. A deputy cannot appoint a deputy.
Vice versa. On the contrary.
Vicini vicinora præsumuntur scire. Neighbors are presumed to know things of the neighborhood.
Vinculo matrimonii. In the bond of wedlock.
Vis legibus est inimica. Force is inimical to the laws.
Vitium clerici nocere non debet. Clerical errors ought not to prejudice.
Viva voce. Verbally.
Voir dire. Witnesses are sometimes examined upon *"voir dire"* previously to their being examined *in chief;* this is done to ascertain whether they are interested in the cause at issue, or labor under any other incapacity which may render them incompetent to give evidence.
Volenti non fit injuria. He who consents cannot receive an injury.
Vox emissa volat, litera scripta manet. Words spoken vanish words written remain.

TABLE OF BRITISH REGNAL YEARS.

SOVEREIGNS.	Commencement of Reign.	Length of Reign	
William I.	Oct. 24, 1066.	21	Maurice.
William II.	Sept. 26, 1087.	13	
Henry I.	Aug. 5, 1100.	36	
Stephen.	Dec. 26, 1135.	19	
Henry II.	Dec. 19, 1154.	35	Glanville.
Richard I.	Sept. 23, 1189.	10	
John.	May 27, 1199.	18	
Henry III.	Oct. 28, 1216.	57	Bracton.
Edward I.	Nov. 20, 1272.	35	
Edward II.	July 8, 1307.	20	
Edward III.	Jan. 25, 1326.	51	
Richard II.	June 22, 1377.	23	Arundel.
Henry IV.	Sept. 30, 1399.	14	
Henry V.	Mar. 21, 1413.	10	
Henry VI.	Sept. 1, 1422.	39	Fortescue.
Edward IV.	Mar. 4, 1461.	23	Littleton.
Edward V.	April 9, 1483.	..	
Richard III.	June 26, 1483.	3	
Henry VII.	Aug. 22, 1485.	24	
Henry VIII.	April 22, 1509.	38	Wolsey.
Edward VI.	Jan. 28, 1547.	7	
Mary.	July 6, 1553.	6	
Elizabeth.	Nov. 17, 1558.	45	Bacon.
James I.	Mar. 24, 1603.	23	Coke.
Charles I.	Mar. 27, 1625.	24	
The Commonwealth.	Jan. 30, 1649.	11	Hale.
Charles II.	May 29, 1660.	37	Clarendon.
James II.	Feb. 6, 1685.	4	Jeffreys.
William and Mary.	Feb. 13, 1689.	14	
Anne.	Mar. 8, 1702.	13	Holt.
George I.	Aug. 1, 1714.	13	Hardwicke
George II.	June 11, 1727.	34	Mansfield.
George III.	Oct. 25, 1760.	60	Blackstone
George IV.	Jan. 29, 1820.	11	Eldon.
William IV.	June 26, 1830.	7	Brougham.
Victoria.	June 20, 1837.	—	Denman.

CHIEF JUSTICES

OF THE SUPREME COURT OF THE UNITED STATES,
FROM MARCH 4TH, 1789.

JOHN JAY, of New York, appointed by the President, with the advice and consent of the Senate, September 26th, 1789. Nominated 16th, and confirmed 19th, of April, 1794, Envoy Extraordinary to England. Resigned as Chief Justice.

JOHN RUTLEDGE, of South Carolina, appointed July 1st, 1795, in recess of Senate, in place of Jay, resigned, and presided on the bench at the August term, 1795. Nominated 10th, and rejected by the Senate 15th December, 1795.

WILLIAM CUSHING, of Massachusetts. Nomination confirmed and appointed, etc., January 27th, 1796, in place of Jay. Declined the appointment. He was then an Associate Justice.

OLIVER ELLSWORTH, of Connecticut. Nomination confirmed and appointed, etc., March 4th, 1796, in place of Cushing, declined. Appointed Envoy Extraordinary and Minister Plenipotentiary to France, February 27th, 1799. Presided on the Bench at the August term, 1799. Proceeded on his mission to France November 3d, 1799, resigning as Chief Justice.

JOHN JAY, Governor of New York. Nomination confirmed and appointed, etc., December 19th, 1800, in place of Ellsworth, resigned. Declined the appointment.

JOHN MARSHALL, Secretary of State. Nomination confirmed 27th, and appointed, etc., January 31st, 1801, in place of Jay, declined. Died in 1835.

CHIEF JUSTICES.

ROGER B. TANEY, of Maryland. Nomination confirmed and appointed, etc., March 15th, 1836, in place of Marshall, deceased. Died in 1864.

SALMON P. CHASE, of Ohio. Nomination confirmed, appointed, etc., December 6th. 1864. Died in December, 1873.

MORRISON R. WAITE, of Ohio. Nominated January 19th, 1874, and nomination confirmed, appointed, etc., in February, 1874.

www.ingramcontent.com/pod-product-compliance
Lightning Source LLC
Chambersburg PA
CBHW022105290426
44112CB00008B/554